Mr Manchester and the Factory Girl

The Story of Tony and Lindsay Wilson

Mr Manchester and the Factory Girl

The Story of Tony and Lindsay Wilson

Lindsay Reade

Plexus, London

Foreword copyright © 2010 by Mick Middles
Copyright © 2010 by Lindsay Reade
Published by Plexus Publishing Limited
25 Mallinson Road
London SW11 1BW
www.plexusbooks.com

British Library Cataloguing in Publication Data

Reade, Lindsay.
  Mr Manchester and the factory girl: the story of Tony and
Lindsay Wilson.
  1. Reade, Lindsay. 2. Wilson, Anthony H., 1950-2007. Sound
recording executives and producers–England–Manchester–
Biography. 4. Impresarios England–Manchester–
Biography.
  I. Title
  781.6'6149'0922-dc22

  ISBN-13: 978-0-85965-456-2
  ISBN-10: 0-85965-456-7

Cover photo by Ged Murray
Cover and book design by Coco Wake-Porter
Printed in Great Britain by the MPG Books Group

We would like to thank the following for supplying photographs:
Granada Television; Kevin Cummins; Jimmy Hynd; Ged Murray;
Ged Murray; Kevin Cummins; Granada Television; Ged Murray; Ged
Murray; Annik Honoré; Kevin Cummins; Annik Honoré; Annik Honoré;
Annik Honoré; Suttons Estate Agents; Vini Reilly; Vini Reilly; Martin Hannett
and Susanne O'Hara; Annik Honoré; Vini Reilly; Ged Murray; Kevin Cummins;
Ged Murray; Ged Murray; Sydney Wilson; Sydney Wilson; Kevin Cummins;
Gene Simon Taylor; Gene Simon Taylor; Nathan Cox; Katja Ruge; Katja
Ruge; Katja Ruge, taken from the book *Fotoreportage 23 – In Search of
Ian Curtis*, www.katjaruge.de. Special thanks to Tosh Ryan. All other
photos are from the author's personal collection.

Contents

This is *not* a book about a record label; nor spotlight on a musical scene, a city or an era. It is also, and most resolutely, not some quick-fire celebrity biography aimed at making the most of one man's enduring legacy. In fact, it is not a biography at all and, frankly, the late Tony Wilson's celebrity status does not sit easily within the crass framework of 2010.

It is a love story, albeit one set in a broad and colourful cultural context. It's a culture that is recognisable to many and here it serves to illuminate the heart of the story . . . and yes, it is a story with a *big* heart. Although it centres on a three-decade relationship between two people it is, of course, more complex than that might sound. It is the pleasures and pains of two tangled lives . . . and of many lives beyond.

It is also a book that has grown organically during the best part of a decade. I feel qualified to claim this, having enjoyed a close friendship with Lindsay Reade throughout this period. During this time, Lindsay and I co-authored *Torn Apart: The Life of Ian Curtis*. Researching that project proved to be an emotive process and, through that, a curious thing happened. The book sent Lindsay spinning through her own back pages; as a woman working within the heart of the male-dominated music industry, at Factory Records, as co-manager of the Stone Roses and beyond, flickering between the music business and, well, normal life.

It was partly because of Lindsay's background, and partly, I strongly sense, because of her infectious personality, that she discovered a niche. She loved conducting those interviews, drawing out aspects of their lives – and her own life. It was partly because of this process, perhaps, that any distance that had developed between herself and Tony also appeared to diminish. Although it was unknown at the time, Tony was also moving towards his tragic and untimely demise. Poignancy seemed to hang in the air during the final years and months of his inspiring life. Tragic as it was, it all fell naturally into a story, *this* story.

And Tony always loved a story. I was also convinced that Lindsay was the only person who could truly write it. I knew that she would.

Of course, so much has happened during the past decade and much of it has been warped into myth and, in some areas, into self-serving anecdote – be it in films, documentaries, books, elongated magazine articles, radio shows, and the continuing innovative allure of the city of Manchester. That story continues.

For Lindsay and Tony, elements of their story had already surfaced in filmic form as the basis of the first half of Michael Winterbottom's fast-paced *24 Hour Party People*. It was fun, though hardly illuminating, and the notion that Tony and Lindsay's relationship was all sexual spark and fiery banter did seem rather simplistic. The truth is more complex, and often more painful – and, I know, it was not easy for Lindsay to relive it all for the purposes of writing this book.

It only recently dawned on me that, while I knew Tony and Lindsay separately, I never really knew them together.

Well, I do now.

What's more, through this unique telling, I have learned far more about the past thirty years in Manchester than I have from any of the elevated tomes and articles that have surfaced on that subject in recent times.

Mick Middles

'How much so ever I valued him I now wish I had valued him more.'

Dr Samuel Johnson

'The life of every man is a diary in which
he means to write one story and writes another.'

J.M. Barrie

'I miss him so much it does my head in some days.
He was the enthusiasm fuel.'

Elliot Rashman

1 Indomitable Spirit

t is 11:33pm on Tuesday, 17 July 2007, and I'm watching the movie *Hideous Kinky* on TV. I have bitten a thumbnail off because Tony promised to ring me this evening with the results of his CAT scan. It is now one and a half hours after the time he usually goes to sleep these days and, though I've given up hope he'll call now, I'm still desperate to learn what's happened.

The phone rings.

'I'm in hospital darling.'

Christ, I think, it's even worse than I thought, but he sounds cheery.

'It's good news,' he continues.

I'm incredulous.

'I've got a clot on my lung.'

I'm even more incredulous. I'm still waiting for the good news but Tony is already celebrating.

'I've been feeling weaker and weaker these last ten days.'

This is news to me.

'Those last few steps walking up the Opera House completely wiped me out.'

I'd guessed this.

'But it's good news . . . because now I know why.'

I'm speechless. How many people can you think of who would be happy they've got a clot on their lung?

'It's all good.'

Somehow he manages to convince me to feel relieved – and he continued to make me feel that way, to say things were 'all good', until he died twenty-four days later.

That was Tony Wilson for you – indomitably cheerful, optimistic and enthusiastic. Always.

The night at the Manchester Opera House was three days before that phone call, on 14 July. It was a 'surprise' outing for Tony in order for him to hear a small segment of the set performed in a group show called *Il Tempo del Postino*, which was part of the last weekend of the Manchester International Festival. Tony had told me it had 'something to do with art' and that, whatever it was, it had moved Factory Records designer Peter Saville to tears. A car came to collect the two of us, together with Tony's son Oliver, from Tony's loft apartment and waited outside the theatre after we'd arrived, since Tony planned to be present for only ten minutes.

Unfortunately there was no lift and Tony had to walk down the stairs into the theatre and back up again. It was only a few minutes, maybe twenty at the most, but it seemed frustratingly protracted to me. Sitting beside him, I could sense how difficult it was for Tony to wait, but we were eventually rewarded with Douglas Gordon's beautiful portrayal of Joy Division's 'Love Will Tear Us Apart', rendered for several captivating minutes by a female vocalist; a haunting, disembodied voice from the darkness. The singer wasn't visible, unlike Tony's tears in the car afterwards. This was to be our last outing together.

Early in June 2007 Tony and I had gone out for dinner on a Saturday night, something that had become a regular occurrence by then. Although I offered to drop him outside the restaurant, he said he wanted to walk from where we had parked the car – just off Manchester's King Street – over to Piccolino's near Albert Square. It was odd that such a simple act as this short walk could seem so magical when Tony's failing health later precluded walking altogether. His voice was clear that night and he seemed to want to talk about his ancestral background. It occurred to me that he might be telling me this for his children (in case they didn't know or might forget), or for posterity. I rather wished I had a notepad or tape recorder but I lacked both. This is what I recall him telling me.

Tony's grandfather, Mr Knupfer, came to Salford from Freiberg in Germany after a short spell in New York, which he had decided was too far away from home. Settling in Salford, he became apprenticed to a watchmaker on Regent Road. When his employer later died he managed to scrape together just enough to buy the business. He had three children by his first wife. One day Karl, the eldest boy, was playing with the youngest in the back yard when the latter fell from a wall and died.

Following the death of his first wife, Mr Knupfer remarried and his second wife gave birth to Tony's mother, Doris, and her brother Edgar. The two siblings remained unusually close from beginning to end. (This pattern seems to have been repeated with Tony's two children and Doris's grandchildren, Oliver and Isabel, who are also extremely close.) Mr Knupfer's second wife died young, when Doris was eight, and he married a third time, fathering Tony's uncle John.

Mr Knupfer bought a house in Douglas on the Isle of Man, and when he died he left the business in Salford to Karl, a second watch-making and jewellery business in Eccles to Edgar, and the house in Douglas to Doris. Doris sold the home and bought yet another business on Regent Road, a sweet shop and tobacconist she called McNulty's, after her husband Ted McNulty. Doris ran it alone after Ted's death in the 1940s. Ted had been a passenger in his brother-in-law Karl's car when Karl crashed it. Although Ted seemed to be all right afterwards, he died two weeks later from a brain haemorrhage.

I hadn't remembered hearing this story before that night in June. It was always common knowledge to me, though, that Doris was heartbroken to lose Ted. She subsequently met Sydney Wilson, who was a friend of her brother Edgar and, it has been speculated, might even have been his lover. Certainly he and Edgar were both gay. Nevertheless, Doris and Sydney married and their son was born in 1950. Her marriage to Sydney was a compromise, as Ted remained the love of her life. Yet she was always grateful to Sydney, he was a pleasant companion and gave her a new great love in the form of her child, Tony.

By the time of his birth Doris was forty-six, which was unusually old to bear a first child. Even more unusual, especially for the repressed fifties, was the fact that, as Tony was growing up, all three of them – Sydney, Doris and Edgar – lived together happily and harmoniously in the same house. Tony had all the attention a child could possibly wish for.

I have become convinced that this unusual upbringing was the foundation stone of Tony's character. He only ever knew what it was to be totally loved and adored by three grown adults. There was never any doubt of that in his world. Among his earliest memories was being pushed along in his pram and watching another child in a pushchair yelling at the top of his voice. 'What are you crying about?' he thought to himself. 'It's not so bad in here.' Tony held as an absolute, irredeemable truth the certainty that this world – his world – was good, which may go some way in explaining that even when he was dying of cancer over fifty years later he was able to view his illness as 'an adventure'.

Wherever he went, Tony was cushioned by the great love these adults had for him. The adoration was logical – Doris would have given up hope of a child and another true love, and children were an extra special rarity in the world that Sydney and Edgar inhabited. How exceptional that must have made Tony to them all.

It was therefore only natural that they should care passionately about Tony's upbringing and education. Tony continued his tale by telling me that this began at Monton Preparatory School, but Doris didn't want him growing up on the back streets of Salford so she, Sydney and Edgar bought a plot of land in Marple and built the home they called Oberlinden. Tony remembered how they would picnic on land overlooking the house to watch it being built. Here Tony attended Marple Primary School, where he was taught by Brigid O'Dwyer, who would become a formidable influence. Miss O'Dwyer introduced him to his first adult book, Charles Dickens's *Dombey and Son*, to which Tony would often refer, particularly the chapter about death. That chapter, entitled 'What the Waves Were Always Saying', apparently had such a profound effect on Dickens that, unable to sleep, he walked the streets of Paris every night during the writing of it.

Miss O'Dwyer became a family friend and when she retired to her hometown of Dunleary, or Dun Laoghaire, south of Dublin in Ireland, the family was able to visit her for their summer holidays.

I learned at Tony's funeral that it was on such a visit that he met the man who became his best friend, Shaun Boylan, as a result of Sydney and Doris offering Shaun's parents a lift in their Morris Minor when they encountered them walking up a steep hill in their hometown of Dunboyne, Co. Meath. Tony always said that Shaun was the Alex Ferguson of Ireland, but in addition to his contributions to football Shaun is also a medical herbalist. Tony told me that some herbal remedy Shaun gave him, quite soon after they first met, got rid of his sore throat. Decades later Shaun tried to help treat Tony's cancer with herbs, but the first time Tony took them he had such a strong reaction that I don't think he attempted it again.

Despite his weakening voice on the night of that dinner in June 2007, Tony reminded me that, notwithstanding the lasting literary influence Miss O'Dwyer had on the young boy, he appeared initially to have more of a leaning towards the sciences. At the age of ten his favourite magazine was *Knowledge*, with its articles about atoms and the universe, and he obtained a distinction in Maths and Physics at 'O' level. He had decided to become a nuclear physicist – and knowing his unshakeable belief in himself he would no doubt have achieved this – but his career plans changed after he saw a production of *Hamlet* at Stratford-on-Avon. So affected was he by this performance that he decided there and then that his future lay in the literary arts, and he went on to take a degree in English Literature at Cambridge.

Of course, much of Tony's past was common knowledge to me. I knew that Tony's mother always said that going to Cambridge ruined him (and also that women would be the future ruin of him), though he must have been somewhat infuriating even before this because, although Doris was a devout Catholic, she once threw a statue of Our Lady of the Sacred Heart at him!

I also knew that in 1968, the year Tony began at Cambridge, he felt somewhat lonely and homesick at first. He used to listen to the track 'America' from Simon & Garfunkel's *Bookends* while staring out of the window of his tiny college room, and would count the cars passing on the road in front (rather than on the New Jersey Turnpike).

Going to Cambridge was a core moment in Tony's life. His years there always meant a great deal to him and he loved to reminisce and revisit. I can remember a sunny day when he enthusiastically showed me his old haunts and his friend and colleague, Nick Clarke, recalled a day when he accompanied Tony around Jesus College: 'Tony had this big coat on, we went through the door and he went, "It's okay, don't worry, I'm an old boy!" I was looking in awe, there's Coleridge on the wall, all these great writers and he took it all in his great stride. He was totally and utterly comfortable there. I saw something that day in his eyes that very few people would have seen unless they were close to him. He actually loved that place to a solid heart for all the right reasons.'

Apparently Tony also showed Nick the precise spot where he took his first ever acid trip during his first year there, and then the position where he'd vomited from the experience – they weren't too far away from each other.

To accompany his love of literature and music, theatrical and performance genes appeared to have been handed down to Tony. Sydney Wilson was an actor, mostly amateur, throughout his life and had been brought up in Hulme, Manchester. Sydney's mother, also a thespian, worked at the Hulme Hippodrome, located a short distance away from the yet-to-be-born Russell/ Factory Club. The Hippodrome was built in the early 20th century next door to the Hulme Playhouse and boasted a beautiful theatre. Sadly in the 1960s the building was used for bingo and, I am told, was also at one time a 'review theatre' featuring shows such as 'My Bare Lady' and the like. Currently it is disused, and it is a great pity that such buildings go to waste.

The first I heard of Tony Wilson was when he got his break running a kamikaze section on *Granada Reports*. This career twist came about somewhat by accident, as do so many things in life. It was two weeks before Christmas 1975, and, with the show calling for something Christmassy, the crew went off to the Mottram Hall Hotel. They decided on two shoots, one of Tony on the roof dressed as Father Christmas arriving, and the other of him emerging from the chimney into the fireplace. The staff cleared the grate from the fireplace and he was told it wasn't hot. 'They lied,' he told me later. 'It was.' He climbed a short way up the chimney, balancing himself on a brick protruding slightly out of the wall, out of sight of the camera. He could hardly breathe and thought he might suffocate, and when he heard the cry 'Action!' – his cue to emerge from the chimney – he couldn't as his clothing had become caught and he was well and truly stuck. Tony said this was the most dangerous kamikaze he ever filmed; he really thought he was going to die in there. However, the seeds of an idea were born and Wilson's kamikaze series – in which he did dangerous sports without any proper training – became a weekly event.

Most famously, Tony was filmed hang-gliding on the edge of a moor. The dramatic impact, on the audience and Tony himself, captured attention both on television at the time and also thirty years later when Steve Coogan re-enacted the scene for the film *24 Hour Party People*. The movie cuts to the original, real-life footage of Tony scaling down the Welsh mountainside where *Granada Reports* was filmed in 1976. It was his third or fourth attempt, by which time he thought he might be able to joke in the commentary that he was getting the 'hang' of it. But then things got somewhat out of control, and it looked hilarious when a sudden gust of wind lifted him up and threw him precariously off course in the direction of a barbed-wire fence. Luckily there was just enough wind to carry him over, but he landed upside down in a ditch.

The ratings demonstrated the show's popularity. People enjoyed seeing Tony Wilson – the man they loved to hate, perhaps because of his total self assurance and a confidence amounting to near arrogance – end up face down, arse up, having narrowly missed a body wrap with barbed wire. It certainly livened up a rather dull regional news programme.

My first sighting of Tony was on this very programme on Granada TV when, during a round of teaching practice in early 1976, I had been invited to tea by the class teacher. Having recently become hooked on it herself, the teacher asked me if I would mind if she tuned in to watch Wilson's weekly dance with danger. She had probably enjoyed his brush with the wire fence that nearly broke his ankle or, equally captivating, the water-ski jumping/parascending episode that would see Tony narrowly miss smashing into a wooden jetty. Tony's description of this in his book *24 Hour Party People* is really funny and I recommend reading it for a laugh.

Sitting watching Tony's 'Kamikaze Corner' (as writer Paul Morley later referred to it) that day, I was struck by an absolute intuitive certainty that someday I would come to know this man. It felt like recognition. This conjecture of mine occurred despite the logical improbability of our meeting – I didn't know anyone who knew him and we occupied entirely different social circles. Amazingly, weeks later, I watched, almost open-mouthed, as Tony, accompanied by a girlfriend and mate, walked into a party I was attending in Altrincham. As I too was with a boyfriend we politely held our distance, but when Tony's male pal came over to me I knew that a connection was being made. It was. He got my phone number. His name was Nick Lander, a bright fellow who'd studied at Cambridge and who later became an acclaimed restaurateur at L'Escargot in London's Soho. He has even appeared on *Masterchef*.

A week or two after the party I met Nick in town for lunch and happened to mention some unusual and fresh Thai sticks that I'd gotten hold of (certainly I have never seen the likes of it before or since). Nick laughingly said his friend Tony would be interested in that and I offered to pass some on. The next thing I knew Nick inadvertently played cupid when he rang to say that Tony had asked to try it, but could I ring him myself as Nick was going away? Once I'd got Tony's phone number I knew our fate was sealed.

Tony and I met for the first time on 15 May 1976, in the car park of the Ram's Head pub in Disley, Cheshire, on the edge of the Peak District. He was sitting behind the wheel of a Ford Escort RS 2000, the pale blue racer model with a darker stripe down the middle. I thought it the ultimate in cool. I jumped into the passenger seat and we drove a short way up the hill, whereupon he parked the car and we smoked a joint of said Thai grass. I couldn't take my eyes off his jeans, patched up with all manner of interesting stickers and badges, and his blue eyes. It was love – or, to the cynical, lust – at first sight. I knew Tony felt the same way. I drove away absolutely certain in the knowledge that we belonged together and that my time with my boyfriend – with whom I'd been in a live-in relationship for two years, which had been heading towards marriage – was already over. I was sorry for that as the guy in question, Michael, had done nothing wrong, but my future was no longer with him. Categorically.

How many times in a lifetime does something like this happen? Probably only once or twice. In several letters Tony referred to this first meeting. An example was: 'That "love from above" which we both felt survives . . . In me it is a recognition that beyond infatuation and friendship, there is a thing, a kind of relationship that is rare, almost a twinning of souls in one destiny, that I felt soft intimations of that afternoon in Disley.'

And, being Tony, this was illustrated with a quote from his favourite poet, W.B. Yeats, who he had loved since first discovering him aged sixteen:

. . . it seemed that our two natures blent
Into a sphere from youthful sympathy,
Or else to alter Plato's parable,
Into the yolk and white of the one shell.

Tony was always very fond of literary references – much to the annoyance of some, since it often appeared that his ego was coming to the fore but, speaking for myself, I really enjoyed them. That said, the way he sometimes assumed intellectual superiority could be infuriating. Tony read the classics throughout his life. Shortly after we met he steadfastly read his way through all seven volumes of *À la Recherche du Temps Perdu* (often translated as *Remembrance of Things Past*) by Marcel Proust. He never tired of literature, even when seriously ill with cancer. The last classic book he read was *Moby Dick*, a story full of symbolism about a man who battles with a great white whale while all but one of his crew suffer a watery doom. The narrator floats to the surface clinging to a coffin, so the symbolism here is very heavy indeed. But I am often told off (in the past not least by Tony) for reading too much into symbols.

It seems odd to me now that I hadn't realised then what a good writer he was. Although when I look back on his career it is hardly surprising that he had a way with words. After Cambridge, at which he edited the student newspaper, *Varsity*, he went to ITN and was there for two years as a journalist and scriptwriter. Then he went on to Granada as a TV reporter, which he always described as 'my job, my craft, and my career'.

Bob Dickinson, a writer, musician and producer for BBC Radio and Granada TV, recalls: 'As a serious journalist, Tony was just as much at home behind a typewriter in the *Granada Reports* newsroom as he was in front of the cameras. Granada's news and current affairs output during this period was – unlike the BBC's – leftwing, and unafraid to launch campaigns, or ask awkward questions.'

Again elsewhere – when we were apart – Tony wrote about the powerful connection we both instantly shared: 'So many people are strangers, even people you love. Vonnegut calls it your "karass", all these people you are tied to by family, job, situation, even tenderness, *but* not your people; maybe you don't meet your people except very occasionally. To me, this silly absence is the lack of one of the few non-strangers I've ever met; I knew you weren't a stranger that first afternoon on the hillside in Disley. Funny how clear you can see from 200 miles.'

Tony was referring to *Cat's Cradle* by Kurt Vonnegut, in which the narrator ends up on the make-believe Caribbean island of San Lorenzo, where, of course, the natives do things differently. Their dialect is odd and their religion, called Bokononism, encompasses unique concepts, with San Lorenzan names such as karass – a group of people who, often unknowingly, are working together to do God's will. The people can be thought of as fingers in a cat's cradle.

After our first encounter in Disley and knowing we had to meet again as soon as possible, Tony invited me to travel up to his house the next day. Charlesworth seemed to be miles away – en route I kept thinking that I must have gotten lost because surely he couldn't live so far from Manchester – though I would have driven anywhere to reach him.

I was surprised to find him in the company of two friends when I arrived – and the house was tiny! I'd expected someone in the public eye to have a much bigger place. But I was pleased by that, since I had thought that his place would be flash and large. His modest terraced cottage seemed cosy and unassuming materially. Nonetheless there were clues to his 'hip' lifestyle in evidence. In the small living room there were the dramatic Lichtenstein *Whaam!* prints on the wall and two guitars on stands – an acoustic and a red Fender Stratocaster. Tony and his friends (one of them was Alan Erasmus, later to become a Factory director) were also playing pool on a small table that totally dominated the front room. When I visited the bathroom I noticed funky pictures – such as a caricature an artist had drawn of Tony and a photograph of him at a stock car race, helmet atop his head and his arm reaching out in a symbol of victory. (Actually this was taken before the race – it transpired that his car got turned over, but that all added to the drama of another kamikaze episode.) Even the kitchen had unusual crockery – shiny green hexagonal coffee cups with matching saucers and plates, like those made by Apilco.

The atmosphere that evening was charged and the energy was high. Everything announced to me Tony's love of craziness and music – something we shared. Actually, guitar-playing turned out to be one of the few things that Tony was modest about. I thought he was rather good and, though he dismissed it, I enjoyed listening to him strum. Quite often he would play acoustic melodies, anything from Bob Dylan to Beatles tracks and so on. Clearly he must have known from an early age that music would play an important role in his life. His parents paid for guitar lessons in town to reward him for his graduation, aged eleven, from Marple to the Catholic grammar school De La Salle in Salford, and later bought him his first guitar – a red Watkins Rapier – to celebrate his becoming a teenager.

That night (our first date, you might say) I'd expected us to be overtaken by passion right there and then in Charlesworth, but instead we went out to see Wythenshawe glam-punk band Slaughter & the Dogs at some dingy club in Stockport. We drove separately and behaved as if we were just close friends. Tony was tripping on LSD when I arrived that night – a drug that interested me, which I'd taken several times.

We listened to the band – I thought they were pretty terrible but loved it all the same. Tony later told me he thought the band were exciting and that Martin Hannett (the producer of this band) had rung him up and told him to go to the gig. Tony seemed to remember it was held at the 'Garage' and in general thought the gig was kind of 'interesting – if not brain-defying'. He said he thought it was punk – 'punkily glam' – and that one member of the band was wearing a women's blouse or dress. Tosh Ryan, who released the group's early records on his independent punk label, Rabid, assures me that they never wore women's clothing and that Tony may have been getting this gig mixed up with Ed Banger and the Nosebleeds. Mick Middles, who interviewed Tony extensively for his book *From Joy Division to New Order* (repackaged and updated in 2009 as *Factory: The Story of the Record Label*), wrote that 'Wilson decided he had just experienced his second truly historic rock happening' (the first being Lou Reed), but I'm now not sure whether he meant Slaughter or Ed Banger. Memory is, of course, a subjective affair at the best of times, and is certainly affected by drugs such as LSD and marijuana.

Afterwards Tony and I said goodnight in the car park. Exactly what happened after that is somewhat lost to the mists of time (and a subjective memory). Our first kiss, date – all uncertain. But what I do know is that our mutual obligations to our existing partners seemed like something that had to be sorted out immediately. My two-year live-in relationship was over there and then, and I was ruthless about it, adopting Shakespeare's maxim: 'If it were done when 'tis done, then 'twere well it were done quickly.' Tony preferred not to let the axe fall on his affair so harshly and chose a more diplomatic way of ending it. This demonstrated a difference in our natures. I believed in ripping the plaster off quickly; he wanted to spare the pain by peeling it away more gently. Also, he was more devious than I was!

Tony said his girlfriend was travelling to India in about six weeks' time and it would be best to leave it until she got back to break the news. Then he and I would travel to Thailand together. I could see his logic, that it would be kinder, but I still had my doubts. It seemed dishonest somehow, to her and me. My own relationship was already over, yet it had gone on a lot longer than Tony's had and he was still pretending. Still, I agreed we wouldn't see each other for the six weeks but only on condition that he wrote to me every single day in the meantime. He said he would and kept his word. His first letter referred to this plan:

Darling,
The first of many . . .
. . . I know you don't think much to my plan . . . but like the man sang, 'trust in me babe'. So for the first few weeks of this 'could-be-eventful' summer (this is the first summer of the rest of our lives) I'll write, each day, I'll wake up as I did this morning trying to imagine how lovely your sleeping face would look on the pillow, I'll get my show and my thing together as they say on the west coast of Scotland, I'll become a small but contented gun, oh and I'll also miss you but you already know that. And don't give me any of that 'I don't believe it for one minute' crap. You know it like I know it, that's why we're acting so crazy.

Tony went on to quote Donne ('Think that we are but turned aside to sleep') and the letter ended on a literary note:

It's a long time before the dawn Mr D. Crosby used to sing, but then again some sunrises can be worth it. Oh and one more lovely quote, I've just been crying my eyes out – yes, I'm not as hard as I appear . . . my dear – while watching *David Copperfield* on the TV. My love for Dickens and Aunt Betsy can wait for another time but there was one lovely moment, where Mr Micawber was venting his worries about the future and the difficulties to be faced therein. Mrs Micawber turns on him and, with a voice that is as loving as it is scolding, says: 'You are going to a distant country expressly in order that you may be fully understood and appreciated for the first time.'
The Micawbers went to Australia; us, Bangkok.

As it was quite a tall order he had taken on, he sent postcards after this (with a capital 'A' cut out of them for Anthony). A card was easy to fill with a literary brain such as his – one addressed to 'Lady of My Life' simply quoted: 'Anything I ever desired or got, 'Twas but a dream of thee.'

Another advised me not to worry and promised that one day we would 'roll around in bed all day'. Yet another card told me: 'June is going to India early – running away – I'd recommend the same for you but you're not the type that takes advice.' He signed it: 'Yours "as this machine is to him" Anthony'.

Tony was re-quoting a letter from Hamlet to Ophelia that ended: 'Thine evermore most dear lady, whilst this machine is to him.' His card also explains why we didn't make the six weeks apart (we didn't make Bangkok either, as it happens). In fact within days of sending that card he came to visit me at the place I was renting.

This same month happened to be a time of infamous change in Manchester's musical landscape, a hinge moment if you like, although no one realised it at the time. In fact two relatively minor gigs would become momentous in Manchester's history that summer. It was an energy flash that took place, intriguingly, in the same area where the 1819 Peterloo Massacre occurred. (A cavalry charge and attack on thousands of hungry yet peaceful civilians who were gathered in the name of democracy.) Something was changing fast, both personally and musically, but it was only with hindsight that it became apparent. Although Tony and I were portrayed as together at the first of these two gigs in the film *24 Hour Party People*, in reality we were still distanced. As the punk scene in Manchester was invisibly germinating underground, our relationship was also invisibly intensifying. We'd met, we'd had the thunderbolt, but we weren't quite together on 4 June 1976, when the first famous Sex Pistols gig took place at the Lesser Free Trade Hall in Manchester. Howard Devoto and Pete Shelley had arranged this gig and – inspired by the Sex Pistols but lacking a bass player and drummer for the occasion – rapidly put together their band, Buzzcocks, who played with the Sex Pistols at their next gig at the venue in July. Tony had been in London working at ITN and expected not to make the gig, but he caught an earlier train and managed to race across town from Piccadilly to the Free Trade Hall and by himself witnessed something that changed his outlook, if not his life.

David Nolan speculates in his book *You're Entitled to an Opinion* that Tony wasn't actually at the first Sex Pistols gig but rather the second on 20 July. Perhaps that would be like Tony – to bend the story to make a myth. Personally I don't give a stuff which gig he was or wasn't at, although there could be something in Nolan's argument. It occurs to me that surely if Tony had attended the first gig he would have made certain I attended the second one? Still, even Ian Curtis missed the first Pistols gig. In point of fact I think the second more historically interesting in any case, because the Buzzcocks played their first set that night. During an early interview with Tony for research into *Torn Apart*, the book I wrote with Mick Middles about the life of Ian Curtis, the following dialogue took place between Tony and I about that first Sex Pistols gig:

TW: So, then the point is which members of Joy Division were at the gig?

LR: We've all heard enough about that gig, haven't we?

TW: Are you writing a book about Ian Curtis or not?

LR: Yes, he was.

TW: I don't think he was. Are you sure he was?

LR: I'm not sure which one it was. Could have been the second one. Does it matter?

TW: Yes. Piece of advice – it matters enormously if you're writing a book about Ian Curtis. It does matter.

LR: But does it matter in terms of the history of Ian whether it was June or July?

TW: Yes. Whether he was at the first or second gig – it's called a fact.

LR: Well, true.

TW: I'm sorry, it's actually very important. Just trust me.

LR: Okay, I'll find out.

The night in question was depicted in the film *24 Hour Party People*, but as Tony later commented: 'Nobody actually pogoed at the Pistols Lesser Free Trade Hall gig – it was invented later – everybody just sat and stared.' In my own view this wasn't the only thing that became myth rather than reality. The Sex Pistols were the undoubted catalyst in changing the music scene and inspired others who pushed forward with a DIY creative energy of their own. These doubtless included others present in the audience, amongst them Ian Curtis and members of the yet-to-be-formed Joy Division, the Fall's Mark E. Smith, and Morrissey. The group onstage became lightning rods for the avant-garde musicians and mavericks who happened to be in the audience. But if the Sex Pistols themselves were a catalyst for the changes that were happening, the reasons for those changes can be traced back even further.

3 The Hippies' Revenge?

The 1960s was a vibrant time for music, and there are some who would argue that for sheer creativity, originality and influence on future generations it has never been equalled, let alone bettered. Tony was a folk-music fan at the dawn of the decade but then, like everyone else with a brain, he was swept along by the magic of the Beatles, the Merseyside pipers who led the parade of countless other groups from around the world. Tony once told Tosh Ryan that he thought the greatest tune of the 20th century was 'Love Me Do', the first single by the Beatles, released at the tail end of 1962. 'I think he was being contentious,' says Ryan of Tony's opinion of what is not generally regarded as one of the Beatles' finest works. 'It negates everything that happened from Ravel, Charlie Parker, Stravinsky, Sinatra, Duke Ellington to Plastic Bertrand – it's a crazy thing to say.'

In the early 1960s EPs were a common currency in the record world. These were seven-inch, 45rpm vinyl discs containing four or five songs, packaged in an attractive full-colour sleeve made from good quality shiny card, and Tony was enthused by one of many EPs that the Beatles released, this one containing four songs from their film *A Hard Day's Night*, which influenced him to issue the first four-track EP on Factory later down the line. He was a fan of all this kind of music – and in another part of Manchester, so was I. My girlfriends and I had regular 'disco' sessions, dancing around the Dansette. I loved the new releases and was always the DJ on these evenings, playing a stack of 45rpm vinyl singles (which, by the way, in my opinion have a far superior sound quality to CDs). *Top of the Pops* began broadcasting from an old church on Dickenson Road in Rusholme, Manchester, from 1964, and was not to be missed. It was always exciting to think that the Hollies, the Rolling Stones, Dusty Springfield and many more were all performing a mere bus ride away.

Although at age thirteen I was astounded by a local group when they played 'Louie Louie' live at a church fete, unfortunately I was too young to go out to the many clubs and cellars operating all over Manchester, where live beat groups played virtually every night of the week. There were as many as 200 in the early 1960s and some, like Oasis and the Twisted Wheel, have become legendary. The Twisted Wheel was based on Brazennose Street from 1963-65, and its cramped stage played host to artists like Ben E. King, Georgie Fame, the Yardbirds, Long John Baldry, Edwin Starr, and Junior Walker & the All Stars.

The resident DJ was Roger Eagle, with whom Tony and I would one day become well acquainted, whose love of R&B and soul turned this hip basement into an important, pioneering venue. Indeed, it was Roger who created the genre known as Northern Soul, though he did admit to a slight ambiguity of loyalty as far as his personal taste was concerned. 'At heart I was a Teddy Boy amongst a load of Mods,' he once told us.

In 1965 the Twisted Wheel moved to Whitworth Street near Piccadilly Station and ran until 1971. However, many believed that its early, underground (literally and metaphorically) years were the best. All-nighters generally took place on a weekly basis, no doubt helped along by the use of amphetamines more commonly known as 'purple hearts', which were, in fact, not purple but blue. All in all it seemed the most exciting place for the 'in-crowd' to be, even if it was dangerous, forbidden and certainly out of bounds to me. No Manchester club would become as well known as the Twisted Wheel until the Hacienda in the 1980s.

By 1970 many of the live venues in Manchester had been closed down by the police, led by the city's chief constable, who cited health and safety issues but in reality was waging an unwinnable war on drugs. When they reopened many of the remaining clubs became discos, not least because it was cheaper to hire a DJ than a band. This resulted in a relative lull in the Manchester live scene in the early seventies, with live music moving to venues that served the city's student population or the 2,000- to 3,000-seater halls like the Apollo, the Free Trade Hall, the Opera House and the Hardrock in Stretford, which hosted shows by visiting Americans or UK big-hitters like Led Zeppelin and the Who. With the mass unemployment the seventies brought, many young kids couldn't afford to see these super-groups, a factor that led directly to the rise of the DIY punk ethic.

A musician's co-operative called Music Force was formed in Manchester in 1972 to support the now struggling jobbing musicians and benefit gigs were held at the Houldsworth Hall on Deansgate. Music Force's promotions were mainly publicised by fly posting, and in the early days the posters were designed and silk-screen printed by members of Music Force at Mayfair Mansions on Mersey Road in Didsbury, a stylish building that used to be the Italian Consulate. Several musicians lived on the premises and others gathered here in a spirit of mutual support to exchange plans and ideas.

Tosh Ryan, along with Bruce Mitchell and Victor Brox, co-founded Music Force, and remembers Tony Wilson hanging around them there as early as 1971-72. 'In those days Tony was more inclined to be sycophantic to these musicians, whereas in later days it was the other way round,' he says. 'He wanted to be part of it.'

Martin Hannett, bass player and producer with a scientific background, was soon co-opted onto the committee of Music Force and became involved with booking bands, and writing for their magazine *Hot Flash*. He wrote some clever things. For example, a singer and guitar player called Kevin Ayers had run off to Tenerife with Richard Branson's wife way back in the seventies. Martin wrote an article headed up with 'Record Mogul's Wife Splits With Ayers, Branson Left in Pickle'! Martin turned his hand to anything useful, as soundman and roadie, and procured musical and PA equipment which undoubtedly led to his fascination with, and understanding of, electronic gadgetry. Of course, his sound engineering talent was soon to flower in the form of studio production technique.

Tony mentions seeing Martin at the Sex Pistols gig in his book and describes him up rather well: 'Mad professor eyes under hippy haircut, the town's wannabe producer and knob twiddler: one of the true geniuses in this story.'

Martin had co-founded Rabid Records with Tosh Ryan and Lawrence Beadle using money from Tosh's flyposting operation. Tosh recalls that Martin referred to himself as a wizard and noted that the name Merlin spelt backwards was nil rem, or Latin for 'no thing'. This could well be the origin of Martin's penchant for calling himself Martin Zero. Tosh and Martin promoted a few gigs before this time – under the name Ground Zero Promotions.

In 1996, Tony said that he thought any book about Factory (he was referring at the time to the first and only book then available, which was by Mick Middles) should really be about Martin Hannett. 'Manchester music only has two stages,' he stated, 'the Harvey Lisberg/Danny Betesh phase and then the Martin Hannett phase. Whatever the next phase is hasn't happened yet.' Tony's observation, like many of his almost 'sound-bite' phrases, sounds clever if a bit over the top, but it got me thinking about what a huge compliment this was to Martin, particularly since the pair had a spectacular fallout in the early eighties, culminating in Martin's legal action against Factory.

Lisberg and Betesh ran Kennedy Street Management, and their involvement with Manchester music is in itself a story for a whole book. They had success with so many of the Manchester acts that became big in the sixties – Freddie and the Dreamers, Wayne Fontana & the Mindbenders, Herman's Hermits and so on. There was a collection of Manchester Jewish kids in addition to Lisberg and Betesh – Lol Creme, Kevin Godley, Graham Gouldman, Harvey Rose, and Ian Starr – who also marked a successful phase of musical output in Manchester. Gouldman wrote for the Yardbirds and together with Godley, Creme and Eric Stewart from the Mindbenders, went on to form 10cc. In

Stockport in 1968 they opened Strawberry Studios, which would play a major role in the history of Factory Records.

Music Force began arranging their own gigs around 1972 at various venues such as the Cavalcade Pub in Didsbury, Mr Smiths at the back of Whitworth Street, the Midland Hotel, and the Houldsworth Hall on Deansgate, the corner frontage of which is now the Bella Pasta opposite Kendals Department Store.

In many ways the emergence of this movement was a reaction to the mainstream rock of the 1970s, the dinosaurs and 'old farts' who became so reviled by the punk movement. In the beginning, the press latched onto it and called it pub rock because many of the gigs took place in the back rooms of pubs. The London-based music press, as ever curiously reluctant to travel north of Watford, implied that pub rock was a London-based movement but it was actually a nationwide phenomenon. Its independence, operating outside the traditional influence of agents and managers, became, in its own way, the forerunner of punk. Young musicians got their start with the help of older musicians playing the same gigs. Buzzcocks, for example, had no idea how to make a record and came to Music Force to find out.

While the pub-rock scene was largely apolitical and concerned purely with playing good live music – with much of it based on traditional genres like R&B and country – there was a political edge to punk that was driven by the disaffection felt by its leading lights. Punk stood for change, and under its banner there appeared other left-leaning pressure groups like Rock Against Racism, the Right to Work campaign, the Anti-Nazi League, various factions opposed to the proliferation of nuclear arms and, at its most extreme, the rather shady Bash the Rich group.

'I think punk was deliberately targeted by these organisations,' said radio and television producer Bob Dickinson, 'because some punks were parading around with swastikas without really understanding the implication of what they were doing. Then some punk bands like Skrewdriver actually started using racist language, and that was that. In other words, there was a politicisation of punk around 1977-78.'

Music Force's benefit gigs were often supportive of various protest movements. Tosh Ryan explained: 'The kids who wanted to be in bands substituted musicianship for outrageousness in dress and lyrics – i.e. the spectacle – as they hadn't got the musical ability. Then punk was exploited by the right wing. The BNP and National Front fascists turned up at the gigs taking advantage of the imagery the naive punks had embraced. It was further exploited by the likes of McLaren and Westwood with their shop Seditionaries, and justified by Wilson in his defence of Joy Division's Nazi imagery as "post-modern irony".'

Liz Naylor, co-editor of *City Fun* magazine, once said of punks: 'It would be accurate to describe them as a bunch of still-born hippies from the tail end of an era which had trashed its promises and rather disappointingly fizzled out.

Punk provided the perfect vessel for their thwarted ideas.' Tony often referred to her words, saying that punk was the hippies' revenge – implying that hippies had been disappointed that the world hadn't changed and so got their own back with punk. He quoted Naylor in his book and went on to say, 'Dead right, honey. We were a little bit stardust and a little bit fucking golden and some of us refused to believe that the Garden didn't exist.' (This was a reference to Joni Mitchell's song 'Woodstock'.) On the one hand he agrees with Naylor, but he seems to be defending the hippie trail and finishes by complaining that she and her mate Cath fucked off with the £200 he gave them to produce Manchester's first colour-photocopy fanzine, so 'fuck you' is his final statement to her. (He always liked to have the last word and usually did.)

I asked Liz and Cath Carroll about this, and writer and performance artist Cath gave an interesting response: 'Tony ran everything and everyone through the Mythologiser. When he paid his first visit to our flat in North London in the late eighties, he took one look around and took up the entire meeting talking about the horrible flats inhabited by Jagger and Richards, pre-success. Our flat was basic, but wasn't so bad that I thought it warranted comment or a quick re-spray from the Mythologiser. It was like bringing in a conceptual interior decorator. Now we had a construct for our cheap lino and railway view. And actually, yes, it did make the flat more exciting. He knew what he was doing.

'He once gave us £50 to do a one-off fanzine with full colour and posh paper. As in "gave" us, not "lent" us. It sold five copies but looked great. He liked it. In later years, the story grew and eventually it turned into we had taken £200 from him and never returned it. At first I thought he was joking, so I never countered with a request for Miaow [a band fronted by Carroll who released two singles on Factory in 1987] sales figures etcetera, but apparently he was quite keen on the story and put it about a lot.'

With all this going on in the background it was only natural that the mad, staring eyes of Johnny Rotten, leering over his microphone into a startled audience, screaming about anarchy, would capture the imagination of so many, not least the young Tony. He later derided the music of the early seventies, saying that Rotten's Sex Pistols had shown us just how 'bloody dreadful' it was and how we had needed something to destroy all that 'Rick Wakeman bollocks'.

I don't agree entirely with this view, not being such a huge devotee of the Sex Pistols nor totally averse to Yes; nor do I recall that he really had such an intense dislike of all seventies music (at the time at least). Tony often tended to see things as either black or white – brilliant or shit – when in fact the truth might lie somewhere between the two. The differences in our musical tastes would emerge later but at that time it was clear that a passion for music was something we both had in common. Tony was a self-confessed musical snob, he sneered when he saw an album by the Eagles in my collection but in reality I don't think our tastes were all that far apart. I always thought I couldn't go out with someone if we didn't share a similar appreciation and taste for music and still do – it's very important. I think the punk thing created one of the cracks in the proverbial lute of our relationship, so that one day it couldn't play. I disliked the scene that eventually built up around punk. Also, I didn't trust Tony's wavering musical taste, which seemed to have more to do with fashion – and changed a bit too dramatically when punk came along.

Initially though, in 1976, punk did seem vital. There was something healthy and moral about the people of Wythenshawe making a stand, the inverted snobbery even, and all this appealed to me as well as Tony. I was ever the supporter of the underdog. Women, black people – the punk movement seemed to stick up for those repressed by the system, those whose anthem might be 'Don't tell us that just 'cause we've got nowt we're not talented'. There seemed to be something revolutionary about it. Personally I find it extremely disappointing that thirty-odd years later two of the leading protagonists of this movement, Iggy Pop and Johnny Rotten, can be seen advertising insurance and butter. But then punk seemed to stand up for the socialist values that Tony and I shared, although I wonder if the punk movement was not in fact exploited by the middle class, if not right wing. Designer Peter Saville responded to that idea with: 'It was an intellectual gesture, class wasn't the issue. It was about the politics of youth rather than international politics. Tony cared about what a young generation were trying to express. To me, Tony's relationship with pop music was as the poetry and politics of an upcoming generation.'

So Tony and I both loved the scene early on, and both of us were, in our own ways, supporters. It took another year or two for the division in our tastes to become evident.

LR: You've proved to me what an exceptional man you really are,
truly heroic.
TW: I'm just getting on with it you stupid cunt [*said with some fondness*].
LR: Yes, but don't you see that's exactly what I can't do.
TW: That's true.
Transcription of phone call, 12 July 2007

As soon as we both became free of our mutual emotional entanglements in June, Tony arranged for us to spend the weekend at Portmeirion, an Italianate village by the sea in North Wales. I had no knowledge of this place at all (although the TV programme *The Prisoner* had been filmed there in the sixties and my brother-in-law was an extra in it). I can still remember my amazement when we arrived in his RS 2000, pulling in to park outside the hotel – parking was a cinch in the seventies – checking in and going off to our little cottage. I thought this must be heaven. Not only was the place exquisitely charming and magical but the sun was shining, the sky was as blue as Tony's eyes, and we were in love. From our room I could hear people splashing in the outdoor swimming pool. In North Wales! It genuinely seemed like Italy. It *looked* like Italy. Oddly this blue sky remained intact every single day for almost the entire summer of 1976. Portmeirion has a plaque on a tree in honour of that year's summer that reads 'None such'. Tony called summer 1976 the summer of love. For he and I it most certainly was.

It was only a month or so after our first meeting in Disley that I moved into Tony's house. My mum strongly advised against this happening so soon. I knew that deep down she had doubts about the whole thing, although she never actually came out and said so. I chose to completely ignore her in any case, despite the fact that she was my wisest ally. It all seemed terribly simple to Tony and me – this was what we wanted. I hadn't so much as a nanosecond of doubt about it. Neither did he. His first gift to me was a door key inscribed with my name, the least expensive yet most generous present I could wish for. Attached to the key was a card that read: 'Is this the key to your heart I ask myself. Can I stay here for awhile if it is? Anthony x'. Also, because I said I liked two and he only had one, he presented me with a duck down pillow.

The night I arrived with my stuff we decided to celebrate the occasion by taking LSD. Happiness doesn't really require stimulants but they can give it an interesting edge. Tony and I both had a penchant for changing our consciousness with psychedelics. I can't speak for Tony, but I think I was looking for answers to the meaning of life. Since then I have heard it said (rather wisely, I think) that taking drugs to find that out is a bit like trying to open a door with explosives. But, having said that, I had my moments of truth. I don't remember anything dramatic about this particular trip except when the flashes of colour and quirks of consciousness started to wear off and we both knew it was bedtime. He went ahead of me and I lingered for a while in his little study, taking quiet pleasure in the affinity I felt for his books that lined the shelves. Located between the small galley kitchen and the living room, the room I was in was an obvious choice for a dining room. Certainly most people would have made it so, but not Tony. I loved him for that. His practice of always assigning one room in his home for use as a study or office remained with him throughout his life, from this humble beginning in Charlesworth to wherever he lived thereafter; the only aspect that varied was its size.

I think he was referring to a poem I had written him when, in a subsequent letter, he wrote: 'I know that image of the warm house, the cosiness, that step down into the study at which point I'd first see you in the kitchen . . . yes.'

On 27 June 1976 we went to the King's Hall at Belle Vue to see Bob Marley & the Wailers. King's Hall was more commonly used as a circus venue in the round, although on this occasion the stage was opposite the front door. Artists couldn't fail to note that the journey from the dressing rooms to the stage was accompanied by a strong odour of animals. The hall was packed but Tony and I were both sufficiently enthusiastic to want to press forward towards the front. I had felt perfectly well until we got there and to this day I have no idea why suddenly, without any warning and while thoroughly enjoying Marley's music, I fainted on the spot. In the event it was terribly romantic, the stuff of movies – in which the lady in distress has invariably just fallen pregnant, though not so in this case – because Tony singlehandedly carried me through the crowd, through the front foyer and out into the cool evening air. When I came around the first thing I saw were his concerned eyes looking down at me. The stuff of pure romance!

Tony was enthusiastic for all sorts of things, but his enthusiasm for music was in the realm of passion. As well as the psychedelic music of the sixties, when the seventies progressed he became attracted to edgier American rock artists. Talking to Mike Sweeney, a prominent DJ on Manchester's Piccadilly Radio, in 1983, Tony said: 'It's funny I have a rather American tradition and what happened with American kids – the reason that '67, '68, '69 the great hippie thing happened, was that they were all folkies, they were all into folk music in '62–'63 just as I was into Peter, Paul and Mary and Joan Baez (I was aged twelve then) and then suddenly what happened with the American kids was they went to see this film called *A Hard Day's Night* 'cause they listened to the radio, liked pop music, but don't love it like they love folk music, and then they saw this film. Every person who was important in American music in the late sixties – who made rock music – went to see *A Hard Day's Night* and thought, "My Heavens, I can sing songs like I like, songs with meaning, but with electric guitars." The same thing happened to me . . . I loved Hendrix and then I got into psychedelic music at university. I stayed involved with psychedelic music. I was one of those idiots who kept buying Jefferson Airplane albums till about 1975.'

Tony was impressed by Lou Reed, the former head honcho of the Velvet Underground. He saw Reed perform at the Free Trade Hall in 1974 and afterwards spoke with great excitement about the riot that ensued when Lou, ever a contrary soul, refused to return for an encore.

When in June 2007 an occasion arose that enabled me to see Lou Reed on his Berlin tour, Tony sent me a text message: 'Have eaten loads. Feel I have turned a corner. Enjoy Lou. Can't wait to see you tomorrow. Can we eat out early, straight after work? Shame you're on your own. But enjoy. Xxx.'

A ticket that Mick Middles had obtained for Lou's Berlin tour couldn't be used due to illness, so I stepped into the breach, as it were. By that time I couldn't remember much of *Berlin* and was therefore surprised to discover I still knew most of the words. Even after so many years without the album, the words to the songs that I had played so often at Charlesworth came chiming back to me.

I couldn't fail to be impressed by the optimistic tone of Tony's text. It was sent six weeks before his death. Tony was eating very little at this stage. But I believed him. I thought he was getting better. Maybe *he* even believed it.

In the early seventies Tony became fascinated with the States and was one of a tiny handful of people lucky enough to catch Bruce Springsteen perform in a small bar there soon after he was signed to CBS. Long before Bruce's triumphant, barn-storming tours with his E Street Band, Tony recognised something in him that he saw years later in Ian Curtis; a weirdness, the future of rock'n'roll perhaps.

Tony had also been much taken by Patti Smith after the 1975 release of her debut album *Horses*. 'Suddenly there was an album that was fresh and didn't sound like all that other shite.' He told me that her gig at the Apollo in 1977

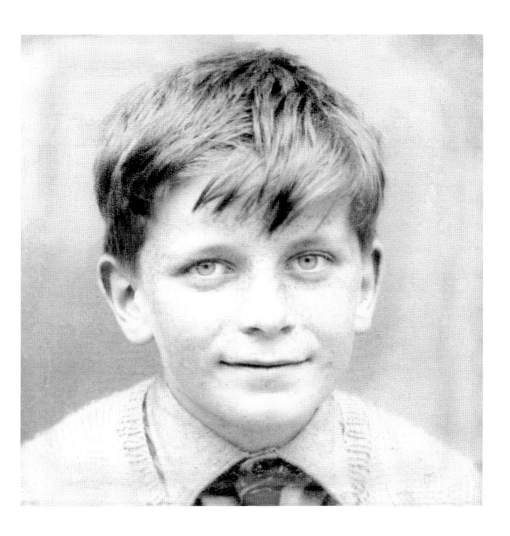

Above: The childhood photo I kept by me
throughout Tony's illness, taken in around 1957.

Opposite left: Tony on the set of *So It Goes*, 1976.

Above: Tosh Ryan leads Tony to Slaughter (& the Dogs), outside Wythenshawe Social Security Office, 1976. **Left:** Martin Hannett, aka Zero, on his way to a Greasy Bear gig in the early 1970s.

Opposite above: Holiday hallucinogenics, November 1976. **Opposite below:** Blue skies over a blue RS 2000, taken by Tony on a visit to my rented house, June 1976.

Above left: The trip to the bullfight, France, July 1976. **Above right:** En route in France the same month. **Below:** Au revoir to the car in France, July 1976.

Above: Our two natures blent, 1977. **Below left:** Passion in Portmeirion and (right) me posing among some sculptures, as instructed by Tony during the same trip, July 1976.

Above and below: I can't remember where this photo of me was taken, but Tony is pictured during our trip to Tenerife, November 1976.

Above: Tony's scarf serves as a bikini top (after my suitcase failed to arrive), Tenerife, November 1976. **Below:** My modelling card from the Lucie Clayton School featuring some kids from Hulme, spring 1977.

was where he first met Peter Saville (although Peter disputes this, and believes their first meeting was at Granada). 'In '76 she was great because then she was a New York poetess playing at being a rock star,' Tony said, 'and by '77 she was a rock star playing at being a New York poetess.' *Horses* was the forerunner of punk for Tony, and his unfettered enthusiasm for the movement, even if he hadn't yet got the tag to label it.

So with all his enthusiasm overflowing, and with the pre-punk world simmering below the surface and becoming visible at last, it seemed unbelievably lucky that summer of '76 when, having made a reasonably successful pilot show, Tony was able to present a new TV series called *So It Goes*. The name was inspired by Tony's reading of Vonnegut's *Slaughterhouse-Five*, in which the echoing motif 'So it goes' is used every time a passage deals with death. It was enormously exciting for me that my boyfriend had been given such a fabulous opportunity; to be directly involved with a music programme. It seemed a logical progression from his *What's On* slot on *Granada Reports*.

Tony had joined that programme in 1973 and enjoyed tea-time banter with broadcasters, mainly Bob Greaves but also Richard Madeley and Judy Finnigan, Gordon Burns and Brian Trueman. Although Tony's contributions to *Granada Reports* made it an entertaining show, he was in reality a serious journalist, having pursued a career in journalism after leaving Cambridge.

Bob Dickinson remembers: 'At that time [1973] Granada defined something very important about the North-West of England. It wasn't just because *Coronation Street* had put the region on the map, or because Hughie Green made affectionate jokes about "Granadaland" on *Opportunity Knocks*. It had more to do with the fact that Granada made great TV programmes that reflected the people and the culture of Manchester, Liverpool, Lancashire, Cheshire, and bits of North Wales and Cumbria. Granada's regional television coverage was as good as, if not better than, the BBC's, providing the region with its own documentary strands, such as *This England* and *Celebration*, as well as news. Many of Granada's networked programmes were also better, and more successful.'

Tony always thought it was really quite accidental that he went in front of the camera as a news reporter rather than remaining behind it as a journalist. It hadn't been his initial intention, at least. Immediately after he arrived in front he succumbed to what he called 'the red light syndrome', an addiction to the buzz of adrenaline that shot through him the minute the red light on the camera filming him turned on.

Tony's involvement in the *What's On* show – which really got the musical ball rolling in his career – involved another turn of fate. Trevor Hoyle had presented *What's On* from 1973 to 1975, but was moving to further pursue his career as a novelist in the tranquillity of the Lake District. Tony suggested himself for the job since film and music were his hobbies. His selling points were having majored in English and his training as an art critic at Cambridge.

This gave Tony a perfect niche to present his fun artistic side, put bands on, and generally enjoy himself.

Granada, like Tony, thought that Manchester was a really important region and did much to cultivate it. Tony worked at Granada when the company was at the height of its creative powers, as Dickinson recalls: 'By Tony Wilson's time, every TV viewer was aware of Granada's weekly current affairs programme *World in Action*, their quiz contest *University Challenge*, their press review *What the Papers Say*, comedy shows like *Lovers*, groundbreaking social documentaries like *Seven-Up*, ambitious drama productions like *A Family at War* and *Brideshead Revisited* – and the fact that Granada had been the first TV company anywhere to film the Beatles, in the Cavern Club, Liverpool, back in 1962.

'As a rock fan, Tony was well aware of the important music documentaries Granada had produced, including *Stones in the Park*, *Johnny Cash Live at San Quentin*, and *The Doors Are Open*. Many of those who'd worked on those programmes were still around at Quay Street during Tony's time, when Granada continued to make pop shows for ITV's unstuffy and non-middle-class children's schedules, including *Lift Off with Ayshea*, *Shang-A-Lang* [with the Bay City Rollers], and *Marc* [starring Marc Bolan]. Granada employed plenty of people who were well-versed in producing pop for television, and unlike the BBC, these personnel weren't permanently attached either to regional or network output. As a Granada employee, you were moved about, and you mingled with, and met, everybody in the building. That's how *So It Goes* got off the ground, with talented directors like Peter Carr and producers like Geoff Moore.'

One Sunday lunchtime in late July, 1976, Tony met my parents and his future in-laws for the first time at the house in Charlesworth. When they arrived he lingered upstairs rather than face them directly which, given Tony's TV profile, seemed to indicate an uncharacteristic lack of confidence or insecurity. Later I discovered that he often dealt with circumstances that made him feel uncomfortable by simply being absent. After lunch we took a walk across the nearby hills, admiring the local scenery. Attempting to break the ice, my mum uncannily tapped into one of Tony's favourite subjects when she asked him what he was reading. He mentioned *The Romantic Exiles* by E. H. Carr, a book about the Russian political writer and activist Alexander Herzen and other suspected revolutionaries who had been exiled. Though it wasn't the sort of thing I would read, Tony was fascinated by it, not least because of Herzen's complicated love life, which involved more than one wife and various love triangles. My mum cynically joked that perhaps this sort of thing – to be an activist with two or three wives – might appeal to Tony, whereupon he grinned as if that was exactly what he had in mind (at the tender age of twenty-six). Odd that it sort of came true.

Perhaps out of a desire to win over my mother, whose doubts about the suddenness of our living together he was aware of, Tony presented a copy of the said book to her. He always wrote inscriptions in books, and this was no exception: 'For Mrs Reade, just 'cause your daughter won't read it, doesn't mean you won't. Says it all. Always does, I suppose. Anthony x'.

He was right. At the time, I never did. But in 2008, six months after his death, I was looking around for something to read on my bookcase and found this. It was somehow comforting to find after so many years forgotten, and I was glad of one more opportunity to spar with Wilson, so naturally took up the challenge at once.

'Pfff!' I thought when I read his note. I always enjoyed a battle with Tony, particularly if I won of course (which I rarely did). And heavens, I wasn't going to let a thing like death get in the way of it. So I picked it up with a determined mind (thinking, 'Oh God, this may be as bad as attempting *War and Peace*'). In the event no such effort was required. The book was actually a pleasure to read. And it brought me comfort knowing it was a book that Tony once considered valuable. I found parallels in the lives of Herzen and Wilson; both men of letters. Tony, like Herzen, had ambitions and visions beyond his private life, which I failed to grasp at the time.

Reading the book brought frustration, that damn, damn, damn feeling that I had missed out on an enriching conversation because I couldn't talk to Tony about it. We weren't going to have any more one-to-one conversations. Sadly they were all history now, but that history had a beginning.

Before Tony and I met, he had fallen madly in love with a lovely lady named Thelma from Liverpool. Their love affair had lasted two years and together they might well have gone the distance but for one thing: she was married to Roger McGough, a performance poet and member of sixties group Scaffold (who also featured Paul McCartney's brother Mike McGear and comedian John Gorman), and they had two young children, plus one much older – Nathan – from Thelma's earlier marriage. That said, her relationship with Tony was not clandestine or hidden. Tony asked Thelma several times if she would leave Roger 'for someone with a smaller kitchen'. This was a pun on one of Roger's lines from his poetry collection *Summer with Monika* – about her leaving Roger for someone with a bigger kitchen. Tony called Thelma his 'Maud Gonne' (the name of Yeats's muse, with whom the poet shared a turbulent relationship), something that puzzled her since their love was reciprocal. She says, 'These literary fantasies of his took various guises – he imbued me with qualities, which in truth I did not possess.'

Tony and Thelma used to meet at Birchwood Service Station, which was roughly midway between Manchester and Liverpool, and Tony told me that 'their' song was 'When Will I See You Again' by the Three Degrees. Thelma told me there was one other by Gram Parsons, they used to play it in the car and sing along very loudly. It was somewhat prophetic, 'We'll Sweep Out the Ashes in the Morning'.

The two lovers went to London twice, one time to discuss Tony's prospective job at Nationwide. Showing typical unselfishness, Thelma didn't try to deter him from accepting, although Tony promised her he would be back at weekends in any case.

The day he set off from Charlesworth he was snowed in and had a horrendous road trip over the hills of Derbyshire on the way down to London. In the early evening he telephoned Thelma from Watford Gap Service Station and said, 'I'm coming home, I've phoned Mike Scott [Head of Granada] and he said I can have my job back. Can I come and see you?' He drove straight back without going into London and arrived at her house in Liverpool late, looking very weary. She was thrilled to see him. Off he went to Granada the next morning – all back to normal. Thelma liked the thought that he'd come back for her, but she thinks he didn't want to leave his roots behind. He told her that he preferred to be 'a big fish in a small pond'.

In Tony's case his Maud Gonne, as he later also referred to me, was not to be the only love of his life. He quoted Yeats's poem of the same name on more than one occasion, and in a letter to me wrote: 'I've loved Yeats since he was my "first" poet . . . nice somehow that my experience in life should lead me to feel so deeply and exactly those great commonplaces of love and experience and pain which he sets forth to the love of his youth . . . who, incidentally, and for him, like me, in vain, was to be the only love of his life.'

Incidentally, Thelma was not the girlfriend I first saw Tony with (at the party). Her name was June. June was unfortunate to have met Tony when he was still in love with someone else. Several women have endured that sad fate. A bit like a rebound romance – doomed. His relationship with Thelma had sundered after Roger McGough, 'the Patron Saint of Poets' as Carol Ann Duffy calls him, wrote to Tony and, appealing to his fellow Catholic principles in the erudite language of poets, requested him to return his wife (property) and family. Thus persuaded by the written word, Tony moved on, choosing honour above his personal feelings. He was able to empathise with Roger and respected his point of principle. Honour amongst men perhaps, especially a fellow Catholic.

I met Thelma that summer of 1976 at a function in Liverpool and she was very friendly towards me. Tony wanted Thelma and I to meet, he had told me all about her and her all about me. I could tell at once that Thelma just wanted Tony to be happy – almost in a motherly way, not the jealous-lover way – and I sensed that I had her approval as she had mine. She told me recently that it was an honour to be invited to our wedding, even though for her it was tinged with sadness.

So It Goes ran all of that first wonderful summer of ours, nine weekly shows from 3 July to 21 August. The night of the first broadcast was another special event for us so we decided to take LSD again. *So It Goes* seemed fantastic to me and I thought the phone would ring off the hook as soon as the show was over. Much to my surprise not one single person rang. I couldn't believe it. Had they not seen what I had just seen? What about our friends and family? Not one vote of confidence. Tony didn't seem perturbed and was his usual ebullient self. I felt quite disappointed by the lack of appreciation, but we went out together for a walk and stopped by a wellspring near our house. Gazing down at the gushing water gave me some comfort. Indeed, *So It Goes* was, metaphorically speaking, a wellspring of things to come.

Many years later in 2005, when I was interviewing Tony for *Torn Apart*, the book I co-wrote about Ian Curtis, I asked him why he thought no one rang that night. He replied: 'It was terrible, it was an utter disaster. All our friends thought it was crap.'

'Why?' I enquired

'Because it was disrespectful to music. It was a comedy show.'

'I thought it was quite good,' I said.

'It was complete and utter shite. Be-Bop Deluxe, John Miles . . .'

'. . . Dr Hook,' I said. I always associated a song of theirs, 'Little Bit More', with Tony and I, which obviously wasn't mutual, as he continued: 'Yes, just quite nice pop schlock. It was utter shite. It wasn't respectful to the music.'

'I'd love to see it again,' I said. 'Sounds a bit black and white to me.'

'The night after the first show went out,' added Tony, 'we were at the Portobello Hotel in London on the way for a week in France and we met up with Leonard Cohen. And Leonard said, "Oh, your show was fucking great Tony."'

Incidentally, of all the famous people I have ever encountered, I most value having met Leonard Cohen. I have such respect for him; he seems to be truly wise. Unfortunately the remembered snippets of conversation I had with the great man seem rather trite now – a wasted opportunity perhaps, or just the way life goes. We shared afternoon tea; his partner was there and she struck me as lovely. As we made our way into the tearoom I got talking to Cohen about drugs. He told me that he'd given up smoking dope as he'd got older and I was curious to know why. I couldn't imagine ever wanting to abandon it then, however old I got. He replied that it had stopped working and I remember feeling somewhat dissatisfied with that answer. Yet with age I have come to interpret his meaning differently because of the way I feel about it now. It's not so much that it doesn't work anymore as it doesn't work *the same for me* anymore. With age comes values and responsibilities that dope really doesn't cater for.

'We had a lovely week in France,' continued Tony, 'got home on the Monday and my father rang and said, "Oh, the *Sun* doesn't like you," and I'm thinking why is the only thing he says that one of the critics has got it in for me, but I go to work the next day and every critic in Britain had it in for me.'

Perhaps this is a slight exaggeration – Tony liked to get a reaction, even a bad one was better to him than none. But I remember being astonished at the time that the only comments the show received (from anyone) seemed to be negative. It must have hurt Tony because it upset even me. When Tony was hurt he never let it show. But he was always pretty good at getting his own back, either by punishment or revenge!

Although the formula was pretty much the same for both series – with feature input from Clive James and a row of television sets behind Tony – the first series was arguably a rather tame if quite diverse snapshot of pre-punk, with artists ranging from Tom Waits to the Chieftains to Eddie and the Hot Rods. Nonetheless there was a kind of exciting confusion to 1976, as if everything was up in the air, on the bubble, with impending change around the next corner; whereas in 1977 it was just pretty much all punk and done and dusted. Tony's look – long hair with leather jacket, scarf or denim shirt – seemed to perfectly capture that slightly hippie yet pre-punk confusion.

It was also an exciting time because people could sense that something was about to happen – but didn't quite grasp what it would be despite the clues that were all around. The direction seemed to be leaning toward the avant-garde, the adventurous, the out of the ordinary. As early as July '76 Tony was to be seen interviewing his beloved Patti Smith on location. His last show, on 28 August, featured the Sex Pistols. This was the moment that gave series two its edge and engaged Tony's real passion for the show. 'Bakunin would have loved it,' he said to the camera after the Sex Pistols left the stage. I often wondered how many in his audience realised that Tony was referring to the Russian revolutionary and founding father of anarchism, who argued that the abolition of the state was the best route to freedom.

Tony and I took acid together another time during that summer of '76, while in France. He thought it would be an interesting idea to watch a bullfight while tripping and I went along with it, having no reason to doubt the merits of 'Tony's Tours' up to this point. Speaking for myself, it was the horror of horrors. I sympathised empathically with the bulls in every case and was astonished that no one else seemed to. It reminded me of a football match; the crowd erupted in cheers every time the poor animal got stabbed with a dagger whereas I wanted to cry, 'Stop! It's a beautiful, innocent creature.' I was badly shaken up afterwards, but Tony, as per usual, thought it had been an interesting adventure. Then again, he said the same thing about having cancer.

It was in the summer of 1976 that Tony first took me to meet his father, Sydney, at his house in Eccles. Sydney had been widowed in 1975 and the loneliness he felt was there for all to see. I thought it might cheer him up over tea if I quoted something Tony's mother had apparently always said; that, because she was quite a bit older than he was, Sydney would marry again after her death. This went down like a lead balloon. Indeed, judging from the scowl on Sydney's face I thought I had seriously offended him, though at the time I took it to mean that, in his grief-stricken frame of mind, he was horrified at the thought of taking another wife.

Tony's mother had died very suddenly while he was away in California. Sydney and Doris had been to the theatre that very evening, and I remember Tony telling me about this terrible day and how he had bought himself an ice-cream near Santa Barbara pier and noticed his tears falling down onto it. This image stayed with me for some reason, perhaps because even in his extreme sorrow he still showed a certain zest for life by buying the ice-cream in the first place. Tony loved his mother as dearly as any child could. He also admired her, and as such she was a role model to him through her love of the arts, her Catholic faith and her fondness for the city of Manchester. I never met her, of course, but Tony spoke of her often in our early years together. One image of her that remains in my mind is the night they boarded a bus after an outing to the theatre. Doris was wearing her finest fur coat and jewels but seemed unconcerned about travelling by bus or climbing up to the top deck, where she accidentally spilled some change from her purse onto the wooden floor, yet thought nothing of getting down on her knees and foraging for it in her finest!

Another image is of this devout Catholic woman on holiday in Paris with Tony and Thelma. Thelma describes Tony's mum as having been as open, welcoming and inclusive as her son. Doris knew that Thelma was married (twice) and had three sons, yet it mattered not – she made her son happy, which was all she cared about. I had thought that Doris often used the name Anthony (especially when angry with Tony), but Thelma said, 'I did not want to call him Tony because that was the name of Nathan's father and I didn't want to be reminded of that association, so I always called him Anthony. He liked it and later began referring to himself as Anthony; his letters are all signed "Your Anthony". Doris called him *Tawny* – at least that's what the Manchester accent sounded like to me.'

(Indeed, although I never once used the name, all Tony's letters to me were signed Anthony, or, in the case of Factory documents, Anthony H. Wilson.)

Doris loved stylish hotels, an influential habit that stayed with Tony for the rest of his life. One of her favourite hotels, to which the family would return every year, was the Grand Regina in Grindelwald in Switzerland. Tony took me there for a week one spring, during which it rather disappointingly rained most days. We had to go up higher to get snow and sun. Tony told me the story of how one year Sydney took it upon himself to book the second week in another hotel, which turned out to be rather in the package style, both in terms of the hotel and resort. Apparently they were going up in the lift to their rooms when they heard a man remark to his wife as the couple were about to leave the lift, 'Let's make tracks luv,' in a broad Manchester accent. Doris at once pronounced, 'I've not come all this way to listen to that,' and insisted that they check out immediately and go to stay at a pensione, away from the rabble as it were.

So it was a given that the hotel they all shared in Paris was elegant, stylish and very grand in a baroque kind of way. Doris bought Thelma a bouquet of red roses on arrival. Tony loved to relate the story of how his mother barged into the lovers' room the next morning, tired of waiting for them when there was all of Paris to see. She couldn't help but notice that the roses were now crushed, with petals strewn across the bed and around the room! Tony was amazed by how matter-of-fact his mother was in a situation which the lovers were obviously rather embarrassed by. Thelma describes Doris as 'a no nonsense, down-to-earth type of woman, funny and forgiving too'.

I think Tony believed to the end that his mother was near him. Or at least I must assume so because, on 14 May 2007, over dinner with me, Tony spoke of a higher kind of genetic love and said that he cared for his children more than anyone else, more even than his partner Yvette. Being without either children or parents I remarked, 'What hope is there for me to find this special love then?' He said that my mother was still there.

'Where?' I asked. 'She's not here.'

'In the place where death is,' he replied.

Tony often visited his mother's grave, opening his heart and making vows to her. I think it a great shame that she wasn't physically present, especially during those early years of ours – I suspect she would have knocked some much-needed sense into the pair of us.

Looking back to 1976, the odd thing is that neither Tony nor I knew at that point that his father was gay, even though it was blatantly obvious really. What innocents we were! Of course, homosexuality had only been decriminalised in 1967. I do know, however, that whatever his sexuality Sydney was a perfect gentleman and behaved so towards his wife from start to finish. He died on St George's Day and I think that somehow fitting for a man of his calibre.

Nonetheless, as a child Tony had sensed something about his dad that somehow didn't fit. He told me that he once got annoyed and asked his mother what on earth she was doing with Sydney, implying that he wasn't good enough for her. Doris pulled Tony up immediately. She explained that she had lost the true love of her life in the war and that since then Tony's father had been enormously kind to both her and Tony, that he was a good man and she would not allow Tony ever to speak like that about him again. He never did. He kept his thoughts to himself. He confessed to me that he had always felt closer to his Uncle Edgar, his mother's brother, who also lived with them. Looking at photographs, Edgar seems more masculine. Sydney wore bow ties, loved to act – we saw him perform at Eccles Theatre – and was perhaps a shade more effeminate.

It must have come as a great shock to Tony when, within a year of our meeting, he discovered that his father was gay. In this regard, Doris's prophecy about Sydney remarrying did in fact come true, after a fashion. The year after her death Sydney met Tony Connolly – a very rough diamond – in a pub in Charlesworth, probably the summer we were in France, when he kindly called at our house to water the plants. Their relationship was kept a secret from us until Tony Connolly came to our door one day in 1977. Despite elements of wildness, especially in Connolly, they remained together until Sydney's death in 1997.

I'm not sure if Tony ever fully dealt with, or worked through his odd heredity. It fell to me to make Tony face up to the fact that his father was gay, something I felt impelled to do. But a bigger shock lay in wait for Tony on a day not that long afterwards. He was sitting in a parked car round the back of Kendals Department Store with Rob Gretton (who became his partner and manager of Joy Division) and Donald Johnson (who joined Factory band, A Certain Ratio, after Tony began managing them). Sydney worked at the nearby tax offices and Tony suddenly saw him enter the adjacent public lavatory (on St Mary's parsonage, I think). After at least half an hour or so Rob, who had also seen Tony's father go in but not come out, suggested that they move on. Even I was rather shocked by this, although I'd rapidly come to terms with the fact of Sydney being gay. It smacked of a taste for casual sexual encounters – a quality I would never have associated with someone like Sydney. Perhaps it was the illicitness of it that was exciting to him, perhaps it was partly because in those days there were fewer places for gay men to meet, and so many more of them were still pretending to society that they were straight. Or maybe he was meeting Tony Connolly down there – I later discovered Connolly's penchant for wildness, sexually and otherwise, and he told me that he sometimes brought a third party home to 'share' with Sydney.

In September 1976 I began work as a primary school teacher in Gorton while Tony carried on with his day job at Granada. Every evening I would come home and make the tea while watching Tony present *Granada Reports*, feeling proud of him. He'd usually make it home by 7:30pm in those early months, but because I had to leave early for work I would often fall asleep before we made it upstairs to bed.

During this same month Tony and I went to another Slaughter & the Dogs gig at the Forum in Wythenshawe. Their profile had grown since May, to the extent that they now had a support band, a group called Wild Ram who, within weeks, would become Ed Banger and the Nosebleeds. It was Ed who would have been wearing a dress, so perhaps it was this show that Tony may have mixed up with our first date and Slaughter gig. Although not an earth-shatteringly memorable night for me, oddly the forces of fate were at play as producer Martin Hannett was present. Vini Reilly, who was to become a huge catalyst in the formation of Factory, was playing guitar with Wild Ram. I loved his electric-guitar playing on 'Ain't Been to No Music School', a slight against another Manchester band, Sad Café, and their pretensions of superior musical knowledge. Vini's technique is absolutely brilliant yet quite unlike the style he became better known for during his esteemed career with the Durutti Column.

This night obviously made an impression on Tony as he invited the group to appear on *Granada Reports*. John Crumpton, a founding member of the Film & Video Workshop in Manchester, made a film entitled *The Rise & Fall Of The Nosebleeds* in 1977 and reported that the group manhandled Tony during the performance of 'Ain't Been to No Music School', saying, 'Whether such opportunities exist for a present-day bunch of working-class lads from Wythenshawe, to have their fifteen minutes seems highly questionable in the era of ITV without its regional connections and the increasing sanitisation of rock music through the dull blandness of *Pop Idol* and *Fame Academy*. Unfortunately the band weren't able to capitalise on their brief moment in the spotlight and their failure to make money created further tensions. Without success they carried on regardless, but the splits within the group were ever widening.'

Tony and I both enjoyed the evening at the Forum, so I was surprised when it was abruptly cut short and he ushered me out to the car park. He seemed somewhat agitated. What had happened I wondered? It wasn't until we drove away that I found out he'd had an 'encounter' with Martin Hannett, who, under the name of 'Zero', had written in listings magazine *The New Manchester Review*: '*So It Goes* is Granada's answer to *The Five O' Clock Club*.' (*The Five O'Clock Club* was a children's TV show in the 1960s presented by Muriel Young with regular items in the style of *Blue Peter*, e.g. about pets and Bert Weedon giving guitar lessons. Young was head of children's programmes at Granada in the late 1970s.)

Martin was being his usual cryptically funny self but Tony took offence. Clearly, even if Tony had thought the first series of *So It Goes* was, in his words, 'a pile of complete and utter shite', the arrival of the Sex Pistols had given him something of which he could be proud. Otherwise, perhaps he might have laughed Martin's comment off. Certainly, Tony had been hurt by the bad reviews of *So It Goes*, even if he didn't show it. Also, it wasn't just the show that had been rubbished – Tony himself was unpopular. Many people thought he was arrogant, annoying, pretentious and smug.

Although I accompanied him that night I wasn't aware until we left that Tony and Martin had crossed swords. Tony later talked about the incident: 'Walking in this guy came over to me and said, "Hello, I'm Martin Hannett," and I said, "Oh yeah, that's right, nice to see you again. Do I take it, it was you who wrote that line having a go at *So It Goes*?" and he smiled and said, "Yeah," and I said, "Well *fuck* off," and walked off. The rest of that night these kids were coming up to me and saying, "Mr Hannett's outside in the car park, he's waiting for you," so Martin was waiting for a fight. He wanted me out there. That was the Mancunian part of Martin. He was really pissed off and expected to have a fight.'

Once Tony and I had beaten a hasty retreat he told me in the car that he'd thought a fight might have happened, hence his nervousness, since he'd never been in a fight in his life before. There was certainly no one screaming 'cunt' at him in the car park or banging their fists on the car as one 'eye-witness report' later suggested.

In some ways Tony wanted to be one of the working-class kids and deny his middle-class background. With the dawn of punk it had become fashionable, but sometimes it irritated me slightly that he spoke with a different accent depending on who he was with or where he was. Speaking on television he tended to go the other way and adopt Queen's English, but one step into Wythenshawe or Salford and suddenly he became a true northerner. Perhaps I should have been more forgiving – he was a performer after all. My mother always said he was a 'showman'.

Tosh Ryan thought that Martin had a thing about Tony from the start. In the early 1970s, '73 or '74, Tosh remembers that he, Martin and several others picketed Granada Studios for not putting local bands on. Tony recalled that Martin rang him up at Granada soon afterwards and did, in fact, come in to the music library there to play him music he had produced by the band Red Brass, who were part of Belt & Braces, a political agit-prop theatre group.

When Tony's passion was engaged with a punk-influenced second series of *So It Goes*, he reverted to the very bigheadedness that had made people dislike him. In 1992 he told *Q* magazine: 'It sounds arrogant and it sounds terrible and it sounds smug, but to me *So It Goes* was like being the A&R man for the biggest record company in the world. I was the A&R man for God's record company. And every group I put on was the right decision. It made me think to myself, "I am clever, I am clever."'

There had always been people around Tony to help him, though. By himself he wasn't the world's best A&R man. Those groups of the seventies renaissance literally fell into his lap, even though he was astute enough to know intellectually what was going on. He made errors with bands – the Wendys, who received a healthy advance when Factory's finances were headed towards critical, being just one example. After Factory went into liquidation Tony's later incarnations of record labels weren't that successful. He may have had posh offices, but the substance in his groups was somehow lacking. Hopper? Who the fuck were they? Tony's complete and utter enthusiasm – amazing though it was – didn't of itself make it happen, even if he did have magazines on the table and a secretary in a city centre office. Not with Raw-T either, even if he did believe they were the best band in the world. But I'm not saying that Tony's bands were necessarily so bad. I think the last two decades have been sufficiently materialistic to stifle the natural creativity of young bands in favour of naff commercial enterprise and talent shows.

For my school's half-term break Tony booked a week's holiday in Tenerife. I wasn't sure what the weather would be like and so packed virtually everything I owned. The night we left we went to a party in London and I was wearing a red dress. I will never forget that dress since it was the only garment I had for the whole week – my suitcase went missing and was never found. We enjoyed the holiday, although Tony was a bit scathing about package tours and swore he would never go on one again. Actually I don't think either of us ever did. I quite enjoyed the set meals, the buffet lunch outside and dinner in the restaurant. I told my parents about the resort where we stayed – set in a large garden with flamingos, two swimming pools, games rooms – and they liked it so much that they went there many times.

As the year wore on, Tony and I ventured more than once to a dingy club on Collyhurst Street off Rochdale Road called the Electric Circus. It seemed to encapsulate the ethos of punk rock – very anti-establishment – and was somewhere Tony and I both liked to go. That December we went along to witness the Anarchy in the UK tour with the Clash, Johnny Thunders & the Heartbreakers and the Sex Pistols.

The club was teeming with tension then. Previously a prog-rock hangout, its long-haired, flare-trousered clientele seemed to regard it as home turf and were openly hostile to the incoming flood of short-haired, tight-trousered punks. One night in December, the old prog band the Enid – a favourite act at the Circus – had been billed, but this had changed at the last minute and the Damned appeared instead. They were jeered throughout their lively set and exited to a chorus of 'Shit! Shit! Shit!' from the prog crowd. It seemed ludicrous to us that these hecklers were soon dancing to a disco playing Black Sabbath's 'Paranoid', which seemed strikingly similar to the music of the Damned. There was some confusion when AC/DC played because no one was quite sure whether they were rock or punk at that point.

By the spring of 1977, however, the tide had turned and punk enjoyed a regular Sunday-night billing, with bands such as the Jam, the Ramones, and Talking Heads; the Clash's White Riot tour, with Subway Sect and the Slits; Generation X with Billy Idol; the Stranglers – who were prog rock pretending to be punk – and Manchester's own Buzzcocks.

Buzzcocks were not only championing the punk movement in the city but also pioneered the concept of the local independent record label. Their manager Richard Boon came to the Music Force offices to ask Martin Hannett to produce Buzzcocks' *Spiral Scratch*, which was a four-track EP released in January 1977 on the new label. Alberto Y Lost Trios Paranoias frontman C.P. Lee apparently asked singer and writer Howard Devoto what Martin's role in the production was and he replied, 'Merely to add a certain ambience.' Perhaps so, but Martin's main plan was to break into production. C.P. also suspects another reason Martin was chosen for this production was that Hannett claimed he'd got a pressing and distribution deal arranged with Parlophone! Distribution was in fact poor – the record was initially only available from Virgin Records on Lever Street or directly from the New Hormones label by sending £1.10 – but the enthusiasm was there and the group's initiative was much admired. So was the frugal, value-for-money manner in which they went about their business. According to a story *New Manchester Review* printed a few months later, the songs were recorded at Indigo Studios in five hours at a mere £19 per hour. Pete Shelley's dad had put up the initial money and can therefore be directly credited with paving the way for the independent record labels that followed. *Spiral Scratch* was the first successful independent record in Manchester.

The success of *Spiral Scratch* gave Martin and the label Rabid Records, founded in 1977, quite a good foothold. For years Martin had wanted a recording studio and now his dreams were becoming real. Having produced Rabid's first single 'Cranked Up Really High' by Slaughter & the Dogs, he went on to produce Nosebleeds, Jilted John and John Cooper Clarke tracks for Rabid.

Clearly all of this was a vital inspiration for the creation of Factory, which was yet to be born.

6 Amen (So Be It)

Nineteen seventy-seven was a year of change. And we were at an age when the changes that involved Tony and I were generally new and interesting. He'd proposed during our first Christmas together and there was a wedding to prepare for. Changes that involved loss and decline were, so far, rare; certainly to me, although Tony had already lost his beloved mum which – when it later happened to me – was heartbreaking and felt like losing a precious limb.

It is odd that our married life began that May since this was also the month that Tony later claimed Factory Records began. This was the same month that Alan Erasmus went to see a band called Fastbreeder and began managing them. Tony and Alan had become mates through an introduction by Charles Sturridge, who was a director at Granada. Sturridge was Alan's flatmate at 86 Palatine Road, Didsbury, an address that would later evolve into Factory's office. Fastbreeder's name was apt and Alan's involvement with them would lead to the partnership between him and Tony.

This band never struck any chords with me, but it did seem that we were heading into a period when exciting new developments were happening on the music front – a spirited renaissance of some kind, somehow not entirely tangible but present all the same, and appearing at various venues such as Rafters on Oxford Street, the Electric Circus, or Eric's in Liverpool. We also went to some of the bigger shows, including the New Bingley Hall, in Stafford, to see Pink Floyd in March 1978.

My teaching was only a temporary appointment, due to a secondment, and soon ended. Teaching jobs may have been a bit thin on the ground but I didn't try all that hard to find another since I'd felt compromised taking the job in the first place. I'd never really wanted to teach but I didn't know what else I could do with my degree. I'd already tried nursing and then driving Range Rovers –

with Michael, the boyfriend I was with when I met Tony, and his friend Clive –
to sell to Sheiks in the Middle East. I loved to travel but the same road became
monotonous after the first trip. I suppose you could say I still hadn't found
my niche. I probably took the view that my future job was likely to be in the
home as a wife and mother, and although this might sound dated today, less
than fifty years earlier it had been regarded as somewhat shameful for wives to
work. I took on being a housewife like a mantle of clothing – perhaps imitating
the role of my own mother and Tony's – but I soon got bored. I seemed to
remind Tony of his mum (he often made comparisons) and I made a mistake,
I think, in mothering him in similar ways. I spent hours washing and ironing
his shirts, cooking homemade stews, etc. Tony was too busy to notice. He was
highly motivated with a list of ten things to do before even getting out of bed
and then rushing to get on with his day, and I would wonder what to do with
myself in remote Charlesworth other than housework. Years later Tony blamed
this situation in part for the demise of our marriage – that I hadn't engaged
my attention and passion enough outside the home as he had. Yet he was to
completely play down my role in the formation of Factory – if not dismiss it
entirely. He thought I would make a good model and, since it pleased him for
me to do so, I enrolled for a six-week course at the Lucie Clayton Modelling
School on King Street in Manchester. Up until then I'd never worn much
make-up and had never used lipstick in my life, which certainly seems odd
now. After a makeover at the school I walked across town to meet Tony and
on the way a taxi driver waiting by his cab called over to me and said I was the
best-looking girl he'd seen all day.

I never got anywhere as a model. I was too short and too petite. Fashion
work was all in London and mail-order catalogue shoots in the North-West
required a size twelve. I only remember one assignment and that turned out to
be just for my feet! I did produce a model card and went off to a rough part of
Hulme in my best dress and shoes and wore scruffy jeans in a posh restaurant.
But, in truth, my heart could never have been in a career such as this.

If nothing else the modelling course gave me a short-term focus and a few
tips on grooming, and enabled Tony and I to meet up in town every day, which
was fun. I would walk the short distance from King Street to Granada Studios,
and felt at home the minute I walked or drove through the entrance. The man
on reception and the men at the car-park gate all knew me.

It wasn't a given that we were to be married at St Mary's in Marple Bridge,
the church at which Tony had been given his first performing role as an altar boy.
Personally, if I had any religious leaning at all it was towards Buddhism, and
I suggested to Tony that we tie the knot at a Buddhist monastery in the Lake
District. Much to my surprise he seemed to like this idea – a certain wackiness
about it appealed perhaps – but I took it quite seriously. Consequently we
went off one weekend and met with a monk at this establishment. In the event
I didn't get on too well with the monk, largely because we had opposing views

about reincarnation. He insisted that one could return as an animal or even some sort of plant life, whereas I said I thought that once a soul had advanced to the human level this would contravene the basic laws of the evolutionary ladder. Tony just found the whole thing amusing, but as we drove away I told him I'd prefer to be married at St Mary's. We stayed that night with Rita, an ex-girlfriend of his – his first, I think. Tony once told me he was in a car with Rita with his mum driving (a Triumph 1300) when Tony said something that indicated he and Rita might not last. His mum said, 'Then it's not true love. It's thirty-eight years since Ted . . .' She stopped speaking and Tony was amazed to see tears falling down her face. When he told me this story thirty-two years after Doris's death he was crying himself – he remarked that he took after her.

Rita was married with a small baby – we woke to those early gurgling noises that I had diabolical mixed feelings about waking up to. The next day we visited the television presenter Russell Harty at his lovely country home in Giggleswick for Sunday lunch. I detested the way Harty was all over Tony and virtually ignored me; very ungracious, I thought, and in retrospect this encounter had shades of the infamous incident with Grace Jones, who would later slap Harty on air for a similar kind of thing. Tony and Harty actually had much in common, having both studied literature and gone on to a career in broadcasting. Also, Harty had interviewed the Who, for instance, on his show as early as 1973, an encounter that wound up with Keith Moon threatening to remove his underwear on camera.

Tony and I invited far too many people – about 200 – for the wedding and my dad picked up the bill. We'd looked around at various places to hold the reception and the favourite was the venue closest to the place we had first met in Disley – the Moorside Hotel.

Tony chose the date for the nuptials – 14 May – because it was exactly a year to the day we met. The week before I insisted that he and I separate for a week. He was to stay in the house until the thirteenth, when I would return and leave for the church from there.

The Monday before he wrote:

My dearest young wife to be, 'No doubt she was a dangerous woman but I would never be greatly interested in any woman incapable of harm, in any woman who didn't threaten me with loss.' [*Humboldt's Gift*, Saul Bellow] Seemed to strike one of those just right chords. I embrace the days and years to come. The house . . . without you . . . feels like, I can hardly describe it, most like the day after good acid when things look bleak, no colour in anything, washed out and up, cut yourself and you know the blood would be grey not red. If you're not with me, I'm not even with myself. One from one leaves nothing, simple maths; I've always been good at maths but I've also always been good at being simple.

He also referred to that inner knowing we both shared at our first meeting:

> Marriage is one of those crazy expeditions into wild lands, you choose a partner for a trip like that like choosing a gun. With you, as with no other, my aim is perfect, it will save me from all peril, and the stock fits so neat and right into my shoulder. Like it was made for me. I felt like that about you one year ago. I won't say I've grown surer over the year. I couldn't. The certainty I felt that sunny afternoon was quite searing. Few things in this world are definite but I knew that afternoon that the irrevocable had happened.

Then *the* day arrived. Once more to St Mary's in Marple Bridge for 4:00pm. Of course Tony arrived early with his ushers, amongst whom were his childhood friend Shaun Boylan, Alan Erasmus and Charles Sturridge. Charles had been producing episodes of *Coronation Street* – his lucky break as director of *Brideshead Revisited* was yet to occur. My mother was a bit baffled by Charles's choice of footwear – a pair of white trainers – with his formal suit, quite daring for the seventies, albeit more common nowadays. With time to spare before the service, Tony suggested a walk round to the back of the church so he could visit and show his friends the grave of his beloved Uncle Edgar. This wasn't such a good idea as, in what might be construed as an ill omen, Tony noticed the name of the person buried beside Edgar, Lindsay Wilson; even the spelling was the same. Incidentally, Tony had always planned to be buried with Edgar, which prompted a joke from me to the effect that he'd be lying for all eternity next to Lindsay Wilson, but he changed his mind at the last minute, thinking the location at Marple Bridge too far for people to travel out to from the Hidden Gem Church in Manchester. Instead he chose to be buried in the same cemetery as his partners Martin Hannett and Rob Gretton.

I travelled to the church in a vintage car and ostensibly it all went without a hitch. We sang 'All Things Bright and Beautiful', Tony's sole acknowledgement of my love of hymns, which are often strangely lacking in Catholic services. We were both happy and it felt right. But another omen befell us as we left the church. There were two paths leading to the road and we walked – almost danced – our way down to the stylish car waiting for us. Tony even picked me up and carried me at one point. Then, as we drove away, I suddenly realised that something was missing. People! The guests had missed our departure. And we had been too happily oblivious to notice they were on the other path. 'Tony!' I exclaimed in horror. 'We didn't get any confetti! It's terrible, it means we won't have any children.' (The throwing of confetti is symbolic of fertility – it used to be rice in the distant past but the symbolism is the same.) Tony's response was a swift, 'Oh you do talk rubbish' or 'That's utter shite' or something of that ilk. People often look on me as being slightly odd for interpreting signs and I am willing to admit I sometimes overdo it. I'm not particularly superstitious but occasionally feel an intuitive grasp of things, of a primal symbol falling – or not falling in this case – into our path. But I felt certain that this was a sign and – well, sadly, we never did have any children. That is probably my biggest regret in life.

And as if bad omens weren't enough, more trouble was looming at the Moorside Hotel. Everyone sat down for a three-course meal, but I was so distracted that Tony tenderly told me twice to finish up my soup. At the end of the meal Tony's best man, Charles Edmundson – a lovely doctor who had been at Cambridge with him and who was already worse for wear from drink and showed no sign of stopping – stood up to deliver his speech. He began by saying, 'I've been told to keep it short and sweet so I've been holding it under the cold tap.' This didn't offend me and I'm sure it went over the heads of the one or two reactionary elderly ladies present. It greatly amused Tony, so much so that he often referred both to this and a supposed blunder of Charles's, when he apparently referred to me by the name of a longstanding former girlfriend of Tony's from university named Eithnè (who he was also with during his time in London). What offended me was not Charles's speech per se – despite the fact it was not at all short and sweet but somewhat lengthy and appeared to be a biography of the life of Tony Wilson, his education and background. Of course Charles didn't know me at all and could hardly say much on that subject, though I felt slighted all the same by this lengthy analysis on the life of T.W. But what really incensed me was that Tony lent across me at the end and exclaimed, 'Great speech, Charles!' I took this as blatant evidence of his outright egotism; his pre-occupation and love of himself above me on our wedding day. Buyer's remorse struck instantly. 'I shouldn't have married him,' I thought. And of course I was furious that I could love and even marry such a man as this and not a perfectly modest one. The fact that my annoyance was evidence of my own egotism didn't quite hit home until years later. Not just because no one talked about me either. I little realised then the more subtle workings of a strong ego – in this case adopting the role of victim – or a defensive but large ego built on insecurity. At that moment I subscribed to the more usual concept of a big ego along the lines of the generally held public view of Tony as smug and conceited. I was used to and expected Tony to get top billing wherever we went, but *not* at our wedding and certainly not from him. The fact is that I was just too insecure and sensitive and felt rejected by the slightest thing.

Later on we went to cut the cake together, a cake my mum had made and iced well in advance of the day. Consequently the icing was rock hard. Smiling for the cameras we tried to put the knife through it with his hand placed delicately over mine but it hardly made a mark. After one or two failed attempts he rather impatiently yet gently pushed me out of the way so that he could do the job himself. I took this very personally – as though he was stating he was the only one that mattered here – but I can see now that no slight was intended whatsoever. He simply wanted the job done before anyone noticed the trouble we were having. Yet perhaps it was another symbol, for some things that we later needed to share but didn't quite manage to – such as our involvement in Factory Records and choosing a family home.

On a lighter note, Tony had asked Dougie James and his Soul Train to play live at our wedding. Unfortunately, Dougie told me later that just about every wedding he has ever played at ended in divorce! This has included the snooker player Alex Higgins's wedding, along with many other less famous people.

The group seemed a bit cabaret to me but the line-up that day was fairly special and included Bruce Mitchell on drums, who played more usually with Alberto Y Lost Trios Paranoias, and later went on to join Durutti Column, with whom he plays to the present day. He was also next to Tony the day he died. The Albertos already seemed to be gaining success with a comic musical play called *Sleak*, about snuff rock, which Tony and I had just seen at the Royal Court Theatre. It was a memorable night, and I enjoyed the humour and songs even if some of the cryptic cleverness went over my head. Stan 'Red' Hoffman was also in Dougie's Soul Train as backing singer and was way ahead of the game, having had a record deal with Columbia as far back as the mid-1960s, singing with the Measles. The group's set on our wedding night finished with the song 'Amen'.

Yet another tradition went out of the window as Tony and I felt a bit awkward trying to share a traditional dance together accompanied by this lot, and yet their world seemed more familiar to me than that odd wedding world.

When I look back on our wedding day I think to myself that if I managed to feel rejected by Tony on that day there was probably little hope for us! Rumour had it that certain people were taking bets at the back of the room that our marriage wouldn't last. Although I was holding Tony's hand and sleeping beside him to the end, they may have been right – but I consider it bad form to share a wedding feast and make such observations at the same time. Tony always believed that his father, Sydney, was one of those taking bets (against), but knowing Sydney as well as I did I simply cannot accept that and rather think that if he would have stooped so low – which I doubt – he would have been the one taking the bet in our favour. He strongly approved of the match, always adored me and was, according to his partner Tony Connolly, heartbroken when Tony and I split. Oddly, the last time I ever saw Sydney he was still suffering from the aftermath of a severe stroke, which made conversation rather difficult. I remarked that I'd seen Tony recently and I felt we'd end up back together again when we were old. At this Sydney's face contorted into a 'No'. I was a bit shocked – I thought my little prediction might please him. Then he managed to utter the words, 'Tony won't make old bones.' How prophetic. I wonder to this day how he knew that.

7 Thank God for Drugs

From the jazz era of the 1930s through the advent of rock'n'roll to Merseybeat, punk and Madchester, drugs and drug culture have played an integral role in the British music scene. Tony and I both came from a background of psychedelic music and drugs, smoking pot the way most people drink tea (or alcohol nowadays) and using LSD on special occasions, Christmas or during psychedelic light-show gigs by the likes of Pink Floyd. But drug culture, like fashion, moves on – even if it sometimes reverts back to its old ways.

Tony and I always had a history of taking drugs together and, oddly, it finished up on that note too. With the sentence of death hanging over him, Tony was having a great deal of trouble sleeping until a doctor prescribed Zopiclone, a sleeping tablet which really is the best I've ever had. Like Tony, I sometimes suffer insomnia yet conversely seem unable to function without sufficient sleep. In January 2007 I began meeting Tony fairly regularly at his loft apartment in Manchester. Previously he'd usually driven out to my place some distance away but now his tiredness often precluded that.

It is not for me to discuss Tony's relationship with his partner Yvette and yet, in order for my story to make sense, I can't entirely avoid it either. I can only begin by telling you what I know from him: that he was in love with her from the day they met in the early nineties until his death. Nonetheless, he told me in the later years that she was living with someone else and it appeared that this prevented her from being with him most evenings and weekends. Hence, although their relationship continued during the week and on many trips abroad, often connected with their business interests, Tony was usually free every weekend and seemed, especially with the onset of illness, to be in need of my company.

On a visit one Saturday night in 2007 it seemed sensible that I stay over, and I suggested sleeping in Oliver and Izzy's bedroom (Tony's son and daughter with

Hilary, his second wife). This was agreed, but as I was getting ready to turn in he asked why I didn't make it simpler by sleeping in his bed. This was hardly a sexual advance but more a sign of another kind of intimacy that comes with a very long association. I was a bit worried I might get insomnia (although oddly in this case sleeping beside him was remarkably like putting on old comfortable slippers that – despite lying unworn for many years – seemed as familiar as always). I thought it might be best not to risk disturbing Tony with my wakefulness and when he got the sleeping tablets out I joked, 'Come on Tony, we've always taken drugs together, let's not make an exception now!' That first night I hadn't realised that Tony's tablets were much stronger than the Zopiclone I'd had before, and I ended up completely and utterly crashed out beside him. He had taken twice as many as me but still got up in the middle of the night and put the television on. I wanted to go and sit with him but, with the best will in the world, couldn't move off the bed.

From that evening until his death, this was our ritual every Saturday night. I would drive over and we would go out for dinner, although increasingly, and very sadly, he lacked the energy to go out so I would bring food and cook it there. We would retire early after dinner, usually when it was still light, and he would break out the tablets. Then he would tell me a story and we'd both be asleep by around 10:00pm. After he passed I took great comfort from this. It was as if all the bad stuff – the divorce, the rows – had vanished, and here we were, slightly decrepit maybe, but mellow at last and forgiving one another like an old married couple at the end of both their lives. We'd made our peace with one another and were friends to the end. Surely that is the best one can hope for from marriage?

Oddly – in view of the fact that I am writing this book – his stories were vignettes from his own life, such as his first unplanned 'kamikaze' as Father Christmas. But as the months wore on he became weaker and weaker and one night he simply didn't have it in him to tell one, so I asked if he could recite some poetry instead. Then, as with those postcards sent every day in the weeks following our first meeting, in those last weeks he found sufficient energy for a poem. This night he quoted (almost word-perfectly) his beloved Yeats:

How can I, that girl standing there,
My attention fix
On Roman or on Russian
Or on Spanish politics?
Yet here's a travelled man that knows
What he talks about,
And there's a politician
That has read and thought
And maybe what they say is true
Of war and war's alarms,
But O that I were young again
And held her in my arms.

That night I wrote in my diary: 'Dreamt that Tony was so light from weight loss that I picked him up and carried him to bed.' And also: 'We were in a helicopter going somewhere but it became very sinister because we knew we'd been taken hostage – kidnapped and taken prisoner. There were people of different ages but we were all going to the same place.' The place being death, of course.

Tony aged rapidly during this time. His weight loss was alarmingly severe and swift. In looks and vitality, he went from age fifty-seven to seventy-seven, but his brain was right there throughout, drugs or not. Now, like the older people we were becoming, we were taking legal drugs rather than illegal ones. It seemed to me, though, that the times we had spent together could be catalogued by the music of the seasons, and the drugs associated with them.

The drug that followed on from the acid-head hippie 1960s was probably cocaine, which became more available and fashionable in the early 1970s. It was a glamorous drug for the jet set, largely because it was prohibitively expensive, at least in those days. I have a friend who took an executive post in a major record company in the seventies and was told at a meeting one day that it was his turn to obtain the coke!

Cocaine's effect was somewhat similar to speed (amphetamine sulphate) which was soon to become readily available to those on a tighter budget. Simon Napier-Bell, in his book *Black Vinyl White Powder*, posits a correlation between speed and punk rock: 'To complement its foulness, sulphate users needed to find a new type of music as rough-edged and disgusting as the drug itself. What they came up with was punk rock – simple, fast and angry. Leftover acid-heads were still telling us to love the world. Newly amphetamised punks demanded we trash it. The names of the new groups seemed endless – the Stinky Toys, Siouxsie and the Banshees, the Slits, the Vibrators, the Damned, the Clash, the Buzzcocks – all driven by bucketfuls of foul speed sniffed through unpleasant little tubes. The best known, of course, were the Sex Pistols.'

Tony thought it would be a good idea to have a white wedding, by which he meant taking cocaine. It was just like him to take an idea to its literal conclusion. I don't particularly recall Tony and I taking it together before this day, nor at what juncture we adjourned for the festivity, but I vaguely remember it was badly timed – just before the meal I think – and because it was an appetite suppressant I toyed with my food. On top of this it was likely to make me edgy and overreact to all of the foregoing. I did, and shed a private tear in the ladies' loo. Perhaps Tony was treating his wedding day as a gig, a performance. Oddly that was even how his funeral felt to me.

Cocaine is one drug I never got along with. The first time I took it I thought it overrated and actually wasn't sure what the effect of it was aside from keeping me awake. But I soon discovered it was guaranteed to set me on edge a day later, and so it was perhaps a good thing that I was allergic to it. I didn't think whatever little rush it gave was worth getting a streaming cold for. I have therefore avoided it pretty much ever since but Tony, on the other hand, developed a penchant for it right through to his later life. He wasn't especially open about the fact that he used coke, unlike marijuana, but he confessed to me how much he liked using it – and he always seemed to have a runny nose and a handkerchief on hand. He often explained this away as a cold, but as I saw him fairly regularly I had my doubts. He seemed to be nasally challenged every other week.

Simon Napier-Bell wrote about him: 'Tony Wilson loathes cocaine when it's taken into the recording studio. "Nothing destroys creativity like cocaine," he warns. "Never work, think or try to create on it." But when work isn't involved he thoroughly enjoys the stuff. "We all do it at weekends," he happily admits. "It's a party drug."'

I have wondered if his use of cocaine (or particularly the impure chemicals the drug is mixed with) may have been a factor in Tony's demise. He had a mini-stroke about three years before his death and it was then discovered that his blood pressure was very high. Cocaine and amphetamine drugs have strong links with heart disease/attacks/blood pressure problems. Also, cocaine has increasingly been cut with a carcinogenic painkiller known as Phenacetin. The chemical is a popular choice to bulk the weight of the drug since it is cheap and closely resembles cocaine. However, it was initially banned from general use in 1968 after it was linked to bladder and kidney cancer.

This wasn't anything Tony wanted to think about – perhaps understandably – although one day he mentioned that he believed his cancer had been triggered by a plug-in aroma (a plug that sends out a pleasant yet chemical smell) he had been using on his upstairs landing ever since he got his dog, a Weimaraner called William, three years before. Someone had written to Tony about the established links between the same type of plug-in he had been using and kidney cancer, and Tony showed me the letter. Actually I think that many different factors can trigger cancer nowadays, particularly the heavy onset of generalised chemical pollution, and this plug-in aroma may well have been one of them. I personally detest them and whenever I see anyone using one of these plug-ins I warn them immediately.

I'm sure there are always other factors exacerbating or limiting the damage drugs do (such as a genetic predisposition to cancer, heart disease, etc), but given the reports of high current cocaine use it couldn't be a bad thing to inform people as much as possible about what they may be doing to their bodies. The Durutti Column's Bruce Mitchell commented: 'Cocaine gives you several things: bad breath, it makes you psychotic, and your nose is going to run for the rest of your life. Terrible drug.'

One Saturday in the last months of his life Tony and I were eating out when one of his friends joined us. It came out in conversation that this friend used cocaine a lot. I wanted to tell him what I'd learnt but Tony asked me to be quiet. However, his friend said he wanted to hear what I had to say so I went on with it. During the same meal I was talking about how men go almost entirely for the body beautiful in women, Yeats having observed this in his work. Tony said that Yeats never wrote anything of the sort. I insisted that I thought he must be mistaken and Tony asked how I dared contradict someone with his knowledge of Yeats in this way? I thought that was a bit pompous, especially as I was sure I'd read something along these lines by Yeats only the other week. When we got back to his loft I felt ashamed that I'd brought up the 'dangers of cocaine' issue in front of him. It felt as if I was rubbing Tony's nose in it – excuse the pun. As we were getting ready for bed he said to me, 'Do you realise how very rude you were this evening?' I said I was sorry about the cocaine thing. 'No, not that,' he said. '[I mean] speaking about Yeats in that way in front of me. How dare you. You know *fuck all* about Yeats whereas I have been a scholar of him all my life.' But the next day I found the poem, entitled 'A Drinking Song', and texted to Tony: 'Wine comes in at the mouth; and love comes in at the eye – W.B. Yeats.' Tony texted back: 'My humble apologies.'

Another damaging factor was undoubtedly smoking. Tony – like a lot of people I know who carried on smoking pot most days of their lives – mixed the substance with cigarette tobacco and was, I suspect, as much addicted to that as he was to the dope. He denied this though, and never at any stage did he ever resort to actually lighting a fag. Tobacco is such an insidious drug; as addictive as heroin they say. How times have changed since the fifties. My father would sit in our little lounge permanently puffing on a pipe and while passively breathing it in, no one breathed a word against it. We didn't even think it was unhealthy – even doctors used to smoke in front of you then.

Cannabis smoking is hardly the healthy alternative to tobacco smoking, particularly as there tends to be a deeper and more prolonged inhalation with smoking a joint compared to a cigarette. Speaking for my own use of the drug, I think the damage was more far-reaching than anything physical. Mentally and emotionally I was all over the place because of it.

After Tony's cancer diagnosis in December 2006 he stopped smoking dope. I asked him a few months later if he missed it. 'Not at all,' was his reply. Odd that really, especially in view of Keith Jobling's memory. Keith – who along with Phil Shotton later formed Bailey Bros to make films for Factory and another company called Screen Intelligence (which was fifty percent Factory and fifty percent Bailey Bros) – recalled: 'We would be coming back from London all the time. He would be driving at 100 miles-per-hour with a map on his knee, rolling a joint while talking on the phone. Swearing away.'

Tony valiantly fought the case for the NHS to offer a drug named Sutent, which Professor Robert Hawkins, Tony's surgeon and doctor and Director of Medical Oncology at Christie (a specialist hospital in Manchester dealing mainly with the treatment of cancer), described as 'the most notable advance in the treatment of kidney cancer for many decades'. Professor Hawkins added: 'This is not a cure, it is a very good treatment and I would want it if I had kidney cancer.'

Less than one month before his death Tony was campaigning for this drug to be offered on the NHS, including an appearance on *North West Tonight* and press conferences that went on until his last fortnight. I admired him for this and there are many people who have benefited from his fight for funding. He wasn't campaigning on his own behalf since many of his wealthy friends and associates contributed to a fund for him that totalled £100,000 by the time he died. His efforts were for others, so it was particularly generous and brave given his terrible health and accompanying frailty. In Tony's case the Sutent was ineffective because his cancer was so far advanced before it was treated.

In a statement immediately after Tony died Professor Hawkins said that the cause of death was a heart attack and unrelated to his cancer. Though Tony did suffer a heart attack in his last twenty-four hours, I must say I felt relieved that his suffering was cut short when it was:

Thursday, 2 August 2007
Visited Tony in Christie. I thought I was prepared to see him at death's door but burst into tears at the sight of him. He seemed to have turned into a skeleton and I only saw him the other day – he hadn't looked this bad. As usual my mouth went into gear before my brain. 'You're not improving.' (I had so wanted to believe the spiel he had been giving me about that.) He said he'd had a bad day. 'But do you feel any better?' 'No.' It was a false hope about the clot on his lung, the tumours shrinking. I was shocked by something in his face – the death mask perhaps, a kind of vacancy. He said the doc had put him on anti-depressants and they seemed to have knocked him out. I asked him if he felt depressed. 'Not at all,' he said, though he had thought about death today. 'What?' 'Just about it.' 'What do you think happens after death?' 'No idea.' 'Of course but what is your belief?' 'After death is nothing and nothing *is*.' I put the flowers in a vase; he noticed their smell (freesias). We spoke about bringing it to an end – he said if this went on until September he would want his life to end (would take whatever).

To suggest that Tony's death was unrelated to his cancer was, in my own layman's humble opinion, completely untrue, although Professor Hawkins added that 'his cancer was responding well to treatment but obviously did contribute to his poor health'.

Nevertheless, it was wonderful that Professor Hawkins was able to give Tony positive feedback for his efforts on his last day on earth. He said, 'I was able to tell him really in his last few hours that the drug would be made available to a large number of patients in Manchester. He was obviously delighted he had made a difference to those patients and he actually celebrated by asking someone to go out and get him a beer, which I gather was very unusual for him.'

I hadn't found it particularly unusual for Tony to enjoy a beer – and how like him to call for a campaign celebration on the day of his death.

Tony was quite emotional when we left the Moorside Hotel following our wedding reception and the inevitable evening disco. He remarked to me as we drove away that he felt very similar to the way he'd felt when his mother died. That night we stayed at an airport hotel. It didn't feel very glamorous; we slept badly and the alarm call woke us so early that we felt absolutely jiggered. Something I didn't know about myself at the time but have learnt with experience is that when I'm very tired I'm prone to tears and tantrums, like a child. I look back now and wish I could have been different.

Our honeymoon in California was documented to a large degree in a diary that my mum had given us. I began it and Tony eventually became the principal author. It is easy to spot which of us is writing I think, but to make it clearer Tony's entries are in italics. Cut down slightly for the sake of brevity, with contributions from us both, the entries complete this next chapter:

Sunday, 15 May 1977
It was only a short flight to Heathrow and the plane to San Francisco didn't leave till 1:00pm, so we decided to have a proper breakfast. It was during this that we had our first marital altercation! Nothing too serious – although I did consider hurling myself over the balcony onto the milling crowds below – it was just that I was still very upset about the best man's speech. However, after crying in the airport lounge I felt better. Tony was being very sweet by then and the people around must have thought there'd been a death in the family.

Anyway, we boarded the plane and for the next ten and a half hours nothing too eventful happened except that everyone was American so it was as if we were already there. We watched a mediocre film (sound appalling) and I read nearly a whole book – Edna O'Brien's *The Girl with Green Eyes*. Tony read the *Sunday Times*. When we got there the sun was shining and it was only 5:00pm. We got a taxi and drove straight to the hotel. Staggering fare of sixteen dollars! SF looked absolutely delightful but no time for that now – we went to bed and slept zzz . . .

Monday, 16 May 1977

We woke at dawn and saw the sun come up. Lovely view from our window – can see the sea and the city. Had another nap and went down for breakfast. Tony's all right here – they're coffee mad; I'll have to forget my tea addiction for a while. Then we had a bath and ventured forth into SF. Forgot to mention the TV – about ten channels and adverts on nearly every one.

Oh dear, the hills in SF and me with only my stilettos! There is a particularly sheer drop right outside the hotel. We staggered down it and whilst waiting for the bus looked in at a supermarket – jammed full of enormous fruit and lots of nice goodies. Then got the bus down into town and then on a cable car (one of those where you hang off the side).

I think she's more impressed by the bumper-sized apples – but despite the cold wind off the bay she seems to be loving the cable car – good.

We walked round Fisherman's Wharf and shared some shrimps and then walked to Chinatown. My feet were killing me by then so I bought some flat Chinese canvas shoes ($4). Mind you they look stupid. We ate lasagne somewhere and then headed home to watch *The Boston Strangler* on TV. Unfortunately in two parts. In the evening went to see *The Realm of the Senses* – a Chinese film, its main attraction being that it's banned in England. It was quite exceptionally rude, but I fell asleep during it and woke up to see the end where she chopped his penis off.

Tuesday, 17 May 1977

Slept late and missed breakfast. Set off and my shoe snapped on the big hill, so I behaved like a four-year-old child for half an hour and then we set off again. My shoe was mended quite easily in town. We had coffee and toast and 'jelly' (they don't call it jam) and then got the ferry boat to Sausalito. The sun shining brightly down, it was a lovely journey. Went past Alcatraz. We looked round the shops – Tony bought some sunglasses – and had hamburgers for lunch. Then we got the ferry again and bus back to the hotel to watch *The Boston Strangler* on TV. Well, it was either the wine at lunchtime or jet lag catching up on me, but that was the end of me for Tuesday. I slept through the film and Tony put me to bed.

Wednesday, 18 May 1977
Due to sleeping so early we woke just before dawn. Tony dozed and then bathed and we had an early breakfast. We got the bus over the East Bay Bridge to Berkeley University. Had lunch and then viewed the students, saw a march about anti-apartheid and went up the Sather Tower. Lovely view. Got the BART (their name for the underground) back. Saw Tony's old hotel and then came back to our lovely room where I fell asleep again. Tony forced me to wake up and go out so we went and had a snack in a café but I couldn't wake up. Picked a sweet-smelling blossom for our room.

Thursday, 19 May 1977
Brilliantly sunny as we set off to go to the Palace of Fine Arts. It was a long steep walk, and as I was wearing heels I was nearly crippled when we got there. It was a lovely building (Hollywood Egyptian, Tony says) and there was this weird low cloud drifting around it. It was built early this century to exhibit technological advances like the telephone, and we looked around the Exploratorium with things to play with on the senses and tricks of perception. The walk did me in – Tony watched the Nixon/Frost interview in the evening and I slept.

Friday, 20 May 1977
Lovely day again and (wearing my new flat shoes) we set off and got a greyhound to 'Africa USA'. It was like a spectacular zoo. Safari raft and all kinds of shows – best of all was the dolphin show and the killer whale one. We had a great time and then when we got back to SF we went to see *Annie Hall* with Woody Allen and Diane Keaton. That was thoroughly enjoyable. 'The food's so poor and there's so little of it' – Allen's view on life. Afterwards we had a small tiff, probably because we waited ages for a bus that never came.

Definitely – Tony.

Saturday, 21 May 1977
After the usual delightful breakfast I had a bath and wrote some cards home and Tony went to collect the hire car. We both got ready for this wedding of an old friend of his, but before going there we drove over the Golden Gate Bridge and then up the mountain for the view. The wedding was very high society – rich and boring and service very short in the garden. We met this actor and went in the evening to see his play *Equus* the horse, but Tony and I kept dropping off – it was terrible, so we left at half time and went to bed.

Saturday, 21 May 1977 (cont.)

*Reflections on American money: there was a lot of it at our SF society wedding.
Such opulence – tennis courts through the grove behind the pool etc – makes
me ill at ease, till I remember Chandler's descriptions of such unease as his
hero Marlowe waited in just such dollar palace vestibules – marble cool – to
receive work from the hands of the deathly rich. The American hero is not the
man in the Hollywood Mediterranean mansion – he's the loser like Marlowe.
Soul-rich etc. Lindsay says she doesn't want to be rich – good job I say and slip
out to the tree-lined drive to roll another number for the road/groom.*

Sunday, 22 May 1977
*Missed breakfast – start with the relevant details, in my darling's eye that
was the big (bad) move of the day. We leave hotel – we also leave one leather
coat, one white jacket, one flashy skirt. Seventy-five miles south, en route for
Monterey we realise – small discussion ensues. Decide to go on – correct. Hit
Santa Cruz – give café, shoe shop, and bakery a little of our money. Give
boardwalk and big dipper a miss. Bel Air Motel in Monterey, basic but for
the 25c-a-hit pulsating bed. Give me a 25c-a-hit pulsating woman any day.
Ooops I married one – last week – only this evening we're not pulsating.
The recommencement of oestrogen ingestion cycle and the blocking of the
'true channels of nature' – thanks Vatican II – render madam a mite fidgety.
Make contact with local family – friends of Patrick and many others back
in England. Very stoned evening four blocks from Cannery Row – Bob grows
his own. By the end we – like his lofty garden – are fluorescent. His fourteen-
year-old daughter cooks Taco's and pumpkin cake – gimme more – and his
estranged wife returns in a camper with 'a pretty smile' (that's me) and 'wild
staring eyes' (that's him).*

Monday, 23 May 1977
*Left the rather chatty Bel Air and moved on to the south down the Coast
Highway via a run in with a host of squirrels who enchanted and then bit
(and then further enchanted) the new Mrs Wilson; via the seventeen-mile
drive around the flat but beautiful Monterey Peninsula; via Carmel, [an] old
Spanish Mission town established, like the lovely old Mission itself, by Catholic
refugees from Majorca in 1760 – yes Majorca and yes 1760; via Big Sur, as
lovely and unflat as ever; via the waves, rocks and separate orgasms of Mill
Creek where the twenty-three-year-old Mr Wilson had spent ten bored minutes
on a previous hitch-hiking hol, but aged twenty-seven remained for two hours
and was, in all, delighted and absorbed; via Hearst Castle, monument to
personal greed, and charging $5 a time for a tour – we didn't tour.*

*And then we were south, in San Luis Obispo where [Timothy] Leary was
jailed before snitching on his friends to the FBI.*

*We stay at a quite trippy motel – pink – all over the lampposts even. The
Madonna Inn it was called, every room thematically designed and usually*

pink – a veritable Californian Portmeirion, and as befits this gross land, done with utter lack of taste. The word that best describes this country's greatest lack is 'GRACE', maybe even the people aren't gracious – Dick Nixon isn't gracious, that's for sure – and that's the most annoying thing about his Frosties special.

But it's nice to be gross on occasions – occasions like when you stay in the 'morning star' room (the same star we saw crouched on bedroom floor of day two in SF??), with pink walls, gold chandeliers, and Lindsay Wilson in smilingly athletic frame of mind.

Enjoy.

Tuesday, 24 May 1977

Wot a lot of rot he writes. Left the pink room and drove to Santa Barbara. Stopped for breakfast somewhere that seemed rather like Morecambe. Walked on the pier (bit freaky with stiletto heels). Checked in at the Motel 6 and bought some suntan cream and got an hour or two of sun. Then we dressed and went to a drive-in movie – the film being Mohammed Ali's life story. I loved seeing the screen against the open sky; the whole thing was great, even the film had me nearly in tears when his wife got upset about his boxing.

Tuesday (cont.)

Some rot about Morecambe; in fact it was called Pismo Beach and marks the cultural beginnings of that phenomenon known as Southern California – this seaside town had the spaced-out buildings of S.Cal for the first time.

The towns are not more spacious in terms of intentional aesthetics; rather they are built not to the scale of man, but the car – from place to place, house to house, shop to shop, you always drive, never walk. Town planning by Detroit.

Forgot to mention we went on the amusement arcades at 'Morecambe'.

Wednesday, 25 May 1977

Woke up and Tony said why was I in a bad mood? I wasn't but I soon was. Went into Santa Barbara and had breakfast. I ordered bacon and tomatoes and the girl was confused and I remarked how unimaginative Americans are or something and Tony went mad at me so I went mad at him.

This is half the recipe for disaster – part two came with a visit to lovely atmospheric SB bookstore where occurred the – aagh, disaster, tremble, shake – PURCHASE of Norma Jean the Termite Queen, the new soap-opera novel for housewives where the soap stings the eye – 'cause these housewives are depressed, massively.

Now – you've guessed it – the newly married young lady has found a voice;

an empathetic spirit. As of lunchtime Wednesday 25 May the heavens opened. We also went to the beach – reddened our skin on the Pacific shores – and got specific sores on legs, face, the lot. And we got sore at each other. Back at the motel, Lindsay took off on a private expedition in the car; did well – came back with news of bluegrass music in a downtown bar. We sorted out together, decided to get drunk, got drunk, and ended up at Mom's Place – an Italian restaurant – drunk – and had a monster meal. For dessert – a monster row. Went home, passed out. The test of strength – nay, friends of the occult – 'the darkening of the light' had begun.

Moral: Women should never have been given the right to read books – make for an easy life.

Thursday, 26 May 1977
Woke up and the sun was not shining – in our hearts. Of course [it was] in Santa Barbara – lots of it. Had breakfast – a BLT, figure it out – in El Paseo, a Spanish courtyard downtown. Thence to the beach for mucho bronzo.

In the evening went to the beautiful Arlington Theatre – Spanish village in the Gods, like a small Chicano version of the Rainbow. The concert was appalling – Marc Almond and Jesse Colin Young, cheap sentimental lyrics plus efficient, workmanlike musicianship; less original talent and improvisation. We had a similarly uninspired hamburger which beat the music and our stomachs.

Back at the motel the cold war got colder and the shoulders got harder. They've also got browner which means at heart some things are going to schedule.

Friday, 27 May 1977
Tony moodily went out to wash his shirts and I read *Norma Jean* in the sun and packed. This young lad who kept saying 'neat, real neat' to and at everything was there. We left the motel and went and had a rather grotty Mexican meal. Tony was really in a bad way, he said, 'I want to do nothing and I don't even want to do that.' We went on the beach for about one hour and then got in the car to drive to Los Angeles. After a long silence (almost whole journey) Tony cheered up a bit and told me about things in Los Angeles. And actually we weren't too bad from then on, although Los Angeles was pretty horrific – like a cross between Hulme and Soho. Checked in at [the] Saharan Hotel and then went to see a film (French) called *L'argent de poche* – small change.

Saturday, 28 May 1977
Slept quite late (we meant to go early to Disneyland but didn't make it). Had lunch and went to see the 1:45pm showing of *Star Wars* at the Chinese Theatre. The queue was a mile long last night and was fairly packed lunchtime. It was great – 'The force is always with you,' good

overcoming evil. Was pretty hot when we came out. We had a joint and drove to Universal City – a Hollywood movie lot. We were queuing to go on a tour and it was funny because I was feeling very weak and then Tony says he thinks he might faint. His eyes started rolling and his body was giving way. 'Don't worry darling,' he says. DON'T WORRY! Stretched out on the floor, all the people around looked quite amused, as if it was part of the show. I thought he might be dying, and I was afraid I might fall on top of him. But hey presto his eyes opened and his face visibly changed colour from white to grey and broke out in massive perspiration. My heart wouldn't stop thumping for ages. We got in the tramcar thing and started the tour. It was great, we saw lots of things, e.g. a room where they do the bionic woman. And there was the lake and scenery from *Jaws* and a big plastic whale. The thing we both liked best was this cylindrical tunnel – the car stopped on a platform and the walls whirled round it. It felt as if the car was falling over.

Talking about falling over – I don't think I've ever fainted before – it was wild. Like going under Valium except fifteen [seconds] before I collapsed, everything – Lindsay, the queue – began flashing from grey tones to pure white neon. Finally the throbbing reached overexposure like in a picture and I whited out – mucho fun only in retrospect.

Highspot of LA was the beautiful Grauman's Chinese Theatre and the fine film Star Wars *seen there – oh, the land of movies, everyone's a star.*

Sunday, 29 May 1977

Decided to give Disneyland a miss and we drove out to Redondo Beach instead. I had my palm read. She said drawbacks – I had been emotionally confused, I was easily influenced by others and there has been a lot of jealousy around me. But she said it was good I married Tony and that I didn't nearly get married before, that he'd be very successful – money and health no problem (except some sickness in my family?) – we'd have three children and I'd live to be about eighty-two! We sunbathed on the beach for a while (after nearly losing the car keys in the sand).

Only nearly – God on our side – we drove thirty-five miles through industrial Los Angeles; Trafford Park times ten. The FA Cup Final was on the PBS channel that afternoon and I was hoping to find a bar to watch it on. Eureka. Happy Days – a Chicano hang-out in a district called Alhambra. Lindsay chatted to the immigrants, I watched the game, we both drank Budweiser. As for Wembley – I didn't miss a thing. Utterly uninspired though our much maligned defence did well. We did well to drive on into the night, out of LA, and head into the desert, our heads not a little befuddled by all the beer the Mexicans had thrown at us while watching the football. We end up at a

Above: The girl on his arm. Our wedding, May 1977.
Below: Sealed with a kiss.

Above left and right: Wedding daze.
Below: Tony sees the patter of little feet.

Above: Tony with his ushers, left to right: Alan Erasmus,
Charles Edmundson, Charles Sturridge and Shaun Boylan.
Below: We couldn't cut the cake due to rock-hard icing.

Above: Big Sir on the Big Sur, our honeymoon, 1977.
Below: Yosemite wildlife, 1977.

Above left: In these shoes? Practical footwear is a must in San Francisco, honeymoon or no honeymoon, 1977. **Above right:** Man at C&A above the Golden Gate Bridge, on our way to a society wedding in Marin County, 1977. **Below left:** Our honeymoon suite in San Francisco, 1977.
Below right: A girl in Vegas, 1977.

Above: San Francisco's El Drisco Hotel, where we spent the first part of our honeymoon. **Below:** Tony's model girl, San Francisco, 1977.

Above: Automatic exposure on the beach, 1977.
Below: Arizona heat on London Bridge, 1977.

Above: Tony, me and music publisher Andrew King at a party, 1976.
Below: Bruce Mitchell holds court at a party, 1977.

cheaper Motel 6 in Barstow – the cicadas at last are in evidence, the night is hot and the desert awaits us – ooohh, heat.

Monday, 30 May 1977

The desert indeed. We had driven in darkness on Sunday night and though we had a bad – hot – night's sleep for the first time, we weren't really aware that the desert was all around us. Set off for the main drive east in heat and all it did was get hotter. Just a motorway and then desert stretching off either side through grey scrub up to mountains which always seemed to keep their distance. There was one service station eighty miles out – well, a roadside café – just one, the Friend's Coffee Shop. Other than that, the odd shack and some scorched dry bones – no doubt. Finally our Chevrolet microwave oven arrived at Needles, which we had thought to be just a town in California – instead it's the hottest town in California, as we were told frequently in the coming week; today it was 105. And that temperature was about par for the rest of the week.

Feeling that 'let's get into some cold water' urge which afflicted us throughout our desert days, we turned south at the Arizona border and went twenty-five miles down the Colorado River to London Bridge. Yes indeed – a double-decker bus, an English pub, one main street, three motels, 3,500 power boats and, of course, desert. We swam in the lake, filched a small lilo which was drifting downstream and which later became the most important thing in Lindsay's life – well, it kept her afloat.

Lake Havasu City is a tourist trap in the making. Now the sand mixes well with the concrete stubble of a yet-to-be-built town and the English ambience harmonises with the green and blue of grass and lake – all utterly out of place in the middle of this endless desert.

As life cools down in the evening – ninety-five – put a jacket on. We set off into Arizona – 100 miles into Kingman where I thought we could stop. Lindsay is on for further passage – she drives, which is nice for both of us in a role-playing way. As the driver madam seems more fulfilled therefore happier; me too. Arrive late in Williams – a large village, small town, in fact a big truck stop.

We do like the trucks. At the Grand Motel – very nicely run by a nice old couple. Now of the opinion that Arizonians are the most courteous of Americans. Indian jewellery for sale – must be getting near the reservations – and boy you'd need a reservation. $500 for a necklace in turquoise though he has another name for it. 'Squashed' something – must be Indian, Lindsay insists [to] T but doesn't buy. We both buy a good night's sleep. We are temporarily in HIGH DESERT. Less low – less hot.

Tuesday, 31 May 1977

Drive straight north to the Grand Canyon – just fifty miles. Stop at Fred

Flintstone enclosure in middle of forest – kiddies' fun fair, very basic – but we press on for a mediocre breakfast at a sub-mediocre café. The owner advises sitting on porches in the shade. We agree and I make second fatal mistake of holiday (remember Norma Jean) – I fail to purchase a MOO COW MILKER. I'll give you that again – a Moo Cow Milker, an extremely tatty plastic milk jug with a brown plastic cow's head which slurps out milk; and yours for only $3.50 at this tourist trap. For Lindsay it is love at first sight. I refuse to pay the inflated price. Will Lindsay ever forgive me?

On to the Canyon.

Like Niagara Falls, it is indeed a wonder of the world. Few media-acclaimed spectacles live up to their promise – like the smell of coffee – but the Canyon of the Colorado is IT. Lunch at a less than exciting restaurant – real tourist hotel, only one allowed on the west of the Canyon, good advert for the values of competitive industry.

Helicopter after dinner. Another wonder – in particular [when the] pilot accelerates as he approaches lip and drops a little toward the green roof of foliage – sensual effect is that of being shot out into the wilds of the universe. Lins in front seat, very excited.

Set off late afternoon to go round the eastern rim of the Canyon and up to the north, something like 250 miles to bring us to the edge of Utah for a drive back to Vegas. It's one of the most out of the way spots in a world of wildernesses, but the big pull of the big cliffs means maybe 1,000 people a day and that means this is 'tourist desert'. Hot – empty of everything but sand, stone and mountains that litter the horizon. In England you measure how far you drive by the passage of major junctions and lights; here you measure your long straight line by the range, by the range of mountains whose perspectives pass you by in maybe twenty minutes to half an hour, and each time there's a new row of peaks, one side or the other, which shadow your part of the plain. And there are the Indians near the rim and the white man's traffic, every quarter mile a sign saying 'Indian jewellery' another hundred yards and in a patch of flat dust, just spare enough to pull off for a couple of Chevvies, old women sit, squat position on the floor beneath a cloth laid out with trinkets. They are sitting inside makeshift scrapwood pyramids – only the top section filled in with boards to shade them from the sun. The jewellery was blue stone and very, very expensive – aquamarine.

Away from the holiday in the sun the Indian scene changes. Much more desolate landscape, every ten miles a village; a few shacks and some wooden eight-sided huts with conical tops – tepee of the 20th century – and debris, broken old cars and bits of metal, just like the Irish tinkers, the cannibals of mechanical trash.

As night falls we cross the North Rim at a bridge over the canyon called Navajo Bridge. What else? It goes dark – we hit the forests and start to run out of gas. This increasingly becomes a feature of the trip. My uncle always refused to buy petrol till the last minute, the last garage – I learnt my ways from him – but in Northern Arizona the next gas station can be a long way away. Much tension – much horrible imaginings of a night in the desert – final relief as we find a garage just closing. In high spirits we drive on to Fredonia on the Utah border – small town, 100 buildings, and very Mormon. Clean and honest – cheap and quite lovely wooden motel room. Have a non-alcoholic nightcap at a sparkling clean stand-up café – spick and span – open, smiling, but somewhat empty faces (religious prejudices) are everywhere. Sets Lindsay thinking about Mormons or about the religious prejudices.

Wednesday, 1 June 1977

Wake up and it's hot. Leave Fredonia – great name, Marx brothers used it in their films – and head north into Utah. Ahead of us and then beside us as we turn east towards Nevada, the ROCK MASSIF formations of the Zion National Park. Away in the distances, big rounded rectangular bare pieces of rock that are as big as mountains. Wind down from the highlands for a lunch stop in Hurricane; two miles out of town on a boiling hot hillside overlooking the town. Pssst, a puncture; we get out and I confidently go for the spare tyre – and whaddaya know, this is one hire car that hasn't heard about punctures. No spare. Sometime around the discovery of the negative state of affairs in the boot Lins and I have a row, can't quite remember the details but I remember her sitting angrily on the hot roadside stones. One up for the human race; a guy – middle-aged – drove his motorbike over from his house 500 yards away and asked if we wanted help or at least shade in his house. Mormons! We take the dud wheel off and I hitch into town with it. Find a garage; while tyre gets done I have some cold milk from a supermarket, feel guilty about Lins guarding the car and bags back on the hillside. Lug the tyre back to the outskirts of town – hot work in hot weather is more than just hot work.

Tyre on, lunch inside us, we snake through a mountain motorway that follows the course of the Colorado River. Suddenly we're in Nevada, and suddenly its 105 when we stop for gas. Lins proceeds to put legs out of windows and we search for a swimming site en route for Vegas. End up at a campsite on the northern tip of Lake Mead. Stony beach but okay water and a nice little holiday café with a veranda and jukebox. Lins is getting on well with the lilo – it's getting to be part of the family.

About six o'clock – Las Vegas, past the suburban rows of cheap food chain cafés, past a commercial district of garages and one-storey factories, past the rows of wedding massage parlours – 'd'you want it quick or slow – it's the same in the end', the catchphrase of both – and into the hotel land. A six-lane city street lined with block after block of big skyscrapers, blunt, unappealing hotels. They are made bearable – almost 'right' – by the desert backdrop and coloured neon light monstrosities which by day and by night somehow make them work. We go straight to the Circus Circus for a room – spend, spend,

spend – but they're full, full, full and we save, save, save by going to the Golden Key, a quite acceptable alternative motel. Well, not exactly alternative – they didn't have dope in the rooms – but we did and I got ill. Went and bought some Eno's. Lins watched TV a bit and re-examined her flesh.

Thursday, 2 June 1977
Spend the morning driving round Southern Las Vegas looking for a branch of our car-hire firm – looking to put right the spare wheel situation. Find nothing – except lots of mid-morning heat.

Friday – ski resort.
Saturday – cabin.
Sunday – San Fran.
Monday – San Fran.

The Monday we left San Francisco we had a bit of time to spare between checking out of the hotel and our flight. Tony suggested we go and see a 'porn' movie in some theatre he'd read about. I was curious to see what kind of people viewed this type of film and had never seen anything sexual onscreen before. The theatre was largely empty apart from a few solitary men, but I can remember the film's storyline to this day. It was about a young woman whose life was so empty that she commits suicide and arrives at the 'gate', where her life is assessed with a view to her entering heaven or hell. The wise saint on duty concludes that her life was exemplary, that she had never indulged the pleasures of her flesh or senses; never done anything whatsoever that might be considered sinful. Sadly, though, since suicide is a cardinal sin, he has no choice but to direct her toward the door that leads to hell. The unfortunate woman confides that, had she known this, she would have lived an entirely different life and indulged herself with every wicked pleasure known to man. The saint considers her situation and points to a third door. He tells her that although he has no choice but to send her to hell, as she had been so virtuous he will delay the sentence and allow her to experience every single pleasure of the body. She is instructed to go through the third door, where her 'teacher' awaits in the bedroom. It was at this point in the film that Tony whispered to me that we had to leave to catch our plane home. We had been in the cinema nearly an hour and there hadn't been so much as a whisper of sex – a bit like this woman's life – and he was saying we had to leave, just as it was getting interesting. I asked for just five more minutes, during which our heroine enters the door and meets a beautiful young man who suggests she make herself comfortable. Then Tony nudged me again and said we really had to go that very instant. So it was a memorable porn film – a good story and zero sex.

Some of my family – and Alan Erasmus – were there to greet us when we arrived back at Manchester Airport. Alan presented Tony with a bottle of champagne, which seemed a really nice gesture to make. My mum took a rather more cynical view – commenting later on Alan's priorities – she said that although he'd bought the champagne he didn't have the money to pay for his car-parking fee.

That summer of 1977 the vitality and changes in Manchester's live music scene were continuing apace. Of course we didn't call it post-punk at the time – that phrase was coined in retrospect several years later (by Simon Reynolds, according to Mick Middles) – but nonetheless this is what was evolving. One night Tony and I had just finished tea at my mum's house when he got on the phone to Alan Erasmus in the hall and was heard to ask, 'Where's the action tonight then, Al?' My mum thought this extremely rude as by implication he was suggesting there was no action at her house, but, insensitive though it was, there did seem to be a lot going on out there.

The changes in music brought changes in fashion and Tony's appearance was gradually changing accordingly. Out went the long hair, scarves and patched-up jeans, and in came combat trousers, epaulettes and short hair. I wasn't entirely comfortable with this, although it was barely noticeable that summer. What was more noticeable was the number of gigs Tony and I attended, and how very entertaining it all was.

On 21 July Tony and I went to one of our more regular haunts, Rafters on Oxford Street. We had already seen several groups here and I preferred this venue to any other. The club was run by Dougie James (whose band played at our wedding reception), who then employed Alan Wise (later to run the Factory Russell Club nights) to work for him. Tony and I had seen

Dougie and his band Soul Train perform upstairs – directly above Rafters – at a nightclub called Fagins, which was a cabaret-style venue, whereas Rafters was more underground, literally and metaphorically. The club had been host to Sham 69, Siouxsie and the Banshees, Billy Idol and others.

On entering Dougie's club, even before descending to the large basement area where it was held, there was a buzz about the place and we invariably saw people we knew, either outside on the street or on the stairs. Once inside the fun really began. This sultry July evening was a memorable night for me.

The support band were the recently formed Sad Café with the brilliant singer Paul Young, sadly no longer with us. This group had evolved out of the Mandalaband, who had lost both their singer and their record deal with Chrysalis. Martin Hannett had suggested that Paul Young join the band and Tosh Ryan recalls: 'He [Martin] was considering remixing the Mandala tapes the band had got back from Chrysalis. Martin took Sad Café to Kennedy Street, who then began managing them. The name was also Hannett's idea. I remember one afternoon in the office of Music Force. Susanne O'Hara, Martin's girlfriend, was sitting on a psychiatrist-type couch reading a copy of Carson McCullers's *The Ballad of the Sad Café*. Martin suddenly yelled, in his own inimitable style, "That's it!"'

Susanne says rather that it was she who thought up the name for the band: 'It occurred one night when Paul Young was on the phone to Martin and needed a name for the band, they were considering the Vultures, I think. I was reading *The Ballad of the Sad Café* when Paul rang and I suggested the name Sad Café to Martin. He told Paul and Paul liked it.'

Incidentally, Paul and his wife Pat visited us for dinner at Charlesworth and I remember Tony and I visiting them at their house in Wythenshawe. Pat used to work the door at Rafters and Dougie said that 'Tony made Sad Café' (because of his TV and promotional help).

The main Rafters act that night was Elvis Costello, who Dougie had brought over from Liverpool. He knew his father, Ross McManus, a singer, musician and trumpet player who performed with the Joe Loss Orchestra. Dougie remembers how Tony often helped him to plug his acts and in this case Tony said he'd give Costello thirty seconds to perform on his *What's On* show on *Granada Reports* (pre-recorded to go out that very same night). Dougie said that as they were getting in the taxi Costello was 'losing his bottle' with nerves, and so Dougie gave him a lemon to suck (a real one). In the actual event Elvis got a full minute on the programme. The original plan was that Costello would play 'Less Than Zero', but at the last minute he asked if he could sing something he'd just written the week before, and so he sang the classically beautiful 'Alison'. This was actually his very first TV appearance. Costello's second TV appearance was live on *So It Goes* two weeks later. Like everyone else I was intrigued by his name and wasn't sure whether or not he was a fan of the other Elvis. Little did we know that within a month the other Elvis, the one who lived in Memphis, would be dead.

Mick Middles remembers that Tony was wearing a Fedora hat that wonderful July night. I noticed Costello staring at me and was very flattered when he suddenly presented me with a copy of his album, *Armed Forces*. On one side he had written: 'For Lyndsey Elvis Costello', and on the other, 'Tasteful, yes!'

Tony and I probably were a stylish couple, though Mick thought Tony's hat was a bit pretentious! I loved the gig and remain a huge fan of Costello and anything Paul Young sang to this day.

I was reminded of another significant event around this time when I spoke to Cath Carroll. Tony and I went onstage together at Manchester Grammar School. She said: 'The first time I saw Tony was when he came to do a talk on the "punk-rock phenomenon" at the boys' grammar school opposite our girls' school. This was pre-Factory; he was just billed as the "controversial" host of *So It Goes*. I went with a friend; I think there were four girls who went and about 200 boys. It hit home how very male-dominated the interest-in-music scene was, let alone the actual business. Even more shocking was that Tony showed up with his partner in this music business lark, and she was a woman. That would be *you*, Lindsay! That was the first time I realised that women might be allowed to work behind the scenes on an equal footing, you didn't just have to be a secretary or Elkie Brooks at the mic to be allowed into the biz. You and Tony seemed a bit frustrated by the nature of the questions, the lack of feedback. It was a bit *University Challenge*-y and most were there to defend their Genesis albums, not discuss Howard Devoto.'

On 16 August Buzzcocks and Penetration played at Manchester's Electric Circus, and Granada were there to film it for *So It Goes*. This was the night that Elvis Presley died.

Tony later told *New Musical Express* how special this night was: 'It was all wild. There were only two series; one in the summer of '76 and another in the autumn of '77. The Pistols night was a standout, and the night we filmed at the Electric Circus, with Buzzcocks and Penetration. Basically, I got into it because all the way through the summer of '77 I would wake up in a sweat, thinking: someone else is going to realise this is great stuff. I can't believe it's so wonderful, it's gotta be on television. I remember going to see the producer Mike Appleton, an absolutely sweet guy, God bless him, and I asked, "Why can't we have more punk bands?" He said, "Because music is about technical excellence, and if they're technically proficient I'll put them on." To this I replied, "Mr Appleton, you are completely and utterly wrong." But that's what it was like then.'

Mike Appleton was the producer of *The Old Grey Whistle Test* for BBC Two, and they had a reputation for ignoring British punk bands. Of course the whole point of punk initially was to flout supposed technical proficiency. The following year, as punk became much more popular, the *Whistle Test* changed their booking policy and became more open-minded.

The odd thing is that, however much this August night of filming for *So It Goes* at the Circus meant to Tony, I don't recall much about it, although I know I was there. The first show of the second series of *So It Goes* in October 1977 got off on a punk footing and had Pete Shelley singing 'What Do I Get?'. Buzzcocks manager Richard Boon had been in discussion with major labels about a deal for the band. Although they had enjoyed some success with the *Spiral Scratch* EP on the self-funded New Hormones label, Richard tells me that he struck a deal with Andrew Lauder from United Artists at the bar of the Electric Circus on the night Presley died. The deal was for £75,000 over three years.

Whatever went on that night is a bit of a blur to me, merging in my memory with other Circus nights and early Buzzcocks gigs. I do remember the cameramen swishing about onstage and wondering what these guys made of the beer swilling, pogoing mob at the front. I found it mildly disturbing and entertaining in the same measure, standing at the back by the bar. Buzzcocks, on the other hand, put on a great show as ever. Pete Shelley turned out to be a genuinely good guy and friend to me. I loved his lyrics and his tuneful/tuneless vocal over the band's great melodies. Pauline Murray of Penetration was soaked in beer while performing that night. I admired her bravery, getting up there in front of all those beer-swilling blokes. The footage of Penetration shot that night is some of the best ever, and ranks high with footage of any UK punk band in action for that matter.

Pauline had a look of Siouxsie Sioux, of whom I was a fan. Tony and I saw Siouxsie play at the Students Union of Manchester University, a memorable night and one of the best gigs I saw around this time. She also played at the Oaks in Chorlton, on Barlow Moor Road where the Travelodge now stands, a venue that Tony thought very important. In fact in an interview with Paul Morley he said that 'the Electric Circus and the Oaks should be regarded with the same reverence as the Twisted Wheel and the Hacienda'. Hmm.

Tosh Ryan remembers a Siouxsie and the Banshees gig at the Oaks: 'At the side of the stage three clowns suddenly appeared playing rubbish – Kevin Cummins, Paul Morley and Tony, and for some reason they were being showered with feathers.' He thought Tony might have been playing bass. Perhaps because of this, Tosh has always thought that Tony was in the Negatives, a group that also featured Cummins, the Manchester rock photographer, and Morley, but I cannot recall Tony ever playing onstage and Morley doesn't even remember this night at all.

Of course, memories are always suspect, especially of events that may have involved alcohol and drugs, but speaking for myself, the fact that I don't remember something doesn't necessarily mean it never happened. Then again, some things I do seem to remember may have become jumbled up, especially in regard to time and place. This becomes especially apparent when sharing memories with others – then one is rapidly aware of a collective false memory syndrome! It's a case of 'same world, different reality'. Or as Andy Couzens, early member of the Stone Roses, states: 'You can put five people in a room and then ask them about what they experienced in that room and every one of them will have a different story.'

Tony remembered being a roadie for Wayne Barrett, the singer with Slaughter & the Dogs, at the Oaks. This probably just meant we gave him a lift home, especially since singers don't really have any equipment beyond a microphone. We were often in the habit of dropping musicians off before making our way out to Charlesworth.

On 19 August Tony and I travelled to Wolverhampton to yet another rather seedy venue to see the Sex Pistols. By this time, despite having appeared on *Top of the Pops*, the group had been banned from playing many towns in the UK, largely because of their swearing on Bill Grundy's TV show and coverage of their antisocial behaviour in the press. For this reason many of their tour dates had been cancelled and the Pistols appeared under a different name, Spots, which stood for 'Sex Pistols On Tour Secretly'. This night was the opening show of their secret tour and Tony and I were there to give our support.

I remember feeling that it all seemed a bit surreal – as if it was somehow a theatrical performance as opposed to a rock gig. There was plenty of enthusiasm amongst the audience, which seemed, as was so often the case with punk, to be largely male, and was considerably bigger than expected considering the show was supposed to be secret. I didn't share this wild enthusiasm, and Tony and I stood together rather sedately, enjoying the antics of the crowd almost as much as the band. I especially liked the fact that the gig was underground and flouted that silly ban. Afterwards we went backstage to say our hellos. Tony, of course, was highly favoured. There was an element of male bravado in the dressing room. Sid Vicious was standing there, bare-chested, and I noticed several cuts slashed on his front and shoulders, none of them especially serious, but deep enough to have drawn quite a bit of blood. I asked him – perhaps naively – what had happened? I wish I could remember his reply but I don't exactly. All I know for certain is that it was a lie, something like, 'I fell down,' or some such nonsense. It was only afterwards that I realised what the marks probably were – fingernail slashes.

On 2 and 3 October just about everyone played a full weekend at the Electric Circus to commemorate its imminent closure; I was not particularly sad about this as it had become so raucous, uncouth and predominantly male. Mick Middles remembers 'Big Dave' walking out of the gents' lavatories (which were swimming in urine, beer and God knows what else) holding aloft a toilet seat that he had just ripped out. Perhaps this helps paint the picture! Tony and I were in our usual place at the back, near the bar, at a safe distance from such mayhem, and enjoying the bands who were, when all was said and done, definitely enjoyable.

Then, without warning, Tony left my side and mounted the stage to make an announcement, perhaps to comment on the closure and talk to the audience, as was his wont, given his new and important role as a figurehead of the Manchester music scene. Of course, the minute he got up there the lads at the front started chucking beer all over him, but worse – much worse than that – they were gobbing at him as well. Rumours also abounded that it wasn't always necessarily beer they were chucking. I just thought this was revolting. However, when Tony came off the stage and walked towards the back, getting wetter as he did so, he looked absolutely exhilarated. I had just been about to sympathise with him and help dry him off in some way, but he looked as if he'd just had the best orgasm of his whole life. 'That was amazing!' he exclaimed, much as he had about Charles's speech at our wedding. I felt pretty disgusted with him at that moment. I thought it meant he was perverted – to actually enjoy such a thing. I left immediately and drove to my parents' house for some down time. I think Tony saw himself as a champion of punk, which was something he wanted to be, whereas I took punk as I found it and couldn't see anything worthwhile about being drenched in spit and beer.

Maybe the event triggered a form of jealousy in me in some weird way. I had imagined any intimacies that occurred ought to be shared with me only, and it seemed to me that there was something intimate in the pleasure he took from these young men lavishing him with the contents of their glasses.

But Keith Jobling noted, 'In some ways Tony kind of wallowed in the fact he could go onstage and they'd all be shouting at him, "Wanker!" and afterwards he'd be saying fucking amazing. It was the spectacle he was interested in.'

I agree with this – Tony was fascinated with youth culture. It was the spectacle, not some kind of weird perversion. I wish I had understood that then.

Perhaps, with hindsight, this night was some sort of watershed, the beginning of a kind of a musical – but only musical – split between us.

It wasn't that I was anti-punk. For instance, I loved Iggy Pop at the Apollo and was thrilled to be present with Tony when he interviewed him in the dressing room there. This performance went out on 30 October and, whereas to us it seemed that Tony's show was finally offering something truly valuable and important, paradoxically this night was in part responsible for the downfall of the programme – because Iggy was parading around with a horse's tail in his arse.

Clearly I wasn't listening carefully to Iggy's words (much as we all later realised we weren't listening to Ian Curtis's words until it was too late). In interview with Tony, Iggy said, 'The only reason I'm in this is to get my face on more screens, get my name in more papers and more print, to expand my fame.' Well, I feel somewhat cynical about such an ego-bound desire – rather disappointing for a hero of punk. But Iggy had an attractive face then and his songs were great. In the end perhaps music really does just come down to good songs.

Tony and I were still united in sympathy towards an anti-establishment stance and were both pleased and amused when, later that month, the Sex Pistols released their album *Never Mind the Bollocks*. Tosh Ryan remembers putting up posters that featured the album's title all over the country and recalls: 'There was a town – Nottingham I think – that decided to go to the law and sue Virgin on the grounds that "bollocks" was an obscene word. Virgin engaged John Mortimer to deal with the case. We also would have been fined a lot of money for sticking these posters up. I had to meet Mortimer with details of the background to our campaign. Anyway, Mortimer won and the word bollocks was deemed not to be obscene so the posters were left up.'

The era seemed to be declaring a policy of 'anything goes', which seemed necessary at the time and yet now I wonder where it has got us. I saw it then as healthy that boundaries were being stretched. The Manchester rock satire troupe Alberto Y Lost Trios Paranoias were making controversial headlines in 1977 with their play about snuff rock. They had appeared on *So It Goes* back in '76 and in October '77 clips from the play were shown on Tony's show, including the song 'Gobbin' on Life'. While the group were enjoying great critical and popular success during this period, they never really 'made it' in a commercial sense. Yet the band's drummer Bruce Mitchell remembers their arrogance:

'Nobody was returning Tony's calls . . . He'd wanted us to do a show but he had a vision of what this show had to be. He'd phone me on the payphone 'cause I was sort of producer of the show: "Is Bruce there? Bruce, we've got this slot here that you could [. . .] the band could come in and do this. My concept is . . ." He was making this plan to persuade the band to come and do this gig for him. The band were saying things like, "Tell him to fuck off, that creep," all that sort of usual guff that you got in those days. But we did the gig and his concept was that all the band had to be dressed in choir boys' outfits. Maybe it was a Christmas thing, we were all being angelic, and singing.'

It's funny to look back and be reminded of how many musicians thought my husband was kind of uncool. It rather exacerbated my own doubts about him. And so many people thought him arrogant and smug. Even Tony himself said in his book that at age twenty-five he was 'a prima donna in full flow', and that he'd 'always had that prima donna edge from the age of eleven, when he filled in for Father Quinn on the Novena Rosary when the PP had laryngitis, and come first in the A stream in his first year at grammar school; Christmas, Easter and summer'.

All the same the Albertos' singer, Chris Lee, and Tony had hung out together and this continued, along with myself and Chris's then girlfriend, Fran.

Nineteen seventy-seven closed with the second series of *So It Goes*, beginning in October. It seemed to Tony and I that there was no going back with this show since it was now undoubtedly successful. Wrong. *So It Goes* found its niche with the second series and was the only programme of its kind to air the likes of the Sex Pistols, Siouxsie and the Banshees, Buzzcocks, punk poet John Cooper Clarke and Ian Dury; along with all sorts of diverse and interesting archive material and culture. Some of the content was a little on the wacky side, but all in all it made for a rounded show.

Mostly these were happy days for Tony and I, possibly our happiest together. He was fulfilled at work and I found a balance between running the home and being very much part of the musical side too. We went to see most of the bands that featured on *So It Goes* together and I got to meet the artists wherever they played. I remember walking behind Ian Dury as he climbed up the narrow stairs at some venue or other – I think it was the Apollo in Manchester, where Ian and the Blockheads supported Elvis Costello. It was memorable to watch because Ian had suffered polio as a child and as a result had a pronounced limp. He wore an orthopaedic boot – a built-up shoe to compensate for one of his legs being shorter than the other. What a lovely man he was. 'Reasons to Be Cheerful' was such an appropriate song for him because he was so cheery, with not an ounce of self-pity either then, or later when he suffered from cancer. Tony loved him from the outset and interviewed him for *Granada Reports* and *So It Goes*. I saw clips of these interviews recently and it was interesting to see their two contrasting worlds converge. The cockney son of a market seller, who Janet Street-Porter called 'The Godfather of Punk' (presumably because Johnny Rotten imitated his style and razor earrings), completely in tune with a well-educated, middle-class, posh-speaking northern guy. I remember my mum posed a question to Tony that he asked Dury on-air shortly afterwards. It was, 'What's your idea of a great night out?' I doubt if she also asked him, 'Which do you prefer – sex, drugs or rock'n'roll?' but I wouldn't have put it past her. In response to the latter question, Ian told Tony that he'd choose rock'n'roll, but I can't vouch for what Tony's answer would have been.

As well as enjoying so many concerts, I often visited Granada. Malcolm Clarke was a studio director on several of the *So It Goes* shows and the three of us had many a good laugh together.

All in all we were loving it. So what went wrong? Tony thought it was down to Iggy Pop and the horse's tail sticking out of his bum in the first series. But then in the second series there was the thorny issue of Iggy using the word 'fucking' in his performance. In the middle of 'The Passenger' he'd told the audience that when he asked a girl called Lucille if she liked Cadillacs she'd replied, 'I hate fucking cars.' During a meeting over this issue Tony remembered screaming at his boss, 'Art, art, this is fucking art.' I wonder whether this was when Tony's fondness for the word 'fucking' began, because in later years it was quite rare for him to utter a sentence that *didn't* include the word. As well as the Iggy problem there was the ban on the Sex Pistols. Tony loved that group with a passion and wanted to give them more live coverage, but a memo from on high informed him that he mustn't even refer to them for one month. Tony tried to rebel, understandably, even threatened to leave. I sympathised with him. How could Granada not see how important this show was? But Tony had to shut up and put up. After that he never had any sympathy with me if I had trouble with my own bosses. He used to say that they were all twats – that's how they got into the position of being a boss in the first place. Also, he was philosophical about it: you get paid to do what they say, if you don't like it, run your own business. Which is true, of course, and when Tony himself became a boss he embraced these same notions with a vengeance.

When the Iggy show finally went out there was a dubbing error: the 'fucking cars' weren't the problem, but a loud clapping overdub ran out just before Iggy was heard to shout, 'Clap your fucking hands,' over the credits. Sadly, this may have been the final nail in the coffin for *So It Goes*. The show was axed. Fortunately, Tony was intelligent and robust enough to turn that ending into a beginning.

As a late celebration for my birthday that July, ever the one to do things differently, Tony spontaneously suggested we hold an LSD party in our little cottage. Others might like to get boozed up, but the kind of celebratory touch we liked was a psychedelic one.

So it was that 45 Town Lane became filled with assorted young men. I was the only girl present for some reason. I'm not sure who they all were except that they were musicians. I remember that Pete Shelley (singer with the Buzzcocks) and his friends Francis and Eric Random (soon to emerge as the Tiller Boys) were among them.

We all took a tab of LSD. It seemed stronger than usual – I was unable to speak or interact with anyone and felt alarmingly antisocial. Tony's dad, Sydney, called round with his friend Tony Connolly – what a time to meet the gay equivalent of your new mother-in-law! Fortunately Connolly was sufficiently wild himself (mostly alcohol induced) and probably thought our gathering somewhat tame. They both seemed to understand what was going on and didn't expect the social niceties such an occasion would usually bring. This was just as well, as I couldn't even talk to them. They probably went off to the pub to get completely plastered, laughing about how weird we all were. I remained glued to a sofa totally absorbed by the workings of my brain. Others were interacting but I was too busy. It was a bit like trying to work out a fascinating mathematical equation. After about four hours or so something clicked for me – it was a Eureka moment. I jumped up exclaiming, 'Everything is opposites!' and charged out of the house to sit on top of the hill, gazing at the stars in wonderment. I believe at that moment I had briefly transcended the oppressive duality in life and hence experienced a feeling of utter freedom and joy.

It is impossible to put this feeling into words but the following quotation from writer Paul Brunton describes it rather well:

'Living in time and space as we do, we perforce live always in the fragmentary and imperfect, never in the whole, the perfect. Only if, at rare moments, we are granted a mystical experience and transcend the time-space world, do we know the beauty and sublimity of being liberated from a mere segment of experience into the wholeness of Life itself.'

But if everything – or nearly everything – is opposites in this time-space world, then the second half of this trip would find me behaving as the extrovert to the introvert I'd been for the first half. Feeling liberated of all oppression, I skipped back to the house. I felt love for every person on the planet and wanted to inject a bit of life into our gathering. I'd witnessed chess games going on and it was hardly what you'd call a happening party. Tony was standing on the pavement outside the door, and the minute he looked at me I could see *fear* in his face. I couldn't understand why when I was smiling at him. Some say fear, not hate, is the opposite of love, and at that moment I could see why. It put a block on everything. My heart felt open, I wanted to share something good with him, but he announced that the party was over and he was taking everyone home. I felt really disappointed as, to me, the party was just beginning. I wanted to talk, dance, and celebrate life with everyone.

He duly piled in as many of the young boys as his car could hold and drove off. But he couldn't fit them all in. There were two left behind – named Barry Adamson and Willie Trotter. Barry was soon to join the group Magazine as their bass guitarist, and Willie also went on to join a group called Ludus.

I was in a dancing mood and would have done so whether alone or not. I got the records going – Donna Summer's 'I Feel Love'; Blondie's '(I'm Always Touched by Your) Presence, Dear' (I had that particular single framed because I played it so many times that it wore out); Joan Armatrading 'Love and Affection' – I was relating to women on vinyl since they were not in evidence around this odd, nether-boys'-club music world Tony and I now inhabited. Record producer Yvonne Ellis noted that in her experience of the music industry, ninety-nine percent of the 'girls' in it are generally singers.

I felt a particular affinity with Blondie back then. Tony always spoke about the night Debbie Harry appeared on *What's On*, singing 'X Offender' with her group. Our memories differ about what happened with a red rose. In his book Tony said that she was fingering said rose and handed it to him, and that I therefore assumed something was going on ('and was pissed off. More than normal, which is more than enough'). Actually, that's bollocks (the myth, rather than the reality). What I seem to remember happening is that he threw something towards her – I can't remember what, it might have been a dandelion or something he just happened to have in his hand – and said to her, rather romantically I thought, 'It should have been a rose.' I'd be interested to see Granada's footage if they have it. Obviously Tony fancied her – she was gorgeous – but I distinctly remember thinking it was a good job he and I had arranged to meet at Granada at 7:00pm that night, because then he wouldn't be able to carry on chatting her up. And so I wasn't worried. Though you never know when people might just fall madly in love. The way we had done.

I got hot dancing that crazy acid night, my clothes were getting in the way and, feeling liberated of constraints and inhibitions, I took them off. I can only swear on all that is precious to me that this was not a sexual thing. I've often seen young children do the same thing, run around naked because they want to. I wanted to and I was in my own living room. That said, I must admit I was enjoying the attention – as a child I never got any, and now this childlike woman had the full concentration of two people all to herself. But then I saw that familiar expression of *fear* on the faces of Barry and Willie. They both sat forward in their chairs. Barry nervously shouted out, 'Put something on, Tony will be home in a minute.' So I put a belt on and carried on dancing.

Barry's recollections of the evening, given to me in 2009, contain a couple of surprising elements:

'The way I remember that night: It was 4 July 1977. It was a very "trippy" evening.

'"You Yesyesyes" from the album *Fingerprince* by the Residents plays out across a room full of laughter – people crying with laughter, notably Pete Shelley and me; crying over some splashes of black and white paint on a badge which we decide looks like a dog wearing a mask and therefore must be a burglar's dog! Of course, this is all heightened by the acid we had all taken earlier that evening peaking and inducing a lowering of boundaries all round to the point that you – yes yes yes you! – felt free enough to strip naked and dance when Tony had taken Pete and Francis back to Manchester, or at least the station.

'Now Miss Reade, I cannot think you would be so naive as to totally believe that a beautiful naked woman dancing, iconically, while one of the boys is known to be besotted with you and the other is consumed with working-class guilt, could be interpreted as nothing more than a display of childlike free-thinking and not have ramifications we would still be talking about thirty years later? (Well, perhaps – my five-year-old son regularly wants to get naked and I have to explain to him why it's not a great idea too!)

'To me it was perhaps one of the most scintillating displays of a woman in her sexual prime, turning boys into men, Mrs Robinson. The icing on the cake being a moment of sheer brilliance on your part, when yes I said to put something on, as indeed Tony would be back soon – you put on a brown suede belt and carried on dancing! As this scene played I went to the window to confirm both my protective urges and quell my paranoia, and maybe get some air! When in the light of early morn I moved the curtain a spy-like inch and saw what can only be described as the very first ever wave of paparazzi!

'Stood outside were some ten photographers and I could almost see the headlines... "TV Presenter's Naked Wife and Teen Bass Player in Acid-Fuelled Dancing Romp (Well, She Was Wearing a Belt)".

'It was indeed a shocking sight in those days, and a delicious moment of the Bret Easton Ellis kind to see that many people with cameras. Then out of the corner of my eye I see . . . Tommy Docherty!

'T'was the morning of 5 July and Manchester United had sacked him for having an affair with the wife of United's physio – hence the paps.'

By the time Tony arrived home in the early hours of that morning, I had in fact thrown some clothes on because I was sitting down by then and felt a faint chill. But bits of clothing were still strewn where I had left them. The boys looked apprehensive when Tony's key turned in the lock. I wasn't frightened in the least. I suppose if I'd thought about it I would have expected Tony to ask me what had happened, and I would have told him the truth. But he didn't ask. He sat beside me and surveyed the clothes on the floor and looked over at the boys. Then he got another look I recognised – a sexual look. It was as if he had just walked in on a swingers' party or something. I was sorry that he had misread the situation and didn't really understand me. That was naive of me – I doubt any outside observer would have seen me as an innocent. Yet when he tacitly suggested, in front of the others, that we might go upstairs, I felt slightly repelled. That hadn't been the point of it at all.

11 LSD and the Consolation of Friends

Drugs get such a bad press nowadays but, speaking for myself, the times I drank when I was younger were ultimately the most destructive – i.e. done when the 'game of life' was given up as lost. Young people now appear to be more hedonistic about it. I can be hedonistic about it now too and enjoy a glass or three. But there's nothing hedonistic about punishing the body, is there?

I don't know about Tony, but I didn't take LSD for pleasure, it was more complicated than that. I suppose you could say I was a quester or a seeker after truth. I wanted to know what was in there – deep in the layers of the mind and maybe the soul. It wasn't always an easy ride. I had moments of bliss but equally moments – that felt like lifetimes – of sheer hell. The ultimate lesson from that perhaps being that we ourselves are heaven or hell.

I was a big fan of eminent writer Aldous Huxley – still am in fact. He advocated the use of LSD. I particularly admired the fact that his last written request on his deathbed was for an injection of LSD. This makes total sense to me.

One night Tony and I had taken acid, for no special occasion this time, it was just an ordinary night in Charlesworth.

Unfortunately some people I didn't know arrived unexpectedly and I got an impression of a sycophantic air towards Tony. Perhaps that was my paranoia, as Tony always claimed he disliked any suggestion of sycophancy and shunned it. Maybe he did – but I was never so sure about his ego. My ego certainly snubbed it, on this occasion anyway. I felt I didn't belong and absented myself, retreating to our bedroom. LSD really is a trip into your own mind and that was where I wanted to go. Have any of us got more than our mind? Life really is a conversation in your own head.

Lying on the bed I could hear chatter and laughter coming from the room below. It was so far removed from where I was at. At this point the trip took on a horrific aspect. My mind was still mine, but my body – and ipso facto my life – was someone else's. In the first place, I wasn't young anymore – I was very old. In the second place I wasn't female either. I was a stick-thin man – even thinner than I then was and, by God, I was thin then. Every single bone in my body hurt like hell. That was all I was – a bag of hurting bones. There were no two ways about it. I was dying. Expiring. The breath – my breath – was literally leaving. I felt panicked but I couldn't even do that, it took every single ounce of my strength just to take a solitary breath.

I heard someone laugh. It probably came from a passerby outside, or perhaps one of the people downstairs. It brought home how alone I was in this death. Not one person sitting with me by the bed, and people so removed and uncaring that they were laughing.

It is sad to die alone. This poor bugger, this old man, was dying entirely alone. There aren't many people who care really, are there – I mean *really* care? That's the great thing about family. You don't have to doubt that your family care – hopefully. I never have in any case. What is a true friend? Basically, it's very simple. It is just someone who is genuinely on your side. I think a handful of true friends is about as good as it gets for most of us. Some of us have partners and family who are not real friends – how perfectly dreadful. I think I may have more true friends on the 'other side' now than this one. That's the trouble with getting older. As John Updike said, 'The more dead you know it seems the more living you don't know.' Maybe that's how so many of us finish up dying alone.

Friends. I thought I had loads and loads but then, after Tony and I publicly split, how they fell away. It was a rude awakening. People who I thought really cared – some of them didn't (and still don't) even have the time of day for me. People who I broke bread with, or rather frequently made homemade casseroles for, became as cold as ice. Other sycophantic fish to fry.

I was glad I'd been given the opportunity to see through false friends. Other people continued to be fooled by them but I knew it was an act – a self-interested act. That was always a difficult thing for Tony. How many could he really trust? Funny that I worried back then that he had virtually no true friends. By the end of his life he had several. And there was no doubt he was really loved by them.

Tony's closest friend in the seventies and eighties was undoubtedly Alan Erasmus. As Elliot Rashman, who managed Simply Red amongst others, observed: 'You couldn't have put a Rizla paper between them.' Tony and Alan travelled a long road together and, despite not speaking for over a decade, when Tony became ill their friendship was rekindled. If I had ever had any shadow of a doubt about Alan's love for Tony – which I honestly didn't have by the end – it would have been dispelled one night in July 2009. I was spending my birthday evening on my own, but I wasn't going to let that stop me from doing something different. On the recommendation of a friend, Fran, I went to see *It Felt Like a Kiss* on its opening night at the Manchester Festival. She'd seen a preview of it and recommended it highly. It was sold out but I managed to get a ticket and it was absolutely brilliant. Driving home I was thinking about Tony, remembering how I messed up my last birthday meal with him. So on the way back, I called in at Tony's grave. As I walked towards it I was astonished to see someone else already there and nearly left, but carried on regardless. It turned out to be Alan who, on this sunny evening, had his car parked right beside the grave, door open, and was playing Bob Dylan very loudly. It seemed like a party! I sat by the grave, it felt as it Tony was there, the three of us together again. Alan said he'd brought Tony his favourite Chinese dumplings and a joint. I couldn't remember if I'd ever had these dumplings. He asked me if I'd like to try one – there it was on the soil, it was still warm! I felt a bit peckish, took a bite, and it was delicious so I ate the lot.

Designer Peter Saville, another of Tony's best friends, also recalled bumping into Alan at Tony's grave on the evening after Tony's funeral. Saville remarked that later, because Alan is such a frequent visitor there, a sign went up on the grave that said something like, 'If you see Alan Erasmus here please contact the office.'

I can think immediately of at least five men who also love Tony and, as Bruce Mitchell said, think of him every day.

Tony was a real friend to me. Sometimes it didn't seem like it. The time he sacked me, the time he walked straight past me without letting on at Urbis because he was with his partner, Yvette. (Tony and I had shared a dinner less than a fortnight before this public snubbing.) But at key moments he was always there.

Back to the bad trip: perhaps Tony sensed my 'death'. He came into the room and sat by the bed. It was like a fairytale – he woke me from my dream, or rather nightmare. He cared. I wasn't alone.

Other key moments when Tony was there – odd, it was as if he had an unconscious sixth sense. I went through a particularly bad time after my mum died in 1997. I also had a miscarriage and subsequently broke up with my then boyfriend (and knew I'd now never be able to have a child). Because Tony always said I was similar to his mum he was convinced I'd give birth at the same age. The odd thing was that if that child had been born I would have been the same age as she was when she had Tony – forty-six. The pregnancy was threatening at my mum's funeral and I told Tony this at the wake. He'd come to the funeral with Tony Connolly, who also loved my mum. Tony said, 'No, no, you'll keep it.' He seemed certain, but it wasn't to be.

I'd been completely broke and hence had been living with my mum for three years before her sudden death. The music business had cast me aside (despite signing the Stone Roses and Orchestral Manoeuvres in the Dark, and co-founding Factory) and I became unemployed in 1993. In 1997 I had just about picked myself up off the ground, studying homeopathy and earning money as a Feng Shui consultant. The studies went out of the window and I became too depressed to work. Plus, I now had to sell the house and share the proceeds between my siblings and me. This house had been the rock I'd clung to when all else failed – my marriage, my job, my relationships. Now even this was going. My sister and brother weren't pressing me and the market was quiet in 1998, but in '99 the house sold. I worked out I'd have to go and live in some horrible house and decided I'd rather be dead. When it came to it my sister saved me from the awful house scenario, but on the night in question I didn't see any way out of it. I thought to myself, 'Well, the easiest suicide would be toxic fumes from the car so you'd better go and do it while you've still got a garage.' I knew I wouldn't ever want to fiddle about with a hosepipe – too technical, it might go wrong. So I made my way out to the garage. I laugh about it now – how ridiculous, I'm sure I didn't mean it, but sometimes the drama helps give a perspective on things. I think it was important to me to know that I could do it if I so chose. It still is actually. I'd hate to be kept alive, rotting in an old people's home with no quality of life, for instance, and think a person should have the right to choose when they go.

I got to the garage, intending to go ahead, and then noticed that there was a hole in the glass of the side door window. *Drat!* There'd be no point trying it because it might not work. As I made my way out of the side door, I glanced up the driveway and saw Tony walking nonchalantly toward the house, carrying my coat. How utterly bizarre to see him at that exact moment. I hadn't been expecting him. He didn't have the slightest idea what I'd just been going through – but he was there. He was bringing back my coat that I'd accidentally left in his car. And my coat was in his car because he was there for me – in his way – through this difficult period.

Another time later on I'd moved from that house and was now living in a terraced cottage in the country (not dissimilar to the house we shared at Charlesworth). I was surviving with two part-time jobs, one of which was at the weekend. But on Saturday 9 August 2003, and not that long after a whiplash injury, I woke with the most dreadful dizziness – vertigo, I think it's called – such that I couldn't lift or move my head without being sure I would vomit. I managed (out of sheer necessity) to go to the loo and grab the phone but had to lie completely still for half an hour before I could call work to say I wouldn't be in. The girl there kindly offered to ring the doctor since I didn't feel up to dialling anyone (I couldn't see the numbers without feeling dreadfully sick). The cat was hungry but there was nothing I could do. To this day I still wonder how it came about that Tony called me at home that morning around 11:00am. In the first place I was supposed to be at work, and in the second this period preceded our regular dinner evenings. When I explained the situation to him he drove straight over. 'In sickness and in health,' I marvelled. He checked on me, fed the cat and then went across the road for a lager. Soon after he got back, a lady doctor arrived. It must have looked a bit of an odd situation; Tony Wilson in a little two-up two-down and me white-faced in bed. She prescribed Stemetil, an anti-nausea drug, and Tony fetched the medicine.

He was a great nurse. He had not one iota of pity or fussing, but just got on with the business in hand. Much as he did when he was a patient.

'I collapsed outside Dimitri's,' remembered Vini Reilly. 'I was doing some music for Derek Jarman's last film, *Blue*. Jarman was dying and this guy from his office had come up to listen to what I was doing and give me an idea of the film, which was very radical. I met him and I smoked loads of weed and I collapsed. I was hyperventilating and Tony physically picked me up, put me in his car and drove me to casualty. Even though he had a busy schedule he sat with me and got them to sort me out with Valium and oxygen and all sorts of stuff so I was all right. That was what he was like, he was very hands-on – there was no question of telling someone to get me to hospital, he got me to hospital.'

'If you were in trouble, he was there,' Elliot Rashman recalled. 'Lots of people either can't cope or short-circuit or whatever. Tony was always there for people, whoever it was. I was thinking about all those years when he would visit his friend Neville, who suffered mental health problems. Whenever Neville had an incident, Tony was always there for him.'

Elliot had personal experience of Tony being there. He told me: 'I remember when I got seriously ill with depression he came with this book, Boethius's *The Consolation of Philosophy*. He said, "Look, this philosopher was really depressed, he wrote a lot about it, read up on it, it will help you." The day that Tony found out I was ill he turned up in Hebden Bridge. He would find time . . .'

Tony also told Elliot he'd found the book helpful himself. Boethius was quoted in *24 Hour Party People* when a homeless vagrant, sitting on the pavement, said to Tony, 'It's my belief that history is a wheel. "Inconsistency is my very essence," says the wheel. "Rise up on my spokes if you like, but don't complain when you are cast back down into the depths. Good times pass away, but then so do the bad. Mutability is our tragedy, but it is also our hope. The worst of times, like the best, are always passing away."'

'I know,' replied Tony in the film.

Of course he knew. The homeless person was expressing one of Tony's core philosophies. Tony reminded me of it every time I was cast down to the depths. 'You never know what's round the corner,' he used to say, and he really meant it. When you feel depressed it is hard to imagine things improving. Tony walked his talk and, like Boethius himself, he often took comfort from a chat with Lady Philosophy.

One of Tony's stock phrases (which, incidentally has become one of mine) also captures the *impossibility* of resisting change. He often referred to the 'ineluctable modality of life'. As ever he took his inspiration from one of the classics; in this case James Joyce wrote about it in *Ulysses*. Stephen Dedalus, an important character in that novel and even more especially in Joyce's *A Portrait of the Artist as a Young Man*, ponders the subject of impermanence while walking on the seashore; the rolling in of the waves, breaking and disappearing, ineluctable and ever changing. By trying to hold onto any shape, even one's own, one is against life. Even the mountains themselves rise and fall like the waves over millions of years.

T.S. Eliot's *The Waste Land* came out the same year as *Ulysses*, but Eliot had read the latter before he wrote the former. There are constant echoes in *The Waste Land* of themes and images from *Ulysses* – the drowned man, the voice of thunder, and others.

The more I understand Tony's appreciation of such fine classics, and the more I see how he truly tried to embrace such philosophies, perhaps never more so than when he was dying, the more I honour the man he was.

The roots of Factory Records began to come together in rather uncertain ways as 1978 unfolded. Tony always reckoned that Alan Erasmus started it all after the group Alan had been managing, the aptly titled Fast Breeder, broke up that January. Tony, Alan and C.P. Lee had been to see an earlier incarnation of this band, called Flashback, in May 1977 on Tony's stag night (apparently having consumed Dutch speed and/or LSD). Dave Rowbotham and Chris Joyce were thrown out of the band. Alan left at the same time since the remaining members of the group chose to be managed by Bruce Mitchell and Les Thompson, who ran Thompson Trucking with Dimitri Griliopoulos.

In the early seventies, Music Force had a list of members fortunate enough to own a van, who were then able to obtain work with jobbing groups. Later on Les and Dimitri took this niche market for their own with their two four-tonne trucks. Dimitri had been in a group named Drive In Rock and owned an old ambulance as well as musical equipment – a PA, microphones, etc – and spent many hours on the road as Alberto Y Lost Trios Paranoias' ambulance-driving roadie. Alongside drumming, Bruce also went into a similar line of work as a fixer for gigs – he'd sort out a PA or fix the lighting or find a bass player if needed. He helps run Manchester Light & Stage to this day.

Tony told writers Andy Zero and Bob Dickinson about the Flashback dismissals in an interview for a feature in *City Fun* fanzine: 'I felt a bit pissed off about it because I thought those two [Rowbotham and Joyce] were good musicians, they had ideas. It seemed a bit unfair so I said to Alan, "I'll join up with you and we'll start managing." *So It Goes* was finished. We needed another guitarist, Alan said, "What about Vini?" [He meant] the kid out of the Nosebleeds. "He's ill at present but he'll be all right." Then Tony Bowers was added and Phil Rainford was the singer.'

Tosh Ryan had a big cellar in Withington where rehearsals for the Nosebleeds were held. One day Vini had sent his then young, buxom girlfriend around with a note. It read: 'Unfortunately I will not be able to make Thursday's rehearsal. I'm afraid I'm going to be ill.' Tosh fell about laughing. Later on he questioned Tony about the wisdom of having a band based around a musician who sent sick notes in advance of being ill. Tony thought it was all part of his genius.

Tony suggested the naming of the Durutti Column as homage to the Situationist movement – something Malcolm McLaren and punk rock had already borrowed from. If Situationist means creating situations, then that seemed to be what McLaren was about (although others disagree that he manipulated these situations).

Tony was a fantastic catalyst for new ideas, for making things happen. He encountered Situationist ideas in 1968 at Cambridge as they were filtering back from Paris. The Situationist process concerned the reinvention of life in the city and our relationships to one another. I believe that the Situationist uprisings had such an impact on Tony that it inspired him to shape Factory and the Hacienda in the way that he did.

The Durruti Column were a group of anarchists who followed the leadership of Durruti in opposition to Franco during the Spanish Civil War. *The Return of the Durutti Column* was a piece of provocative art created by the Situationists in the 1960s, as Tony explained in his book, *24 Hour Party People*:

'In 1966, a bunch of proto student revolutionaries, fired with the cult brand of anarchist theory that goes by the name Situationism, took over the student's union at Strasbourg University, just by turning up for the elections. They spent their entire annual funding on creating a massive comic strip which they then fly-posted overnight in their city. The Strasbourg morning rush-hour was brought to a halt by a city-sized comic strip. One of the panels featured two cowboys talking about reification. This panel was called *The Return of the Durutti Column*. So now you know.'

In the comic strip, one of the cowboys asks the other (in French) if their occupation involves serious books, and the reply is, 'No, basically I just drift.' I personally could always relate to the idea of drifting; the idea that physical and psychological freedom are inextricably linked; roaming over the hills on horses and having the freedom to play. Though I'd never totally understood what this drifting (or *dérive*, as it is called in French) has to do with reification.

'Reification is a Marxist concept – to do with the capitalist process,' Bob Dickinson explained. 'One of the things capitalism does is it creates material fantasies. Another important process involves the way work becomes a commodity, and that's one definition of reification. In other words, your labour under capitalism becomes a quantifiable "thing" that capitalists can manipulate. Another process involves the appearance and disappearance of material objects – goods, buildings, landscapes, people – that are "invented" by necessity, then swept away again, so that, in Marx's phrase, "all that is solid melts into air". The changes wrought by capitalism bring about change – reification – on many different levels and in many different ways. The whole world is still changing because of capitalism, which is of course now global, and change is happening faster because of technology.'

Drifting or *dérive* denotes a way of escaping the overbearing characteristics of an urban space that limits freedom of movement and freedom of thought. To my mind, working just for money, or even fame, can enslave us; but work that comes out of experimentation, play and spontaneity can fulfill us. This can apply to music as much as anything else. As Barney (Bernard Sumner, guitarist with Joy Division) remarked when later working with New Order: 'Everyone wants to be a bloody pop star these days and no one is doing anything leftfield and interesting. Martin [Hannett] really encouraged experimentation in the studio. I think the results he got out of us were great.'

Tony told Bob Dickinson that he saw himself as an armchair anarchist, and that the sentiment between the two horsemen depicted in the comic strip entirely summed up his belief.

Tosh Ryan often sparred with Tony on political issues and even now has an inclination towards it. For instance, Tosh told me: 'Drifting is not participating in social change and the Durruti anarchists got in the way of what the socialists were trying to achieve. I see the Situationists as being somewhat middle-class art provocateurs. Wilson was paying homage to the Situationists, who were paying homage to Durruti, and it's like second-generation plagiarism. The way that Tony justified Joy Division's use of Nazi imagery was that it was a post-modern ironic statement because it was provocative, and that's the way the Situationists tried to provoke people by events and situations. It's really a middle-class and safe way of creating some kind of societal activity, but without any kind of useful political commitment.'

Tony would doubtless have had words to say in reply to that, and I'm only sorry I can't invite him to comment. Tony embraced the philosophy of anarchism, whereas Tosh sees solutions in socialism – in structured political activity, not through anarchy. I thought Tony was a socialist with a predilection for anarchy, but Tosh stated: 'A true socialist would not embrace anarchy. Socialism believes in political structure, order and the state, whereas anarchy believes in no state.'

Whatever the political machinations, the timing was ripe for Tony to preside over his chosen musical protégées. He thought Dave Rowbotham had the makings of a star and was now able to build his vision, in partnership with Erasmus, to form a group around Dave. Dave reminded Bruce Mitchell of Dickens's Artful Dodger. I thought Dave was a nice guy but didn't see what Tony saw and, besides, if he was the star shouldn't he be at the front? Being Tony, he went into this venture with characteristically annoying fervour; after all, the bands with whom he was associated were always the greatest in Great Britain. But after the debacle of *So It Goes* perhaps he had something to prove, as if he was on the rebound from a love affair. Granada may have stymied him but Tony wasn't going to depend on them to make things happen. His belief in rebellion and rock'n'roll coupled with his utter enthusiasm would drive it. To be fair, I was enthusiastic too – I liked all the individuals involved in the group and thought they had talent. But my enthusiasm was never on a par with Tony's.

With his usual aplomb for titles, Tony named his management project with Erasmus the Movement of the 24th January, or M24 for short, since that was the day the idea was conceived. The more this project of theirs began to take shape, the more frequently Tony drove round to Alan's flat after work, which meant he wouldn't make it home to me until the best part of the evening was gone. I little thought he was planning to build an empire – rather I took it as a personal slight, that he preferred to socialise with Alan rather than with me. Perhaps that was the case, since Alan never gave him a hard time whereas I sometimes did. If we had a row – which was now becoming more and more likely – then I could guarantee I wouldn't be seeing him. He worked late enough hours with just his day job.

In our honeymoon diary, after a tiff, Tony wrote: 'The test of strength – nay, friends of the occult – "the darkening of the light" had begun.' He was referring to an *I-Ching* reading, the first that we had done together some weeks before our wedding. The *I-Ching*, sometimes called *The Book of Changes*, is an ancient Chinese text often used as a system of divination. We were both familiar with this book before we met, but I was perhaps the more avid of the two of us, and the more our marriage ran into trouble the more I slavishly referred to it. I was always trying to get a handle on the future – probably because of my insecurity. Tony often joked about this reading, with its warning of difficulties ahead in our marriage. I just took it as yet another accurate bad omen. Another time that the two of us consulted the *I-Ching* together resulted in the naming of a track on *The Return of the Durutti Column*. Tony and I had received the hexagram entitled 'Conduct', and Vini couldn't think of a better title. So 'Conduct' it was.

During the period when Tony and Thelma's relationship had been in full force, Tony featured a clairvoyant named Ivor on *Granada Reports*, and on live TV Ivor announced to Tony that he could 'see' an older woman with whom Tony was having a relationship, but that she was married! Tony tried to change the subject and panicked; fearing that something pertinent might be given away, especially when Ivor went on to say that she was associated with someone else in the public eye.

I was always very impressed with Tony's story about Ivor's prescience in this matter and decided that I would go and see him for myself. Indeed, this I did many times. I don't believe now that it is a good idea to dabble with such things. The danger for me was in believing so much of what Ivor said – when in fact he got a lot wrong.

One day, Tony told me about a time when Ivor and Pat Phoenix, who played the famous Elsie Tanner of *Coronation Street,* were present at the same party. 'Do you remember that party we went to in a big house [with] Ivor's friends?' he asked me. 'All the guests are assembled when suddenly the doors are thrown open and in walks Pat Phoenix in a fur coat. The chatter of the guests falters for a moment – everyone is watching her whether their eyes are on her or not. She pauses with great dramatic effect. Then suddenly she makes a beeline straight towards me. She walks up and embraces me and – whilst in this embrace – whispers in my ear, "Have you got any dope, Tony?"'

While I was courting clairvoyants in the hope of gaining some insight into the problems surrounding our marriage, Tony was becoming more and more involved with the Durutti Column. As 1978 wore on it got to the point where a venue was needed for their first gig, and Tony, in typical maverick style, didn't fancy the usual Rafters or Band on the Wall. His sights were drawn instead to an Afro-Caribbean social club called the Russell Club. Alan Erasmus already knew the promoter there – Don Tonay, a man of Irish gypsy descent with black wavy hair – and was familiar with the club because his Jamaican father, Aubrey, had taken him there. Don Tonay looked like a big Mafiosi character. Tosh recalled accompanying Don's right-hand man to collect Don from the airport after a trip to Italy. The first thing Don said was, 'Anything happen?'

'5 Mitten Street got torched,' came the reply. (This was a shebeen that Don owned.) To which Don responded, deadpan, 'Anything else?'

Alan Wise thought that Don Tonay had great humanity and kindness, however much of a gangster he may have been.

'We wondered why no one ever goes to the Russell,' Tony told *Zero,* '"cause we liked it and everyone was saying, "Uh, no one'll ever go there, it's in the middle of Moss Side, it's no good, people will be scared to go." So Alan and I thought, "Well, screw it, who cares, that's not really relevant." So we went round to see Don and he said, "Yeah, have Friday nights if you want it." So we thought we would. Alan said call it the Factory. Nothing to do with Warhol, I think he'd seen a sign walking down the street. If it had come from me it would have been a Warhol quote.'

Factory was in fact the perfect name, coming as it did out of industrial Manchester, and I personally believe Tony was attracted to the name in part because of its Warhol connection. His heroine Patti Smith also went to Warhol's Factory in New York.

Dancing to reggae music, and the ganja-smoking culture that went along with it, appealed to the young Wilson and Erasmus, and me. The Russell Club on Royce Road in Hulme was perfect. Walking in there drew you immediately into a dark, womb-like room with tables and stools dotted around a stage in the corner, and the ambience of a rather seedy community social club. In later years the venue accommodated the public service vehicle drivers in the area (hence its name, PSV Club). The sign as you entered – 'No Tams allowed' –

made you jump erroneously to the conclusion that the place was racist. Until you discovered that a Tam is a tam o' shanter – a Scottish tartan hat made of wool with a pompon in the middle.

The Russell Club was in many ways the ideal club, being intimate enough to work with small numbers of people, but also able to hold a crowd reasonably well. The Electric Circus had finished, Rafters was temporarily closed, and there wasn't anywhere else at that level to go and watch gigs.

Tony and I often went over to Liverpool, where Roger Eagle was running a post-punk club called Eric's, situated in a basement on Mathew Street opposite the Cavern Club. There were some great nights and happening acts there around this time. Roger's rather sophisticated taste in music was evidenced by the jukebox, on which he placed records by the likes of Charlie Parker and Ornette Coleman. I recall sitting in Roger's curiously cluttered room, the animated conversations about music, and Tony gleaning firsthand knowledge about the ups and downs of running a nightclub. Indeed, from where I was sitting it looked like these two were loosely toying with the idea of a partnership, sharing bands if not venues. One of the Liverpool acts that came to the opening Factory nights shortly after this was Big in Japan. Jayne Casey, who also DJ'd at Eric's, was the striking lead singer and the band are particularly notable for the subsequent careers of members Holly Johnson, Bill Drummond and Ian Broudie. In August of the same year Durutti Column would support Big in Japan for the last gig they performed at Eric's.

Tony decided that, to help establish the identity of his club, it would be as well to do an initial run of four Factory nights in succession at the Russell. Yet he had already encountered someone who would achieve the branding of Factory almost singlehandedly. Peter Saville had approached Tony and said that he was a designer at art school who wanted to get into the music business, and was Tony doing anything interesting? Tony was only managing a band then, but he had a vision and recognised from the start how to get the machinery moving. Saville, despite borrowing inspiration for several Factory images – including 'Use Hearing Protection' – from a sign, proved to be a master of image creation and style. His first Factory poster, using this industrial safety image and promoting the four gigs, may have been late (delivered two weeks into the four-week run), but it forged the beginning of an identity that outlasted the club as well as the record label and survives to this day.

Actually, Saville confesses to a perpetual lateness throughout his career, and reminded me of Tony's standing joke with him that Tony thought analogous to their relationship, which was taken from the 1965 film *The Agony and the Ecstasy*. In it, Charlton Heston plays Michelangelo, who is painting the ceiling of the Sistine Chapel. The Pope often appears and shouts up at him, 'When will you make an end?'

'When it is done,' shouts down Michelangelo.

No prizes for guessing who the Pope was.

Funnily enough, Tony's grave is still without a headstone nearly three years after his death. Tony would be amused by the lateness of it, as Saville is designing it (along with Ben Kelly).

This is how Tony described Saville and their next meeting in his book *24 Hour Party People*: 'A sort of twenty-year-old Brian Ferry look-a-like with searingly intelligent eyes turned up at the Granada canteen to see Wilson. Over a cup of GTV coffee, Peter showed Wilson a book on Jan Tschichold. He showed him the Penguin Crime covers from 1941, the constructivist play posters from the 1920s, and the cover of the 1965 Hoffmann-La Roche catalogue (the Swiss chemical boys who did so much for the neural pathways in the second half of the century in question). Wilson was entranced. Another fucking genius. The utter commitment of this kid said soul brother.'

Tony was so driven to create something, somewhere, somehow that doubt – the merest scintilla of pessimism – never entered his mind. In fact quite the reverse, as if the three-way family of his childhood was still hovering, as ever rewarding everything he did. It does often seem the case that the formative years of a person have far more impact on their entire lives than anything that comes along later. Hence, in contrast, I had zero confidence in everything I did and even assumed the delicious pastry I was making for Tony's dinner, for his favourite steak and kidney pie, must be inferior. He was always very late coming home for dinner and then when he appeared he'd seem hypnotically unaware of it, eating the food whilst staring at the television and ignoring me. I was hardly the innocent either, since I let my feelings be known. Looking back, it seems to me that here was reason enough for me not being driven to produce a child. Then again, surely this was the year when it would have been an obvious step. Because we never talked about it, I wasn't really sure how much Tony wanted a family. It seems obvious now, staring me in the face as I look at a wedding photo where he glances lovingly at Alan Erasmus's little girl. Perhaps that was really the point of marriage to him. I knew I wanted children – eventually – but it was a bit like the sentiment expressed in Augustine's wayward prayer: 'Lord make me pure . . . but not yet.' I was more interested in my freedom than I was in babies. I was scared to death of becoming trapped or, worse, abandoned and left to raise a child on my own. Our marriage didn't feel stable enough to cope with the extra stress and I was determined not to bring up a child in a house where rows echoed from room to room, as I had been. My mother warned me of the mind-numbing boredom and unbearable tiredness that went with young children. She wasn't wrong, as I would find out for myself.

A radio presenter called James Stannage lived near us in Charlesworth. At the time Stannage had a phone-in show on Piccadilly Radio and was renowned for his rude and aggressive manner towards callers. Tony and I rather admired this and we became friendly with James and his wife, Kerry, occasionally meeting them for drinks at a nearby pub. Soon after they had their first baby Kerry went back to work, and for some reason had no childcare on Tuesdays.

I volunteered (unpaid) to look after their little boy since I thought I would really enjoy it. So James dropped the child off at 8:00am and collected him at the end of the day. As the weeks wore on I noticed I wasn't especially looking forward to Tuesdays. This was nothing to do with the child – he was a perfectly lovely little boy – but I just found baby-minding tedious; long days with no adult companionship were not much fun, and I simply didn't want my life to be like that. In reality, of course, babies grow up, and nothing remains quite as it is. Yet children are, as it says in the Bible about the poor, always with you.

In truth I had more interest in music at that stage of my life. I thought Tony recognised this, but with hindsight I believe he was, like the music industry itself, if not the world – especially then – rather chauvinistic about it. If he was planning a musical enterprise then it began, as it continued, with a masculine bias. My role to him was as a housewife and mother-to-be. I played along with the role to a degree (behaving as I thought his beloved mum would have done) but became utterly bored and frustrated by it.

Tony and I were both present the night of the Stiff-Chiswick challenge at Rafters on Friday, 14 April 1978. Stiff and Chiswick were two independent record labels offering local bands the chance of winning a contest; the prize was the opportunity to release a record. Some of us, though curious, rightly took a bit of a dim view of the event. The idea of a talent contest in itself smacked of tastelessness, a forerunner of the dumbed-down Britain of today. Certainly I don't recall people queuing outside trying to gain entrance, as is depicted in *24 Hour Party People*, unless they were musicians perhaps. Joy Division didn't appear until around 2:00am, and had become increasingly wound up by all the other bands (fifteen to be precise) going on before them. Perhaps it was this, in part, which led to the group making an impact and the exchange of words between Curtis and Wilson that evening. According to Tony, Ian showed a belligerent side to his nature, accusing Tony of being a 'fucking cunt' for not putting the band on television. Tony said that he thought to himself, 'You're next on the list you stupid twat.' It's odd that in the nineties Tony told Mick Middles that Ian had scribbled his abuse down on paper. Several years later it became something Ian actually said. Much of what is written in Middles's book came from Tony – he repeated his stories so often I think he believed them himself without question. But he, like most of us, suffered from false memory syndrome. Still, whether it was written or spoken, yet again, as with Hannett, controversy kick-started an important relationship in Wilson's life. I would argue that without these two – Ian Curtis and Martin Hannett – Factory would never really have got off the ground.

Bob Dickinson, who was a DJ that Stiff-Chiswick night, along with Rob Gretton, remembered some backstage arguing going on – particularly when it looked as if Joy Division might not even get the chance to appear. Yet when they finally did, it was electrifying. Ian in particular was compelling to watch.

After such a dire evening it was apparent to any onlooker that this group were different. I can still remember their performance. They weren't trying to entertain anyone, they had all this pent-up energy and they were serious to the point of aggression. Tony always said that the other groups were there out of choice, but that Joy Division 'had no fucking choice'. Tony might not have had the best ears for music, but that was something he was good at recognising – bands who really meant it and had something new to say.

Bob says that Rob Gretton approached him after the gig and delightedly announced that this group were the big break he'd been looking for. Rob had very good, credible musical taste and, like Roger Eagle, was into Northern Soul. Rob used to go to the Spin Inn Disc Shop on Cross Street to swell his collection for DJing at Rafters, amongst other venues. Before encountering Joy Division, Rob had been involved with Slaughter & the Dogs – he wrote their fanzine *Manchester Rains*. He'd also roadied for Slaughter & the Dogs and the Nosebleeds. He was doubtless desperate for a bona fide chance to get into the music business. Joy Division were it, and he knew it that night – he was like the cat who got the cream.

Barney recalled two things coming out of the Stiff-Chiswick night: 'Rob Gretton was at the gig. I met him the next day in town and he said, "I saw you play last night, I want to be your manager." I said, "Yeah, all right, you can do it." Also, Tony Wilson was at the gig and he got interested so the two guys came together. It just shows you how important it is to play live!'

The first four Friday nights at the Factory Club were an eclectic mix of sounds – Jilted John, Cabaret Voltaire, Big in Japan, Joy Division and, of course, Durutti Column (as they were before the break-up). Tony and Alan originally staged the gigs to present Durutti Column, who played the opening night on 19 May along with Rabid Records' Jilted John. Thelma's son, Nathan McGough, remembered that first Factory night at the Russell Club. Tony had written to Thelma after their split to say that he missed Nathan and, with her blessing, Nathan remained very much in contact with Tony from then onwards. Tony looked on him a bit like his own son. He told me he would've been entirely happy to have taken all of Thelma's children on, had they stayed together. Nathan was often at our house and I welcomed him because he was good fun and kept me company. In truth I was a bit isolated and lonely in Charlesworth.

Nathan told me that he and I went together to the club that night (no doubt he was staying in Charlesworth at the time) and that I DJ'd and he did the lights. 'I flicked some strobe switches for Margi Clarke, or something,' Nathan said. (Margi, or Margox as she was known, was an eccentric, attractive character with a broad Scouse accent who, like many others before and after her, got her first break into show-business via Tony by presenting on his *What's On* show.) 'But you DJ'd . . .' Nathan continued. 'I know you put a 45rpm record on at thirty-three and a third. It was "Shake Some Action" by the Flamin'

Groovies. Tony had an amazing collection of seven-inch singles because all the record pluggers would send them to him. One of the reasons I loved being at Charlesworth was that I could just sit and play these singles.'

It was, however, to be Joy Division – playing on 9 June, the last of the four nights – who were destined to become the jewel in the crown. Rob Gretton had begun managing them by then, and had written to Tony at Granada to ensure they weren't forgotten. I can remember seeing Ian perform and recognising something really extraordinary and compelling about him. And yet, offstage, he just seemed like a nice, ordinary, rather shy young man.

Supporting Joy Division were the Tiller Boys – consisting of Pete Shelley (of the Buzzcocks), his friend Francis Cookson (about whom I believe Pete wrote 'Ever Fallen in Love'), and Eric Random. I got along pretty well with these three (and also Karen, who lived in their terraced house in Gorton but generally never came out with us), and we frequently got together before the Factory nights and drove up there together in my Karmann Ghia. I recall we also had a penchant for picking magic mushrooms together and boiling them up to drink with Vimto before going to the Factory. This might, in part, have been a factor in the Tiller Boys' performance conveying a certain artistic or theatrical wackiness.

It had been Tony's idea that I buy a Karmann Ghia. Ever the man with an eye for style, he thought it would suit me. Although a VW, the car bears a strong resemblance to a Porsche design (definitely the old banger version of it, however). I began in 1976-77 with a blue one and, after it gave up the ghost, ended up giving it to the boy who lived next door to us in Charlesworth – a tad unwise perhaps, since I then bought a red Karmann Ghia and kept that going until the mid-nineties. Oddly, even nowadays, if I dream I'm driving a car it is always a Karmann Ghia.

Meanwhile, Tony had changed his RS200 and bought a Peugeot Estate. I loathed that car. It seemed as un-sexy as his last car had been sexy and, worse, a symbol of all the doom I felt was coming to us. I called it the 'hearse' from the outset because it was long enough to fit a coffin in. I used that word so many times even Tony referred to it as a hearse in his book. It was a horrible maroon colour and felt like a family car for a much older person. Tony got it so he'd be able to ferry his groups around, as it could either fit seven people including the driver, and/or hold a lot of equipment.

After the first four nights at the Russell Club there was a short break, and then the Factory nights were resumed regularly until June 1980.

Mick Middles wrote about those initial Russell Club nights: 'One recalls, in the early days, an eight-piece Durutti Column, complete with [Vini] Reilly's surging solos, thrashing through a pub-rock set, with Alan Erasmus flitting around the crowd, offering free smokes to anyone who looked as though they might be from the music press. And backstage, afterwards, with Erasmus and Wilson injecting the unbecoming fit of giggles, puffing on various cigarettes, and generally screaming about the exaggerated genius of that particular, short-lived version of Durutti Column and claiming that this would be the birth, the true birth, of Factory. Whether they meant the club or the forthcoming label, it was impossible to tell.'

In effect, Tony was doing exactly what he'd done on *So It Goes* – putting bands on. It had taken him less than six months to get back to where he was and where he wanted to be. And he had only just started.

And while all this and more was going on, what happened on one of those summer Factory nights was to mark the beginning of the end of our marriage.

The slow birth of Factory seems now to have run parallel with the slow death of our marriage. As is often the case in deteriorating relationships, I began to despise the very things that had attracted me to Tony in the first place. I had loved his confidence, which I now viewed as arrogance; his intelligence, which I now saw as smug superiority; and his romantic nature, which was now directed away from me and towards 'his' projects.

I wrote in my diary: 'His childhood was one of those "too much care" syndromes. Three adults and himself, the only child, who all worshipped and built their worlds around him rather than have him incorporate into their world. The child – now adult – expects everyone to do likewise, still believing himself to be the pivot around which their worlds revolve.'

Oddly, this almost perfectly describes the model that Peter Saville later devised to explain Factory Records (which was also used during *Newsnight*'s coverage of Tony a couple of months before he died). Saville said, 'You take a large body of energy and gravity, such as the sun, and other bodies come into orbit around it. The thing that brings all of these disparate elements together is the large mass of energy and magnetic attraction at the centre of it. So what Tony does is he brings together the bodies that are then able to act on the platform of Factory. His energy brings life. I told Tony I didn't like to give him this analogy because it makes him the fucking sun, but I drew it for him and he smiled and said he liked it. It's a good way to see it. Yes, he's the speaking head, he's the spin doctor of it – but he's not a contract person, he's not a business person, he's not a producer, he's not an artist, he's not a songwriter, he's not a musician, he's not a designer, he's not an architect, he's none of these things – but without him all of those skills, people and personalities don't come into play with one another.'

My diary continued: 'The ideas and beliefs I hold dear are just that – my beliefs, which I don't expect anyone else to adopt. But Tony assumes his ideas to be the most important conceptions since time immemorial. The only people he can be in tune with are those that may agree. Those that don't, well, their ideas must be annihilated from his mind – sometimes even the people themselves, as in the case of Phil.'

Phil was Phil Rainford, the lead singer with the Durutti Column, who Tony sacked in July 1978. I'd actually gone round to Phil's flat in Chorlton with Tony many times before the sacking – we were quite friendly with him and his girlfriend – yet I think I accompanied him for this unpleasant task. I thought it was a bit harsh, but Vini tells me he'd demanded it be done. Vini says he thought Phil was 'ineffectual', that he made 'funny gestures posing as a frontman' and that he was 'too nice'. Phil performed with a Doctor Who scarf – he kept flinging it round his neck, and indeed was a very nice person. I suspect the feeling was that he was a bit too ordinary to be a star.

Tony certainly thought that Dave Rowbotham was weirder and therefore a better candidate as a frontman. Vini agrees with this, he said Dave 'looked dangerous, on the edge'. Dave played guitar, but the idea was that he could be moved to the front. Vini says, 'Dave was supposed to be co-writing songs with me, but he could barely play, let alone write. At least he had a strong character though.' Horrifically, in 1991 Dave was found murdered in his flat.

Tony had backed this group (with Phil) to the hilt. Music promoter Phil Jones recalled an early gig with this line-up of the Durutti Column. He said, 'The Knives played a gig in some West Indian community centre and Durutti Column were the support (with Phil Rainford). Oz was doing the PA. DC were in the middle of this really loud soundcheck and I said to Oz, "What's going on? We're the main band," it was getting a bit late. He said Tony had given him £5 to make sure Durutti Column get a long soundcheck, "So unless you can match that, that's how it's going." When Tony turned up I said, "What's going on, this isn't how it happens?" And, I'll never forget this, he said, "Look son, when you've got a band that's even half as good as this then you can tell me what to do, but until then fuck off." When Durutti Column went on it was just too loud, there was no subtlety in there and everyone thought they were shit.'

In 1980, Tony told writers Andy Zero and Bob Dickinson about Rainford: 'He's a very good singer and a wonderful guy but he wasn't right for that sound, according to my mind. It was the worst thing – that and the way we messed Elti-Fits around were the only two bad things I've had to do. Just because in the end it wasn't right. Those are the only things I regret, one had to behave unpleasantly and I found it abhorrent and I still do. It seemed to me that Phil would be right for more of a pop band and whatever else, so he had to go. It was horrific, absolutely horrific.'

When it came to it, the next incarnation of Durutti Column had an even shorter lifespan than this one and imploded almost from the start. In light of this it was a pointless exercise, but Tony had the kind of brain that, once fixated on something, wouldn't be shifted. Yet, since Vini had apparently told Tony 'it's either him or me', what looks like a hatchet job on Tony's part could have been belief in and loyalty to Vini, something he kept until the end. Incidentally, neither I nor Alan Erasmus remembers what happened with the band Elti-Fits.

Alan Wise, who became the promoter of gigs at the Russell Club, thought that Tony was a dominant person who liked to get his way. 'If he didn't get his way you were out,' he said.

Wise remembers Tony going into partnership with him around this time (or possibly earlier). Their company was called Shopfloor Entertainments, and they opened a joint account at the Shanghai Bank (now the Midland). Alan laughed to recall that they could both sign cheques on this account, but if Alan signed a cheque he needed Tony's countersignature, whereas Tony could write cheques by himself if he wanted!

I always found it significant that the Durutti Column's first recording, the first of many for Factory Records, was called 'No Communication'. This seemed to be the way my marriage was going. Actually, it seems to be the classic way for men to deal with conflicts in relationships – they don't want to talk about problems and prefer instead to go into their 'cave'. It was also perhaps ironic that this track sounds a bit like an early Magazine song. The vocal (which was actually by Colin Sharp), though reminiscent of a Devoto-esque delivery, is a bit flat but fits quite well with a post-punk sound. The song, along with 'Thin Ice' (which has more of a distinctive Reilly guitar sound on it), became one side of the four-track EP *A Factory Sample*, originally due for release on 24 December 1978, although in the event the first thousand records had been pressed up in Ireland and, due to a dock strike, got stuck in transit and didn't actually surface until January 1979. The line-up of the Durutti Column who'd made that recording had entirely gone by then.

Colin Sharp wrote a book entitled *Who Killed Martin Hannett?*, published in 2007. I mentioned this to Tony at the time and he couldn't remember then that Colin had ever been in the Durutti Column. Certainly Colin's association was short-lived.

A disagreement had arisen after Rainford's departure. In 1980 Tony recalled: 'So then we said we'd try out a guy called Colin Sharp. I also asked Martin to come up to Cargo with this guy Colin, and he put some weird talk, speaking vocal on it and Martin fiddled about with the mixing desk. We don't actually have that – that was lost unfortunately, it should have been what it was but it was lost – got wiped, so I told the band I wanted Martin to produce the sampler and Tony Bowers said no. There is a great residue of hatred musicians have for Martin because of a) the Didsbury scene and b) musicians don't like producers [because] they think they can produce themselves but most of them can't. All they produce is demos.'

(The Manchester scene was awash with cassette demo recordings which were largely low-fi, cheaply produced and quickly recorded versions of a few of the band's songs, but they were limited in production value.)

'Musicians, if they produce themselves,' continued Tony, 'they have all the instruments up there – they can hear themselves, they love it but it's not a record, you hear it three times [and] you don't listen to it anymore. It's like a demo tape. Producers make records you can live with that have depth and space and atmosphere and all the other stuff. This is a row one constantly has with bands.'

This observation was also applicable to Joy Division, who, with the exception of Ian, actually disliked Martin's production.

Tony went on: 'With that band [Durutti Column] it got to the point where – I did what I've done since then again – Martin did his version and the extra money was paid out of my pocket so the band could do their mixed version. I never even heard what they did – they wouldn't even play it [for] me. So we had this final meeting. Vini wasn't there because he was ill. He got ill again with all the trouble. And the band said they didn't want Martin Hannett's production to go out, and as they weren't happy with what they'd done they didn't want anything to go out. I said we're going ahead with this record and it's going out. So we basically agreed that Sunday afternoon that was it and those three fucked off. The Durutti Column ceased to exist in that sense – they went off to form the Mothmen, Vini was ill and we just mixed the track and put it out as part of this record.'

Bruce Mitchell remembers hearing about this turning point during a meeting held at Alan Erasmus's flat. 'There was a typical disagreement about what they were going to record, etcetera. The band said they were being dictated to by Tony. Eventually Tony shouts at them, "You should listen to what I'm saying to you. I haven't made a mistake since such and such a year. That's why you should listen to me, I never make mistakes." The band just walked out, led by Tony Bowers. Bowers later said to me, "How can you deal with anything like that?"'

Penny Henry, who worked on the door at Rafters and later at the Hacienda, was Tony Bowers's partner at the time. She remembered another example of Tony dictating terms: 'Durutti Column were playing at the Russell Club and Tony Wilson said to Tony Bowers, "I don't want you wearing that hat, it's not cool." He was referring to a bowler hat. He said, "Just stick to what you're good at, playing the bass guitar."'

I knew nothing of this; Wilson was hardly on the cutting edge of fashion himself. Chris Hewitt, who owned a music shop downstairs from Cargo Studios called Tractor Music, reminded me that Tony Bowers also wore a green boiler suit (Pete Townsend had started a trend for these by wearing a white one).

That said, Hewitt claims that he took the very first Factory cheque out of the book, which was for a Yamaha bass guitar for Tony Bowers. He thinks the price was £200.

It would seem that Tony Bowers and I were somewhat likeminded on these issues. Such opinions gave justification to my own doubts and feelings. If a band weren't prepared to put up with Wilson's bloody-mindedness, how was I supposed to cope with it in an intimate relationship? I sometimes felt as if our marriage was a dictatorship, not an equal partnership. I just thought there was no way I was going to go along with his bully-boy tactics. Nonetheless I have to hand it to Tony that – with regard to Hannett – he was right! The musicians Martin worked with may have had their crosses to bear, their egos might have taken a battering, but with hindsight one doubts if they would ever have prospered without him.

It was doubtless after some kind of battle with Tony that, feeling unkindly towards him, I wrote about his self-important convictions in my diary. Tony gave a more balanced description of this characteristic of his in an interview with local Piccadilly DJ Mike Sweeney. This was in 1983, after we had split but were working towards a reconciliation. He told Sweeney he was an extremist and went on: 'I never have grey areas of doubt, no. I'm very extreme and I know what I know and I know what I think. I don't think it's the truth but I think it's my truth and therefore I'll stick to it and I treat everything from that truth. I don't think it is the truth but it's my truth and I have to live by it 100 percent. People think you're sardonic and critical and extra cynical but I don't think that at all, I'm really a romantic. I know what I like, and if the rest of the world liked what I liked it would be a lot better place.'

'So what you're saying,' Sweeney said, 'is other people might not conceive your ideas of the truth, but to you they are the truth and you believe in them so much that if everybody else took them up, everybody would then think it was the truth.'

'Oh yes,' Tony replied. 'I don't just think I'm right. I think that everybody else is wrong.'

Well, at least he was honest and knew himself and his own mind! But God help those who crossed him. Martin Hannett was one such who, in spite of a near set-to in the car park, went on to produce the Durutti tracks at Graveyard Studios. Tony recognised something special in Martin, and time has proven Tony's perceptiveness in this.

He told Zero and Dickinson: 'Hannett had done Slaughter & the Dogs, which was great, and *Spiral Scratch*, which was great – so I said what you doing? He was obviously working with Rabid and he said, "Yeah, sure." He's like that now he's working for Factory, anybody who'll put him in a studio with a desk in front of him, he'll do it. So he recorded Durutti Column – actually the very first thing was with a friend of Tony Bowers's from the Townhouse, called Laurie, he put the track down, not for a single, for a demo.'

Much later, Tony stated: 'Apart from television, the thing I enjoy most is hanging out with very clever people who are far cleverer than I am, and it was very clear that as '76 and '77 went on and our friendship remained that Martin was a desperately clever person and something of a genius. Then we started working with bands, with Vini and Joy Division and Rob in '78, and we got towards having a record label. Here with us was Peter Saville as genius graphic designer; here was Martin Hannett, genius record producer. Everything was there for us so it was natural to want to work with Martin.'

Alan Wise doesn't agree that Tony enjoyed the company of people cleverer than him. He told me: 'Tony was most at home amongst people with very low educational levels, where he could be the more erudite one and teach them and be showing them, lording it over them. He liked people who essentially were a bit thick. He had a club round him of know-nothings, and I think that let him down in that respect because at heart he was a generous, warm-hearted, nice guy, but perhaps he had low self-confidence, and in that respect he thought he needed people around him that he was intellectually superior to. I didn't notice any signs of intellectual superiority. Tony had gone to Cambridge but he'd got a second-class degree and he'd probably bummed around. I knew academics that were the real McCoy. They had an erudition but not the same excitement that Tony had. He was very full of life – strange now that he's dead – I thought he was a very, very nice person.'

Personally, I think Tony was actually ridiculously clever, and he could identify and enjoy spending time with a different kind of genius to his own. On the other hand, he did always seem to want to be the most erudite one in a group of people, and any insecurity he had was almost certainly eased by the knowledge that he was ostensibly the cleverest in the room.

Since Alan Wise is himself extremely clever, I wondered if Tony may have felt threatened by that. Alan replied, 'I don't think he would allow me to be cleverer. I think he was a little bit challenged by the fact that someone else perhaps had a different perception. He didn't want someone else to have a different perception.'

Nonetheless, Tony had struck gold with Hannett. Factory's gain was Rabid Records' loss, especially since Rabid had invested quite a bit of cash in the man and paid for his rapidly expanding collection of audio equipment, which included Revox tape recorders, top-of-the-range HiFi playback amps and speakers, and an AMS digital delay line – a piece of studio equipment that virtually defined Joy Division's early Hannett sound. Tosh is philosophical about it, and appears to have no bitterness about what happened. His view of Martin was that 'he was a major innovator in production and drew on the past merits of the likes of Phil Spector and Joe Meek. He was also influenced by the production skills of Abba, such as [on] "Fernando".' Nevertheless, Tosh also said that 'Tony and Alan worked on Martin to poach him – to take him away'.

If that was so, their ace card would have been Joy Division, since Tosh refused to have anything to do with them having taken offence from their name and the cover of the record *An Ideal for Living*. He thought the imagery was used irresponsibly, but said that Martin shrugged this off and saw Joy Division as anarchists, playing around with provocative information, not the fascists Tosh perceived. Yet Tosh remembered that Martin had himself referred to the band as anarcho fascists, despite stating that Joy Division were the 'dance music of the eighties'. This description became a running joke at Rabid, where Joy Division and the Fall were collectively known as the Miserablists. Before this Rabid had unintentionally been thriving. Jilted John sold 500,000 copies and yet cost only £108 to record.

During an interview with journalist Jon Ronson, Tony was asked if there was any particular record that made him realise that Martin was the right producer for Joy Division. After some thought, Tony replied: 'No. I'm with George Martin on this one. He didn't like the Beatles tapes, he just liked the way the Beatles stood in a room – that's what genius is. It's just the way people are and Martin reeked of it.'

Tony felt the same way about Joy Division, or Ian Curtis at least. It was something 'in the eyes', he said to me. Prior to 1978 the group hadn't made much of an impact on Tony. He claimed that the first time he saw an earlier incarnation of the band – when they were calling themselves Warsaw, at the closing night of the Electric Circus – they made an 'absolute caterwauling of sound', but that the lead singer was 'a bit weird and interesting'. He told me he decided then to put them on television, although they performed at the Factory Russell Club before this, and it would be September 1978 before the group actually appeared on *Granada Reports*.

Tony had surprised himself by becoming the manager, with Alan, of a band, and surprised himself again by running a club. The first record release to be supervised by him was also a surprise, though when you look back and piece together the steps that led to the formation of Factory Records, it can seem like a natural progression, with one thing leading inevitably to another. In reality, most of the events were random and disorganised. Tony may have been cultivating a vision, his passion even, but he put his career as a television presenter first. He told me soon after we met that he saw himself when older as a Robin Day kind of character and that this was his chosen career path. Day was a renowned television journalist and political broadcaster, celebrated in later years for wearing a bow-tie and being provocative and bad-tempered, so I can see why he was a role-model for Tony.

In view of Tony's long-held but not quite realised dream, it was perhaps fitting that his very last job on TV – and very last TV appearance – was on *The Politics Show* for the BBC. He loved the job and was proud of it from the start. That last Sunday, less than a month before he died, he could barely walk or talk but he still went on, which showed what guts the man had. I helped him to dress for it, as he was unbelievably weak. As I was helping him into his clothes, I knew without doubt that it had to be the last time he would ever appear on television, and sent my love and admiration along with him for his swansong.

On one of those early summer Factory nights, there seemed to be quite a buzz going around for an out-of-the-way place only recently started up. This unknown club night was already proving to be quite a draw. It was as if people could sense something important was happening. Soon after the club opened, when people were appearing from nowhere, I noticed Tony staring towards the door with a look of rapt admiration. I followed his gaze towards a beautiful girl who was walking in at that moment. It was as if he was silently greeting her, having been alerted by Alan that she was there. Knowing Tony as I did, I knew that beauty in women was his 'thing'. I was yet to realise that infidelity wasn't also necessarily his 'thing'.

Unfortunately, the same insecurity that caused me to doubt myself and to question the merits of anything I did couldn't accept that. My paranoia snapped into action. I had also learnt by then what rats men can be when it comes to infidelity and lust. It may seem cynical, but I discovered that men who are faithful are, generally speaking, the same men who don't get the opportunity to sleep with the most beautiful girl in the room. Tony had the sort of profile and good looks that meant he could be exposed to such opportunities. It wasn't rational, but I was sure, sure without a shadow of a doubt, that he was betraying me with this girl, particularly since, without taking his eyes from that direction, he appeared to be smiling with Alan and looking pleased with her and himself. I imagined a male conspiracy, and it took me a long time to accept that this was pure imagination on my part. I learnt later that the two men were actually congratulating each other. As Tony said rather eloquently in his book: 'Wilson looked over and saw one of the most beautiful sights a man can see. Forget the *Water Lilies* or the Vatican *Pietà*. This was a queue.' So they were grinning together as they watched people pouring through the door, and an attractive girl just happened to be among them. But I made straight for the bar.

Perhaps he *was* betraying me in some way, even if not with another woman. He wasn't sharing his dreams with me. He was sharing them with Alan Erasmus.

In an interview, Alan Wise commented: 'Tony lacked close male friends. When he did have a man as a friend it was like a boy and girlfriend [relationship]. But he found it hard to have a man as a friend. He expected people to be two-faced. He didn't really trust them.'

If this insight possesses truth, then Tony and Erasmus were like boyfriend-girlfriend. They were inseparable, almost visibly joined at the hip.

I did feel somehow excluded, despite ferrying musicians about and cheering them on, making beds and cooking for them; despite discussing Tony's plans with him and dealing with daily telephone calls in the pre-mobile era. Also, my passion for music was as great as Tony's, and I believed I had a feel for A&R talent, which I would later demonstrate.

I threw back a double brandy and surveyed the room. 'Who here do I fancy the most?' I asked myself. Revenge is a dish best left unserved, but if it is, never hot like this one. The face that most appealed to me belonged to the enigmatic Howard Devoto, aka Howard Trafford. He looked interesting. I was not consciously aware that the attraction was anything beyond physical, but my choice may subconsciously have had an added piquancy in that Tony and Alan were hatching exclusive music-related ventures of their own. I had no particular knowledge of Devoto apart from the fact that he'd been in the Buzzcocks, and little knew that he was the person who told Tony to go to the Sex Pistols gig – that, in fact, he and Pete Shelley had arranged it. But I knew he fronted a group called Magazine and that I liked them. This band had appeared on *So It Goes* as far back as December 1977, and I went to the specially arranged gig for this at Belle Vue, although had no designs on running off with the man at that point. Interestingly, I got to view this particular programme recently. It was clear their music hadn't dated and still stands today. I'd forgotten that Tony wrote his own scripts and links for this show and how good they were. He said that Howard had thrust a copy of his *Spiral Scratch* EP into Iggy Pop's hands and said to him, 'I've got all your records, now you've got all mine.' I believe this exchange occurred the night Iggy played – and was recorded for *So It Goes* – at the Apollo.

I had also seen the group at their official Rafters debut in October 1977, although Rafters was such a long, narrow venue that it was sometimes difficult to see the band even if you were present. When the Factory nights resumed regularly at the Russell Club on 7 July, the first band to play were Magazine, and it's possible that this triggered a further interest in him on my part, although I honestly don't remember the exact order of events. I do know that I loved the way Howard strutted about the stage. The band sounded amazing. Here was something I could really get enthusiastic about – compared to a band on the point of disintegration because Tony was sacking the lead singer. I thought Tony was way off the mark.

I had made my mind up but I wasn't sure what to do next. Maybe Howard noticed me looking at him, I don't know, but less than half an hour later I was sitting alone at a table when he approached, put down his pint and asked me if I would watch it while he visited the gents. When he returned we engaged in some sort of conversation. I don't remember much of what we said, but felt it was a bit phoney chatting away like this and wasting time. I didn't want to play games – I mean what was the point of playing around with the body language of 'I fancy you, do you fancy me?' – honestly, I couldn't be bothered with it; my mind was already made up. So, cutting straight to the chase, I just said, 'Basically, all I'm trying to say is that I'd like to fuck you.' If he was shocked he didn't show it. I thought punk was supposed to be about shocking people, so that was okay anyway. This was my version of punk; to speak my mind. His reply seemed to me to contain an odd sort of poetry, something along the lines of this being as easy as rolling down a sand dune onto the beach (or perhaps it was onto the pebbles). He didn't lose his cool for a moment.

Chris Charlesworth, who was the editor of *Torn Apart*, commented on an earlier draft of this book: 'What a brazen hussy you were!' The funny thing is I truly wasn't like that. Self-destructive is nearer the mark.

I wasn't driven by a desire for sex but rather the belief that fulfilment was to be found in a relationship. (Just as others imagine it is to be found in a career, money, property, etc.) I know now what an illusion this was and how fundamentally destructive such yearning notions can be.

I was dreadfully shy and lacking in confidence, and because of my striking looks had endured years of being stared at by men such that I'd had to develop a technique of staring back to make them look away. I'd attracted all sorts of guys – usually the wrong sort – and observed them try, with all manner of trickery, to take advantage of me. Whilst I didn't allow myself to be seduced I was often taken in, being terribly naive. I even wondered if my marriage wasn't born solely out of Tony's desire, for love of my body and face more than love of the person underneath. A lovely object to be owned and taken out on his arm as a boost to a huge ego. I still believe that – although he did genuinely love me – he put the appearance of women above anything else, and that this is prevalent among the majority of men to this day. I find it disappointing that the media is still dominated by men and that ageing, intelligent women are sidelined to make way for younger, less interesting sex objects.

I felt stripped of power, Tony had me where he wanted me and had all the control. For once I wanted to take it. Rather like an anorexic or bulimic, who at least has control of what they digest – if little else – however destructive that control may be. I didn't want to flirt, curtsy around some animal attraction, or attempt to seduce the way men had tried to seduce me with dishonest ploys. I simply thought I might as well be direct. I would have respected that approach more in the men who had tried to bed me with deception and lies. And it wasn't that I wanted sex for its own sake. It wasn't even that I wanted sex at all. I wanted to fall in love elsewhere, to be with someone who wouldn't let me down, to make things equal. It was my way of coping with Tony's betrayal.

Tony simply called it revenge fucking. That was what he later embarked on, at any rate.

Despite Tony's own fantasy and myth-making about Howard and I consummating the act there and then in the Russell Club toilets (as portrayed in *24 Hour Party People*), that is not what occurred. Incidentally, this scene in the film was a last-minute alteration after Tony visited me and showed me a screenplay that had me having sex with five men in a row (four of whom I had never met; the other one was Vini Reilly!). When I threatened to sue, Tony responded with, 'Well, we'll just have to have you having sex with someone you did have sex with then.'

'Why the hell do I have to have sex with anybody?' I retorted, to which Tony had no reply, but I suppose they needed something to go with the drugs and rock'n'roll.

Although nothing happened between Howard and me that night, a dangerous exchange of words had taken place. Ironically, Tony remarked that Howard Devoto commented to him at the end of the evening that he must be very pleased with himself (given the popularity of the club so early on). Perhaps Devoto could afford to be complimentary to the man whose wife had just told him she wanted to fuck him.

At this point I knew that a) I'd set something in motion that would not be so easy for me to stop – thoughts don't often take long to become words (seconds in this case) and deeds often follow even if they do take a bit longer – and b) Tony was absent for far too long, always returning later than he said, and I didn't entirely trust him. For instance, I had already caught him out not telling the truth. And yet he was so good at it that most of the time I was taken in. It wasn't until the end of Tony's life that I found out how noble it can be to be sparing with the truth, and how pathetic my own slavish adherence to truth can also be. (Besides, I was a genius at deceiving myself.) Tony lied about his health, always having me believe that once he got past something – be it chemo, taking Sutent, or a clot on his lung – he would be getting stronger. He pretended he was eating when he wasn't. All very noble really – it helped me to stop worrying so much anyhow. Perhaps others weren't so gullible. I've always been a sucker for lies because I can't tell them.

That said, I was sometimes able to hold back on certain information, to be economical with the truth, as they say. Tony and I drove home that night and nothing was mentioned or done about any of the foregoing for months. It could almost have been forgotten about except for one thing: Magazine's album *Real Life* had recently been released and I began listening to it. Over and over again.

All I could think of was what I had said to Howard and how incredibly cool and intelligent he was. And, being a girl (in the seventies, maybe not today), it felt like this had to mean more than basic physical attraction. It had to mean I was in love.

The fact is I spent a lot of time on my own in the country during the day and Howard, with the eloquence of poetry, seemed to be talking to me via *Real Life* more than Tony. Charlesworth was miles from anywhere and often bleak and grim with a mizzling mist if it didn't rain sideways. When Tony finally arrived home from Manchester after his various attempts at conquering the world, he'd come in and flop on his rocking chair (aka throne) and basically become incommunicado, absorbed in television while eating the food I'd been playing around with for hours. It was understandable, perhaps, after a full-on day in the studio, then on camera, and chatting and rolling joints with Alan, but I was eager to have a conversation, eager for some stimulation. His work and play had been sorted but I was a bit short on both, and the distance that now afflicted our playtime disturbed me. My every attempt to reach him, to engage him, failed. The more left out I felt, the more left out I became. He was interested only in what they had to say on the TV, whatever it was. And then the next morning he'd be off again, leaving me to housework and country isolation. And words from Howard's album, lifted by the fabulous keyboards of Dave Formula and the stunning guitar of John McGeoch, excited me and transported me to another world.

'Time flies, time crawls, like an insect, up and down the walls.' It did.

One day I decided to change the arrangement of the furniture in our lounge. My sister and mum helped me. I put Tony's rocking chair to one side so that it no longer occupied the commanding position in the room and moved the sofa into that place (thinking we could now share this space). When Tony got home he went mad and wouldn't do anything until it was all put back as it was.

I couldn't even take charge in our home.

In the absence of a fulfilling outer life I began to look within for some kind of inner inspiration. Devoto seemed to address even that. 'We stay one step ahead of relief.' I thought he was a genius. This was how my obsession with Howard began. I fell in love with his words. I even imagined he might be my soul mate. I adored his face. He looked like someone I'd always known. I loved his thin and agile body. Tony seemed to be getting fat.

That summer of 1978, Alan Wise and Nigel Bagley took on the running of the club every night of the week and, though Tony and Alan Erasmus remained involved, this was mainly only on Friday nights and Tony never at any stage took a wage from the club. Alan Wise told me that Nigel booked the bands and that Alan Erasmus took a small wage. Wise said, 'We ran the club for the whole week – that's what used to make us laugh about Tony and that. He came in for one night of the week – we ran it seven nights a week, as the Factory. I remember once, one week we had six strong things, but not the Friday. By chance it was packed for six nights and [there was] nobody on the Friday, and it was always advertised and sold as the Factory, not as the Russell Club, that came later again. We leased it from Don Tonay for £500 a week, we kept the bars; the bars were ineptly run. The bar manager was pinching all the booze and I was the licensee and didn't have a clue what I was doing.'

Around the time that Wise and Bagley came onboard, Tony and Alan began drifting away from the club and towards a label. I'm fascinated for a moment now that even *I* am writing this – just like every other account ever written – as though I wasn't involved when I was. Though from what I have been writing it would perhaps seem that Tony and I had already drifted away from each other. The truth is that I was like Scarlett O'Hara in *Gone with the Wind*. I was beginning to imagine I loved someone I didn't know, and thought I had stopped loving someone who I loved very much. I was soon to learn the tragedy of mistaking infatuation and romance for love. Between Tony's bloody-mindedness and my pride, between his obsession with groups of young men to go on a record label run by men, and my emerging obsession with just one man, things were to spiral downhill, even hitting rock bottom more than once, but in truth Tony and I were never really all that far away from one another throughout our lives.

There were major catalysts at this stage moving the label forward. One of them was Roger Eagle – who had been resident DJ at the Twisted Wheel and was now running Eric's. As mentioned, Tony and I frequently drove over to Liverpool to meet with Roger and check out the bands, although it could be a bit hit-and-miss as to whether Tony's car would still be there when we came out! Roger was a real enthusiast for music, and he and his partner at Eric's had decided to revive their idea of a record label. Having shared notes and band ideas for their respective clubs, Roger suggested to Tony that they collaborate, the plan being that there would be two of Tony's artists from Manchester and two from Liverpool.

Part of the reason this never came about was because Tony really wanted to make a double seven-inch – the only memorable double seven-inch release up until then had been *Magical Mystery Tour* by the Beatles. Roger, an expert in Northern Soul, with the biggest record collection (vinyl, of course) I had ever seen, naturally preferred the idea of a twelve-inch. It wasn't just the size; Tony had a fixed idea in his head about how the sleeve should look, having taken LSD one night and become lost in admiration for the texture of a Far-Eastern import of the album *Abraxas* by Santana, at the house of Chris Joyce (then drummer of Durutti Column). The regular version of this psychedelically-sleeved album lay at home in Charlesworth, but Joyce's copy from Thailand had a sleeve that was made out of tissue paper and double-sealed in plastic. Thus inspired, Tony was very specific about how the first release was going to look.

Alan Wise remarked that 'Tony was interested in style more than content. He had an interest in how a thing looked more than how it actually was. That's associated with the gay thing to me. But he was right because a club should look good and the handbills should look good.'

And they did. Thanks to Saville, who provided a stylish consistency to Factory's identity. As writer Paul Morley observed in his book *Joy Division: Piece by Piece*: 'Saville kept up the illusion of method. He gave coherent visual shape to the endless, almost slapstick improvisation. He produced a pattern, giving a private order to public mayhem.'

Elliot Rashman remarks: 'There were two great artists in the Factory set-up – Hannett and Saville. The truth of it is that those album covers have outlasted ninety percent of the music on Factory. No one's going to know who Crispy Ambulance are, Stockholm Monsters, Section 25 etcetera. There were a whole host of them who elevated graphic design to art at that point (the art design of the eighties) as well as Saville – Malcolm Garrett, Barney Bubbles, Neville Brody. They were all influential and those covers were vital in making Factory stand out because ninety percent of the music has been and gone. There are only two and a half or three acts that you remember: Joy Division and New Order – which is really the same band, less the singer – and Happy Mondays.'

Tosh agrees with the style versus content theory: 'Factory had to define themselves with a new style as they hadn't evolved, the way Music Force had, from the ground up with bands. They were plagiarists from the start. Thatcher, who was voted in in 1979, tried to produce enterprise out of everything, presentation was all important. It was the era of the Enterprise Allowance Scheme. People were doing anything – travelling hairdressers, community jugglers and punk bands – all sorts of ideas were being invented to show they were in business.'

Tony would argue differently. In 1980, when Bob Dickinson asked him about the idea that what Factory were creating was not just a product but an art object as well, Tony replied: 'The original thinking was a) Saville is a very classy and brilliant designer, b) if you're charging someone a quid for something then if you can choose if it should be beautiful or not beautiful, or interesting or not interesting – if they're paying a quid for it, make it look interesting. It's part of Dexy's [Kevin Rowland] attitude that the way you look onstage and the way you talk and the way you advertise is every bit as much a part of what you're doing as a band as your music. We are aware that we are presenting people with an object, so why not do something to people with it, why not make it attractive?'

Or to put it more simply, as Tony once remarked, 'Would we put the holy wine in a mouldy pot?' Except that quite often Factory's offerings were far from sacred – unholy more like it!

There was another major catalyst in moving things forward – easily overlooked but nevertheless absolutely vital. It was Rough Trade Records. This independent label was formed in 1976 and ran in conjunction with a shop and burgeoning distribution arm. In 1976 there were only about twelve independent record labels in England, but by 1980 this number had exploded to around 800, and Rough Trade were at the very epicentre of this revolution. Every time Tony and I went to London – which was virtually every fortnight – we called in at Rough Trade. Then it was based at the record shop, but we would enter a cluttered room at the back where Tony would pick the brains of a highly intelligent and sensitive man named Geoff Travis and his associates. It was Geoff who made the whole independent label business look possible, not to say idealistic – politically and aesthetically – and even downright simple to achieve.

However, as well as the style and mechanics it was important to have something of musical value. It all seemed perfectly simple. As well as Durutti Column, why not release records by the bands represented by the initial four Factory nights? Most of them seemed to be up for grabs. Except for Jilted John, but it was easy to substitute something for them. A different kind of comic relief, perhaps.

On 9 June Joy Division played the Russell Club and Rob Gretton came up to Mick Middles and said, 'You can interview them if you want, come down to the rehearsal.' (At T.J. Davidson's, a rehearsal studio on Little Peter Street.) So at 7:30pm that Sunday night a somewhat reluctant Mick trundled along to Little Peter Street, whereupon the band played their whole set just for him. He little realised the significance of this at the time. Afterwards they walked up to the Gaythorne pub on the corner and sat around the tap room eating pies. This was to be their first interview for *Sounds*. Mick rang Kevin Cummins (the only photographer doing anything for the music press at that time from Manchester) and asked him to take some shots to accompany the article. These would be the first photos Kevin took of Joy Division, later to become iconic shots, along with other photos for *Sounds* and *NME*. (Worthy of note: Mick got paid £80 – a one-off fee for his article, whereas Kevin's photos continue to make a lot of money to this day. He's also made a name for himself.)

Inspired by all the musical talent at his fingertips, and using the model of Rough Trade as his own (i.e. after costs share the profits fifty-fifty) whilst relying on them for help and distribution, Tony made up his mind to put a record out himself. This has always been documented by Tony as a decision he made with Alan Erasmus but, since our money was to be used, it was obviously going to involve a discussion with me as well. Actually, Tony could have gone ahead without my agreement – the money wasn't in our joint bank account and had been left to him by his mother. In a colder climate – such as our marriage was heading towards – he doubtless would not have sought my opinion. But things hadn't deteriorated that far yet, and he sincerely believed the money to be ours. I mean, hadn't he endowed me with all his earthly goods before his God less than a year before? But, then again, hadn't we both promised to forsake all others, and – already – how long had it taken for that promise to fade?

I remember the conversation that took place in our bedroom. Tony did have some reservations about using the money and wondered if his mum would have approved. He also respected the fact that it was there to support us – for our home, family, whatever. I didn't aspire to a bigger house or even a garden (there was only a shared space at the back and we never went in it). Nor did I see the point in savings when Tony had such a good income. Actually, I was politically opposed to sums of cash being locked away.

Besides, worries about money were not on our agenda. Apart from his Granada salary, Tony sometimes went on a public appearance at a cricket match or something and got a ridiculous amount – say £500 – just for a Sunday afternoon in the sun. I was amazed at how easily he could earn money. I usually accompanied him on these jaunts. I remember soon after we'd met sitting on a deckchair in the sun, thinking it was good he had hobbies such as cricket because soon I'd be absorbed in motherhood and he would be in need of another activity. Ha!

I didn't expect us to get the money back from the *A Factory Sample* venture but it simply didn't matter. Commercialism really wasn't the point of it. If anything it was supposed to be anti-commercial. It just felt right. I told Tony I thought his mother would be glad that her money was being used for something creative rather than being locked in a dead stone vault, as her earthly body now was. And seeing how genuinely excited he was about this record, I figured that she, like me, would think the money was worth chucking away just for that.

The nice thing about Joy Division and Vini Reilly is that they also put art before money. Money wasn't the object of it then at all. In October 1978 Joy Division recorded 'Digital' and 'Glass' at a sixteen-track studio in Rochdale called Cargo Studios. It wasn't an especially nice neighbourhood but the rates were good. Tony asked Hannett to produce and Rob agreed to contribute the songs to the sampler. Although Tony was orchestrating things and had the cash, I wonder how much of a hand Martin Hannett may have had in cajoling him into it. Hannett had been convinced that Joy Division were going to be big long before Tony and Rob came on the scene. He had positively pestered Ryan and Beedle to put them on Rabid, and even given Ryan's aversion to the band's suggestive artwork, Rabid did in fact distribute *An Ideal for Living*. Also, according to both Terry Mason (the manager of Joy Division before Rob – his suitability for the job being somewhat compromised by his lack of a telephone) and also Vini Reilly, Tony viewed Joy Division as useful to the furtherance of Durutti Column rather than the other way around during the early Factory days.

Keyboardist Steve Hopkins had worked with Martin Hannett as the Invisible Girls, a collaborative team of musical director and producer who drew on the talents of other notable musicians of the time. Undoubtedly Martin dreamed up the name after being inspired by John Cooper Clark's brilliant lyrics in 'I Was a Teenage Werewolf'. It's a referential post-modern poem about pulp culture – B-movies, actors going nowhere and cult heroes. Interestingly there is a Marvel comic character named the Invisible Girl/Woman. The lyric includes the lines, '*Invisible girls go haywire, I'll be their go-go guy.*' The name speaks of anonymity, much like Martin's oft-used name Zero. The Invisible Girls worked on John Cooper Clarke's albums and went on to write and produce for Pauline Murray.

Steve Hopkins recalled his first meeting with Tony, when in Cargo Studios working with the Durutti Column and Martin: 'Tony seemed like a quite sprightly sort of puppet master, who appeared to have total faith in Martin. He didn't interfere with his artists. He was very "hands off".' Interestingly, this is a comment I have heard said about Tony over and over again by artist after artist – that he left them to it.

The next time Hopkins met Tony was at Granada when the Invisible Girls and Vini Reilly appeared on *What's On*. Hopkins said, 'It was just the three of us and this pile of drum boxes. It was very brave of Tony to let us do the play off. We turned up at Granada with this pile of ARP synthesisers, which were the bee's knees at the time. Some sound effects boxes and drum boxes. Vini had his guitar, Martin had his bass. We completely flummoxed the Granada sound people. Tony said, "Right, we are going to have some avant garde musical happening." He always had some way of selling something. He was a bit of a spin doctor. We set this up and Granada technicians were very used to having little combos. Guitarist, drummer, bassist, maybe a sax player. They knew where to put the microphones. But we had this pile of crap basically. They had no idea. The old guys were giving up in despair. We gradually built up this vaguely industrial rhythm track. I thought, "It's going to be hard work, this." Vini did his usual ambient doodling over it. I think my job was just to keep these machines running. The young sound guys seemed to get into it. The old guard disappeared. That was Tony . . . willing to risk everything to put this on.'

John Dowie recorded three tracks for *A Factory Sample*, with C.P. Lee producing, as the offering for side three of the record. Tony liked the idea of having a comedy break. And then lastly Cabaret Voltaire, who had already recorded a single for Rough Trade, donated a couple of tracks. Saville designed the sleeve.

We spent weeks packaging the sleeve, just a handful of us making thousands of them. I enjoyed it though – Tony, me, Alan, sitting hour upon hour, week after week, listening to music and endlessly folding up the sleeve, inserting it into a bag with four stickers and two records in the package. All very home-grown. Ironic that I now don't even possess one, having destroyed my copy in a fit of anger.

In late 1978 Tony took me to see a band he was quite interested in. We arrived at a rehearsal basement somewhere in Stockport, whereupon we encountered three pathetic-looking specimens of yet-to-be-manhood who could barely play a note. I smiled politely, after all they were nice enough young lads. In the car on the way back I was astonished at how excited Tony was about what we'd just witnessed and told him I thought they were rubbish. He simply wouldn't have that. 'They're fantastic, you don't understand,' he told me rather patronisingly. Damned right I didn't understand. It was as if they were the greatest discovery he'd ever made. Tony's enthusiasm was such that I wondered if he was a closet gay – for what the hell else was attracting him to these young boys? They had a kind of teenage boyhood beauty. I couldn't find anything else credible about them.

They were called A Certain Ratio (or ACR for short). Tony had missed their first gig, which he said Mark, of a guerrilla-funk band called the Pop Group, had told him about. This was at the Band on the Wall, and was bass player Jez Kerr's first appearance along with Simon Topping and Pete Terrell. Prior to that singer Simon and guitarist Pete had performed together, but that had pretty much been the sum total of the group's gigs thus far. Martin Moscrop played with the support band that night – Alien Tint – but defected to ACR, having decided they were a better bet. Rob went to this gig and told Tony ACR were good.

My opinion concerning their lack of talent counted for nought with Tony. Perhaps he was taking a kind of punk view of it – that the look and attitude were everything and the group would soon learn to play their instruments. He (and Alan, of course) became their manager at once.

Management was something that Tony felt very strongly about. He told DJ Mike Sweeney about it: 'The Beatles without Epstein, the Stones without Loog Oldham, it's a role and it's a really vital role which I don't expect people to appreciate or like or anything else, but it's vital. Now there's a particular generation that I'm proud to be part of which began with Malcolm McLaren and Bernie Rhodes [who managed the Clash] and we're all a particular generation, we're all in our thirties. Bob Last who manages the Human League, Dick O'Dell of Pigbag – there's this group of people and it's natural for us to do it. I don't know anyone in their early twenties doing it, and we do it and we know what we're doing. It's just a role in music that the audience needn't know about – they needn't know about Colonel Parker or Brian Epstein.'

Yes, great reasoning – just the wrong band, perhaps? Tony would later argue that it was Simon Topping, the lead singer, who would have vouchsafed success for the group had he had not left in the early eighties. He was the one Tony thought had 'something in his eyes'; that weird star quality he saw in Ian Curtis. In the early days of ACR the band were often outraged to be compared to Joy Division, but Simon did have a certain presence that was reminiscent of Ian. Whether or not Simon was badly affected by the death of Ian, it was after this that he took a backseat with the band, playing percussion rather than singing. According to Tony, after drummer Donald Johnson joined the band, 'Donald's significant psychic presence was one of the reasons Simon, the main man, began to retreat. He retreated behind the trumpet and then behind the timbales and then behind a girl singer called Tilly.' He finally left the group when, having become enamoured with New York and electing to learn percussion there during an intensive six-month sabbatical, Martin and Jez wouldn't wait and told him he was out of the band.

Tony once observed that, as a manager, he spent half his time trying to get Vini Reilly to stop singing (with Durutti Column), and the other half trying to get Simon Topping to start.

That said, A Certain Ratio are still performing and are an accomplished group of musicians. After so long this is hardly surprising, but they can make for a fantastic gig. Tony would probably be amused to learn that the original line-up – Simon Topping, Jez Kerr and Pete Terrell – reformed as the Sum Ratios in 2010 and played a gig at Hooky's FAC 251 Club, situated in the old Factory office building on Charles Street.

Also Durutti Column, the other band Tony managed, are still playing thirty-one years later and (with an entirely different line-up from the early days) sound better than ever. In July 2009, the group paid tribute to Tony and their long association with him for the Manchester International Festival. The performance was entitled 'A Paean to Wilson', a piece of music I personally found quite moving, and one of the best works I have heard Vini, Bruce Mitchell and friends ever perform. Of all the many tributes to Tony since his death I thought this one of the best. And Vini didn't sing at all!

A contemporary spiritual teacher called Ram Dass once remarked that 'relationships are the yoga of the West'. I take this to mean that relationships can help us develop spiritually, which is difficult to comprehend when ugly scenes of resentment and anger occur. I remember once rowing with Tony about something and angrily smashing a plate in the kitchen. It seemed odd – given the advent of punk and all things outrageous – that he took particular exception to this. Pete Shelley of Buzzcocks laughed when I told him about it later and called it 'kitchen punk'. When any argument developed after that, Tony would pin me to the floor so that I couldn't throw anything except a punch. This resulted in us rolling around the floor fighting one another, and I thought that worse than breaking crockery.

All the same, I think Ram Dass had a point. Or, as my mum used to say Confucius said: 'Marry well and you'll be happy, marry badly and you'll become a philosopher.'

I think one of the hardest things in a long-term relationship is not to take the other person so much for granted that you have no idea of their true value. Worse than that, it can become quite a task not to magnify the things about them that disappoint you. I wonder if getting married and/or living together makes this more likely to happen. In older age it is perhaps easier to appreciate our partners and indeed life in general. (After all, there is less and less time.) Also, by then one has hopefully had time to gain maturity and develop beyond destructive shortcomings.

My partner for most of the last five years has been Anthony Ryan Carter, aka Tosh Ryan, co-founder of Music Force and Rabid Records, described by Manchester media guru Andy Spinoza as 'semi-legendary'. That said, Tosh and I broke up in the spring of 2007. We were apart for four months – didn't even speak except once – and it perhaps turned out to be a blessing in disguise, because that was such an important and special time for me to be emotionally with Tony. This was the time when Tony and I made and found our peace together – as I believe couples often do at the end of their lives. I admired the way Tony handled his final journey more than *anything* else he had ever done. I could relate when Elliot Rashman told me that 'Tony taught me how to die. He taught me how to die because he got on with it. It didn't stop him getting on with it. I never saw, and I am sure he had moments of fear and doubt, but I never saw. He said, "Death . . . it's a pussy." Meaning it's something you have to do. But his spirit was great. He kept his humour. He kept his pride. He kept total dignity.'

The time I shared with Tony seemed so precious – as in reality it always was – but this is hard for the young to feel. We take life itself for granted, never mind each other. Added to that are the myriad hang-ups we bring to the table that have not yet been worked through.

I now bitterly regret how Tony and I behaved in 1978, when in truth we really were in love. Death had been little thought of. Even separation hadn't occurred to us. We were married, in it for the long haul. Films always end at the point of marriage – probably because after that the story becomes uninteresting. And after our wedding I suppose Tony had carte blanche to pretty much get on with his career and assume our relationship would take care of itself. I was always there in the house at the end of his long day, and I felt he didn't really see me even then. I in turn stopped appreciating him. He was just someone to make a meal, wash and iron for – but he didn't even care about that as long as I had sex with him. Which, increasingly, I didn't want to do. He once said that he could put up with no sex if there were no rows, and rows if there was sex, but he couldn't stand rows and no sex.

Tony and I really ought to have had a happy life together with children. Perhaps it was the drug-taking that messed things up. We never went a day without them and, speaking for myself, despite the highs, I think overall it caused more lows – depression, mood swings and volatility. It was also yet another factor that prevented me from making a commitment to a child. But we were just young hippies who did so like getting stoned, and drugs and music seemed to go together. I couldn't imagine life without it then, but in truth it probably wasn't doing much good. Of course marijuana these days can be quite a different thing from the more natural stuff common in the seventies. I think super-skunk is quite likely to make you go completely bonkers if you're not careful.

Drugs are like illusions; it's better if you can live without them.

Once we were playing cards with my mum and during the game Tony and I smoked a joint. My mum never moralised about that, or anything in fact, but she did remark that our skill at the game had suddenly taken a turn for the worse after the smoke – that we didn't seem as sharp. Tony's response was to quip that his brain was so super-sharp he needed to smoke to dull it slightly so that he could be more in line with other people!

As said, despite enjoying endless activities connected with the burgeoning music scene at this time, I didn't feel a true ownership of, or identification with, the Factory concept. At this point in time none of the bands seemed especially thrilling to me. ACR, Durutti Column, even Joy Division were yet – by mid-1978 – to make a strong impact on me. Much fuss is made about the Stiff-Chiswick challenge night – how fantastic Joy Division were – but this wasn't obvious to everyone, including the judges, and there wasn't much in the way of competition. Joy Division did explode onto the stage with a pent-up energy bordering on aggression, and it was perhaps this, along with Ian's performance, that made such an impression. Still, I don't remember Tony especially raving about Joy Division from then on, even if he did put them on at the Russell Club and *What's On*. Rob Gretton rightly recognised talent in the band and became their manager, but then again he was ripe and ready to grasp onto something, anything in the music arena. In 1977 he had released a single by the Panik called 'It Won't Sell' on Rainy City Records. This was a short-lived association for both band and label (the record lived up to its name).

Though the budding Factory bands seemed a tad dour to me in 1978, going to Magazine gigs became the absolute highlight of my life. It wasn't just because of my infatuation; I honestly found their performances exciting. I think that was about as enthusiastic as I have ever been for a band. I saw them at the Russell, Rafters, Eric's, and I remember the Ritz in May '78. That night they played with John Cooper Clarke. It was memorable to me because I went right up near the front, and the wooden floor there was sprung and bouncy. I lost myself in the heart of the crowd that Howard wormed his way into. Every gig after that I went close up to the front, pushing my way through the volume of people. This is how Joy Division gigs were portrayed in the movies *24 Hour Party People* and *Control*, yet there were never huge numbers of people in their audiences early on, and in any case they weren't the sort of band you danced to. It was more of a spectacle that held visual interest because of Ian. I was transfixed watching Ian but his movements scared me slightly. The rest of Joy Division seemed nice but rather shy, submissive boys. When Tony and I were with them in the early days there was a fair amount of toadying going on – they all kept quiet and kowtowed to the master, as it were. I thought this spectacularly un-rebellious and un-punk. I liked them but it wasn't really until I heard them in the studio with Martin that their music had a profound impact on me.

In 1978 I was unaware of Hannett's rare talent, and whilst Tony was focusing on that my sights were set elsewhere. My obsession with Magazine and Howard was even affecting the way I dressed. The carnival style of music, something clownish about Howard's clothes – I remember I got this outfit that was vaguely and tastefully harlequin shaped. My heart pounded when Howard was in sight. Tony was unaware of it all – we would call briefly backstage and I would be unable to speak, on the point of passing out, while Tony got on with the pleasantries.

Being in love is like that. Crazy. I would think of him from the minute I woke up and throughout the day. And yet I didn't know him at all.

Thirty-one years later, on 14 February 2009, I went to see Magazine play live at the Academy in Manchester. I was stunned it was such a great gig. Their songs have not aged; there's a timelessness there – or, even better, the music has improved with age like a fine wine. Howard sings clearly, 'I don't know if I ever knew you, but I know you, you never knew me.' How true. He could have written it about me. Interestingly, this song was on the album *The Correct Use of Soap*, which was originally released in 1980 and produced by Martin Hannett. Martin said it was his best technical production. I think it was made before its time.

How ridiculous my fixation seems now (although I got a glimmer of understanding when I heard the power of the band that night in 2009). I was a married woman. Did my vows count for nothing? The sad fact is that infatuation and obsession can feel a hell of a lot stronger than love. It is only a fool that mistakes the former for the latter. I was a fool. I rationalised. I had already betrayed Tony with words and now my heart was involved. Did our marriage mean anything anymore (to either of us, I wondered)? Should I not follow my heart and be with Howard? I pondered this question day and night. I knew all I had to do was pick up the phone and call Howard to make something happen. But months went by before I did.

Then one night Tony had gone off somewhere after work as usual, running about with his boys, and I knew he'd be very late back. I decided to take LSD on my own. I was searching for the truth. What should I do about this disappointing marriage? During the trip I happened to watch an episode of a series running about Lillie Langtry. I was always impressionable, but the drug made me see this programme as if it were somehow holding up a mirror to my own situation. Lillie found marriage dull, despite her husband's wealth, but consolation was gained from a society that opened up to her because of her beauty and association with the Prince of Wales. In the episode I watched that night, Oscar Wilde and she appeared to be smitten with one another. Wilde was appreciating her artistic qualities, and in fact it was he who helped her to find a career as an actress. My impression was that because she and Oscar were in love then happiness was being with him and not with her husband. It seemed to me that Oscar was Howard, I was Lillie and the husband was Tony. Of course, Tony was not a bore as Lillie's husband was, but to me – in this period of history – he had become so. In reality Tony was a literary sort somewhat in the vein of Wilde, who loved beauty for its own sake. They both understood Keats's point that 'beauty is truth and truth beauty'.

I had turned to drugs for help. I wanted to know whether I should follow up on my feelings for Howard – perhaps if I never did I would miss out on something incredibly important. How wrong that was. With the maturity I now have I know that it would have been better to wait until my feelings passed, to have weaned myself off them, however addictively strong the pull I felt was. Infatuation, obsession – these are unhealthy feelings that, like candy floss, although very much in your face, have little substance and ultimately vanish into the nothing that they really are.

But I was immature – I imagined it was my heart speaking.

I wasn't looking for an affair. Believe it or not I wanted to share my life with someone – a fulfilled relationship, the kind I felt I wasn't getting with Tony. To think I would find that with Howard only demonstrates how far off the mark I was.

Some psychic voice made itself heard on this night. Actually, it was the only time in my whole life that I have literally heard a voice speak to me. It sounded human – as if coming from outside my body. It told me: 'He'll be the first of many.' So my fate was already written? I didn't believe there could be many – but took the message as an agreement that the marriage was doomed, and therefore in some way a green light to the new liaison. The voice seemed to think all this agonising of mine was a waste of time – guilt was superfluous to the drama of my life.

The next day I telephoned Howard. Without any hesitation he invited me over to his flat in Chorlton. I took this as evidence that he felt the same way as me. Yeah right – how naive could I be? It wasn't difficult for me to slip away unnoticed. Tony was out as usual. And he didn't seem interested in my activities. He probably thought I was over at my mum's house (where the action was not). He didn't telephone, mobile phones didn't exist, and I didn't need to lie. This was just as well, because I've never been any use at that.

I remember it was dark when I drove into Manchester. I stopped on the way to buy a bottle of wine. Odd to think, but Tony and I very rarely drank alcohol. We never had wine with a meal unless it was a dinner party. It just wasn't our thing. So consequently I didn't have a clue about what kind of wine to buy. I was so uneducated in that department I didn't even know if I preferred red or white. (No such problems now, of course. A lovely red rioja goes down a treat.) I looked helplessly up at the shelves. The man behind the counter smiled at me kindly. 'You wouldn't if you knew what I'm up to,' I thought, but still couldn't turn back. I chose a white wine that I thought had to be tolerable and, besides, it was the only one I'd heard of. Blue Nun. I only became aware of the irony – that I was at the same time naively innocent and adulterous – later on.

As I walked up to Howard's door, I wondered if anyone might have seen me. I knew loads of people who lived in Chorlton. Something I'd read that Oscar Wilde had said came into my head, something about the things we do in secret one day having to shout out to the world. I could never have imagined then that my secret would appear in a film, or that I would write about it for anyone to read.

I was so excited I felt nauseous.

'How was it?' he asked.

'You tell me,' I replied, momentarily lost for words.

'It was . . . fine,' he said.

As I was leaving, Howard asked me if I was going to tell Tony. I got very concerned hearing this – it didn't quite tally with my expectations of him proffering undying love and suggesting we run away together. My imagination hadn't got to the part where I would return to Tony. I looked quizzical, so Howard went on to say that he thought if I did tell Tony it would just be to make myself feel better, since I would be unloading my guilt onto him. But I was ready to leave Tony for this man. I wouldn't have made love to him otherwise.

Clearly Howard was not convinced of this. Doubt entered my mind. I don't recall being aware then that Howard had a girlfriend, but I soon would be. Maybe I'd been mistaken – the awful realisation that I was probably just a one-night stand to him, that there was no great romance beyond the obsessive romantic tangent I had gone on. I kept thinking of his words – that it would be selfish of me to tell Tony. A few weeks went by, and I received a really nasty phone call from Howard's girlfriend. So Howard had told me not to say anything but done so himself. I feared that Tony might hear it from some other quarter.

So it was that on New Year's Eve 1978, I made an even bigger mistake – probably the biggest yet – and told Tony I'd been unfaithful. Now the light really was getting dark.

Although I still had feelings for Howard, it was clear that they were not mutual and our relationship was never going to develop into anything. It seemed sensible to let it go. I made up my mind to tell Tony about the affair because not telling him carried a certain deceit. I still didn't know if he'd been unfaithful to me and thought it would be an opportunity for us both to come clean. Wrong, wrong, wrong. I should have listened to the Austrian writer Vicki Baum: 'Marriage always demands the greatest understanding of the art of insincerity possible between two human beings.'

We were on our way to a New Year's party, just before midnight, when I told Tony. I was contrite and wanted us to start again, to make a clean breast of things, begin anew, restore our trust and try to make our marriage work this time. I had suffered and truly learnt my lesson.

His reaction to my news was very, very bad. So bad, in fact, that I understood I must have been mistaken in thinking he'd betrayed me. I had hoped – naively – for forgiveness. I thought he might understand my mistake; recognise that our relationship needed more to survive and see that my affair – for such it had turned out to be – was over, and let it go. The reverse was true.

He seemed genuinely shocked, then angry, and then just icy cold. The coldness was the worst. If I had hoped for more from him, in fact I got even less. His trust in me, something very sacred, now seemed to be broken. He didn't get angry the way I would have done. He held it in and made me feel ignored – which I did anyway, but now with an edge of a biting cold wind.

When *A Factory Sample* eventually surfaced after Christmas there were no celebrations at 45 Town Lane, Charlesworth because things between us had turned as frosty as the weather. My contribution to and support of the project might as well have been nought. I'd voted with my body for another musical concept.

Tony became even more absent. My hope had been that we'd both give more to our relationship, but in fact he now had carte blanche to have a love affair of his own, on top of his obsession with his newly formed label and male bravado partners. I, on the other hand, felt even more cut off from it all by him (although not by the musicians and the gigs). The most painful thing for me was being aware when Tony was off to be with another women – he displayed a streak of cruelty by telling me about it. I didn't necessarily know if his new friendships were sexual or not, but had a feeling they would be if it was left up to him. Ironically the first woman he told me he was meeting after our debacle was Linder Sterling, an artist who had formerly been a long-time girlfriend of Howard's. Perhaps it wasn't ironic. Perhaps it was a deliberate choice. Actually, Linder's group Ludus (along with Willie Trotter) had appeared at the Factory Russell Club on 19 January 1979. Her friendship with Tony seemed to develop from then, although the two must have met prior to this since she told journalist John Robb: 'I was asked to do the artwork for Factory. I said, "I've got another friend who can do it for you," because I didn't want to make sleeves. I told them about Peter Saville. I was quite good at match-making!' That said, Linder had already designed the cover for Magazine's *Real Life*. In light of this, I wonder why Tony's memories are the only ones we pay heed to and ponder that, of course, I was not the only woman to be denied credit for her contribution.

I didn't then know the extent of Linder's connection with Tony, but he seemed to take pleasure in telling me he was seeing her, something I found very painful. She told writer James Nice: 'Tony and I were good friends for a while, but when he made an advance I firmly and politely refused.' That is all very well, but I knew that he wanted her and would have taken her. The betrayal was there, whether consummated or not. Then he quirkily scheduled one of her creations as a Factory art object – Fac 8 was to be an abacus, a menstrual egg timer (so that you'd know which day of the twenty-eight-day cycle you were on). I vaguely remember Tony bringing home some sketches and the beginnings of a prototype of this, and enthusing madly about Linder's brilliance. In 1992, *NME* ran a page that included Tony's Top Ten Factory Experiences, and Number One was this egg timer: 'We never actually did it but it was there . . .' (A bit like the thumb track on a Stone Roses song produced by Martin – the bass guitarist, Pete, spent hours on it but it wasn't audible in the final mix. Martin assured Pete, '*You* know it's there and *I* know it's there.')

I'm not surprised that Tony was rather smitten with both Linder and her concept. Apart from her being immensely attractive, her creations were intriguing and she was obviously independent and very bright. The menstrual timer seemed like a good idea, artistically as well as practically. It could have come in handy – Tony and I were, like all good Catholics, adopting the rhythm method of contraception. Also, he had decided by then that all my problems were down to premenstrual syndrome. I laughed the suggestion off – don't men always say that? 'Oh God, you must be getting your period,' when in fact it is they who are being as annoying as hell. But I have to concede defeat, at least in part (even if he could be infuriating). Tony was right – my mood swings most definitely were cyclical and hormonally based. I just didn't know it at the time. Doubtless the drugs were exacerbating the problem.

Meanwhile my own Factory offering – Orchestral Manoeuvres in the Dark – was released in May. The previous year Tony and I had been driving along listening to cassettes together in his car. It was a bit like the Stiff-Chiswick challenge, wading through the piles of cassettes Tony was regularly sent because of his position at Granada. But just as Joy Division had stood out that night, on this day OMD jumped out at me. I asked Tony to play it again. He did but wasn't convinced. I told him I could hear this group in the charts. I felt certain, so much so that he told me he'd release the record 'just for you' (he wasn't so keen on it). It was slightly patronising, the way he patted me on the leg as he said this. Probably because it wasn't quite his 'thing' – i.e. not oedipal rebellious rock. It turned out that OMD had just then decided to give up pursuing a career in music and go back to their day jobs in Birkenhead because they weren't getting anywhere.

The record was called 'Electricity'. Saville designed a clever sleeve – a black-on-black thermographed (embossed raised ink) sleeve. I got the impression that – as the graph under the words 'Electricity' and 'Almost' (the name of the B-side) was raised – the idea was that it was a sort of Braille. Saville said it was something you could feel in the dark. Whatever it was it worked. It was very much the marker of a Factory style. It also led to Saville becoming Art Director for Dindisc, an offshoot of Virgin Records.

One afternoon my husband came home and informed me that he'd 'sold' OMD to Dindisc. For £3,000. Although there was no contract with the band, the rights to the record were owned by us since we'd paid for the recording costs. The £3,000 may simply have been a licensing advance, but, whatever it was, Dindisc now owned this group's future. I was appalled. I thought I might at least have had some say about that? Wrong. The phrase 'thirty pieces of silver' came to mind. Rob gets made a partner because we're spending our life savings on his band, but my band just gets sold on after one single. It was all out of my hands. By coincidence the person Tony dealt with at Dindisc was called Carole Wilson. My middle and last name. I felt betrayed. This really was *my* act and he'd given them away. I wondered if he objected to the fact that they were more mainstream and commercially interesting rather than possessing the rebellious punk attitude that he worshipped? Certainly they were more my taste than his. Or might it have had something to do with the fact that the band hadn't been able to see eye-to-eye with Martin Hannett, as they rejected his mix of the track? Tony was always almost perversely loyal and saw the emerging Factory as a family firm (wives not necessarily included), with Martin very much a part of the family. Saville told me that Tony 'didn't have the partiality for the

Kraftwerk link. The thing that interested me about OMD was the electronic dimension, but Tony wasn't a fan of that so there was nothing left.' But, as I remarked to Saville, Tony was a fan of it when New Order took that route later.

Or was it a punishment? Whatever it was, the way he went about it was a slap in the face for me.

Saville, who had been languishing in Manchester for months at parental expense, had been told by his father to find a job within two weeks or have one found for him. As the options in his field of work were mostly restricted to London, he was consequently obliged to up sticks and take on a job for design company Acrobat. He subsequently went on to work for Dindisc.

Later, in September 1979, for the Factory 'Records and Shareholder's Analysis', Tony wrote regarding the single 'Electricity': 'Cult hit, discos even. 5,000 May '79. Sold out. Record now licensed to Dindisc, Virgin's new label; to engage in the chart game. Necessity for licensing "the best example of this to date" (*NME*) is regretted but the big stall holders seem to fill the square (chart shops) and subletting is an enforced activity.'

I couldn't really see the logic of this. To be fair, in an interview with me in 2005 Tony said: 'The whole idea of being an independent record label in 1978-79 was to get your band or your mate's band signed to a major label – 'cause that's what everyone wanted. There had been a tiny period when we may have felt differently, but I can remember interviewing Tosh [Ryan] – this was before Factory, and probably around spring '78, after he signed Jilted John to EMI and Gordon the Moron, and he signed John Cooper Clarke to CBS. I interviewed him in a Granada cutting room and I asked him why he'd signed the bands to majors and Tosh laughed and, quite rightly, said, "You're living in the past" – i.e. this idealistic past of summer of '77 when everyone thought we could do it ourselves.'

'So it seemed possible then?' I asked.

'It did, yes,' Tony replied. 'Early '77 there was a period. Late '77, no – the whole idea then was to get your band signed to a major. So by the time we put a record out it was because we had a band that we wanted to sign to a major. The band was the Durutti Column, and the way you got your band signed was the system where you could put out independent records and you did it to get your band signed. That was what everybody was doing.'

Fair enough. The thing is, though, that a) Tony didn't discuss the sale of OMD's catalogue to Virgin with me until it was a done deal and b) in February 1979 Tony had already mapped out the future of the Factory label to a large degree by agreeing to Rob's suggestion that he record Joy Division's first album on Factory.

I might add that I don't particularly remember him discussing that with me either – the fact that all of his (ipso facto our) savings were now to be jeopardised on a musical venture.

Tony was entering a different league and leaving me behind. But after all, I had sinned and I was to be punished. Tony was pretty big on punishment. Meanwhile, I didn't know whether he was playing away or not. That was the worst thing – not knowing what he was doing. One night he didn't come home at all, and I was pretty concerned when his other other half (Alan) didn't know where he was either. A bit of a giveaway, that one. It transpired that Tony had slept with someone in the Didsbury area. He didn't deny it. He even told me – after my jealous questioning – that he slept with her twice (once in the morning as well). I didn't find out who she was until years later. When interviewed by Mick Middles, Tony announced that his first 'revenge fuck' was with a girlfriend of a singer with an early Factory band. He said she had Sellotape on her breasts and, although it was difficult, he shagged her out of politeness. A gentleman through and through. It served me right I suppose.

In 2005 Tony told me the oft-repeated story of how Joy Division came to be a Factory stable mate: 'Then suddenly one night, must have been February '79, in the Band on the Wall, having a drink, Rob and I were talking so there mustn't have been a group onstage at that point. Rob suddenly turned and said, "Why don't we do our first album with you and then go to Warner Bros?" I remember my response was, "Are you sure?" The point is that no one understands that Rob created the independent record movement. His was the first group of any stature that wanted to stay independent. About three or six months later we did *Unknown Pleasures* ourselves.'

'You're saying that no one else had done this?' I asked.

'No one,' he replied. 'I might get confused now – Rough Trade – certainly that was the idea at that point in time.'

Actually there *were* others, e.g. Rabid, Stiff (with their great slogan, 'If it's not stiff it's not worth a fuck'), even Virgin started out as an independent originally. But not many of the independents risked money on an album, that much is true.

Tony's over-glorification of Rob's contribution to the independent record movement slightly annoyed me. My cynical mind couldn't help but ponder how much self-interest might also have been a factor. Tony reckoned that Rob's reasoning was: 'We'd done the *Factory Sample*, a double seven-inch single works, and if we did an album (he understood the economics that albums make real money as opposed to pin money which singles make) we could do it ourselves and, who knows, if it really worked, he could be in the record business with his band and he wouldn't have to get on a train every week and talk to jerks in London (which is how Rob described it in *Time Out*, although the term he actually used was cunts).'

Rob no doubt said this to be amusing (which, by the way, he often was), but Tony frequently latched on to lines like that and turned them into some kind of major historical event.

Not wishing to directly create conflict with Tony concerning his account, I led with my chin another way (repeating Tony's views back to him):

LR: So why did you call Rob a tosser a few minutes ago? [before the tape was turned on]

TW: Because he's my mate and he repeatedly fucked me over.

LR: In what way did he fuck you over?

TW: Having invented what I call the modern independent record movement, exactly about twenty seconds later he said, 'Here's the deal we will do,' and then this kid from Wythenshawe proceeded to sketch out a deal . . .

LR: . . . using our money . . .

TW: . . . which I agreed to on the spot – because why not? This turns out to be the most generous record deal ever done for musicians – in history. His other thought was Tony's a fucking idiot and I'll get a fantastic deal out of him, which he did that very day.

What made the deal totally in the band's favour was that Factory were to pay mechanical royalties out of their share of fifty percent. In other words, Factory would be out of pocket before the fifty-fifty split. I doubt that Tony knew much about mechanical royalties then; I hadn't even heard of them. But this is where the major money in recording can be made. It is the fee the record company pays to the publisher on behalf of the songwriter whenever a copy of their songs is made (i.e. for each record manufactured). Factory's accounting in this department must have been a bit hit-and-miss, however. Andrew King formed Blackhill Enterprises in 1967, managing several acts including Ian Dury, and went on to amass a publishing catalogue in 1976. He recalls representing Blurt's publishing and speaking to Tony about their unpaid mechanical royalties. I think Tony took the view that, since the band were in negative equity, why should he be liable to fork out any more? I could actually relate to this since the principal of Factory was supposed to be to share *profit* fifty-fifty. The mechanical issue was perhaps a bit of a grey area. However Andrew, who remains committed to protecting the rights of songwriters to this day, explained the proper, if not legal, procedure to him. Tony apparently replied, 'Would £500 be all right?' and wrote out a cheque there and then.

So Joy Division couldn't really lose with the deal Rob had hatched. Another point worth bearing in mind is that Rob was both a manager and a Factory director. A double-whammy really. But Tony didn't care about money; he was too excited about the next phase. Perhaps it was as Tony described it after I suggested to him that 'the working-class ones were more motivated to make money'. He replied, 'Very true. I was your typical middle-class wanker who didn't need to make money.' Or perhaps, as he told James Nice, it was because 'I'm a Catholic, I don't give a fuck'. Cardinal Arns, who Tony once interviewed, told him that being rich was in itself a sin.

Thus began a bit of a love-hate relationship between Tony and Rob.

Tony also told me during this interview that Rob was 'ripping me off even in death'. I asked him what on earth he meant. He said that the organisers of the 'Hacienda' New Year's Eve party that year had paid £10,000 for the use of the name just for one night. He told me the name was owned jointly by Rob Gretton's estate and Hooky. This was news to me, but it's the name 'FAC 51 THE HAÇIENDA' (with a cedilla placed under the C) which is a licensed and protected trademark. He also said that it cost £5,000 to buy it, but at the time of the purchase (soon after Factory went bankrupt) Tony and Alan were in financial difficulty and couldn't afford to buy in. Later Tony demurred and said that Rob wasn't ripping him off; he'd just got the most amazing deal in history.

'I have reservations about how New Order see Tony's role in the Hacienda – as Tony pissing their money away, which is very unfair,' said Elliot Rashman. 'I don't think the others would have carried Tony. Tony, once enthused, ran with it. I don't think they fully give him the credit for helping to make them who they were.'

I asked Hooky if he'd like to comment on this and he said, 'I suppose my recollection is that everyone said no [to purchasing the trademark], not just Alan and Tony. I wonder if Elliot would feel the same if it happened to him?'

Elliot responded: 'All I know is that at the end of the week when Factory closed, Alan Erasmus had to sign on. He got nothing from it, Tony got nothing, they [New Order and Rob Gretton] all went off to work with one of the biggest multinational companies in the world and Tony had spent every minute of his waking day promoting everybody on Factory, not just New Order but Peter Saville, Ben Kelly – Tony was the evangelist and they benefited from it. When he struggled all they did was moan about him.'

I believe that in 2010 Hooky bought out Gretton's share of the Hacienda trademark name and that Alan owns the trademark FAC 51. Hooky's new club is called FAC 251 – 251 being the number given to the Factory offices in Charles Street which have now been converted into said club. Alan has prevented the club from trademarking the name FAC 51 since he believes it should be shared by everyone, and was involved in discussions regarding this at the time of writing.

I broached the thorny subject of money with Tony more than once during my interviews, which included the following conversation:

LR: In spite of Rob's amazing deal, the band never had that much money until they left [Factory] though?

TW: The band had loads of money, always.

LR: But not like they've got now.

TW: You don't get money until you've got back catalogue and amass all that.

LR: I thought it was because they get proper royalties now. They were propping up the Hacienda before and things like that.

TW: Yes, but that was their club. Rob pointed out to me in the late nineties that they'd made more money overseas out of Factory's system than out of Polygram. They made fantastic money out of Factory.

Later in the same interview Tony commented, 'I can remember giving Rob a cheque for £450,000 in the car one day [in the mid-eighties].'

After *A Factory Sample* came out, Joy Division were getting attention because of their work with Martin on 'Digital' and 'Glass' and were offered a deal by Genetic/Radar/Warner Bros – for £35,000 or £40,000.

If they'd gone to this subsidiary, it is likely that Martin Rushent would have produced the album. Perhaps Rob had the perceptiveness and/or loyalty to see that Hannett had to be the man for the job – although there's no doubt that Rushent's production would have been excellent, if different. Or perhaps Rob also sensed that if the group signed to a major and became successful he might rapidly be ousted to make way for a big-league manager, which is what usually happens. Whatever his reasons, it was astute to think long-term and not take the money at this stage. Saville set to work on the sleeve. And *Unknown Pleasures* was to make Rob's point.

A Factory Sample paid for itself. Tony has quoted different figures in respect of this. He told me in interview that 'it had cost £4,870 to do and we got £5,300 back. Joy Division made £200.' However, he told Andy Zero and Bob Dickinson: 'Factory Records made £58 out of the *Factory Sample* 'cause we were on five percent – the bands were on twenty percent each, Martin was on four percent, Saville was on four percent – or three percent – [engineer] John Brierley was on ten percent for his studio time, so it was like we'd only made £85 but we got the money back. Having had that experience – it had cost £3,000 and getting £4,600 back – you suddenly think this is how it's done, you get your money back so it's all right.'

The percentages Tony quotes here really don't make sense. Apart from the fact they literally don't add up since they total 103 percent, and that two differing amounts – £58 and £85 – are quoted in the same paragraph as Factory's profit, John Brierley told me: 'There was never a deal between me and Tony/Factory. Tony called round to see me at the studio not long after it had been opened. He told me about this new band he'd found called Joy Division, and as Factory didn't have much money would I be interested in agreeing to a deal to get royalties on all future Joy Division releases, or alternatively he would pay just the normal studio cost (around £120 per day). I said it depended on what they sounded like and if I thought they were a commercial proposition. Tony had some demos – or at least I assumed they were demos – of the band which I listened to, I thought they were awful, so I declined the offer of royalties. However, when the band actually came in to record "Digital" and "Glass" for the *Factory Sample* EP the band had improved a lot and my opinion of them changed, and I could see they really had something and a real future and by then I was really into their music, but the offer of royalties was no longer on the table.'

Peter Saville told me that after he moved down to London, 'Tony said this is ridiculous, you're not even here. I completely agreed, by which time Factory was a company that had shares. He said he didn't really see the point of me having these shares. I said I didn't either, and I didn't really expect to have any. I said I should keep some, so I kept five percent. Apparently, in James Nice's book Martin Hannett was under the impression I was paid £20,000 for my shares in Factory. In his legal suit against Factory it says this. I was never paid anything for them.'

A Certain Ratio began gaining momentum, propelled forward by Tony's enthusiasm. Why was he running around after those boys, I asked myself? It seemed somewhat peculiar to me; the huge amount of energy he was investing in these kids. And the way Tony spoke about them as though they were the best in the country annoyed me – quote unquote 'one of the truly great bands of the era'. I thought he was deluded. He just thought he was right. Actually he always irritated me with the way he thought that, because he believed in a group, they were automatically the best. But that egoistic determination of his certainly got things moving. ACR would soon find themselves on the crest of a wave.

ACR rapidly went into Cargo in Rochdale to record 'All Night Party' backed with 'Thin Boys'. Orchestral Manoeuvres in the Dark also recorded their single here – both groups under the direction of Martin Hannett. In the event, OMD and Martin weren't simpatico with regard to their respective musical ideas and went their separate ways. Martin was, even then and even before anyone knew it, almost custom-made to work with Joy Division. He also wasn't able to do anything especially spectacular with 'All Night Party', but I could tell that something interesting was developing with ACR. And by this point in time I had become quite fond of the lads. They were good fun.

On 5 May 1979 yet another night of craziness began with my decision to take LSD by myself. I knew that Tony was going to be out the whole night. Maybe he was in London, maybe with ACR, maybe with a lover or maybe all three. All seemed to be lost between Tony and I. We hardly ever saw one another, and when we did we rowed all too easily. He hadn't forgiven me and his coldness had continued. I was confused and lonely, probably panicking, and taking a tab of acid was doubtless the last thing I should have done. Pure recklessness. Yet again I was looking for help, for some insight into the truth of my situation. Should I stay, should I go, that sort of thing.

I don't remember a great deal about the evening except that I began thinking about Howard again. And about Tony. I looked at pictures of them both under the influence of the drug. It seemed that I could see cruelty in the shape of Tony's mouth. And how he was making me suffer, hardly ever coming home, flaunting his newfound status as a free man while carrying on with the day-to-day marriage. And Howard just looked like my familiar, like he belonged with me. I decided I'd made a mistake in attempting to make a go of things with Tony – that the marriage was already over. That was why I had driven over to Chorlton that night after all, infidelity always being proof of the death of the previous relationship. And then I went on to imagining a future with Howard – this time we would be together for real. Howard had only been cautious, he wanted me really. He'd as good as told me so when, the last time I had seen him, he'd shown me a piece of paper with some lyrics he'd just written. The song was entitled 'I Want Your Heart'. I thought he must have written the song to me. So, as it neared midnight I got an idea. There lying on the floor was the *NME* and I quickly turned to the gig guide. I knew Magazine were on tour but had no idea where they were on this particular night. It turned out to be Leeds. I didn't want to waste another moment. I'd given four months to trying to get things back on track with Tony and this just wasn't how I wanted to live. In my past when things went sour with a man, or one of us wanted someone else, the relationship categorically ended. So the marriage must end. Before I left I broke a vinyl record into pieces and placed it on the big low coffee table in our lounge (which I'd polished every day for the last three years). What the record was I honestly don't remember, but I do know I smashed my personal copy of *A Factory Sample* at some point. It could have been that I suppose. I left a note on top of the broken bits. It read: 'My heart – you wanted it.' That was my goodbye to Tony. It seemed to sum the whole situation up. I had no intention of ever returning again.

When the song that Howard showed me eventually appeared on the album *Secondhand Daylight* it was re-named 'I Want*ed* Your Heart'. I look back at the crazy artwork I left on our coffee table that night and think that really, in my drug-crazed, mixed-up mind, I left the message for the wrong man. It should have been sent to Howard, not Tony.

I arrived in Leeds about 2:00am and went to every single hotel I could find. By 4:00am I seemed to have visited them all. It was a mystery, there didn't appear to be any other hotels left. Maybe the group were staying in an obscure B&B somewhere. The streets were deserted. Then I saw a couple of lads – punk-looking – wandering along. I pulled over and asked them if they knew Leeds well. Yes, they said they were locals. Somewhat foolishly perhaps, I asked them if they could help me and they cheerily agreed and jumped in the car.

They showed me every hotel they knew. Still no luck. Then they suggested I go back to their place and have a cup of tea and toast. Perhaps even more unwisely I accepted, but they seemed like really nice lads and fortunately they were. And besides there were no all-night cafés open.

The grey dawn came and the grey city awoke. As Tony had so eloquently described that feeling the day after acid: 'Feels like, I can hardly describe it, most like the day when things look bleak, no colour in anything, washed out and up, cut yourself and you know the blood would be grey not red.'

I'd lost hope of finding Howard and set off once more for Manchester. Just as I was about to drive on to the M62 – there, right by the slip road, I saw a hotel I'd not been to. I turned back and could see the group's van parked beside it. It was still pretty early but I pulled into the car park. I got Howard's room number and knocked. For sure he must be in bed, I thought, and will be shocked to see me. In fact he was dressed when he opened the door and didn't bat an eyelid. He looked at me as if I was another tour member who'd just popped out to get some milk. He didn't invite me into his room but took me down the corridor to the cigarette machine. Then we went to get a cup of tea or whatever. Conversation was a bit stilted. He said they were going to Liverpool for the gig that night. I offered to drive him there. He accepted. He got his stuff from the room and we set off.

But I knew it – or I – didn't mean much to him really. I'm not in love, he seemed to scream at me. I'm not even all that interested. What are you doing here? Shouldn't you be with your husband? What *was* I doing there? All these thoughts were going around my head. In fact we said very little. We stopped for lunch at a service station. I think we ate fish and chips.

I realised I'd just gone off on a ridiculous romantic tangent again; adopted some absurd notion that he would save me. Is it not the case that all of us – everyone – are looking for something? Something or someone to make us whole. Where we look for it varies – some think they'll find it in their career, or home, or family, or money. I always thought I'd find it in a partner. Now of course I know, only too well, that the only place we can find this thing is not outside of ourselves at all, it's inside ourselves. And whenever I've observed a man who imagines I am the solution they are looking for I run a mile! There's nothing worse than desperation.

We pulled up outside his hotel in Liverpool. I knew it was over since it could never be more than an affair to him. We seemed to have reached an understanding on that point. I didn't want an affair. I expected him to jump out and that would be it. I didn't respect either him or myself when he asked me up to his room and I accepted. I thought I would let it happen one last time. The truth had dawned on me that sometimes sex and love don't have anything to do with one another. So this time it would be with the knowledge that it was just sex, the exact same act but merely a physical thing this time. I tried to see it from that perspective, but it seemed worse than meaningless to me.

I left immediately afterwards and knew I would never, ever repeat this. I felt sick at heart. My life might as well be over. I drove home and thought I would end it. Where was home in any case? I had no future with Tony or without him.

Later Tony wrote about this journey I went on and compared it to *War and Peace*: 'Natasha's flight of infatuation with the horrible Kuragin had a lot to say about a certain trip to Leeds in the early hours,' he wrote, 'and I always thought I was Pierre. In that instance Natasha fucked-up Prince Andrei.'

It actually seemed to be me that was most fucked-up by it. I wonder, in fact, if fucking and fucked-up are not somehow related. I gathered together all the Valium tablets I could find and took the lot. I thought that might do it. Alan Erasmus rang, or did I ring him looking for Tony? Maybe it wasn't for Ian Curtis, although he did write it for the song 'Colony', but in my case it definitely was 'a cry for help, a hint of anaesthesia'. Definitely the latter, and perhaps also: 'Tony, let's stop destroying each other and ourselves.' Or maybe it was self-disgust. How could I have got so mixed up and sunk so low? And meanwhile I did hope for oblivion. Alan gathered straight away that all was not well with me. His advice was poignantly simple and kind: 'Just put some sounds on and you'll be all right.' I've often thought about that. In times of despair would 'some sounds' save the day? Maybe so. They had before, so why not now? But I felt it was 'sounds' that had got me into this mess in the first place. Alan must have been able to get hold of Tony – he was more in touch with him than me, because he always knew where he was. Tony came home straight away. He looked at me with probably the tenderest look I'd seen all year. Not that it was tender, it just wasn't cold. Plus, he'd cared enough to come home. He checked I wasn't going to die. And so we lived to fight another day.

There was in fact a short lull, an uneasy truce in the battle zone between Tony and me after that incident. It was helped perhaps by a kind of mutual therapy – we both shared a common interest in Joy Division and loved going to sit in with Martin at Strawberry Studios and listen as the great album *Unknown Pleasures* came together. All of our problems temporarily evaporated in that field of creativity, and I never once showed the slightest concern about the money it was costing. I can honestly say I never even gave it a second thought. Tony said later that Martin estimated the album would cost £10,000, but in fact it ended up costing £20,000.

We always went quite late in the evening to Strawberry and sat in the control room rolling joints. I don't remember the band being in there much at all – they'd be downstairs playing pool or watching TV. Occasionally Martin would call them in, but he seemed very much the man at the helm, whether the band liked it or not. The dynamic between Tony and ACR was somewhat similar. It seemed as if they were children and he was almost like a father figure. Actually, for the main part, musicians are like children. But he seemed to have the upper hand – there were obvious reasons, such as him having money and influence while they had very little. Then there was his Cambridge education and his constant quotes, which could be undermining. The boys might be cheeky or rude or complain – in the manner of children – or sometimes even flirt, but it never seemed like a relationship between equals. I noticed this particularly with ACR but also with Joy Division to some extent, though Joy Division had Rob to contend with.

I loved those Strawberry nights, I felt completely at home there. My favourite times in the studio with Martin were when he was mixing and there was no one but him, us and his engineer Chris Nagle. He seemed much more relaxed then, almost as if musicians got in the way of his craft! Little did I know that he even resorted to playing tricks to keep the band away.

Sometimes hours would pass with the reel going backwards and forwards over the same small section of song over and over again. Martin's attention to detail was hard to understand, but it was part of his craft and I appreciated it. C.P. Lee recalled how Martin, being a former Catholic, was fond of a certain ritual that had to be observed in the studio. At a time when punk tracks could be recorded and pressed up within twenty-four hours, Martin was obsessed with specific sounds, and the ritual required that days be spent getting things ready. With typical humour C.P. goes on to say, 'Part of the ritual obviously involved massive intakes of ganja, almost like the incense burning in the thurible before high mass.'

I had explained to Tony what had happened with Howard in Leeds and Liverpool. He understood it was over with Howard and me, but still maintained his right for retribution – to carry on with an affair or embark upon a new one as he so chose. Why couldn't he just forgive me and let my mistake go? Why did he have to continue punishing me?

I was insecure and somewhat paranoid at the best of times. This ongoing threat was complete torture. Plus we were both so completely volatile. We'd shout and roll around the floor fighting. It got to the point that, whenever it kicked off with Tony and I (usually weekends), our neighbours would get in the car and drive away. Sometimes Tony would suggest going out to Edale or somewhere to see the beautiful country. But it was hardly ever peaceful. We'd be rowing before we got there. I used to look at families enjoying a day out. How did they manage it? We couldn't spend a day together without war breaking out, and I'd get upset. So many tears shed. Terrible.

One day, after a row, Tony drove off down the hill. I used to get so desperate. As if he was running away with someone and would never come back – the thing that I'd intended to do to him. On this occasion I ran after the car pleading with him to stop. He didn't. I fell down into the middle of the road, weeping in a crumpled heap. A neighbour (I don't know who he was but I think he lived next door to football manager Tommy Docherty, who also lived on our road in Charlesworth) came over to me. Concerned, he said, 'Why do you go upsetting yourself over a jerk like that?' I thought, 'Is that what people round here think of him?'

On the positive side, *Unknown Pleasures* seemed to be coming together as in a dream, effortlessly. Barney and Hooky didn't see it that way – they had struggled with Martin's vision, it didn't quite sit with their straight-ahead rock music angle. 'When we wrote that album in the rehearsal room it didn't sound anything like it did when it came out,' Barney said. 'I remember hearing the album after it had been mixed and being absolutely shocked at the sound of it 'cause it wasn't the way the band envisioned it. We just wanted quite a hard rocking sound and Martin used all these ethereal sound effects, such as he miked up the elevator shaft with the lift going up and down and stuff like that, broken bottles – and he played down the hard, in-your-face-rock-album of the album.'

But, as Tony ironically told James Nice for a DVD entitled *Shadowplayers*: 'We were clever enough to know that musicians know fuck all about music. They're given the gift of writing it, but their attitude to it is bollocks.'

The sleeve of the album came about because Barney had found an image of a pulsar graph, or Fourier analysis, in a book and shown it to the others and then, since everyone approved, Peter Saville. After that the group, and Rob, didn't seem bothered about what else went on the cover, although Mick Middles thought their vision was for the graph to be large and white. In the event, it was black – Factory black – and diminutive. Perhaps part of Saville's cleverness was more in what he left off the album artwork rather than what he put on it. In the end there were no names or titles on the front cover, not much on the back either. It didn't need them – it looked somehow better without it, and the music made enough of its own mark.

No sooner had the album been finished off at Strawberry than the recording of a seven-inch single, 'Transmission', followed that summer. Tony got really carried away by this particular song. He thought all Joy Division songs were iconic, even the first two, 'Digital' and 'Glass', but as he told me: 'I suppose the first real track was "Transmission". That was the track that made me go, "Oh fucking hell, this is a hit single." I drove off to London to try and get a plugger. I did get a plugger arranged, played him the song, he loved it. Came back to Manchester and Martin Hannett said, "We don't treat music as a commodity; so we don't use pluggers." Rob and Alan didn't disagree.'

I didn't disagree either. I thought we were supposed to be non-commercial.

Still, it didn't stop Tony from ordering boxes and boxes of the singles that endlessly took up space at Alan Erasmus's flat. They were floating around there for years. In fact Tony had 10,000 copies pressed up, and often told the story of how he would visit the pressing plant every month and see how this big pile of singles sitting in a wired pallet refused to budge very much. Joy Division fans may be amused to learn about the pallet next door to 'Transmission', which Tony noticed went down much more quickly. It contained a single by the Normal called 'Warm Leatherette', recorded in Daniel Miller's living room apparently. Daniel Miller founded Mute Records because of his own music, but the work he did under the name the Normal was not destined to enjoy the fortunes his record company did. He went on to host an absolutely brilliant roster and continues to do so to this day.

The funny thing about Tony is that, no matter what mistakes were made, he always managed to turn them around as positives. As Bruce Mitchell observed: 'The most important thing about Wilson – if someone was to invent positivity, it would be him. There wasn't a negative bone in his body that I ever saw. Anything that ever happened – stuff falling apart, something going wrong, whatever, he would always have something positive, like, "That's a learning curve." It went on and on and on, there are so many examples of that.'

Indeed. This is what Tony wrote in his book about the mistake he made with 'Transmission': 'So sometimes great records don't sell. At first. But they infect. They seep into the water table. They change the world. "Transmission" and the *Unknown Pleasures* that preceded it were John-the-Baptisting for Joy Division for a good year before the releases of 1980; they were ploughing the ground and they were sowing the seed.'

He never once reproached himself for any of his mistakes or appeared to have any guilt about anything. Sometimes that would really annoy me – it seemed to be part and parcel of his arrogance. But later in life I learned another way of seeing this characteristic. It had more to do with his indomitable spirit and ability to put a shutter down on any negativity. A quality I try to emulate, but usually fail in. Guilt is generally a waste of time. Hours before Tony's beloved Uncle Edgar died, the man he regarded more as a father figure than Sydney, Tony told me that he and Edgar had rowed about something. That was the note things were left on. But he didn't let it bother him – he knew that it wasn't relevant in the scheme of things. It has taken me a lifetime to learn the value of not beating yourself up. (Besides which, other people will probably make a good enough job of it.)

That said, sometimes it is only right and proper that we should recognise our guilt. Despite being one of the few non-Catholics around Factory, much of the ritual appeals to me, especially the concept of confession. Not necessarily to a Catholic priest, but without the act of confessing to someone the error may never truly be faced.

Still, useless regret is a bike-ride into negativity and Tony never rode that way. Negativity is a disease, sometimes of the ego. By complaining and making others wrong we increase the ego's sense of righteousness. Tony's ego may have been huge, but at least it was turned towards the sun. Of course, he was sometimes inclined to demonstrate his superiority by making others appear to be wrong. But he didn't indulge in excessive *mea culpa*, as I am wont to do over mistakes, and he lived true to Edith Piaf's '*Je ne regrette rien*' (unlike my own '*Je regrette tout*').

'Transmission' wasn't a hit, but things were indeed gaining momentum for Joy Division that August. For the first time they were getting attention outside of Manchester and there was quite a good turnout at the Electric Ballroom in London. But up the road towards Liverpool that same month, it was a different story for an event in Leigh.

As 27 August 1979 approached, Tony was getting all geared up about a live Factory event to be held (it seemed to me) in a nondescript field in the middle of nowhere. As it was my mum's birthday I didn't plan to be there much that day. Tony and I were at loggerheads in any case, and I didn't want to be near him (nor he me, to be sure). Whilst it irritated the hell out of me, I secretly admired his enthusiasm for arranging this event (along with several others he threw himself into), but I found out many years later that he in fact hadn't been the original organiser of this at all. Mick Middles explains: 'Tony rang up me and Savage for press coverage. [Jon Savage was a journalist working for *Melody Maker* and Mick represented *Sounds*] As far as we were aware it was a one-day festival where Factory met Zoo halfway.'

Following the splintering of Big in Japan, Bill Drummond was by this point a co-founder of the Zoo label in Liverpool. Early in his career he managed Echo & the Bunnymen and the Teardrop Explodes. Later he formed radical band the KLF with Jimmy Cauty and released some fascinating music, such as the Justified Ancients of Mu Mu (another earlier name for the KLF). Things got really interesting when the two guys left the music business and formed the K Foundation, which famously burnt £1,000,000 – a piece of conceptual art that didn't get the media exposure I thought it deserved.

Tony, with his nose for talented and interesting characters, was already working with Bill Drummond. Quite impressive really. However, as Mick continues: 'What we didn't know is this was the last day of a three-day festival organised by a carpet seller in Leigh – nothing to do with Factory or Zoo. Tony and Bill hijacked it, they took over the last day, which was a great PR coup but not so great for people who have spent a year organising it.'

Bill's account of the story is as follows: 'Tony Wilson phoned me from Factory Records. They had started at about the same time as Zoo. There was some sort of friendly rivalry between the two labels, which mirrored the less friendly rivalry that existed between the two cities of Liverpool and Manchester. There had even been a rather sad and pathetic attempt at a festival in the summer of '79 – "Factory Meets Zoo Halfway" – on some derelict ground outside Warrington. The bands featured were A Certain Ratio, the Teardrop Explodes, Orchestral Manoeuvres in the Dark, Echo & the Bunnymen and Joy Division. Tony Wilson tried to dissuade me from signing the Bunnymen to a major label. He told me that it doesn't have to be this way, that Joy Division, as we spoke, were recording an album to be released on Factory. We should do the same with the Bunnymen. Up until then none of the rash of indie record labels that had sprung up around the UK in the wake of the punk DIY ethic had produced anything but seven-inch singles. As far as I was concerned, this was part and parcel of some vague ideology. I assumed that most other people out there running small independent labels must think the same way. That they too were going for the eternal glory of pop and the seven-inch single. The Alan Hornes, the Bob Lasts. So when Tony Wilson implied I was selling out and buckling in to the power and money of London, I didn't get what he meant. As far as I was concerned he was the one compromising, by giving in to the indulgent muso tendencies of Joy Division and letting them record an album for Factory. There is another side to this: we were skint. Tony Wilson was on telly every night earning loads of money. We needed the cash the southern bastards could tempt us with.'

Not many people went to the festival – not that that would daunt Tony. 'How many people were at the Last Supper?' he might have said.

Mick Middles went to the event with Kevin Cummins and friends. He said they and Tony spent a lot of the day in a pub, mainly because there was nothing much to eat or drink at the event. There was no sense of the kind of commercialisation that would become synonymous with latter-day festivals. There was also a perfunctory police presence at the entrance; cars were searched and pockets emptied. Cars were parked at the rear of the field and you could actually watch the entire festival without leaving the car. The festival was just a field lightly splattered with a few sundry punks.

Mick had sold the day to *Sounds* as a big northern festival, but when they got the pictures from Kevin they said it was just a few punks in a field. Mick, with his penchant for a good title, called it, 'The Movement with No Name,' and *Sounds* added, 'And a festival with no people.'

Mick recalls that Tony was wearing a beige suit and green wellingtons as he strode through the so-called crowd towards Mick and Kevin. He was very, very friendly. He thanked them for coming and told Mick that ACR were really pissed off he was there since he had slated them so much.

'Tony had pushed ACR really hard,' Mick said. 'He was a great PR man – his actual line was "I have the new Sex Pistols". Looking back it seems ludicrous, ACR did have something but it wasn't that. It was a mental way to sell them. When you've been told that and you see these guys playing funk really badly and looking shy – it's not the Sex Pistols. Tony sold it as a rock thing, and yet they were like club guys. It was more about going to discos and going to funk and soul clubs, listening to Northern Soul, than it was rock. Not Iggy & the Stooges. So Tony didn't sell it well. I guess what Tony was saying was they had the zeitgeist; seize the day; the next day would be seized by ACR – but it never was. Happy Mondays did it better years later with that northern-lads-doing-the-soul thing.'

Comparisons were inevitably drawn between ACR and Joy Division. But ACR member Simon Topping told Mick Middles: 'We are nothing like Joy Division. We are a funk band, truly . . . I mean, that is why we were formed. We would all be down at the best Manchester clubs, listening to Funkadelic, Parliament, Bootsy . . . these are our roots. Not fucking Iggy Pop and the Velvet Underground.'

Oddly, in 2002 Tony described ACR as 'the nearest a Manc band really got to the Velvets, which after all is what every real band on earth wants to get close to'.

There may have been some confusion in terms of ACR's direction, but when drummer Donald Johnson joined the group their funk style became rather distinct. In any case, to me Tony and the boys seemed simpatico from the outset and he really took this band under his wing. His mind was always racing away, plotting an imaginary great future for them. He'd have a brain wave from some unlikely place – a chance remark, and then he'd hatch a scheme. Always making great plans. One of them was to get ACR to support Talking Heads, which, in late 1979, came to pass.

David Byrne really liked ACR (in fact Martin Moscrop claims that Talking Heads were much influenced by them afterwards), and apparently suggested to Tony that he produce them. In interview with Zero and Dickinson, Tony said, 'I said nice idea David, how nice. Then I thought what was great about that was they had a cheap studio in New York, and then I thought what a great buzz it would give them, because more than any band I know they're going to love it, New York is their town. I love New York and I wanted them to love New York, [which was] probably why they didn't, well they did but they had a hell of a time. So the idea settled in my brain – let's record Ratio's first album in New York 'cause the environment will react on them and it may react on the album. In fact the environment reacted on them enormously and it will react on their next album. In fact this first album is probably what they would have done in England anyway, although the next album won't be. But that's why we went out there. Also, because there's a recession and if you look around – like we went out to New Jersey – you can get cheap studio time.'

I don't know if it was on taking the advice of David Byrne, but, according to Bruce Mitchell, Tony did in fact produce an ACR track – indeed their biggest-selling track – 'Shack Up'. Bassist Jez Kerr, however, thinks it was Stuart Pickering at Graveyard Studios who was mainly responsible. Perhaps it was a joint effort? Moscrop noted that Tony was to all intents and purposes executive producer. I do vaguely remember being with Tony in the studio, with ACR and him playing around with the faders and a new mix – of something!

Joy Division returned to Cargo Studios in Rochdale to record one of their finest works, 'Atmosphere', at the end of 1979. The choice of studio was in the name of economy, since the Strawberry costs for *Unknown Pleasures* had been so high. Tony spoke of differing amounts of money in that regard – in one interview he says the album cost £20,000, in another £12,000. My own memory is that Tony inherited £15,000 from his mother and the whole lot got spent, and a bit more besides.

'Tony had some kind of deal going with the owner – John Brierley,' Barney recalled. 'I think there was some big conflab. I remember us recording "Atmosphere" there and all of a sudden this big row broke out in the studio. I think the problem was that John Brierley was supposed to be co-producing the record with Martin, and because of that we were getting a deal at the studio or something. The band didn't know anything about this and some big argument broke out and I don't think we worked at the studio after that.'

John Brierley, however, was at a loss to see where Barney's story came from. John told me: 'As I've said [before] there was never a deal between me and Tony/Factory, so the story Barney relates is odd to say the least. Martin was always the producer, I was the engineer and as such we got on very well together. When we recorded Joy Division, Martin would leave me to get the Joy Division sound. He would come into his own on the mixes, when he'd have all his effects units, delays and reverbs. Thinking back I could understand if there had been a row between Tony and Martin. We had mixed "Atmosphere" at Cargo and it sounded amazing, and Tony came round to listen to the final mix and he was just blown away by the track, as we all were. He once said that on the first time of hearing the final mix he was moved to tears and [it] was one of the highlights of his life. But I remember Martin wanting to do another mix at Strawberry and Tony vehemently disagreeing. I don't know why Martin wanted to do another mix, but that could have been what they argued about. As it happened Martin got his way and did another mix at Strawberry, which apparently wasn't as good and was never used. The one that made it to the release was the mix from Cargo, so Tony won in the end.'

Barney thought that Martin Hannett did his best work when the studio time was limited. He said, 'You'd end up with this basic almost monitor mix, but it was great and we often preferred that. "Atmosphere", for instance, which is my favourite mix of Martin's, sounds the way it does because of two things: 1) The tape machine in that studio was a sixteen-track valve tape machine, which was very rare and it gives you this big fat warm sound. With it being sixteen-track you're squeezing those sixteen tracks into two-inch tape, which is very good for the transience you get in drums so the drums sound really good on it. 2) Because of the argument with the owner of the studio, Martin only had about four hours to mix in and he did a great job.'

'Atmosphere' was released by a French independent label called Sordide Sentimental. Created by Jean-Pierre Turmel the year before, the label had already released another limited edition by Throbbing Gristle. Ian Curtis was friends with Throbbing Gristle's Genesis P-Orridge and the two shared an anti-commercial stance – art over money, in other words. It is ironic, perhaps, that this most anti-commercial, artistic release was limited to about 1,500 copies yet was one of the greatest songs by Joy Division, if not *the* greatest.

Terry Mason, who managed Joy Division before Rob Gretton and subsequently became their road manager, remembers the last time he saw Ian, days before his death, and Ian wanted to give Terry his copy of 'Atmosphere'. Terry only had a white-label copy. Rob curtailed Ian's typical generosity and advised him to keep hold of it.

I asked Tony, when researching the life of Ian, who he thought the boss of Joy Division was. I expected him to say Rob, but he said it was Ian. 'That's Peter's [Saville] point of view. He's got used to working with bands over the years and he says that when you offer artwork to a band, you pretty soon ascertain how the mechanics of that particular group work and there is always someone who makes the decision. He got used to the fact that it was Ian. He says, for example, that day when he presented those pictures of the graveyard in Italy [which later became the *Closer* sleeve and "Love Will Tear Us Apart" twelve-inch sleeve], Ian said he liked them and he caught Ian's eyes and thought, "Okay – so it's done." So very much the boss of the band in terms of the way a band works – it was Ian. But these things change in bands – if you think of the Beatles in the early sixties it was John Lennon's band and the Rolling Stones was Brian Jones's band, and yet by '66 the Beatles belonged to McCartney and the Stones belonged to Jagger, so it does change, but as long as they were Joy Division that was it.'

In the studio, of course, it appeared to be Martin who was the boss. But

Ian, unlike the others, didn't seem to have problems working with Martin. Ian's wife, Debbie, wrote how seriously impressed Ian was by Martin's work and that he came home enthusing about it all, such as the hand-clapping and glass-smashing samples. Ian wrote to a fan that '*Closer* is a disaster', but this would have been when he was depressed and perhaps taking stock of the words he had written – and meant. As Peter Saville noted, 'It is authenticity which is at the heart of the contract between Factory and their audience. That's why Ian's death is the fundamental act of authenticity in pop culture, and that's why it resonates still and generation after generation – the ones who care – have to know about Joy Division. It's in the canon of pop history. He underscored the song "Love Will Tear Us Apart" with his own life.'

I've often pondered the meaning of this song, the virtual anthem of Factory. After one of our pizza nights out, on 8 January 2005, I wrote the following about a mash-up Tony played me in the car, which never saw the light of day due to copyright issues, I believe:

> Driving along in Tony's Jag listening to the brilliant brainchild of Malcolm McLaren. The raw vocal of Captain and Tennille's 'Love Will Keep Us Together' alongside Ian's deep, powerful, naked voice reminding us that 'Love Will Tear Us Apart' (again). McLaren's music wasn't taken from either of the two tracks, but was written specifically for the 'duet'. I thought it was the best thing Tony has played in years and a radio hit. The song moved me privately, whatever the public might think. The reason – it seemed to give hope, to be optimistic even. It felt like a kind of message. That even torn apart we can be put back together. That none of us are lost or apart from love. That Ian was okay. It might be twenty-five years later but everything is fine now. I looked up and saw that we were in Macclesfield, within walking distance of the house where Ian lived and died.
>
> Looking at Tony after a turbulent twenty-nine years, mainly apart but together in that moment, I realised that perhaps the song gave hope there too.

Back in 1979, our moments of togetherness were becoming a rarity. That Christmas day was, like all the others Tony and I shared, subject to trouble. Tony always expected Christmas to be something really terrific. He approached it wide-eyed like a child, with his expectations running high. Of course we're all a bit guilty of that, and consequently the day itself can be disappointing. Expect nothing and you won't be disappointed, the saying goes. Tony could be imaginative with his gifts – although for our first Christmas together he bought me a washing machine (prior to that I was going out to the launderette). With time his gifts to me became musical. He saw me as an artist rather than a business partner, perhaps. One year he bought me a green melodica (the only instrument I could ever play was the recorder) and another year he bought me a synthesiser. It was a beautiful thought, but I ended up giving them both away to real musicians. I'm not sure where they finished up. But I believe that the melodica was the same one that ended up in Ian's hands (via Tony). There is a picture of it on the Joy Division Central website and if it's not the same one then it's an exact replica. New Order apparently threw it into the audience after they inherited it from Ian. It was used on 'Decades' and 'In a Lonely Place' – the two songs I'd put in my top three Joy Division list, along with 'Atmosphere'.

My attempts at playing instruments never bore fruit. I went to African drumming lessons with Peter Terrell from ACR one year (thinking that surely anyone can make progress with percussion). The reason I stopped was, after several months of regular attendance, I asked the teacher if he thought I was making progress. His reply, 'Musically, you are a virgin,' was apt and eloquent. No point flogging a dead horse.

As Tony's family were in short supply (only his father and father's boyfriend, Tony Connolly, remained of his immediate family), we generally shared the Christmas meal with my family. That year my sister pulled out all the stops for a great dinner, along with the magical ingredient provided by her new little boy, Ross, who had just turned two years old. Late afternoon, early evening, we got into Tony's 'hearse' to set off toward Eccles and visit his father. Before turning the car engine on Tony looked out through the windscreen and said rather ungratefully, 'Well *that* was boring.' I shouldn't have got so mad but I took it as an outright rejection of that shrinking arena wherein I could lay claim to anything dear to me. He'd already taken the control and monopoly of the world of music – that was *his* (and his cronies'). Whatever thoughts were shooting through my brain in that split second, however rude and uncalled for his remark, it didn't excuse my outright volatile reaction. Sitting in the passenger seat I kicked my right booted leg at his windscreen. A small crack appeared. Suddenly Tony wasn't bored, but doubtless would have preferred it to this. We drove in stony silence to Sydney's house. Once there we sat reading magazines and ignoring each other. As ever, Sydney tried to pour oil on troubled waters.

A good thing about Tony and me was that we never bore grudges (unless it was infidelity of course). We forgot about the row the next day, though generally found something new to fight about.

The only thing that really seemed to be working well was Joy Division. That was going from strength to strength. But at what cost? Tragedy was lying in wait just around the corner. Nineteen-eighty had barely begun before the first session for 'Love Will Tear Us Apart' was recorded.

I was unaware that Ian had become epileptic relatively recently. I knew he had fits but wrongly assumed this was something he'd been born with. In fact I didn't even know then that someone could *become* epileptic. It wasn't really until 2005, when I began researching the life of Ian for the book *Torn Apart*, that I really got to learn about him and the stresses he was under. His mother said he had never had a fit, or indeed any kind of ill health, until December 1978 when he was twenty-two. He had divided loyalties at the time, being pulled one way and another, which put him under great stress. Stress is a known trigger for epilepsy. The band were gaining momentum and Ian had the foresight to know where this was leading. Despite their growing success, the band were earning very little money as yet. At that point in time they were each receiving £35 per week. But in Macclesfield Ian had a wife who was then five months pregnant. He was yet to meet and fall in love with Annik Honoré. Those two first met in August 1979.

Joy Division had performed twenty-six gigs in 1978, but in 1979 there were sixty-six. So many late nights, on the road, drinking, Ian drumming himself up with his unusual dancing onstage. On top of that Ian was on medication for the epilepsy, which obviously had side effects and didn't mix well with this lifestyle. Little wonder that the fits didn't abate. In fact they escalated in both severity and frequency. Ian's baby daughter, Natalie, was born on 16 April 1979 but Ian was called away the very next day for a gig in London; a gig that was considered too important to cancel. Crazy. Awful.

All the work and creativity of 1979 led to a pinnacle musically in 1980. Yet the year became, paradoxically, a total nadir. It was black, black, Factory black. We hadn't got there yet, but we were getting closer.

Feeling a bit frustrated with Tony running Factory as a boys' club, it seemed a good idea when the suggestion of becoming involved with starting another one presented itself. As already mentioned, I was friendly with Eric Random along with the other Tiller Boys. Also, Tony and I hung out with Richard Boon, and I was friendly with Martin Hannett's partner, Susanne O'Hara – Tony and I visited the couple at their flat in Didsbury several times. The formation of a club somehow evolved amongst this group – Eric, Susanne, Richard and myself, along with others. I don't remember whose idea it was originally, but it was most likely Richard's. We were able to hold meetings at his New Hormones office and the club was christened – doubtless also by Richard – the Beach Club. This was more Situationist stuff, so it definitely wouldn't have been me that thought of it. That said, I loved the idea of a beach. The Situationist slogan reads: '*sous les pavés la plage*' (under the pavement the beach). Somewhat ironic, then, that the three-storey building that housed the club has now been demolished to make way for a car park. Eric Random did an awful lot for the club – arranging impromptu performances with rotating musicians from different bands and putting unusual or art-house films on. Susanne remembers that it was her job to collect the projector from the Film & Video Workshop. She recalled that the club screened cult film *Pink Flamingos*. Directed by John Waters, the movie featured drag actor Divine and controversial, shocking scenes.

Perhaps we were taking the model of Factory and adding value. I liked the idea of having a chill-out room in a club, somewhere to watch films, and also using film as a backdrop for musicians who were performing somewhat experimentally with one another.

So now I had more of my own club night, all I needed was more of my own man, because Tony had been off with someone or other for too long. If he wanted an open marriage then he could have one. So it was that one night at the Beach Club, a talented, slim, dark-haired musician named John Scott got chatting to me at the bar. Earlier there had been two cars heading from the Polytechnic to the Russell. He in one, me in the other. Our eyes met – a long look. At the bar it became proper flirting. We admitted we fancied each other. So that was that really.

John was off on tour playing sax with Manchester band the Smirks, and I went to Nottingham to watch them play. This group, like John, deserved success, but due to bad luck or bad timing, were not destined to find it. John's real talent was, and still is, for the guitar. But I always found the sax the sexiest of instruments. What the hell was it with me and musicians? Destructive or what? It reminds me of something Bruce Mitchell told me about Tony: 'The only time that Tony would stop and go quiet was if you talked about musician stories. A bit of musician gossip and he'd go quiet and be really interested. You'd be talking about people who weren't fit to lick his boots but he was fascinated in it. He was fascinated by musicians' company and by musicians. It was a weakness; he should have been an MP or something like that.' One more thing Tony and I shared; another of the same weaknesses.

I never attempted to hide this liaison from Tony. I suppose it might have fitted the category of 'revenge fucking', since I decided it was time that it wasn't just Tony who could be open about playing away. The trouble was that I was never entirely sure who he might have been sleeping with since he wouldn't tell me. He only claimed the right to do so whenever he wished. Not a good policy. Hence I suspected every female Tony saw. It was too painful. Since I wasn't hiding John I figured I didn't need to feel guilty about it. With hindsight it seems worse that I was so open. Earlier on Tony and I had seen John play with the Albertos. John tells me that Tony said to him quite nastily one night at the Russell Club, 'For some reason my wife seems to think you're talented.'

Actually, John was and still is an extremely gifted musician. To this day he commands respect for his musical skills, and yet he made little or no money. He was always broke. I identified with that somehow, we were both outside of the system, drop-outs, victims even, with unrecognised talent. I admired it more than someone who had effectively been able to buy his way into the music business and indulge spending money on boys, some of whom were much less talented in my opinion. Two could play at that game. I was lonely, probably more than I have ever felt while living alone, and John kept me company.

Tosh remembers how John's absences began to be noticed: 'We were all having chips one day and wondering to ourselves, "Where does he go at dinner time?" So we used to follow him. We saw him in the Red Lion sitting in the back room. Someone whispered, "He's with Wilson's wife. Do you think he's trying to get a deal? The bastard. He's kept that quiet."'

We spent most of our time in one pub or another. I suppose he was probably an alcoholic, although I didn't know it then. We'd spend hour upon hour laughing and joking, talking about daft trivia, and I loved it; I loved the fact that he didn't take himself seriously, wasn't on a mission, unlike Tony with Factory Records. Perhaps it was Factory that Tony took so seriously, rather than himself. Richard Madeley, who worked with Tony in the eighties and became a true friend of his, told me: 'It was Tony who taught me not to take myself remotely seriously. When all that early eighties Manchester "Tony Wilson is a Wanker" graffiti was in vogue, I once asked him why he was so relaxed about it.

'He looked me in the face and said, "Because I *am* a wanker! So are you! You're on the telly, right? You *want* to be on the telly, right? So that makes you a wanker – just like me!" He was 100 percent right.

'I will always miss him.'

Yes, I believe Tony did have true humility. Richard's story made me laugh and captured a beautiful quality Tony had – or certainly learned – the ability to take the piss out of himself and make it funny. But back then all I could see was an egotist who reeked of self-importance, while I mattered not, except as an extension of his ego. I enjoyed spending time with John because neither of us mattered.

Ironically, John was involved with Absurd Records at the time, a latter day offshoot of Rabid Records. He played with the Prime Time Suckers, who performed freeform music. Tosh made up the name, possibly inspired by the 1976 film *Network*, which put him in mind of Tony: 'In the film *24 Hour Party People*, when Tony sees God and says, "He was just like me," it's like in the film *Network*, where the TV presenter played by actor Peter Finch is cracking up, and God appears to him and says he must go back and carry on. He asks, "Why me?" "Because you're on TV, dummy," says God. I thought to myself: how can Tony's company be successful with so many crap bands? Because he's on TV, dummy.'

Also ironic was John Scott's involvement in a record that gained cult status within Manchester at the close of the seventies. Using the name Gerry and the Holograms, John and C.P. Lee released their eponymously titled single on Absurd Records. Never intended for mass-consumption, the single was nonetheless frequently played by DJs working the club and gig circuit in the city. Although the song's exposure was brief, many remarked that its basic riff was later reflected in New Order's huge-selling 1983 single 'Blue Monday'. This link would be further strengthened in 2009 when the mischievous FUC 59 blog site hosted a mash-up of 'Gerry and the Holograms' 'Blue Monday' and Kylie Minogue's 'Can't Get You Out of My Head'.

The hours John and I spent together couldn't continue, of course. It could never have been more than an affair. He had a girlfriend and that felt totally wrong, as well as my own situation. Tony and I needed to split or both of us needed to stop messing around.

John left for New York later that year. When we said goodbye it was kind of sad but sweet – I can still remember his parting words to me. It was obvious, though, that this had to be the end for us.

It was at this point that Tony and I were finally able to put the revenge-fucking wars behind us. We both put it to bed, as it were. But so very much damage had been done. Both idealists in love and romance, both disappointed. Marriage and romance are two different stories. I think it's nearly impossible to have both at the same time. Uncertainty drives passion, and on some level that was probably what we both desired.

It's a remarkable thing, but there is always something new to learn – about anything or anyone. I realised along the way that I'd never totally understood Situationism, or how significant it was to how Tony ran his business and his life. Perhaps it was my insecurity, but Tony made me feel that it was all very intellectual, that you'd have to be as clever as him to figure it out. Perhaps Tony ought to have remembered a Situationist wall-phrase: 'A man is not stupid or intelligent: he is free or he is not.' One of the times I interviewed Tony more recently I asked him if he could tell me in a nutshell what Situationism is:

TW: I don't think you can say. Love thy neighbour as thyself.
LR: That's Christianity.
TW: It's like anarchism – the destructive urge is the creative urge, pull everything down, freedom.
LR: This sounds like punk?
TW: Well, it became punk because Malcolm McLaren, Vivienne Westwood, Jamie Reed and Fred Vermorel, who shared a flat together, were massive fans of it like I was. All I was was a fan.
LR: So these were the roots of punk do you think?
TW: Well, it was because punk was meant to be a massive practical joke on the system. They were very into practical jokes. The idea of punk was to create the Bay City Rollers of Outrage. To have a group who would be Number One just because they were disgusting. That was Malcolm's idea. Of course he failed completely. Because they were Number One because they were fucking wonderful.
LR: Do you think he was almost a creator of punk then?
TW: Yes. He thinks he was. I think he was as well, but I think it was going

to happen anyway. It was a move that was coming and in the end, whatever you do, you need the great artists, and John Lydon was a great artist.

Needless to say I was still slightly baffled. Anarchism, the destructive urge, love thy neighbour as thyself? I suppose the first Durutti Column album, *The Return of the Durutti Column*, with its sandpaper sleeve, now makes sense; something to damage all of your other records. Nathan McGough told me that the first Sex Pistols album cover was originally going to be made of sandpaper. Tony and Malcolm McLaren discussed this at their first meeting.

He went on: 'Tony later wanted the Durutti Column album to be in a metal box. As it turned out, years down the line, they reversed. Malcolm never did the sandpaper sleeve because Virgin wouldn't do it. The whole idea being that it would destroy all the other sleeves in your collection. So Tony stole it for Durutti Column. So this beautiful, celestial guitar music was put out in a fucking sandpaper sleeve. And the poor women at the factory were saying, "We can't make enough of these because everyone's hands are bleeding." And then obviously it wasn't Malcolm but Public Image Ltd [who] went on to do the *Metal Box* album.'

Joy Division spent a day at Alan's flat gluing these sleeves together, and were rewarded for their labours with £5 each (not paid until several months later) and a porn video shown on Alan's new, state-of-the-art top-loader VCR. When Tony called round after work and found most of them on the sofa with the video on and white glue everywhere, he always joked that it would have made a good scene in a film.

While listening to an interview that Bob Dickinson carried out with Tony in 1985, I was reminded of how Tony set off on this romantic journey in the first place. For, romantic as the Situationists were, Tony was more so.

During Tony's first year at Cambridge, he'd gone to London on the weekend in October 1968 when student protests against the war in Vietnam led to the occupation of the LSE. Tony was more in tune with pacifist John Lennon than street fighter Mick Jagger, who was present at the Grosvenor Square riots that occurred the day after a big march. Tony elected to go to Hyde Park rather than the square. At that time Tony regarded himself as a typical socialist kid, basically unaware of anarchy. All this was about to change when he met, at Jesus College, John and Paul. No, not the Beatles. They were Paul Sieveking and John Fullerton, who together produced the first English translation of Raoul Vaneigem's *The Revolution of Everyday Life*, one of the most important works written by members of the Situationist International.

Thus led into it by John and Paul, Tony became fascinated by the Situationist philosophy, particularly by the cultural end of things.

Paul Sieveking can recall the enthusiasm he, John and Tony shared at Cambridge when reading *Totality for Kids* and *Ten Days that Shook the University*. Paul also helped Chris Gray to assemble the Situationist translations that were published as *Leaving the 20th Century: The Incomplete Work of the Situationist International*. This book, with graphics by Jamie Reid, had a decisive influence on Malcolm McLaren and the general punk scene.

Ah, Jamie Reid, how could I forget him? He came to stay at our house. Tony was absolutely in awe of him and I couldn't understand why. After he left I discovered that he'd just about emptied every single bottle of spirits we had (we kept brandy, whisky, vodka etc in the office) and re-filled them with water – or tea, depending on which bottle it was – so we wouldn't notice. I couldn't understand why he didn't just drink the frigging lot and admit it! He was all right really though, and you've got to forgive the man who designed the cover for *Never Mind the Bollocks, Here's the Sex Pistols*, and the 'God Save the Queen' jubilee portrait with a safety pin through the Queen's nose. Jamie was also politically involved in 1968 and organised an occupation of Croyden Art College along with Malcolm McLaren. I believe the two of them were members of a Situationist split-off group known as King Mob, who took part in stunts such as giving away toys to passing kids in Selfridges, or scrawling clever graffiti around London. King Mob participated in the anti-Vietnam War protest in London – culminating outside the US Embassy in Grosvenor Square – under a banner drawn from William Burroughs that proclaimed: 'Storm the reality studio and retake the universe.'

King Mob had dispersed by 1970, and two years later Guy Debord (the French theorist who founded the S.I. in 1957 along with Belgian philosopher Raoul Vaneigem) dissolved the Situationist International.

Funnily enough, Nathan McGough recalled an almost identical story to that related above when Jamie came to stay with Tony at Old Broadway in Didsbury. Nathan was staying there at the time. 'Jamie said he wouldn't stay long,' Nathan explained, 'he'd just split up with Margi [Clarke] in Paris. He said he wanted to design a mural for the Hacienda and Tony thought that was fucking fantastic. He's iconic and he's going to design a big mural for a wall of the club. Jamie just sat on the sofa all day long, and he designs this mural and it's a fucking rainbow-coloured unicorn. Me and Tony are going like – he's having a laugh. You're joking right? This guy designed "Pretty Vacant" sleeve, his artwork is iconic and now he's drawing rainbow-coloured unicorns. Tony couldn't confront him and say this is a load of bullshit, there's no way we're having a rainbow-coloured unicorn in our fabulous New York-styled nightclub designed by Ben Kelly. After about eight or nine days I said to Tony, "He's got to go," and Tony says, "Yeah, I know but I can't tell him," so I sat him down and told him myself. I said, "Listen mate you need to clear off, you've been here too long and that mural's never going to get painted." I gave him money for a train fare and he went. Tony got home and I tell him Jamie's gone and he says, "Thank fuck for that, shall we have a drink?" So we get a bottle of whisky out and pour it and it's tea. Brandy – tea; vodka and sambuca – it's water. He had gone through a fairly extensive drinks cabinet and drunk it dry.'

During Tony's two-year sojourn in London once he'd finished at Cambridge, he recalled visiting Paul Sieveking in squats in Haverstock Hill. He also remembered going to a meeting of the S.I. in London after deciding to join a radical far-left group, but he was so disgusted by this bureaucratic evening that he ran a mile. He told Dickinson he loved the Situationist phrase, 'Unless you live the revolution every day you have a dead corpse in your mouth.' I looked this up and noted that graffiti of the time read: 'Those who talk about revolution and class struggle without referring to everyday reality have a corpse in their mouth.'

In 1979 Tony decided to embark on another Factory sample, but this time it featured quirky, and perhaps rather self-indulgent, releases of his own making. It is easier to appreciate the content of this release by first understanding his romantic political ideals. Buoyed by the success of the original *Factory Sample*, Tony perhaps rather overestimated his ability for spotting musical talent. Despite a veritable niche for writing – for example, he singlehandedly wrote and typed out Factory's press releases at the table in our living room before he went out to work – in truth I think he had slightly cloth ears. He was more of a maverick of art appreciation, revolution and generally annoying people! Sometimes he managed to do this just by presenting them with something they didn't quite understand. In terms of music Tony believed in rebellion more than aesthetics. He saw the best rock'n'roll as a generation of people making a stand against the authority of their parents and society in general. Hence he called good pop music 'oedipal'. (Oedipus killed his father – mind you, he also fell in love with his mother.) I felt that this was a bit of an uncultured view – almost a yobbish stance. To me good music is timeless and goes beyond rebellion. It's more about love and beauty than a lad's culture. But, all the same, I liked Tony's political views, and since the music was supposed to be anti-commercial it hardly mattered if it was a bit weird.

Consequently this sampler, entitled *A Factory Quartet*, featured some rather second-rate musical material but still managed to retain an extraordinary appeal. Amongst the assorted oddities were the Royal Family & the Poor. Tony enthused madly about them, claiming that Factory now had the only Situationist band in the country. He thought they were stunning, mainly because of Arthur, the rather weird and shabby singer from Newcastle, who valiantly stated that 'all politics is fascism'. Tony told Zero and Dickinson in 1980: 'They played at the Beach Club and Arthur sat in the van. I went outside and took a photograph of him, sitting in the van smiling, 'cause the whole sleeve is done on Polaroids. Wonderful. You too can be John Wayne. My favourite line is: "When it's no longer an advert for the system, all they can do is send in the police." He's very good. He keeps sending vicious letters saying, "Can I have £800 please? You can afford it."'

Personally I couldn't see much mileage in the group but, romantically inspired and led by the Situationist ideal as Tony was, he saw young Arthur as a new inspiration and ipso facto a rising star.

Another off-the-wall debut was made by Blurt, featuring Ted Milton, who hailed from Stroud. Ted was a puppeteer touring with Mr Pugh's Velvet Glove Puppet Theatre – a bit like an anarchic Punch and Judy show – who had appeared on an early edition of *So It Goes* in July 1976. He went on to form the band, Blurt, a trio that included his brother. Ted was the lead saxophonist, and the music was as strange as his puppetry. The nearest comparison I can think of would be Captain Beefheart, although I was more of a fan of Captain Beefheart. (In fact, I once persuaded Tony Connolly to go onstage at the Apollo and give the Captain a flower I was holding. He actually managed it before being thrown off.) I liked Ted as a person, he was unusual – obviously – and clever and funny. He came to stay at our house a few times. One night Tony and I had got into bed when we suddenly heard Ted from the spare room laughing his head off. I thought he must be crazy – to laugh so loudly by himself! But if amusing yourself with your own thoughts is a definition of crazy, it's a pity there aren't more of us around.

Ted became frustrated by the delay between recording this material and its release and, according to his website, went on to record with Armageddon Records after Tony failed to see the humour in Ted's comparison of Factory Records with lifestyle-chain Habitat. It's also likely that Ted failed to be impressed with Tony's ad-hoc method of mechanical royalty accounting. Surprisingly to me, Blurt have enjoyed longevity, recording many albums and still touring today.

The other two contributions on *A Factory Quartet* were from the Durutti Column and Kevin Hewick. Tony chose Hewick's contribution based upon a support slot that Hewick played for a Roy Harper gig that was already running ninety minutes late when he unwisely took the stage. The audience were understandably totally hostile towards him, and he snapped and made some unfortunate comments. As he took his leave a girl came towards him to say, 'I thought you were crap!'

> '**When Ian died it felt like you'd had a limb severed off.**
> **You couldn't get away from that.**'
> **Bernard Sumner**

Nineteen-eighty was the year that John Lennon died. And young Les Prior. Les had added so much to the Albertos and their stage comedy *Sleak* but became ill with Hodgkin's disease – cancer of the lymphatic glands. That was the first Tony and I knew of a young person's death. We visited him in his last weeks and I was impressed that he seemingly had two girlfriends looking after him. Very open and modern, I thought, for the two girls to work together as a team. I admired Les and the fact that he took a copious quantity of LSD when he found out he only had a year left to live, as described by C.P. Lee in his book *When We Were Thin*. At the end of a gruelling trip, Les said he'd 'got it all sorted', and, having faced up to the process of dying, was then able to announce, 'Now we can get on with living!' It also puts me in mind of something Aldous Huxley said, when speaking about heroin, which I have never taken, but it could equally be said of LSD: 'Who lives longer: the man who takes heroin for two years and dies, or the man who lives on roast beef, water, and potatoes till ninety-five? One passes his twenty-four months in eternity. All the years of the beef-eater are lived only in time.'

Les had requested that everyone get drunk at his funeral that January, or so I heard. I obliged. It was a magical day – bright sunshine and crisp snow, and I remember Tosh metaphorically breaking the ice by making a funny joke to Tony about the money he owed him (or perhaps it was true, but it seemed funny). I admired Tosh for that – he got my attention that day. He'd been much closer to Les than we had but was carrying on with the humour regardless, and I thought it honoured Les's spirit better than our long faces. Just because a life is cut short it doesn't mean that it wasn't a happy life worth remembering in a happy way. That's what Ian Curtis's mum, Doreen, thinks.

Oh, the tragedy of Ian.

It still pains me to look back at that terrible time. His nearest and dearest will never recover from it. I wasn't so close to him as I was inimical to Tony and to Factory. Factory suddenly seemed all wrong. I felt that it could never be any good again.

I reached an impasse at this point of the book because I didn't want to have to go over it all again – Ian's death, the events leading up to it – but nor could I leave it out. So much has already been said. Myself and Mick Middles have covered it once already in great detail in the book *Torn Apart*, so it would be a bit much to labour over it all again. Not only that, but since the book there has been a film about it, Anton Corbijn's *Control*. Enough already! What follows, therefore, is more in the way of a summary.

The Lindsay-Tony saga was on a bit more of an even keel as 1980 opened, now that there were no extramarital affairs going on. Mind you, I was still never entirely sure about Tony and it took me many years to discover how skilled he was at telling white lies. But infidelity – that's a black lie, no? Or perhaps not, depending on your point of view, and so many other factors.

During March 1980, Joy Division went down to Britannia Row Studios in London to record the album *Closer* betwixt and between too many ongoing gigs. I visited the studio with Tony and felt an entirely different vibe from the Strawberry days of their last album. The band seemed more visible for one thing. Despite that Martin seemed quite chuffed with himself and in good spirits. He had chosen the studio, having established who was really in charge and, ostensibly, all was going well. I suspect that Martin no longer had to fight for his leadership, as he'd had to at Strawberry. He didn't have to resort to exclaiming 'fuck off you retards' because he'd earned the group's respect for his work. The studio itself didn't feel as cosy, even if London could be described as groovier than Stockport. Strawberry had a womblike warmth about it but Britannia Row reminded me of a school or municipal building, except when in the studio itself.

Martin's partner Susanne described Joy Division as 'intense, shielded and defensive. Now I see they were on a mission. They were very determined young men, especially Bernard, determined to do well. I was often at the studio – and they never spoke to me.'

Ian had said that he needed a break; he'd said he was ill. There had been a meeting at Rob's house and they'd all agreed to stop for a year. But then Ian would change his mind and say the opposite. Then he'd say he wanted to leave the band but change his mind again the next day. I didn't know any of this at the time. I never saw him have a fit either.

And then the dreadful Easter Sunday, 6 April, when Ian took an overdose, totally out of the blue. He'd called for Debbie's help in the middle of it, and that led us all to think he didn't mean it. Though with hindsight I – and others – think he was worried it might not work properly, that he might go on living and be paralysed or brain-dead or something. I had no idea Ian was even depressed. Neither did his mother for that matter. I remember driving to Macclesfield to visit him in hospital with Tony and Rob and Alan, and listening to Martin's mixes of the album for the first time on a cassette. The music made us all feel optimistic. It sounded exquisitely beautiful. I felt proud to be associated with the company that had helped to produce this. I couldn't believe that anyone could make something so lovely and not wish to live. He hadn't meant to die, we thought, but none of us were listening to the words properly. If we had, we might have understood that he was more serious about it.

I made a card for Ian and quoted David Hare: 'There is no comfort, our lives dismay us. We have dreams of leaving and it's the same for everyone I know.'

I wanted him to know he wasn't alone. Heavens, I'd thought about suicide several times. I just thought that was normal. Ian's line about the plea for anaesthesia was a given. We all understood the desire to get out of it.

In *Joy Division: Piece by Piece*, Paul Morley noted a story circulating about Tony's visit to Ian's bedside: 'Tony allegedly joking, laying on the mocking blackness with typical jolliness, that if Ian wanted to be a rock casualty he had better make a better job of slashing/overdosing/suffocating/jumping/shooting/drowning next time.' I wasn't at the bedside since I remained at the house in Barton Street babysitting little Natalie, though the story sounds humorous and quite likely.

It was an easy mistake to assume from Ian's lyric (one of the few we were then aware of) that his attempt must be a cry for help as well as a wish to be unconscious. Hence my instinct was to offer it. Ian seemed to be torn between his wife and child and new love, so I thought it might be a good idea if he had a break from it all for a bit. I suggested that he stay with Tony and me, and was surprised when he accepted (thinking he must surely have had other, better boltholes than ours). He probably had no idea that things were not exactly stable at our house either.

The plan was that Ian would come back to Charlesworth with us after the night of the Bury gig on 8 April. Why that gig wasn't cancelled I do not know. We were all young and stupid. Tony suggested substituting a Factory medley for Ian's performance. People still talk about that night as if it was great. That's Tony's myth-making for you. He thought a riot was a good sign. It actually meant that people weren't about to be fobbed off and could tell the difference between Ian Curtis and Simon Topping, could discriminate between Joy Division and assorted members of ACR, Section 25 and Crispy Ambulance. Did Tony think that Bury people were stupid? A bit of explanation to the audience concerning Ian's ill health at the outset might have gone a long way.

Ian did valiantly come onstage for five or ten minutes, but that may have frustrated the crowd even more after he walked off and left Simon Topping in his place, along with Alan Hempsall and Larry Cassidy.

I witnessed the pint pot being thrown towards the stage. I didn't think it was so bad – it was understandable even. After all, these people were being cheated and, with no clear understanding of why Ian had gone, were bound to be frustrated. Also, it was expressive, like punk. But the second the missile got lobbed all hell broke loose. I clearly saw the expression on Rob's face since he was standing on a raised platform to the side of the stage. He looked like he was going to kill someone, as he literally dived into the crowd to clobber the hell out of the offender.

Twinny, a roadie for Joy Division, then jumped in to save Rob, but his reward for that was to be struck on his head with another glass. Terry Mason, tour manager and roadie, then jumped in to help Twinny and lashed out with a mike stand.

I just stood and watched these boys battle, and thought it all a bit unnecessary really. It was a bit like being at a football match. Twinny had gashes to his head, so I drove him to hospital. Sitting in the waiting room while he had his stitches put in, I was amused to see a few other wounded parties wander in. They didn't know where I'd been but I knew where they had. A couple of them sat near me and I heard them talking about it all. One of them could have been the one that kicked the whole thing off. He said he thought he'd be damned if he was going to listen to that A Certain Ratio again – he'd only seen them a couple of weeks ago and he thought they were rubbish. (Although, in point of fact, Simon was the only member of ACR present.)

Afterwards Tony tried to console Ian, who he found sitting with his head in his hands, visibly shaken by what had occurred and blaming himself. Tony reminded Ian about the famous Lou Reed gig when a riot ensued after Reed wouldn't come back onstage following a rather shortened and ice-cold set. So Tony saw Bury as a major and exciting event. Well, I was there and to me it wasn't. But there you have an essential difference between the two of us. He saw the glass as half-full; I saw it as half-empty or even shattered. Whose vision was best? Tony's of course.

I had no idea how serious Ian's depression was, or that I would be catapulted out of my depth within a few days of his stay.

In interview with Tony I asked him, 'Did you realise how depressed Ian was when he stayed at our house?'

'Nope,' he replied. 'I think I just thought that the quietness had got more serious.'

The quietness, yes. Ian barely spoke and never moved from his spot on the floor with his feet under the low table, ashtray at hand and constantly in use. He never complained, though, and answered when I addressed him. I remember him opening a conversation only twice the whole time. Tony Connolly called

Above: The Electric Circus, August 1977.
Below: Pete Shelley, Howard Devoto and Tony at Granada, early 1977.

Above: Two Johns jamming – Scott and Cooper Clarke, 1978.
Below: A Certain Ratio meet the Durutti Column, 1979.

Above left: Martin Hannett in his natural home – Strawberry Studios
(or just about any studio, for that matter), 1979. **Above right:** Left to right:
Karen, Francis, me, Eric Random and Pete Shelley. **Below:** Alan Erasmus
brews up at 86 Palatine Road, 1979.

Above: The ideas man in action – Tony in his makeshift office at Alan's flat, 1979. **Below:** Peter Saville gets creative, 1979.

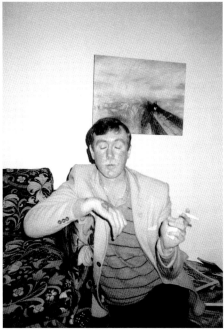
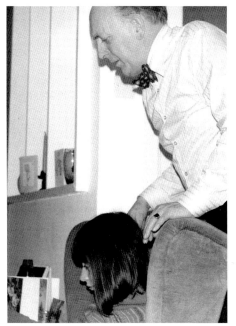

Above left and right: Sydney and his partner Tony Connolly,
both photographed at Charlesworth in 1979. **Below left:** Sydney
observes the aftermath of mine and Tony's row, Christmas 1979.
Below right: 45 Town Lane sales brochure, with Karmann Ghia, 1980.

Above and below: Tony and I photographed by Vini Reilly in 1980.
Vini told us to smile for the second shot. We were on the edge of
a break-up; the doors of 'the hearse' are just visible.

Above left: Tony does the washing up at Old Broadway, 1981.
Above right: Susanne O'Hara and Martin Hannett in a photo booth, 1980.
Below: Rob Gretton shows who's tops, 1979.

Above: Vini Reilly and I planning to get along very well (without you)
– by making a record together, 1982. **Below:** Tony and Alan at
the Factory office (86 Palatine Road), 1983.

round at one point and, while Ian was out buying more cigarettes, Connolly told me that he thought Ian was seriously depressed and even predicted his suicide. I was a bit alarmed, but Connolly was always being doomy and talking about death. I told Tony about it later and he put my mind at rest. 'Connolly is a nutter,' he used to say.

Tony was intensely busy that particular week with *World in Action* amongst other things, and was away overnight in London at one point. Working for this programme was a dream come true for Tony and he was entirely absorbed by it. All visitors and friends of Ian were banished (not by me, I hasten to add – I would have welcomed it). Peace and quiet had been ordered by Rob and Tony. I think Connolly was the only one to flout the ban in the entire week, and he didn't stay long. So for hour upon hour it was just Ian and me. It began to wear me down. I seemed to be fighting a losing battle. Nothing got through to cheer him; if he could only enjoy something as simple as a meal, but he ate mechanically. The closest I got to him was the night Tony was away in London and, as the evening wore on, he opened up more and we talked a bit together. He told me how strange he felt at the Bury gig, watching the others performing without him. Although standing in the wings, he said he felt as if he was looking down on it and it was all just carrying on without him. He said this with expression and amazement in his voice. How prophetic his words later seemed.

He also told me that he had known before he got married that he would love someone other than Debbie. The intuition came to him strongly on the morning of the wedding day. He said he didn't want to go through with the ceremony – because he couldn't honestly make those vows knowing what he then knew – and almost didn't get in the car when it came to collect him.

I hypnotised him that night. I'd recently been taking lessons with the Hypnotist Society. He was amazingly amenable. He went straight under and I was a bit shocked that the techniques had worked. All I could think to ask him was how he felt and he replied, 'Confused.' It's odd that Barney hypnotised him shortly after this. He cleverly took it a step further than I had and regressed Ian back to childhood, then further back to another life in which he was weighed down with study and books.

It was clear, though, that nothing was really helping Ian. I couldn't reach him, he just wasn't responding. I didn't know it then, but I now suspect that he didn't want help. Vini Reilly had a chat with Ian on the phone that week and apparently Ian told him that he really meant it (the suicide attempt), that it wasn't a cry for help, he wanted out.

By the end of an intense week with Ian I felt suicidally depressed. I told Tony Ian hadn't lifted a finger, not even moved so much as a single cup, and that I felt like committing suicide myself and why wasn't anyone doing anything? It was as if they all thought it was just a bit of 'bird' trouble and therefore couldn't be too serious. In my case it *was* a cry for help – Ian and I needed

Tony's support, but as usual it all came out wrong (i.e. blame) and degenerated into a row in the kitchen. He took Ian out then despite my begging them to stay, and Ian later related a story to someone that I threw myself in front of the departing car. Much to my surprise they came back quite soon and Tony said it was best he took me out instead. He left Ian with a bookmarked book to read – the collected poems of W.B. Yeats – and a pile of records, including Jimi Hendrix, for him to listen to. Having been with Ian all week I didn't think he'd bother with any of it. He seemed not to have any interest in anything except cigarettes.

I think it was the next day when Ian left. I tried to stop him, but I knew I'd lost him after the row with Tony.

For the next five weeks Ian stayed mostly away from the house he'd shared with Debbie and lived either at Barney's house or his parents'. His letters declared an undying love for Annik. The laddish mentality of Rob and the group took more of a dim view of it – as if it was just an affair, a bit on the side. In fact the two lovers hadn't even consummated their love.

After a phone call from Debbie, Annik tried to break it off with Ian again. She felt he'd lied when he'd told her it was all over with Debbie and steadfastly did not want to intrude on his life. Ian wrote to Annik: 'Please do not think you are a pressure on me. I would die if I didn't speak or hear from you. Everyone seems to have everything wrong and they've been told so many times before. I have no choice to make. Everything was coming to an end at home and the only thing was when it would actually end and whether I should go before. As it is things have now finished and that worry is gone. These problems were around long before I met you, everyone knows but seem[s] to want to make an issue over them by looking completely out of perspective instead of finally putting it to rest.'

Ian's depression seemed not to be so severe as his death drew nearer. His mum said he seemed okay. There is a theory that the act of suicide requires an effort of will that cannot be raised in the extreme troughs of depression and therefore generally takes place when the depression has lifted slightly. Ian's letters indicated that he was planning a future with Annik as soon as the group got back from their US tour. But on the day of his death he received a letter from Debbie's solicitor concerning divorce proceedings. Of course this wasn't just about him and Debbie; there was his baby girl to consider. He went back to Macclesfield, telling his mother he needed to see Natalie and to sort things out with Debbie before leaving for America. But he never saw his daughter again.

Asne Seierstad writes in *The Bookseller of Kabul* that women's longing for love is taboo in Afghanistan. She quotes the Afghan poet Majrouh, who wrote that the women 'protest with suicide and song', and says that the poems or rhymes of their songs live on.

We drove with Annik Honoré to visit Ian in the morgue. Tony and I went in together. I was aware of a strange, almost sweet smell as I was standing by Ian's body, and without realising the origin of it made an unconscious association between that smell and Ian's death. I even wondered if that was how dead bodies smelled. A day or two later I noticed a lavender tree near our house and the smell was so close that every single year since, when I see lavender in bloom, I have remembered the anniversary of Ian's death. Oddly, nearly thirty years later I found out where the smell came from. I was talking to Susanne O'Hara and she said, 'Martin asked me to call up Interflora in Kings Street. He wanted a wreath made of lavender, it was quite substantial, it must have been over two-foot wide. It was beautiful, purple not white, and we put it in the back of the Volvo before taking it to the Chapel of Rest. I didn't realise then the significance of it.' Martin, like Ian and Tony, was a fan of T.S. Eliot, and Susanne pointed me toward the opening lines of *The Waste Land*:

April is the cruellest month, breeding
Lilacs out of the dead land, mixing
Memory and desire, stirring
Dull roots with spring rain.

Annik's heartbreak was palpable. She wanted to go to the funeral, but says, 'The deal was that I was only allowed to see him in the chapel if I agreed not to go to the funeral. Apparently Debbie thought I would make a scene. How stupid to have thought that. But in a way I can understand she did not want me there. On a trip to Macclesfield a few months or a year later, I went to the cemetery and visited the place where he was cremated.'

The word I got filtering back from 'the family' was that 'Factory people' also weren't welcome at the funeral (although the band attended), so we held a wake at 86 Palatine Road instead. I'd assumed then that 'the family' were Ian's parents. I couldn't say I blamed them. It wasn't until I met Ian's mum nearly thirty years later that she told me they would have been happy for everyone to attend, and couldn't understand why so few of us were there.

Annik didn't attend our wake. I wept for the greater part it. Just as Ian's depression had got to me after a week, now Annik's sorrow seemed to have taken hold of me. (She stayed, coincidentally, for the same number of nights that Ian had.) Also, I was full of guilt. I think that's just how it is when someone commits suicide. Barney said, 'With something as drastic as that, someone hanging themselves, you all think was I in some way involved? You know – was it 'cause I took the piss out of him the other day? You always blame yourself.'

In *24 Hour Party People* Shirley Henderson (in the role of Lindsay Wilson) leaves Tony and Manchester after Ian's death, and as Tony is driving her to Piccadilly Station she makes a remark about the 'bad energy' that prevails. When I saw this scene I took umbrage a bit, because Ian's death had nothing to do with my leaving Tony (and nor did it happen that year). And yet Frank Cottrell Boyce, the lovely man who wrote the screenplay, pitched my character quite well.

If I had been Tony, if I had been in Joy Division, I couldn't have gone on with it. It was all tainted. Nothing to do with Factory seemed worth it anymore. The beauty of it all had turned to ugliness. Even Joy Division's music. Before it had seemed exquisite, like looking at a divinely coloured butterfly – everything from the sounds to Saville's wonderful packaging, all seemed perfectly formed. But now it was like looking at the same creature under a microscope – and it had turned into a monster with the most hideous features imaginable. This particularly applied to the album *Closer*.

With the aftermath comes analysis. Why did he do it? Actually, at the time I didn't dwell on that because it took so long just to accept it. With the passage of time, and when I researched his life much later on, it was easier to take a more reasoned view. Pointless and bloody stupid, I know, but part of me then blamed Tony, blamed Factory, blamed the band, blamed the music and especially blamed myself. Debbie and Annik both had my sympathy with no blame attached whatsoever. Even more so Ian's mother, father, sister, and Natalie.

Visiting Ian's body in the morgue, Tony and I went into the room together. He gently chided Ian. 'You daft bugger,' he said. It was genuine, as if Ian was there, but it sounded a bit like saying 'silly you' to someone who'd played with matches and burned the house down. To me it was devastating and, if Factory was the house, then it had been utterly destroyed. Tony was, as I've said many times, indomitable, and able to move on positively from any destruction. 'Everything is broken, everything is reparable,' he used to say. But of course this just wasn't. He did himself later wonder why they didn't just give up at that point. But no sooner had Tony pondered a negative than he leapt onto a positive. 'Maybe we should have, but I'm glad we didn't.'

Tony took writer Paul Morley to the morgue because he said he knew that one day Paul would have to write the story. Yet again Tony had that talent for recognising the special qualities of others. There are good writers and there are great writers, and I think Morley falls into the latter category. I never thought all that much of music journalists then – I mean, who wants to dissect music when it's for listening to? But when I read Morley's *Nothing* (after Tony told me how great it was) I saw how much he went beyond being a journalist. It's a long while since I read it, but I remember thinking at the time that if I had written it I could die happy as far as fulfilling any desire to be an author went. The book is an insightful and personal view of Morley's past, his growing up in – and desire to escape from – Stockport, and an honest exploration of the impact on him of his father's suicide, pop music, Marc Bolan and the death of Ian Curtis amongst myriad other events. I think that part of being a great writer is the ability to observe and empathise with others, being genuinely interested in *them*, not so much in oneself. Maybe that develops with maturity, but people like Morley seem born with an acute observing eye. As with everything though, practice helps.

This is how an interview I had with Morley began:

LR: You wrote in *Nothing* about visiting the morgue but you didn't actually go in, did you?

PM: I did go in, I did see the body, yes.

LR: At the end of the book you say you didn't.

PM: No, because in a way what I did was replace Ian with my dad, who I didn't see, so it was just a metaphorical thing almost, as if I'd recreated now enough of my father. I never saw my dad's body. At the end of the book I am willing myself to believe that I'd seen my father's body – but I hadn't. I remember getting the train on my own to Macclesfield. Tony was stood outside the church. He was on his own.

LR: Tony must have gone three times in that case. He went with me, then ACR and then you.

PM: He was doing day trips, wasn't he, he was selling tickets. I just remember it was Tony, I was very uncomfortable and I took some flowers and I remember Tony looked at what I'd written on the card and I was really embarrassed because I hadn't done anything special. I think it was just 'missing you' or something, but you know Tony, he was looking for some quote from Dostoevsky or something magnificent. Even though I got the feeling I've done in hindsight, that somehow he was plotting the myth even then and wanting material. It just seemed a very odd situation.

Looking back at the rapid formation of New Order, in the wake of Ian's death, following the odd thwarted attempt to bring in an outside singer, Tony observed: 'You also have to realise how clever Joy Division's manager Rob Gretton was, waiting six months to see what happened before bringing in the girlfriend and not disrupting the family.' Gillian Gilbert was Stephen Morris's girlfriend and assumed the role of keyboard player once the group finally settled on Barney as the singer.

The renamed New Order played their first gig at the Beach Club – sans Gillian as yet – and it seemed more of a tribute to Ian's memory than a gig somehow. But they soldiered on. Although, as Barney said, 'It was very difficult for us as a group to pick up the pieces and reinstate ourselves. It was excruciatingly difficult. We didn't have a clue how to do that. So we really needed help in the studio at that time.' Barney is referring to the group's first album, *Movement*. He continued: 'We didn't get it [help] from Martin. At the time I thought his heart wasn't in it – what we were doing – but looking back on it I think he was pretty screwed up by Ian's death really. He was never the same again.'

I'm convinced that this was where Rob particularly came into his own. He had an indomitable spirit as well. He was a fighter, as already demonstrated. He was determined and propelled the heartbroken lads into continued action. He told them at the wake that Joy Division would be huge in ten years' time. Perhaps, like Ian, he had foreknowledge. Rob and Tony were fellow conspirators in that somehow. Writer Paul Morley's view was that 'Tony needed to make history and you make history by telling it yourself. At that time you just thought he was thinking too far ahead. They're going to be Pink Floyd, they're going to be Led Zeppelin – no they're not. Or the Doors was his big one – this is gonna be our Jim Morrison.'

Tony never spoke this way around me because he knew I would gain no consolation from it. Like the music press, I felt that Factory was now blighted. Yet positivity wins over negativity every single time. And I take my hat off to Tony, Rob, Alan, and especially the band that they were able to carry on so soon in the face of such an overwhelming loss. Because I couldn't have. And, although it would be over twenty years before I could ever bear to listen to Joy Division again, the public felt differently, and the single 'Love Will Tear Us Apart' and album *Closer* were slowly edging their way into the charts.

Although I never spoke to Hannett about it, it seems possible that he shared my feelings. In his book *Who Killed Martin Hannett?*, Colin Sharp wrote: 'Martin's sceptical mistrust of Tony and his cronies hardened into something much more venomous after Ian's death. Perhaps he blamed Tony in some way.'

But, as Susanne said, 'It's difficult to know what someone else is going through. We never talked about anything important really. My father was very ill then and died in June, we didn't talk about that either.' This, of course, is often a trait of the young – to suppress discussion of the things that really matter. Yet Martin was a scientist who liked to experiment with drugs, music and all manner of interesting things and theories.

As Ian had died on the eve of the group's US tour, and since Tony had been planning to take ACR out to America later that year, he thought it would be a good idea to get both bands out there at the same time. The plan was for the two groups to play a few dates in and around New York, in combination with Hannett-produced recording sessions.

Tony suggested I join him out there after the first week; he loved New York so much and thought I would love it too, and that it might be a good opportunity for us to make a go of things. Alas, Confucius says that if you want to make a go of things with your wife, don't expect her to share a two-roomed loft with the lads from A Certain Ratio.

New Order were lucky enough to be put up at the Iroquois Hotel, but ACR were drawn into Tony's romantic notions about a New York loft, which unfortunately meant that this was also my introduction to New York.

Still, like most things that went disastrously wrong, including our marriage, it seemed like a good idea at the time.

Tony and Martin Hannett met me at the airport. I climbed into the front seat somewhat apprehensively, not being sure how Tony was going to be with me. But Martin made me relax instantly. 'Welcome to New York, Lins,' said the cheery voice from the back seat. And Tony was warm and friendly too. Perhaps it was going to be a happy trip despite the foreboding I felt in my bones.

I was a bit crestfallen when I saw the loft. Martin was staying at the Gramercy Park Hotel with Susanne. It was just me, Tony, all the lads from ACR, and a big expanse of unfurnished loft with soulless mattresses. Tony thought it the ultimate in cool; I thought it unwelcoming, unhomely and worse than camping. It was in an area of New York that Tony thought was happening – Tribeca – on Hudson Street above a rather nice café called the Lo-Jan. Other than the café the area had little to recommend itself to me. It was fairly empty of life, vacant warehouses abounded. Tony boasted in his book that he rented the loft from a guy called Chuck, who also happened to be De Niro's loft landlord and, in fact, 'knew Robert well enough to explain how New York Italians hold their balls while they talk to you. Told Wilson Bobby had got him a part in his next movie. A Scorsese movie.' Apparently Chuck later played the annoying barber who gets garrotted in *Goodfellas*. Big deal.

Meanwhile I had to put up with a room off the dormitory-style room the boys were all camped in, which was unfortunately the only way out to the stairs (in reality it was a lobby, I think). The one small bathroom was the most basic you've ever seen and was situated off the boys' dormitory, so I had to walk through their room to get to it. If I were shown this accommodation now I would say thanks but no thanks without hesitation. But I was more modest then, I didn't expect anything and in this instance I wasn't disappointed.

I may have thought the place lacking in comfort, but Tony was nurturing romantic ideas about it. Long-term he was later to choose loft-living in Manchester, but in 1980 such a thing was generally unheard of in the UK. Short-term he had visions to capture. One day an American filmmaker he'd recently met named Michael Shamberg came round and shot a mini-gig with the lads. I watched them at work and thought that the loft worked much better as a film set than somewhere to stay. The boys looked arty, young and almost beautiful, and the result was a mini-movie called *Tribeca*. Subsequently Shamberg became firm friends with Tony and Rob, visiting the UK several times and – as well as producing many videos for New Order and Factory – he eventually headed up Factory operations for the US East Coast.

The lads were naturally made up about all the attention they were getting, psyched, on top of the world. I tried to enter into the spirit of it all, but . . .

The recording studio was in East Orange, New Jersey. ACR recorded most of an album there, while New Order's studio time was much less intensive. Tony remembered: 'There were two ways to drive there. Either we could cross over halfway up the island and go a country way, but if we went through the Union Tunnel there was this forty-five-minute drive through this appalling, industrial New Jersey swamp land. Martin loved that. It reminded him of Trafford Park. So we always drove that way every day for three weeks. He was a very urban person. Yet, if I listen to "Atmosphere" I don't feel urban.'

My days were mainly spent with ACR. I don't remember too much about New Order. I do recall one day being in one of their hotel rooms and everyone was gathered there. The laddish banter was rife. There were some socks sitting in water in the washbasin and someone bet Rob $10 that he couldn't drink it. I was quite amazed when he took the bet on, took a large glass of this filthy water and drank the lot. 'The things some people will do for money,' I thought at the time, but I now suspect it was not money so much as bravado that motivated him. He was the tough guy, the leader. He used different techniques from Tony to get his way. Rob was a Wythenshawe lad and came from the school of hard knocks.

I wasn't sleeping very well at this loft. We'd get back really late from the studio or nightclub and the sun would beam in through giant windows first thing in the morning, right onto our bed. Naturally there were no curtains. Also, our room was on the busy roadside. One thing I've learned about myself over the years is that I'm absolutely no good without sleep. Just like a child I can get really grumpy, if not psychotic! That would probably half explain why a row began one night when Tony was driving the van with just me sitting in the front. This particular night it was so late that I knew the sun would be up by the time we got to bed. I was totally wiped out, plus there was the added horror of anticipating worse tiredness the next day. As he was driving along the tension began to mount and the accusations began to fly. Tony suggested the problem in our marriage was that I'd gone off sex and I quickly retorted,

'Correction, I've gone off sex with *you*,' at which point he pulled over to the side of the road. We seemed to be on a deserted street in the meatpacking district that resembled a murder scene in an American gangster movie. He jumped out, walked around to my door, opened it and pulled me out with the force of ten men. I thought he was going to beat the shit out of me; this was the last straw to him. He didn't, but he pulled me about by my lapels and screamed abuse at me. It sounds funny now but I couldn't stop crying, he really seemed to hate me. I walked off down the street, which actually came to a dead end at the Hudson River. It was there that I learned something else about myself; the calming effect water has on me. I sat down by the water's edge and my tears subsided. The water just seemed to make me feel it wasn't worth it. My dream since that day has been to live near water. And it has come true more than once. ('If you don't have a dream, how you gonna make that dream come true?') Being near water, especially the sea but even a river or lake, never fails to make me feel better. As I took comfort from the lapping noises, I assumed – wrongly, as it turned out – that Tony wouldn't leave me there. He drove up in the van and got out for a minute, but he was still livid. After a few choice words he drove off and I realised, after about twenty minutes, that he wasn't coming back. Oh dear. It wasn't exactly a salubrious part of town. Worse than that, I had no idea where I was. But hold on, this wasn't rocket science. I was by the river. Our street was parallel to the river. I knew I was north of the loft. So, although it was a bit of a walk, I couldn't get lost. Then again, I might get mugged or murdered. I therefore decided to head straight for the main street and walk. And walk. The strap on my shoe snapped. What is it with me and shoes? First San Francisco, then New York. I had to hobble along. This didn't give the best impression. As the dim dawn began to lift I saw one or two cars pass by. To my horror one of them slowed down, looking for business. I gave the male driver a look that could have killed all by itself and he went on his way.

When I got back to the loft Tony was already in bed and the sun was beginning to seep through our big eastern-facing window. I felt his behaviour was unforgivable. However bad things ever are you do not leave your partner in danger like that. So I decided – not for the first bloody time or the last – that this was it, we were finished.

Tony and I weren't ones to hold grudges but some things take more than a day to get over. So the next day I avoided being with him and went out on a bar crawl by myself. Ironically I was actually putting myself in even more danger than I had been in the night before. I decided to get completely and utterly drunk with every fibre of my being. And I wasn't even a seasoned drinker. Isn't it obvious I was still in love with the guy? But no, I *hated* the guy. So I wanted to drink him out of my mind and by bar two it was beginning to work. Some guy – naturally – got chatting to me. He thought the idea of getting drunk was a good one and said he'd join in with it. I told him I'd never been on a bar crawl before (not even a pub crawl come to that), so there we were – two strangers in the night. Except we weren't exchanging glances, though he did show me just about every decent bar in Tribeca.

Fortunately: a) he understood that the last thing I wanted was to pick him, or indeed anyone, up and b) he wasn't a rapist. So we said goodnight in the early morning. That again. Now my tiredness in the early-sunshine room was to be compounded by one of the worst hangovers ever. I was as sick as a dog and couldn't even be ill in private. The band kept politely having to pass through our room – previously I'd usually been the first one up and dressed, but on this particular day I was too ill to even get up. For the whole day. It was awful. I think Tony felt a little bit sorry for me. So we made friends again (sort of). All he ever had to do was try a little tenderness. All I ever had to do as well. I wish it hadn't always been so difficult. At least we learnt how to do it by the end.

I wasn't aware then that Martin had been especially affected by the death of Ian, but still noticed something different, some change in him in New York. He and Susanne returned to Manchester before we did and Tony and I took them to the airport. I was quite astonished by Martin's behaviour in the car. For one thing he seemed completely drunk. I'd never seen him like that before. The other strange thing to me was that, although Martin had clearly been able to handle several altered drug states and appear just like his usual self, it seemed that night that drink was something he couldn't handle too well, because he didn't seem like his usual self. Perhaps there was something else going on with him, I don't know, although as said, Barney thought Martin was never the same again after Ian's death.

Of course years later Martin became a voracious drinker. 'I think drink sped up his demise,' said Tosh Ryan. 'He wasn't a drinker when I met him, he was also thin, his weight ballooned. He kicked one habit [heroin] and acquired another one [drink]. He'd spend all day in the Manor House in Withington and then go home and drink a bottle of Jack Daniel's. I think he could have sustained himself better on the drugs than the drink.'

I had no idea then that Martin used heroin. The drug conjures up images of needles but Susanne told me: 'Martin used to "chase the dragon", he never injected heroin to my knowledge. A heroin addict is mostly thought of as injecting, not chasing.'

Tony and I had arranged with Martin and Susanne that we would go and stay in their hotel room after they left. It just had to be better than the loft. I was longing for a proper sleep in a room with curtains and without boys wandering about. Money seemed to be an issue, but the room was paid for anyway so we made our way there. Once inside the room a scene of devastation greeted us. Things were in absolute disarray; food packaging and towels strewn about, even one in the toilet I seem to remember. The ashtrays were all full and overflowing. I went around tidying and cleaning everywhere up. Finally things looked decent enough to get into bed. But when I peeled back the bedclothes I discovered the bed was strangely full of pieces of cake. Never mind, we were in New York, there were two king-sized beds in this room. But, alas and alack, the other bed was full of cake as well. I'd spent well over an hour cleaning this room and now we had no choice but to drive back to that bloody loft. Plus, it was late. Only four hours before the damned dawn again.

Susanne told me: 'Martin freaked out that night. He didn't want to leave New York. He had been staying in the Village with Lynette Bean [who worked for CBS Records and looked after John Cooper Clarke in the US] for about a week before I went to NY. She was arranging for him to meet Tom Verlaine. The arrangements were changed and Martin would have liked to have stayed to meet Tom at a later date. I had a ticket for that night's plane; Martin could have travelled when he wished.'

The cake has remained a mystery to this day. Could it have been the welcome pack Martin wanted to supply to the man he called, 'That one-way mirror, the Chairman of the Board'? Whatever it was, thereafter my mum always referred to Martin as the cake man.

The first recording sessions New Order ever did were in Orange, New Jersey that year. They recorded 'In a Lonely Place' and one version of 'Ceremony'.

The seeds for the future of New Order and also the Hacienda were planted on this trip. Tony always credited Rob with the idea of the club and, while I'm aware that the Hacienda was very much Rob's baby, I remember asking Tony long before this what he would do if Factory ever made money. I distinctly remember that we were driving in the centre of Manchester and his reply – he said he would give it back to the kids.

'How?' I asked.

'Give them somewhere to go,' he answered.

In Manhattan I recall going to Danceteria and Tony saying that this was something Manchester should have. It was a very impressive club, more up-market than anything I'd seen before and yet kind of wild too. It seemed a bit posh to me, the Mudd Club was more my style – a downtown, less glitzy but still cool live venue. Danceteria had obviously cost a fortune to set up, but I figured that as New York is a much bigger city than Manchester it would be more affordable. Mark Kamins was a DJ at this first venue for Danceteria and has been quoted as saying the club 'was an illegal Mafia club with no liquor license, but we sold drink tickets'. Since the Hacienda was in many ways based on Danceteria, the idea of drink tickets was transported there when it first opened. Tony thought that everything Danceteria did had to be the best, but this scheme – a bit like when you're on the deli counter waiting for cheese but more complicated –

generally caused mayhem and confusion and was soon abandoned.

This was how Tony recalled the dance scene in New York at that time: 'The three weeks saw the team spending a lot of time either playing or hanging out at Hurrah's at 62nd and Broadway, and Danceteria, then on 38th. Cool design. Clubs as venue and disco and style lounge all in one. The kind of clubs that David Byrne could go to the toilet in. Stylish. It was a couple of years before the heyday of the Garage and Fun Factory, which took New Order in other directions, but those first two were enough. They were cool clubs.'

Indeed, after this stay in New York the Hacienda was born, and all that remained was for it to be built.

'One of the good things that did come out of that New York period was going to the nightclubs and listening to dance music and that gave us the metamorphosis that allowed us to continue as New Order,' Barney recalled. 'If you listen to *Movement* it would be a sub-Joy-Division-esque production and record, and I think if we'd carried on that way we wouldn't have been successful. So something good did come out of that New York trip.'

Perhaps it was symbolic that every single piece of Joy Division flight-cased equipment was lost on that trip. I remember how proud Tony had been of these custom-built flight cases he'd organised but, sadly, change or decay is the law, and a sea change was occurring. 'Unfortunately the day we finished the recording sessions and we were due to start a tour,' said Barney, 'we brought all the gear back from the studio, parked it outside the Iroquois and woke up the next day and it had gone. It was *all* Joy Division's equipment, every single bit. Tony Wilson woke me up – he was laughing in my face saying, "All your equipment's been stolen." I said, "What?" Not the news I wanted to hear. He said, "It'll be all right, we'll get it back." Of course we didn't. We had $43,000 worth of equipment stolen. Unfortunately as we didn't alarm the truck – two of the roadies had an argument with each other, they couldn't decide which one should switch the alarm on, the alarm was actually in their bedroom – we didn't get the insurance money.'

Also unfortunate was the fact that ACR's equipment happened to be in the same van, so they too lost everything. 'Tony could be a bit Jekyll and Hyde,' Martin Moscrop recalls. 'He could be really nice one minute and put you right down the next minute. If he was in a bad mood, you didn't know what had turned him but he could just squash you. I remember him doing that to me in New York. After our gear had been stolen Tony took us out to the LP Factory – the people that make percussion. We bought a new set of congas. It was the day we were leaving to fly back to Manchester and we didn't have any cases for the congas – they were just going to get thrown in the hold like that. So I asked him for some money 'cause I'd seen these canvas bags on Canal Street. I said if we wrap some foam round the congas in this canvas bag it'll protect them. So he said something like, "Fuck off you stupid little idiot," which pissed me right off, so I spat in his face. I just thought, "Fuck you." So I ran to Canal Street and managed to get some money together from me and a couple of guys in the band and bought the bags and the foam myself. I've never spat in anyone's face before and I really regret it. I felt really guilty about it for years and years after. I used to see him at South by Southwest every year for four years on the trot before he died. He was always really, really nice to me and I always thought why are you being nice to me? I spat in your face.'

I vaguely remember the row that took place on that last day and thinking, once again, that it wasn't just me who found Tony infuriating. And yet he'd spent a lot of money on percussion for these guys which – despite the fact that their classic recording of 'Shack Up' made it look like they were going places at the time – was generous enough with or without flight cases. At least that's the way I see it now.

On their return from this trip New Order finished off the album *Movement*. Three tracks were recorded at Western Works in Sheffield – the connection here being Cabaret Voltaire – and most of the rest of the LP at Strawberry. Up until this point Martin's drug use hadn't been noticeably debilitating, some might even argue that there could have been an enhancement factor. But perhaps it was around this time that the drugs began to get the upper hand.

'I remember once when I was doing a vocal take on *Movement*,' Barney said. 'I'd already done about three vocal takes and Martin was getting all twitchy and he said, "I've just got to go somewhere, you carry on." I said, "Okay, but what am I doing wrong?" He went, "You'll get it, just carry on, you'll get it." I remember I did about forty takes and he still hadn't come back, I was really pissed off. But he'd gone to score because he was in agony. He really kept that to himself, we only found out later.'

There seemed to be a bit of a decline going on which was affecting Martin's health – both physical and mental – and his work. Sometimes he didn't even turn up for a booked studio session; Barney heard that he was mixing from home down the telephone. Someone would hold the phone out and he'd listen to the mix. Martin also became known for sleeping under the mixing desk.

Although Tony never said a bad word about it, I never much cared for the album *Movement*. It had a coldness somehow. Actually, I find it impossible to say why I didn't like it. But I was scrolling through a community weblog site, named metafilter, recently and found something really insightful that put my feelings absolutely in words. They say a good writer is someone who can say something that you know yourself but hadn't been able to find words for. This is what Jeff Johnston, aka koeselitz, wrote:

> There really are moments on *Movement* which are 'worse' (if you catch my meaning) than anything on *Unknown Pleasures*; like Martin Hannett, who had spent all of these years creating a sonic landscape around what he'd thought was Ian Curtis's dark, brooking art, suddenly felt the trapdoor fall and come to the shuddering realisation that *it hadn't been an act,*

it hadn't been art – he'd really meant it. So suddenly, listening to *Movement*, you notice by way of hindsight that there was a kind of delight that Hannett had taken in all of the dark touches on *Unknown Pleasures*, a secret gleeful evil wink. You notice that because suddenly you realise that the joy he'd had in it – yes (and I don't think this is a coincidence), the *unknown pleasures* that had resided in Joy Division's art, had disappeared. It was empty. As bright and defiant as 'Dreams Never End' may be, the looming, empty, flaccid sadness of Hannett's recordings of 'Truth' and 'The Him' is so stark and empty of pride, of self, of that subtle and masked delight he took in recording Joy Division, that I find *Movement* to be a much more depressing record than anything Joy Division ever put together . . . To me, *Movement* is the document of Martin Hannett's suffering in the face of Ian Curtis's death.

Maybe Martin hadn't realised that Ian's unhappiness was real. Perhaps he simply saw it as part of Ian's creative genius, something he could alchemically transmute for the songs. Martin was a chemist after all. Did Martin feel bad that he might have missed Ian's depression, might he have felt responsible in some way? 'I think we all did,' Barney said. 'With something as drastic as that, someone hanging themselves, you all think was I in some way involved? Martin would never speak about it; he just seemed upset after Ian's death – never the same again. He just sort of wigged out a bit. I don't think it was a responsibility thing. I think a bomb had just gone off in his face.'

Susanne, Martin's partner at the time, isn't sure she agrees. 'I don't think it had that sort of an impact – like a bomb exploding. Martin had lost a creative relationship when Ian died. I don't think anybody really knew each other, they didn't know him, he didn't know them. There wasn't any intimacy except what was implied with the work – which was tremendous – obviously that was very meaningful.'

Closer may have been doing well, but I could never relate to that. Looking back I think it would have been much better if, as Tony himself admitted years later, Factory had shut up shop, perhaps just for a year. I think some of us really needed it, especially those such as myself, who had guilt issues and simply couldn't abide the idea of thriving on the back of a tragedy. It had all been such a disaster. I couldn't see why Tony felt so full of his musical self, as it were. What was there to be proud of? I didn't like his appearance either – all combats like the silly gear ACR had sent him to buy from Laurence Corner, near Euston in London. Tony didn't suit camouflage pants, not that anyone really does, in my opinion. I didn't like them on ACR much either – much worse than their former choice of demob suits. Were we at war or what? Actually yes – Mr and Mrs definitely were. Change was in the air at 45 Town Lane as well, and I could sense it since our return from New York. That hadn't gone well, and after all the trouble there had been our marriage was in no fit state for what happened next.

Tony put our house up for sale having bought 36 Old Broadway in Didsbury. He'd come home one evening at the end of 1980 and announced it as a 'fait accompli'. 'I bought a great house today,' he said. When I objected that he surely wouldn't buy a house for us without my having seen it first, he overruled it by saying, 'It's a great family house.' Family? What family? What the hell was I – chopped liver? 'Fuck family! I'm not having a family with a bombastic controlling bastard like you,' I shouted. At which point he said, 'Well, that's your punishment for sleeping with John Scott.'

'Oh really, and why are you the bloody innocent when you've slept with God knows who?' I asked, adding: 'I'll never live in it.' I meant it. He didn't take the threat too seriously. He didn't mention then that Alan Erasmus had found the house for him. That old partnership again. Those two practically married and even taking over the running of my personal life, as if I was irrelevant. The irony was that Alan was just trying to be helpful.

I remember being particularly upset that day because I'd just finished re-tiling our Charlesworth bathroom by myself. Except it wasn't our bathroom, it was his. As evidenced by the 'For Sale' sign that went up without a by-your-leave from me.

I've looked back at this and tried to see it from Tony's point of view. Did he expect me to be pleased that he'd bought a house in Didsbury? In point of fact, I don't know why we hadn't done just that a hell of a lot earlier. It would have been so much more convenient for both of us. My family lived near there, he was endlessly round at Alan's, all of our friends were close to Didsbury, and it was handy for our town life. Charlesworth was miles away and at that time there was no motorway making the journey shorter. The only way around was the long way around. But I don't remember us really talking about it. I vaguely recall telling him soon after we met that I'd like to live in Didsbury, and he said he hated Didsbury and the scene that went with it (even if it wasn't quite as bad as neighbouring Chorlton). So that was that. A year or so earlier we had nearly bought a bigger, older house up the road from us. It fell through, but then we'd gone looking at others in and around Charlesworth. I'd kind of become resigned to staying there. But then things got worse and we'd stopped looking. Or so I'd thought. Tony wasn't very diplomatic. If only . . . (the two saddest words in the whole of the English language). If only Tony had just said, 'I saw a great house today, would you like to come and see it tomorrow?' Just that little bit of diplomacy would have made a world of difference. But no, this was his decision and his alone. We were moving to the damned house whether I liked it or not. Naturally I hated it, whatever it was, and vowed I'd never live in it. I wasn't going to be bulldozed into my own life.

Although he'd 'bought' this house, I thought he'd see sense, acknowledge our marital peril and pull out of it. However much a move to Didsbury or anywhere might have helped our marriage, surely he could see that this would be the death of it? I couldn't bear the thought of this house that I hadn't seen and never wanted to see. He could go and live in it with Alan Erasmus since they'd hatched it between them. In the event the basement of this rundown house in Didsbury became the Factory video annex, known as Ikon, run by a lovely man named Malcolm Whitehead. Malcolm had initially come onboard filming Joy Division at a youth club near Altrincham, part of which was contributed to *The Factory Flick*, an early Factory foray into the film world. Tony used Factory money to convert the cellars before the house got sorted out (I suspect there were less funds in his own account at the time). The money spent on Ikon's new equipment was a small bone of contention with Hannett that later grew out of all proportion when his own technological requirements were being compromised. The cellar was very high-tech and reminiscent of interior designer Ben Kelly's work, before Ben came along I think. Tony's love of high-tech seemed to match his love of his combats.

I felt that his euphoria about the Factory business doing so well was getting out of hand. It had been less than a year since Ian died. Our little cottage was now under threat, and I objected when he infiltrated it just before Christmas with a black high-tech metal trolley (or, as Tony described them, 'rather obvious Conran hi-tech-manque two-shelf video and TV racking systems'). It most definitely wasn't suitable for the house and to me was a symbol of Factory, the blackness that became Ian's death, and everything I detested about the way Tony was running our lives. This was the style of furniture he wanted in the new house he'd bought for himself. I put my foot down. 'I'm not having that in here.'

'Tough, it's staying,' he said. It was a veritable battle of wills. At one point I opened the front door and put the trolley out on the pavement – and since we lived on a hill it started to roll down. He grabbed it of course. I taunted him, 'Fucking black Factory, fucking death Factory, fucking black fucking death.' Bruce Mitchell remembered Tony telling him that it was at this point he decided he couldn't live with me. David Nolan, author of *You're Entitled to an Opinion*, wrote that I denied it happened which I didn't – I just didn't want the incident to be recounted out of context and asked him to leave it out, which, of course, he didn't. I don't blame him. It's a good story.

Despite our marriage, it was Tony's house and he could do what he liked. It turned out that the very first person who viewed our Charlesworth house bought it. I didn't know where I was going but I made my mind up it wasn't going to be 36 Old Broadway, Didsbury. Tony could be as domineering as he liked, but he was going to be on his own. Ostensibly that was what we both wanted in any case. I knew deep down it wasn't, but my pride insisted. Pride – hubris – does indeed come before a fall and I, like Icarus, was to lose so very much, and plummet to the ground.

Christmas 1980, like all the others, was disappointing, but in this case verged on disastrous. This wasn't really surprising after lurking infidelities, Tony's house purchase and my trolley hysteria. Also, there was now a 'For Sale' sign outside our cottage. I think it might have been the day the sign went up that I threw some of Tony's clothes out of the window as he was going to work and told him to fuck off to Didsbury and not come back.

Tony wouldn't even come with me to my mum's house for Christmas dinner (although he left it until the very last minute to say so). I thought if you can't make an effort on Christmas Day then when can you? I left him at 1:00pm sitting in his dressing gown on his rocking chair about to watch a sleazy-looking video he'd bought for himself. That's what he preferred to do. I felt hurt and arrived at my mum's slightly tearful but determined to make the best of things.

Then Nathan McGough came to stay during a tolerable Christmas week and celebrated New Year's Eve with us. Nathan was a bit like one of our family. He described to me his first recollection of Tony: 'I was thirteen when I met Tony. It was 1973. I had seen him on the TV. I recognised him because he was on *Granada Reports*. But one evening I was upstairs in bed and my mum and dad had been out for the evening and they came back sometime after 10:00, 10:30. I heard some noise and went downstairs and there was this guy off the TV who was sat in this big blue velvet armchair, in our living room. He was wearing a white dinner jacket . . . white tuxedo or something, and a denim shirt. He had long hair and was rolling a joint on the arm of the chair. I had never seen anybody roll a joint before. My dad never had that stuff lying around the house. So I was really impressed with this guy, partly 'cause he was off the TV and partly because he was rolling a joint. He had a genuine charisma which I was attracted to.'

My diary entry for New Year's Day 1981 reads: 'Made bacon, eggs etc before Nathan left and then cooked roast lamb etc – Mum and Dad came. Tony and Dad watched TV – *Dr Zhivago* and the end of another film, me and mum played charades and Othello in a corner.' Obviously Tony was withdrawn and wouldn't interact with us. My dad joined in with it in the name of male solidarity.

Ostensibly our day-to-day domestic arrangements were as usual but Tony and I both knew that, in the game of marriage, we were at a stalemate. I spent the majority of the long, dark January days alone or with people other than Tony. These included Vini Reilly, Tony Connolly and Sydney, my mum and my sister's family. On 14 January I went to the opening of Nathan's club night in Liverpool. I recall telling him that Tony and I were about to separate and his response was that he thought a break would do us good. I mentioned this to Nathan recently and he apologised for this advice – he said he hadn't meant it to be for twenty years! Nathan's club was called Plato's Ballroom, he'd cleverly booked New Order to appear and the club was packed. He told me that Rob Gretton had asked for £200 and a contract, so he went along to New Order's rehearsal room with said contract, but he'd taken out all the vowels because he felt like it. Rob was quite impressed.

Before I left for Liverpool I'd had a massive clean of the house in preparation for both my departure and our first house viewing at Charlesworth. The man looking around had a problem with his leg and I thought the house wouldn't suit him because the stairs were small and narrow and twisted sharply halfway up. But 15 January was the day our little house was sold to him. I wrote that day: 'Short disturbed sleep. Felt upset and in more sympathy with Palestinians (i.e. people who have lost their homes against their will).' On 16 January Tony went to London in an icy mood, wanting the break that had been on the cards since he'd bought a house without me. I didn't argue, packed and took Tabatha back to her original home across the road. Dear old Tabatha. One night two years previously Tony and I came home from somewhere late and Tabatha, a very thin cat, was waiting by our front door. 'Don't let it in,' I said to Tony. 'We'll never get rid of it.' He let her in straight away and I gave her some milk. That cat never left us after that. About two or three weeks later I heard that Mrs Wild, an old lady who lived almost directly opposite us, was asking people if anyone had seen her cat. That's when we found out the cat was called Tabatha. Mrs Wild didn't mind that she was now living with us and, as far as I was aware, Tabatha rarely bothered crossing the road to her house after that.

After a couple of days at my mum's I also went down to London. I stayed with Tony's best man, Charles Edmundson, his new wife Sonia and their new baby. I unofficially earned my keep since there was such a lot of housework to do – shopping, cooking, cleaning, washing, ironing, as well as occasional baby-minding. On 22 January I went to the Rock Garden to see Vini. I'd spoken to Tony on the phone that morning and diarised the conversation as amicable

– 'over, but amicable'. I returned to Manchester with Vini five days later and stayed at my mum's house. In London I'd met a man I really liked when Sonia and Charles invited me to dine with them at an artist's house. Since I now have no way of contacting this man I shall call him K. He was of Lithuanian descent and struck me as cultured, charming and clever; an artistic man who had nothing to do with pop music yet everything to do with art and culture. I was probably unconsciously on the rebound, sensing that Tony had already hooked up with another new girlfriend, Kate. I'd known about his interest in this Belgian girl. Tony wrote about her in a letter the previous August stating three reasons why he'd had no physical contact with her in New York or on his trip to 'Les Belgiques':

1) She has so many boyfriends; and you know how I hate to be one of a crowd. 2) She is one of those women who know they can have any man they want . . . like someone else we know . . . and that makes her very, very dangerous . . . like someone else . . . so she is best observed from behind bolted gates of desire. 3) Most specifically, our New York relationship was entirely non-carnal above all out of FEAR, SHYNESS, AND ROMANTICISM most of all.

To an insecure person like myself, this hardly spoke of his lack of interest in the girl. And yet, reading through the lines, he had spoken of the pain he felt 'to lie night after night beside a woman who wants another and not you'. If he had only made me understand that he loved me, rather than the way I read the letter – as saying that he didn't want to see me anymore, that he wanted to see her instead. His – and my – insecurity was perhaps the reason we could never quite sort things out. I wasn't lying in bed wanting anyone. I think by this stage it was him who was doing that. He made a request in this letter for me to move out of the house for a fortnight so the estate agent could arrange viewings in that time. Did he expect me to be difficult about that? I wasn't, actually. In the event there were no viewings at all in 1980.

That February of 1981 I went back to Charlesworth while Tony was at work to collect some things. I got rather a shock. The house was full of special flowers. He'd mended my wardrobe and it fell on my head. There were two pillows on the unmade bed where before there had only been one (I'd taken mine with me and the pillow from the spare room had gone). And in the washbasin of our bathroom I saw the telltale sign of make-up. It looked as if he'd already moved someone in. So now his relationship was carnal. I had to admit to feeling really upset, but just put it down to anger rather than the fact that I still cared. I poured a brandy even though it was the middle of the day. Clearly it was time for me to move on. Again.

On Valentine's Day I got a card from K (none from Tony) and immediately went back down to London. K and I shared a dinner but he told me that he still held a torch for his last girlfriend and wasn't ready to embark on a relationship with me. He was probably being strong and sensible and mature, all qualities I wasn't able to share. I stayed another week with Sonia and Charles, feeling totally fed up about the way things had turned out. One evening I went out for a drink with John Dowie. He had been the comic turn on *A Factory Sample* but was releasing his own single on Factory around the time we met – a picture disc entitled 'It's Hard to be an Egg', produced by Martin Hannett. John actually made me laugh out loud that night despite my feeling very miserable. I went out with him the next night to see *Stardust Memories*, but that was the end of that little friendship because I didn't want to embark on a romance with him. I wanted to rush headlong into a relationship with K and felt rather besotted with him.

In March I fell into depression. Looking back over my life I see now that a low-grade depression was never all that far from me, but when it took hold it was hell. Feeling suicidal and acutely panic-stricken one day I drove myself to the doctors, got some Valium and swallowed two instantly. Tony, as ever sensitive to our – if not my – imminent destruction, rang and wanted to talk to me. I met him at Granada but we both avoided speaking directly about our situation. I asked him instead if there were any jobs I might apply for at Granada, but it looked as if I'd left it too late. Granada had been looking for researchers a couple of years earlier; Thelma had begun working for them around that time and went on to do very well, eventually going on to LWT to produce *Blind Date*. This meant that she and Tony had been seeing more of each other, which also exacerbated my insecurity. The previous summer Tony had booked a holiday in Sperlonga entirely on Thelma's recommendation and – just as with the house purchase – hadn't consulted me. Although the hotel and Sperlonga were exquisite, the holiday was not. I was furious and felt jealous and powerless that he'd planned our holiday with an ex-lover and not with me. My only power lay in ruining everything.

Now my request to enter the world of TV drew a blank, as did an interview I attended to be an air hostess that same month. (Thank God I didn't get it is all I can say.) I'd been round to see Alan, who was at his girlfriend Annie's house, to get a reference for this interview. I noticed a pile of Factory mail that hadn't even been opened and thought it would make more sense to be working with them.

Shades of Tony's last weeks of life at the loft in 2007. One day Tony asked me to find something he wanted amongst the piles of interesting-looking unopened mail. It was an exciting job – I'm so short of post I even look at my junk mail. Keith Jobling called round as I was in the midst of it. I wanted to open all the mail but Tony was only interested in one particular package. Keith remembered the package in question contained a book about Jesus and when I found it, Tony said that was it, the thing he wanted, I could put the rest down. I said, 'What do you want that for? You're not religious.'

'I fucking am now,' he replied.

The only paid work I could find in 1981 was joining my mum in her market research job but I absolutely hated it. Two days after the meeting at Granada Tony rang and said he wanted to talk. We met, he ate Italian, and it was rather strained as I felt hurt that he didn't ask me to go back. I wrote in my diary: 'I say I don't want him back but I feel differently.' What a pair of clots we were. Both saying we didn't want each other back and both feeling differently but never admitting it. Stupid fucking pride.

On 18 March Tony went to New York. I don't know why he went but I'm guessing it was Factory business, probably to do with setting up Factory US. I moved back to Charlesworth then, looked after Tabatha and cleared wardrobes and cupboards out in readiness for the move. I met Tony's plane on his return four days later, but after he'd slept and I'd worked on the house all day we weren't friendly, so I left.

On 25 March I went to Strawberry Studios as I'd arranged to see Susanne and thought she'd be there with Martin. In fact she wasn't, but Martin was working with Magazine on a track called 'Vigilance' so I stuck around for a short while to listen. It was easy for me to feel at home in the studio with Martin, and I loved listening to Magazine.

The next morning I sobbed on waking. My dad was playing the harmonica and I drove to Charlesworth just to get away. Tony was still there but we hardly spoke. I ironed his shirts. I wrote in my diary: 'He seemed to want me.' In bed in Gatley that night I couldn't get to sleep. I so very nearly got up to go to him. In later years I looked back and regretted that I didn't, it felt like a turning point. Perhaps if I had gone back, admitted I wanted him, maybe we could have put things right. One of those hinge moments when your life can pivot one way or another depending on what you do or don't do. I had a feeling this might be our last chance to rescue the situation. But I didn't go. And my stupid pride would never admit anything. (That's what Tony once wrote on a Hacienda or Dry Bar ticket, I think: 'Admit one, but never admit anything.')

I went out with Tony Connolly the following night, and we wound up drinking cocktails in Napoleons (a gay nightclub) after sitting in the Rembrandt by Canal Street. This was before Manchester City Council designated the area as the 'gay village' as a PC move towards gay rights, but in doing so perhaps rather ghettoised the gay community. In those days the gay bars and clubs were not exclusive in a gay-tolerant area that was rife with all sorts of other interesting venues and characters – robbers, prostitutes, dope smokers, outlaws – anyone who was basically anti-establishment.

I drove out to Charlesworth after the drinks and arrived at 3:30am. I was twenty-four hours too late – Tony wasn't there. Many of life's setbacks are due to bad timing.

He was there the next morning and we awoke around midday. But another fierce and jealous row developed. He said he didn't want us to continue and I went mad and put my foot through a plastic door. I'd always hated that door – it was an interconnecting door between the lounge and little study, a horrible plastic thing. I wished later that I'd destroyed it when I moved in, not when I was moving out.

I stayed away from Charlesworth that weekend and went back on the Monday since Tony had gone to London. Rob Gretton and Section 25 came round. The next day Tony phoned and requested a lift from the train. I made his tea and he told me he'd like me to have a room at his new house. How bloody stupid that was. I should have said I'm either in it or I'm out of it. To my mind he was confirming that it was indeed *his* house and not ours, though perhaps he was just being conciliatory. I did go along with his plan to a degree. I decorated and chose fabrics for 'my' room – a room I stayed in just twice.

Then I went in for a cosmetic operation at Withington Hospital. It seems unbelievable now that I should have been concerned that I didn't look right. I had no idea then what time does to the body! I'd always been self-conscious about my ears, even traumatised when fellow ballet girls held me down on the floor in the changing room so they could look at them. I managed to convince my GP that I needed a procedure to pin my ears back. (The NHS must have had more money then, either that or I was very convincing.) In the event the surgeon took more of a dim view of it and would only operate on the worst ear. As I recuperated at my parents' house, eight red roses were delivered 'from Tony'. The way things were between Wilson and me, I'd assumed they were from Tony Connolly. But I was wrong. If, as they say, red roses are a symbol of true love, why couldn't Tony just say so and stop driving me away? I assumed he'd sent them out of guilt.

I went to Charlesworth two days before the move, cooking dinner, and clearing up. On 7 April I wrote: 'Spent entire morning clearing out kitchen cupboards. Went to Glossop and got fish. It's sad to see an entire chapter of my life over. Tony went to the tip with four bags I collected.' On 8 April: 'All go from 9:00am. Removers arrived and Tony and I worked hard helping them, but they weren't away till 2:00pm. Took Tabatha in car. New house depresses me because of its state.'

Tony insisted on taking Tabatha to Didsbury, but I felt she would have been better being left behind with Mrs Wild. I knew I wasn't going to be able to take care of her because I wouldn't be living with her, and I couldn't take her to my mum's because she already had a cat. Tabatha was eighteen years old and quite frail. I think she hated the house as much as I did. It wasn't comfortable and initially didn't have heating. Ostensibly it was a terrific house – big, detached, and next to the park on an exclusive road in Didsbury (in fact it was the road that Richard Madeley and Judy Finnigan chose to live on subsequently before their move to London) – but I was sensitive to the former occupant and noticed a bad vibe. I sensed something lonely; a woman, perhaps quite old, living here alone. Also it was dirty and pretty horrible. The painters began working the next day, as did I – I spent all of the next two weeks working on the house even though I never slept there.

One afternoon, as the house was starting to look a bit better, Tony offered me money if I would have sex with him. He made it sound like a joke and I played along with it – oh, yeah, so how much then? The humiliating part of it for me was that I did need to make money now – that's why I'd been looking for a job. We'd had a joint bank account but since we'd all but separated, that was effectively at an end. Tony said that the Charlesworth house had made £10,000 during the time we were together there and so he'd opened a building society account for me and put £5,000 in it. The thing was, he was the sole signatory so I couldn't draw on it myself – he gave it to me in dribs and drabs. In the spirit of a joke I agreed to this money-for-sex exchange, and then Tony got some cocaine out (which I took but, as already stated, does not agree with me). Afterwards he seemed happy and I was happy too – in my heart I wanted us to be back together again, and I took this to mean we weren't to separate after all. Tony went downstairs and in a half-undressed state I looked out of the upstairs window and saw Bruce Mitchell and a couple of other musician guys pulling up in the driveway. Bruce was laughing. I realised then that I felt ashamed. I didn't want to see these men and laugh about things because I was just Tony's whore. Tony had bought this house and now he'd bought me. I looked down at Tony talking to them, and it was a bit like the experience Ian told me he had at the Bury gig, when he felt as though he was watching the whole thing going ahead *without him*. I thought I was looking at a future in which I didn't fit. It would be nearly seven years before Tony and I had sex again.

For years I never told anyone about this 'prostitution' play. I honestly felt deeply ashamed. I thought Tony and I could hardly continue to be lovers, having now hit absolute rock bottom. I generally related the most intimate details of my life to my mum but couldn't even bring myself to tell her. How ironic that I am writing it now for anyone to read.

One day, probably about five years later, I still hadn't told anyone about it and I was sitting in an outside café in Paris with a lovely Argentinean man I'd met in Portugal. He fitted the pattern of all the subsequent lovers I unconsciously chose by this time. He was basically unavailable. But I liked him, even imagined him to be my great love. What self-deception! How skilful our defence mechanisms can be. I warned him that I was about to relate a dreadfully sordid tale and, in the nature of confession, told him the story of the last time Tony Wilson and I ever had sex. He listened quietly. Then, in that beautiful, poetic, lilting foreign way of speaking, he said: '*Thees ees not a sordeed story.*' He continued by saying that he thought Tony was showing true humility in this way; he was debasing himself, if anyone, not me as I had assumed. He thought it a self-effacing act of love rather than some crude sexual barter. I was quite taken aback by his viewpoint, which was admittedly a male perspective – I doubt a female would have seen it in quite the same light. Years later I felt able to talk to Tony about it. He barely remembered it. He was astonished I could have run away in part because of it. It had just been a bit of sex play to him, not to be taken seriously at all.

And he did like to play. Sex and drugs with the rock'n'roll. We – he – went through a phase of trying amyl nitrate. Tony told me it would enhance the effect of orgasm, but left out the bit about the damage it can do to the heart and lungs. That stuff is dangerous. It didn't do much for me on the pleasure side either.

Despite, or perhaps because of, the only act of sexual congress that had taken place between us at the new Didsbury house, and despite the fact that I carried on working there and even tackled the overgrown garden, we were no nearer a reconciliation. I knew I'd need a job since I was now financially on my own, as it were. I had my building society money but it was going down fast despite the fact that Tony wouldn't give me too much in one go – he said he was teaching me the value of money. Ha! I have to laugh looking back at that suggestion in view of later events. Who was he to talk? Perhaps he saw me as one of his protégés; I was on the drip like his musicians were. Maybe he liked this scenario, in which I was beholden to him for my £40 a week or whatever. In point of fact I never asked, I simply accepted whatever sums he sent my way. But, partly because of his role-playing with me, I felt like a sex object on a retainer.

Regarding Tony in New York, ACR's Martin Moscrop said, 'He looked after us. He was our dad.' Yes, I can relate to that, but he wasn't mine, he was supposed to be my husband.

Vini Reilly was looked after in the same way. He got paid regularly out of the account called the Movement of the 24th January, and looked back with true admiration at the way Tony handled it. 'Tony had this belief, a conviction,' he said. 'I'd make one mediocre album after another and he just kept putting these albums out, even though he wasn't making any money, Factory wasn't making any money, I was getting all the money. He gave me all the money – I've never heard of *that* before – a manager never taking his percentage, *ever*. He did buy a raincoat once. He'd seen this coat and he had to go into the Durutti Column funds because he was a bit skint. He asked me first and I was laughing my head off – it was like all these years you've never taken anything, just buy it.'

I began to wonder about this account – who could write cheques, was it ever investigated? Vini said, rather touchingly, 'Tony was the sole signatory of the Durutti Column cheque book. Tony wasn't about money. He never lied to me about anything.'

Perhaps not, but Tony could be very evasive.

'My dad always used to say to me, "What's Tony Wilson doing about your tax?"' remembered Martin Moscrop. 'I'd say to Tony, "My dad says what you doing about our tax?" Tony would say, "Don't worry Martin, it's all sorted out." This went on for years and years and years. When we left Factory [in 1987 ACR went to A&M Records] I got a letter off the taxman saying, "What have you been doing since 1979? We've got no record of you actually having paid any tax." The letter was quite threatening and we got asked to go to a tax investigation. We were nineteen-year-old kids, we expected our manager to sort out the tax. The tax investigator was quite a nice guy – a proper right-on lefty like you used to get in the tax office in the eighties – not really interested in helping the government that much. He asked me how it worked, how we got paid. I told him we got paid £40 a week – or was it a month – but it was below the tax threshold. Everything we earned went into an account out of which we were paid. We didn't have a clue what was being paid into that account. He asked me what account it was and I said the Movement of the 24th January – that was the account that Tony used. As soon as I told him that he said, "That's all we need to know," and I thought, "Shit, what have I done here?" But we never heard anything off them again.'

This doesn't imply a lack of trust, though. 'I thought he was too naive to be untrustworthy,' Moscrop said. 'Tony was terrible with money, really terrible. He was only interested in the creative, making music, getting records out; he didn't have time to think about the nuts and bolts of it.'

This is true. Besides, Tony couldn't be bothered to sort his own tax out, never mind anyone else's.

One of my regrets from my earlier life (my God, now there are too many to mention) was that I wished I hadn't given up training to be a nurse. I'd got a degree in Psychology and gone on to St George's in London in 1974 to take a post-graduate SRN (training as a state registered nurse), which was shortened to two years, rather than the usual three. I jacked it in halfway through – another story – but regretted it. As a child I'd always wanted to look after sick people. And then, in April 1981, I had nothing to fall back on. Apart from Tony, that is. I felt like all I had to do was have sex with him and I could live in his big house, buy as many clothes as I wanted and never worry about money again. And I thought, fuck that for a game of soldiers. I am not a whore. I'll make it on my own. So I went back to St George's for an interview and was offered a place. I didn't take it up in the end; somehow being a nurse didn't feel right any more. But Tony thought it a good idea since he said our marriage failed because I had nothing going for myself. The fact that I'd be living in London didn't concern him. I think I still had designs on K, but when I rang him to tell him I'd be down for the interview he said he had too much on his plate to see me. So that seemed to be the end of that.

On 9 May 1981 I went to a party and got *very* drunk. I collapsed on the pavement at 4:00am. A friend drove me to 36 Old Broadway (probably not realising that I wasn't actually living there) and I remember stumbling through the front door and falling momentarily unconscious in the hall. Tony looked dismayed. The next day, a Sunday, I wrote in my diary: 'Bad hangover and unpleasantness with T. He resented my having used the spare room. Thought I'd go immediately, but decided to cook the dratted meal first.' I've often thought that my reaction to his house purchase was sufficiently severe that one of the only nights I ever stayed at Old Broadway was the night I was too paralytically drunk to leave. And yet I still carried on with the role of housewife, cooking the bloody tea.

On 11 May, K the artist had a change of heart. He'd categorically decided to abandon the torch for his ex-girlfriend because she'd ignored his birthday. The weather was sunny and he invited me to the country. We spent three glorious days in a beautiful house belonging to a friend of his near Sheffield. He took me to an antiques auction and sketched drawings of me. I adored the attention and his clever conversation. I drove back to my mum's on mine and Tony's wedding anniversary. Only four years. Passing through Marple Bridge I called in at the church and visited the grave of Lindsay Wilson, symbolically placing a flower on it. This felt like the end of her.

Tony was leaving me pretty much to my own devices at this point. Probably busy building his empire. I spent the next two weeks in Manchester but there was little contact between us. On 24 May he asked me to the pictures but said it was just because he hadn't been for ages. I wrote afterwards: 'Gaping chasm between us. So very sad.' I remember he sat throughout the film with his arm up to his chin and I couldn't see his face. He seemed cold and I didn't know why he'd even bothered to invite me. Tony was great at putting on an act, though. He could feign utter disinterest when this wasn't necessarily the case.

And then K and I shared a wonderful week together. I stayed at his house in London, he took me to Brighton for a sunny day, a funky restaurant in Chinatown, a Cocteau exhibition, a boat trip on a friend's barge down the canal, the Tate Gallery, walks on Hampstead Heath, and introduced me to movies I'd never heard of – Fassbinder's *Fear Eats the Soul*, Truffaut – where had I been for the past twenty-eight years? Tony and I never went to see art-house films. After this introduction I became addicted to the genre for life. Funnily enough Nathan told me that when he first met Tony at the age of thirteen, Tony had fed him music and books and film. Initially having called round to see Roger McGough, as an admirer of his poetry, Tony rapidly formed a bond with Nathan's mum Thelma, as previously mentioned, and also with Nathan. Roger was away for long periods and Tony joked with Nathan that he was 'in loco parentis' (in the place of a parent).

Nathan remembered: 'We used to watch French cinema at a small film club in Liverpool on Mount Pleasant – called the Open Eye. It started as a place where you could watch Francois Truffaut films and Warhol movies. He'd take me to see *Dynamite Chicken* – lots of films, or we'd go stock-car racing.'

As well as the cultural feast I was receiving in Tony's absence and K's presence, I loved the fact that my days were now properly shared with someone. Admittedly this was just the first week, but that was how the relationship continued, we lived together in the real sense of the word – cooked, shopped, worked, talked, slept, entertained – we did almost everything together. Even when K was working, painting large canvasses in his studio, I was near him and felt part of his creative life, whereas Tony, on the other hand, was absent and didn't share his life with me to the point of my feeling ignored – that's what I couldn't deal with most of all. But I shouldn't have taken it so personally, always seeing his behaviour as a rejection of me. That's just how Tony was. It's taken me all my life to accept and appreciate people for who they are (or aren't, as the case may be), and work through my own abandonment issues. Tony was an only child; I never knew what it was to be alone as a child. Tony was chauvinistic, but the point is that you can't change people, and how they are – in this case often absent – doesn't automatically speak of a lack of love.

It was for a similar reason that Vini Reilly and Tony fell out for some years. 'We didn't fall out about money,' Vini said, 'it was because he was avoiding me. I tried to get a meeting with him for a year. He was my manager but I couldn't get one, he kept not turning up. I think he was as baffled by the tax thing as anyone else was. I think he didn't turn up because he couldn't have answered my questions. He wasn't a money man, he wasn't a business man. That's partly why I loved him so much.'

Soon after that week, I met with Tony and distinctly recall the conversation that took place. I knew that things between K and me could develop long-term – unlike with Howard or John. I wanted Tony to clarify things with me. He'd said he wanted a break, he'd now got it, but it didn't seem right to throw myself into this new relationship if Tony still wanted to save our marriage. Maybe I was kidding myself, but I wanted to give him the opportunity to speak up. Deep down I knew I still loved him but felt that he wanted me out of his life. So I told him I'd met someone and I thought it might become serious, and could he tell me how he felt about that because it still wasn't too late for me to pull back. He looked at me with loathing and his reply seared itself onto my heart. 'I'm glad – it'll get you off my back at last.' So that was that. There was no point flogging a dead horse. Good night Vienna, turrah T.

I really believed he meant this at the time. He was glad to get me off his back. He confessed later that that was just what you say to a woman you're in love with who has met someone else. You pretend you don't care. That never occurred to me. I genuinely thought he didn't.

So off I went. K and I were reasonably happy and lived together for several months in London. It was K who broke my dependency on smoking pot, for which I remain grateful. He wasn't averse to the odd smoke but said he didn't want to be with a 'drug addict' and disapproved of the daily habit I had. Of course I didn't regard it as a dependency (what addict does?), it was just a way of life to me. I recall one day snatching a joint while walking in Hyde Park because it had got to the point where I couldn't do it in front of him. I realised then that it *was* an addiction of sorts and over time the drug broke its hold on me.

Tony was getting on with Factory and ideas for the Hacienda. Art director Les Thompson, who also ran Thompson Trucking with Dimitri, told me that Erasmus had been going on about trying to find a venue for the club, so one morning he picked him up and drove him to a boat showroom, originally a steel warehouse, that was about to become available. Les was a friend of photographer John Nichols who, as well as playing bass in the St Louis Union, had a huge interest in boats.

And so the vision for a New York nightclub in the heart of Manchester began to take shape. Meanwhile my Hacienda was being built elsewhere.

Tony and I were civil to one another in spite of everything that had gone on. I was concerned about Tabatha and Tony assured me she was very well. In August 1981 Tony was up to the penultimate volume of Proust's *Remembrance of Things Past*, called *The Sweet Cheat Gone*, which he wrote to tell me was now the title of the piano piece that closed Vini's new album. Tony, ever the romantic, saw my departure as coinciding with Albertine's in the story. He wrote: 'At the end of the bit I was reading a few weeks back a subchapter ends thus: "As for the third occasion on which I remember that I was conscious of approaching an absolute indifference with regard to Albertine, it was one day, much later, in Venice."' Tony stopped reading when the next chapter began, 'My mother had brought me for a few weeks to Venice,' since he planned to go to Italy before the summer ended and he believed he would, like Monsieur Swann, find his oblivion there.

I thought he was telling me he was becoming indifferent. In fact it was a love letter.

In September he sent me another one, but the words that jumped out at me were: 'I don't feel bad at all. It's almost like a weight lifted from my chest.' Fine. He'd really moved on, as had I. But no, it wasn't that. He had a new theory. He wrote: 'I lost you many years ago when my lack of commitment created yours. As you say, you are a woman who passes through life and who passes through loves. I am not; my efforts at adultery over the past five years have been merely disastrous attempts at ego balance with the "travelling lady" . . . In that simple difference lies the impossibility, that I have known deep down inside but never dared to face.'

He was saying goodbye it seemed, which was just as well since K and I were quite happy. I worked with him at Camden Market – helping him to put up a massive steel structure that would house antique furniture and hand-knotted rugs, which we had to load and unload out of the van every Saturday and Sunday. It was hard work and my petite frame and weak little arms really weren't cut out for it. Also it was bloody freezing standing around the stall and I hated it. But I enjoyed the creative aspect of it – buying at auction, and we had free time during the week in which we could enjoy appreciating art. Mainly, he shared his life with me and that was what I wanted in a relationship. Then one day I noticed my stomach had suddenly got bigger (and it wasn't fat). I went to a nearby hospital for an examination and a doctor in a white coat brightly said, 'How do you feel about having a baby?'

'What!' I replied. 'I can't be pregnant, I had a period only two weeks ago.'

'Women often bleed in pregnancy,' he announced calmly as my eyes were transfixed by the badge on his lapel that read 'Doctor'. 'I'd say you were about four months pregnant,' he continued. I figured he of all people should know. Unfortunately it was a Friday afternoon so I had to wait until Monday for an official test (no over-the-counter products then). I was numb with shock when I came out to K waiting for me in the car. 'The doctor says I'm four months pregnant,' I said meekly. I saw the beginnings of a smile on his face. It must have lasted all of five seconds before we embarked on the worst weekend ever – shades of the volatility I threw at Tony. I nearly became violent when he made a tacit reference to the possible 'A' word. Clearly he wasn't happy about this at all, but what could I do?

It turned out to be an ovarian cyst, and ever since then I have been a bit wary of doctors. Another stood over my mum six weeks before her death and told me that her illness was not life-threatening.

In November 1981 I went into the National Temperance Hospital in London to have the cyst removed.

The odd thing was that as soon as Tony heard about this he made what looked like a 360-degree about turn in his feelings. I thought he'd washed his hands of me and was genuinely surprised by his sudden declaration of love. It transpired that he thought I had cancer and was at death's door. He went to his mother's grave (where he always went in times of crisis), prayed for my health there and swore that he would let me go if my health could be granted. He sent several long letters while I was in hospital and, reading them over now, I think I was a fool not to have gone running back to him. He was so fucking eloquent. It was he who had given up his earlier love, Thelma, on the strength of just one letter, and here I was with five that all justified a return to our marriage. But there was K. He had integrity and was kind. We'd been happy until this spanner in the works, so I didn't want to leave him. I thought about it – how he might never want children or marriage with me, in fact his reaction had rather demonstrated that. Tony was offering me everything but I felt he had not been kind. Not that I had, I suppose.

One night in 2007, when Tony was poorly and I was staying over, not long after Tosh and I had broken up, I asked Tony why he thought I'd been so spectacularly unlucky with men. His reply indicated a straightforward belief in the age-old concept of karma. He suggested that I make a list of the number of times I'd both hurt and been hurt by men, saying I'd then see it was simple justice – that I'd caused more hurt than I'd suffered. (I did this later and amazingly it came out equal.) Karma is a Buddhist doctrine and, interestingly, Tony read *The Tibetan Book of Living and Dying* soon after this. But he remained loyal to his Catholic faith to the end.

In 1981 I was at the most crucial crossroads of my life. Which way to turn? This was how my agony of indecision began and, over the next two years, it would nearly destroy all three of us.

Is it possible to turn our feelings off like a light switch? I sometimes think it is, and that we do. Or maybe we just have them permanently switched to dim.

It's a bit like the story of *Our Town* by Thornton Wilder. The play moves to a graveyard above the town where the spirits of the dead talk to one another. A new arrival amongst them, Emily, decides to go back and experience a day in her life but the other souls strongly advise against it. They say she will be living in the past but be able to see herself living it, and, though in the present, be aware of the future. She goes anyway and chooses her twelfth birthday. The ordinary activities that comprise day-to-day life then become too much for her because she is on an entirely different level of experience. Her mother opens the curtains but Emily can't bear the pain it brings to see her there, and so young and beautiful as well. The older we get, the more we understand the value of such seemingly insignificant events when, after death, they are gone forever. Emily asks to go back to her grave with the words, 'I can't go on. It goes so fast. We don't have time to look at one another,' and asks, 'Do any human beings ever realise life while they live it – every, every minute?'

Except for a few poets and saints, most of us cannot live at that level of intensity, but that is not to say it isn't always there. We slip into it sometimes, especially when death is near us or someone we love, but we can't stay there for long, the business of life cannot continue there, we must return to the more basic level, where ordinary things get done and where feelings are never so intense.

Not only do we not appreciate the life before our eyes, but sometimes we find it (and each other) positively irksome. Especially in the endless day-to-day, the monotony, the stress of work and the irritation. Life's vicissitudes.

But within it all there *is* something holy. The breath – the most constant and unappreciated thing – that we often only realise is so precious in our last hours. Food. We have become alienated from our food also I think. Tony used to say I was obsessed with food, and it's true I grew up with the idea that food is love. Maybe it is. Now we eat so much processed stuff and hardly anyone has the time to prepare slow food, it's all fast, fast, fast.

My main jobs as a housewife were preparing slow food and cleaning, washing and ironing. How easily replaced I was. Tony subsequently ate out, had a cleaner and had his shirts washed and ironed at the dry cleaners. Job done. All he had cared about was that I had sex with him, but maybe it's becoming understandable why I couldn't. It didn't mean I'd stopped loving him. I never did.

The last meal I ever made for Tony was his favourite meat stew. I was a bit rusty on cooking meat having mostly been a vegetarian, but I think it was the holiest meal I've ever made in my life. It was packed with love. It was a bit heartbreaking when he only managed to eat a little of it. A good friend of Tony's named Ross McKenzie was there and I gave him a mean portion because I'd made it for Tony and wanted him to have it – if not that day, then the next and the one after. (In fact he'd gone into Christie Hospital by then.) I almost believed it could make him strong again. But he'd gone beyond it; I should have let McKenzie eat the lot. I think Tony was more interested in the rice pudding that I heated out of a can. His eyes lit up when I suggested it.

Tony didn't want to know about vegetarian food. He loved shepherd's pie and I asked him in those last months if he'd like to sample my veggie version (most people seem to like it). I got a categorical no from him – he wouldn't even try it. In years gone by, whenever he called round to my house I used to make him a coffee and he never complained, even saying how nice it was once. Then one day I told him it was decaffeinated. He was disgusted – refused to touch it again! It was the same with veggie food. He especially liked doner kebabs and Alan Erasmus brought them round for him when he was ill. That was love. As much love as went into my casserole.

I have to say how wonderful it was that Alan and Tony became the best of friends again. They hadn't spoken for nigh on eleven years (apart from once briefly when they'd met at Rome Airport).

A conversation between Tony and I in 2004:

TW: I was very bad to Alan.
LR: Why? What did you do wrong?
TW: I regarded myself as Factory.
LR: Not him?
TW: No. When Factory was over I never said to [record executive] Roger Ames, 'Fine – but you've got to pick up me and Alan.' He said he'd give me a job running a record company but I never said, 'You give Alan one as well.'
LR: That job didn't last anyway, did it?

TW: No, it didn't. But even so I didn't do that – which I think was wrong.
LR: You think you betrayed him?
TW: Yes.
LR: Does he think that as well?
TW: I have no idea.

Then one day Alan saw a newspaper headline announcing that Tony had cancer. He was driving past the Marie Louise Gardens when he saw Hilary coming the other way. She flashed her lights at him and asked him if he know about Tony. Yes – he'd read that Tony had had his kidney out and all was progressing well. But Hilary warned Alan it could be terminal. Alan went into Flat 4 at 86 Palatine Road and sat in the same place he'd sat in to meditate when his daughter had a small growth. At that time he'd been able to move – or saw – something so that it shifted and he felt she would be all right. On this occasion, though, he couldn't open the door. From that point on Alan knew we were in trouble.

I think we all did in our heart of hearts. But I played along with the idea that Tony was getting better. It seemed to be what Tony wanted and that went for the rest of us as well. Sometimes denial isn't such a bad thing.

At the time Alan and Tony resumed their friendship, Tony actually said that it was worth getting cancer for.

In those last months of his life Tony and I returned to the olden days, when being a housewife felt valuable. I'd arrive and Tony would say, 'Thank God you're here because you take the rubbish out.' Well, it was nice to be appreciated! Actually I'm serious about that; I felt it was an honour. In my grandmother's day it was almost shameful when women weren't housewives but now it has been devalued. Take cleaning for example. How vital is that? Apparently not so, it's considered the lowest of all low-down jobs (unless you're managing a cleaning company and making a fortune), but meanwhile we've got super-bugs to contend with.

On Sunday mornings Alan would call round with Tony's favourite snack – bagels, cream cheese and smoked salmon. This was something Alan used to do in the old days at Charlesworth. *Plus ça change, plus c'est la même chose.*

Perhaps in those trivial little everyday things lies our greatest meaning. Oddly the same minutiae of day-to-day life that drove Tony and me apart drew us together in the end. I looked up notes about *Our Town* on education.yahoo. com: 'Wilder himself emphasises these seemingly insignificant details in order to reverse the usual conception of what is important. Thus, he concludes that it is not the momentous events but the trivialities that become meaningful.'

That is how it felt in those last months between Tony and I, and therein we found our peace. I think in those little things we found a huge importance. In truth, as he was disintegrating before our eyes my admiration and respect for him grew. I suppose I fell in love with him again. That was a beautiful thing for me, because the illness stripped him of all the outer stuff to reveal an incredible inner spirit. Here was a man with the strength to endure this decay without self-pity, to watch his life disappear before his eyes and yet remain enormously positive. He became so much more humble and gentle it seemed to me. All along that was the kernel of the man I had loved and lost and loved again. Miguel Esteves Cardoso, who lives in Portugal, told me of a saying in his homeland: 'If you follow your heart sooner or later, better follow it sooner.' So I followed it later – but at least I followed it.

In 1981 Tony's love letters and efforts to save our marriage seemed like a vain attempt to destroy my relationship with K. I could not see the beauty and truth in his words and I honestly regret that. We should have had a family and a good life together. But my feelings for him were submerged. All I ever wanted was a good man and for us to be happy together. Why was it proving so impossible?

Clearly I still had bad feelings towards the Factory ethos, as evidenced by an account I wrote in 1981 about a visit to Strawberry Studios:

Sitting in the hall at Strawberry, with 'directors' Wilson, Gretton and Hannett, during the recording of their latest effort. I wondered if I might be privileged to some insight into the current state of feeling at Factory Records. True, Erasmus was missing, but then he usually is.

On my arrival I had listened to the song just made by the Stockholm Monsters, a group discovered by Rob Gretton in the Cyprus Tavern. After the hearing I went downstairs, where Gretton was playing pool. 'How is it?' he asks Wilson. 'It's great,' replies the same. 'Have you heard it yet?' 'No,' says Gretton. He obviously prefers to believe in his protégés from a comfortable distance. He oodles good will, though, or is it the will to make good?

Later, Hannett is mumbling about money, as is his wont. 'We've been rather ill lately,' he says, and goes on wittily, 'but now we've got no money left so we're feeling better.' I gather he was referring to the £5,000 the four partners recently had (from the profits of Joy Division). As Factory profits are split fifty-fifty with the group, I presume the band also had £20,000 recently. This isn't to mention other thousands I know of.

Wilson seems to be the only one with any honour motives, as opposed to the money motive, though he lacks common sense, and is outnumbered in any case.

The three slobs were patting themselves on the back. Wilson says that this, the third year of Factory, has been a severe, testing time, but they're pleased to be surviving well. All the others go by the wayside in their third year, he says, citing Rabid as an example.

Sad to observe, in my book, they never made it to the third year to be tested – they had already failed. As a marketing company they're still in the running, but whether they put out 'new fangled' music or 'new fangled' knickers makes no goddamned difference.

Perhaps if I had also been a director I might have seen it differently, but I couldn't stand the male bravado and back-slapping, especially in the wake of the tragedy of Ian. Possibly I could also sense that the bonhomie was a mask, disguising yet more estrangement and conflict. For in fact this recording was to mark the end of the Hannett fairytale Factory days. The single, released in early 1982, when Hannett's relations with Tony had soured even more than my own, was entitled 'Fairy Tales'.

Tony's letters to me may have been poetically beautiful and, like the scripts he wrote for Granada, hand-typed on his typewriter at Old Broadway, but he used Factory notepaper and Factory envelopes (FAC 7). That annoyed me a bit – how can you save a marriage with a reminder of one of the things that helped ruin it? But one of the most heartfelt he scribbled hastily on the train after visiting me at the hospital. He apologised for behaving abysmally and continued: 'As I walked across London earlier on, I felt all that irritability – jealousy of the unnamed man, the aftermath of all the tension. I knew I'd say something or cause trouble – and I told myself to cool it. I tried and I failed. I behaved like a pig. To mention some irrelevant Didsbury cow in order to provoke some truth from you about your life in London. I know your silly, gentle, paranoiac mind, and to put that crap into it was utter stupidity on my part . . . And I deserve to pay the price of loneliness that I offered as my own small "bit" in the prayers for your health.'

Then later he wrote that he had no intention of approaching another woman until his fate was sealed. He continued:

I want you as my wife and mother of my children – and until you seal the death of real happiness, I see no point in chasing the emptiness [and] foolishness of fancy. You find it fun – romance. I find it too unreal, too lacking in soul – all heart, no soul. And while there is still the slightest hope that you'll come back to me, I will avoid contact with such things, which – while marriage is a possibility, even a faint one – seem to me no more than a putrescent sore; a vain and fantastical obstacle to real and lasting happiness. For God's sake read Lawrence's poem 'Fidelity'. Does loving that poem mean I am grown old? If so, I thank God for each year that adds on. Forgive me but I find your espousal of romance childish, immature. Hence, perhaps, my irritability. I have seen too many people who have chased romance – I have seen that strange emptiness of soul grown in their eyes as the years pass and 'romance' leaves them empty-handed and so little at peace. That's why there will be no woman now – or for some time to come. With 'romance' now I can smell the dead corpse even with the first thought of a body desired.

The wisdom in this letter belies his age. And yet, oddly, he was the one who always espoused romance and the feeling of being in love, rather than plain old boring love. In later years he told me he loved me but wasn't in love with me. The latter he considered more important, more vital. But to my mind being 'in love' is a romance in the head; love is more the gemstone he and Lawrence are speaking of here. And you simply can't have marriage at the same time as romance. But I don't think what I had with K was just a romance, it went deeper than that, and therein lay the problem.

Tony argues his point rather well in another letter to me:

> The increasing knowledge that you love someone more than me; or you would say love less, but merely 'in love' more. Isn't that everything? Love is all very well; but it is only happiness. 'In love' is joy. The active emotion is in a realm above mere contentment/fulfilment/happiness. That that is shared with another is the lover's pain, it says so in all the books, and now it says so in all my mind.

I was a fool. I couldn't see or appreciate the good this man had, and how very much he was offering me. I was frightened. It felt like a trap. A trap with children. I didn't want that. But I couldn't vocalise it. I thought I must want children. I thought it was him who was wrong. All along it was me. I loved him. That's the stupidest thing.

'Fidelity' by D.H. Lawrence

Man and woman are like the earth, that brings forth flowers
in summer, and love, but underneath is rock.
Older than flowers, older than ferns, older than foraminiferae,
older than plasm altogether is the soul underneath.
And when, throughout all the wild chaos of love
slowly a gem forms, in the ancient, once-more-molten rocks
of two human hearts, two ancient rocks,
a man's heart and a woman's,
that is the crystal of peace, the slow hard jewel of trust,
the sapphire of fidelity.
The gem of mutual peace emerging from the wild chaos of love.

As January 1982 rolled in and I was still with K, Tony had embarked on another new relationship with a girl who seemed in every way lovely. Her name was Ros and I couldn't see any reason why he wouldn't settle down with her. K and I went to India for six weeks and, after our return, I began to have doubts about our future, and had a bout of depression. Although I was going along buying and selling stuff with him and working at Camden Market, he told me he didn't want to work on a partnership basis. SOS – same old shit. I felt like I was just another enabler.

At the end of March Tony told me he wanted to marry Ros and I had to admit, if only to myself, that I was greatly upset by that. He'd got the house, he'd got the job, he'd got the company, now he just wanted the family to go with it. I jollied along with his idea – even encouraged it – but looking at my diary it is fairly obvious how this news affected me. I wrote the next day: 'Slept badly. Drove into town. Suddenly felt terribly sad. Cried all the way there. As I was getting money I saw Tony leave the bank but didn't attract his attention.'

I soon realised, though, that Tony's talk was more manipulation and pressure on me to go back. Within two days of talking to me about marriage to her he telephoned me twice, and suggested I stay at Old Broadway and look after the cat while he was in New York. On the third day after his little talk I had parked my car in the centre of Manchester and on returning to it thought damn, I've got a parking ticket. In fact it was a piece of a book that Tony must have left, torn from *On Love* by Stendhal. I couldn't think of anyone else I knew who would possess the book, let alone leave a page of it on my car windscreen. I asked Bruce Mitchell about some of the books Tony gave him and he said, '*Red and Black* and the other Stendhal one; *The Brothers Karamazov* by Dostoevsky; Zadie Smith, *White Teeth*.'

Tony hadn't let go, and it now occurs that my low self-esteem might have been another factor influencing me in casting him aside. It's like the old Groucho Marx joke: 'I don't want to belong to any club that would have me as a member.' I was plainly commitment-phobic, though I didn't know it. I cherished freedom. My way of coping with my father's anger was to reject him and it felt safer when he wasn't there.

Whilst I was looking after the cat at Old Broadway, Rob Gretton came round and we spoke about Martin suing Factory.

Susanne told me that she remembered going with Martin to 86 Palatine Road for a meeting with Rob, Alan and Tony at which there was a contretemps about the club. She said that Rob accused Martin of something. Though she didn't remember what that was, she recalled what Martin said to Rob in response: 'The thing that you don't like in others is the thing you've not resolved in yourself.' Basically, he was saying that if you're pointing a finger at somebody, you're pointing three at yourself. She thinks that Rob accused Martin of being selfish. Susanne had a walkman in her pocket and recorded this meeting. She destroyed the tape in 1993.

This was how Tony described to me the falling out with Martin that led to a lawsuit:

'1) Hannett owns twenty percent of Factory. That fifth in the UK is about 2.5 percent, which is what he'd get as a producer, but abroad that fifth of a third that Factory gets isn't two to three percent, and therefore he was suing us; he was being ripped off. 2) He wanted a studio/Fairlight, not a club. Though if you look back on it, if we had bought him a Fairlight he would have been a Trevor Horn to the next phase.' (Horn, also famed for his love of samplers and technology in the studio, used a Fairlight on his commercially successful production of 'Relax' by Frankie Goes to Hollywood.)

Susanne responded to Tony's words by saying: 1) The idea that Martin wanted a studio was news to her and 2) Martin was always aware that if records were licensed abroad then his royalty would diminish, it was normal practice and not something he would argue about.

Martin was clearly frustrated by the fact that Factory weren't paying him proper royalties. As mentioned he'd received £5,000, but this was as a director and shareholder; it was unrelated to royalties. Martin wanted to be paid by his own label at least the equivalent that other record labels were paying him. Clearly the huge sum of money being spent 'building' the Hacienda hugely added to his frustration. Susanne said, 'He saw Factory as being a record label and Tony saw it as owning a club at that stage. Because Martin knew so much about the record business, he knew that there would be a back catalogue and he wanted a part of that. He could see it going on and on for years and years ahead.'

Regarding the Fairlight, a digital sampling synthesiser developed in Australia, Susanne pointed out: 'Martin was at the cutting edge of sound, he needed it to further his development in the studio.'

Tosh remembers Martin banging on the desk and shouting, 'Don't fuck with my budgets!' and Factory were clearly guilty of that.

Susanne said that Martin had been able to find a deal to buy the Fairlight on a hire purchase agreement, and 'Tony had agreed Factory would buy the Fairlight on hire purchase. Time went on. When I asked Tony where the finance was up to he got annoyed with me – he had just returned from New York and rang Factory's office, where I was working that day – and asked to be put back on to Alan. Alan, when he had finished talking with Tony, told me not to "upset Tony when he [has] just returned from New York". I had no idea he had just returned from New York. The deposit was not forthcoming. I left the office shortly afterwards and didn't work there again. Martin began the litigation very soon after this incident. Martin would have stayed if he'd got that.'

She believes this was the straw that broke the camel's back. 'Some time later Tony told me he blamed me for the break-up,' she says. 'Made me very powerful, don't you think? At least in Tony's eyes.'

Alan remembers that fateful day slightly differently. He said that he had advised Susanne not to call Tony immediately after his return from New York as he would be jetlagged and unlikely to respond well to pressure about the Fairlight, but that she did call him and, predictably, Tony reacted badly. Knowing Tony as well as I did, this does sound like him – to make a radical switch if he was tired, stressed and felt his support was not being appreciated. Stephen Lea recalled: 'Tony was very loyal to everybody, but if it went beyond a certain line where he thought they no longer deserved it, he would suddenly do an about turn and go from being your best friend to "fuck you". I saw it occasionally.' The odd thing is, and Alan reflected upon this, if Susanne hadn't made that request of Tony exactly when she did, and possibly feeling slightly irritated and impatient with Tony – understandable given that something so important to Martin yet relatively straightforward still hadn't been sorted out – history may well have been different. Alan said that Tony had every intention of giving Martin the Fairlight until that day.

Although Tony later regretted not helping Martin with the Fairlight, he believed there was another core reason for the falling out. This was that New Order and ACR wanted to use different producers than Martin. Tony told me: 'That was what the big row with Martin was really about. The fact that Alan and I and Rob – when our bands said, "We're moving on from Martin," we went, "Okay, your choice, we understand," and by that we betrayed Martin. So Rob, Alan and I took the impact of the jilted love affair. That was the hurt and pain that underlay it all – the impact of the bands wanting to go beyond that producer.' He added that he wouldn't have wanted the bands to work with another producer but: 'At that point I was getting so tired of ACR's arrogance and stupidity, which clearly was going to destroy their careers and waste everyone's life and time, and for Rob he knew that his group wanted to move on.'

Susanne disagrees with Tony's theory: 'Martin was building his career as a record producer. He did not intend to be reliant on Factory for that in terms of recording artists. He was in demand elsewhere at that time because of the records he produced for Factory, Rabid, Island, Phonogram, CBS and others. Martin was very grateful to be involved with these and other artists at that time. Other bands wanted his production values on their records. He liked to keep his options open.'

Personally, I suspect the jilted love affair theory may have been a romantic notion of Tony's, in line with his idea that Factory consisted of five heterosexual men who were all in love with each other. Saville thought that Factory was in fact simply 'a mutual appreciation society', which is more in line with my own thinking. Martin had produced two great albums and monumental tracks with Joy Division, and he knew their worth even if the rest of us weren't as convinced.

Susanne pointed out: '"Love Will Tear Us Apart" had sold very well, got a chart position. In my mind Martin's production was brilliant, he did some of the effects that he did best and Joy Division also brilliantly came up with the goods. At the end of "Atmosphere", for instance, there is a cascade of bells shimmering down and away in a light breeze. This relieved some of the heaviness of the track and was a perfectly executed effect. Wilson wasn't in Manchester often. Alan was tight-lipped about sales figures. Rob didn't answer the phone, let alone any questions about royalties. Peter Saville, designer and shareholder, resigned and settled up soon after moving away in the direction of Roxy Music et al.'

The lawsuit went on for about a year. I asked Tony about it in interview and our conversation went thus:

LR: How was Martin's litigation resolved?
TW: He got paid £32,000 and acceded all his rights to everything.
LR: You mean he no longer could receive any royalties?
TW: No.
LR: That was a bit unwise.
TW: It was fucking stupid.
LR: Just for £32,000? Mind you, it seems little now but it was a lot then. That was nearly what Old Broadway cost. [Old Broadway actually cost nearer £50,000]
TW: It was a lot then and also, if you look back on it – it was more than I ever saw in the end.
LR: In total – all the years wrapped together?
TW: Yes. So it wasn't that bad really.

And then Tony quickly changed the subject. He went on: 'Me, Alan and Rob would drive to London to see our litigation lawyers and Alan disappears, so we go in to see Mr Mortlock and we're getting deeply into a conversation and Alan appears with a brown paper bag, and after about three minutes we're in the middle of something and Alan goes, "Apple?" "No, thank you Alan." Then it's, "Orange?" I mean it's like can you explain that to me? I'm sorry, I think I treated Alan very badly but good God he would try the patience of . . .'

Speaking for myself, I would have appreciated Alan bringing fruit into the meeting. Tony was never all that fond of fruit, or healthy food in general.

Susanne said that Martin had sued Factory for 'suppression of a minority shareholder'. They went to the Inns of Court in London's Lincoln's Inn and the barrister was willing to take on the case for £6,000 upfront. 'Martin tried to raise this money with his bank and was refused,' she explained. 'Otherwise he would definitely have continued the litigation.'

Even at that stage Martin had to pay his solicitor £16,000, which left him with £16,000. In negotiations there had been three rooms in a solicitors' practice in London – a central room where opposing solicitors faced one another, with Tony et al on one side and Martin and Susanne on the other.

Susanne told me: 'I see Tony as someone who took advantage of people. Other people made money and he took it and did what he wanted with it.'

Oddly, I found myself defending Tony – pointing out that, unlike several others, he hadn't got money himself when he died. Personally I saw Tony as someone who a lot of other people often took advantage of, but I wanted to look at the situation as objectively as possible, and to understand Susanne and Martin's point of view. Susanne has remained more or less publicly silent about Martin and the contretemps with Factory up until now, and it was important to her, I think, to express this viewpoint clearly. What follows is a direct transcript of an email she sent to me after the previous conversation:

As far as I know Tony had control over the money in the bank, he and Rob and Alan, they decided along with New Order how to spend it. They suppressed the wishes of a minority shareholder, and did not allow Martin to develop the production of records in whatever way he saw fit. The Fairlight was intended to be used in-house and on Martin's other productions, it could have been rented out. He felt he had earned the Fairlight with the records he had produced with Joy Division.

Suppression of a minority shareholder was the only way he could claim funds from Factory. The company did not have an agreement with Martin to pay royalties and when push came to shove, and the split happened, for whatever reason he tried for an equivalent amount in settlement to reflect the royalties he generated as a producer, not as a director of Factory.

Because he couldn't afford to proceed with the case to the High Court he was denied the equivalent amount. The barrister we saw thought he had a case for suing for the equivalent of production royalties, as he was leaving the company due to a dispute and suppression of his direction as a shareholder. They were all directors, weren't they?

He didn't want to walk away without any future income and he did wish to leave Factory. The only way he could get future income that he had helped to generate was in the form of royalties.

In the event he was paid as a director at that point in time, according to how much Factory owned I think. Had he gone to a higher court, he stood a chance of getting production royalties in the future for as long as records sold. This may explain what you said about Tony stating that Martin could have been very rich if he had just stuck with it.

They were going in opposite directions.

Yes, and they weren't the only ones. Around April 1982, Tony seemed to be having doubts about his relationship with Ros. I know this was no reflection on her, but simply due to his attachment to me. He told my mum that she was annoyed by his lack of commitment. By May things had clearly become tense between them. I returned to Manchester principally to visit my sister, who'd given birth to a baby girl, but the second I arrived Tony rang, ostensibly because he'd decided he wanted a classic car and was interested in my Karmann Ghia. I didn't really need a car in London, so I met him the next day to give it to him. In the event, however, Tony bought a classic sixties MK Jaguar and I kept the Ghia. Thus began his love affair with the Jaguar, which continued through various models until his death.

We went out together to a small club that evening and stayed out late, talking a lot but not reaching a conclusion. Three days later we went out to 'celebrate' our fifth wedding anniversary. He took me for dinner at a restaurant in Alderley Edge, which was a nostalgic journey for him to the place he had lunch every week with his mother. Clearly he was courting me again, but I was very confused. I could understand how Ian felt trying to choose between two life situations. I should have known that the best thing to do was make a choice and stick to it, but I kept wavering.

Tony and I began seeing more of one another, and this put my relationship with K under pressure. I remember walking around town with Tony one day, bemoaning the fact that I was short of clothes and couldn't afford to buy any. 'Come back with me and you can have as many clothes as you want,' he said. Having always had a weakness for clothes this sounded really tempting, until I decided it was a controlling thing to say. It actually made me take a step back since it reminded me of the 'whore' scenario.

The 'unofficial' opening of the Hacienda was Friday, 21 May 1982. Bernand Manning appeared and told the jeering crowd, 'I've played some shit holes in my time,' and, 'You're not the one going home in a Rolls-Royce.' Tony offered him money afterwards, but he refused.

Tony had arranged to take Ros to the opening night, so I didn't go. However, giving more strong signals that he hadn't given up on me, he had taken me out to a literary dinner the night before. It was one of those dreadful celebrity occasions at which ordinary people pay exorbitant amounts of money just to share mediocre meals with the famous. Tony played more of the sycophant to me than the stars present when he absolutely insisted that I take his place (since we were not seated together). Hence I found myself sitting next to the evening's main attraction – David Frost. Tony seemed to think this would impress me, which it didn't. Actually it was quite the reverse. There's no doubt that Frost wasn't impressed, either, especially when Tony kept coming over to see if I was all right. He and Tony would have had much more in common. I felt miserable and burst into tears between courses (in the ladies). I noticed Frost didn't touch his food – it seemed perfectly edible to me, but perhaps wasn't up to his usual standards. His conversation seemed – well, hard to say, but almost inhuman, or superhuman (like his appetite, in a different league to us mere mortals). I should imagine I'd feel the same if I dined with Prince Charles or someone of that ilk.

I was in an agony of indecision over Tony and wrote in my diary that night: 'I can't let go but I don't want him back.' I felt he was being too controlling, playing games with me and with Ros; that he didn't know the real me – who wasn't impressed by being near famous people, for instance. But I truly loved him and perhaps subconsciously knew that no one else remotely suitable would ever offer me the home and the children. (The family I was sadly never to know.)

The next day (the Hacienda's official opening day), I went into Revolution Studios in Cheadle to record 'I Get Along Without You Very Well'. Suitably ironic. The words are a poignant reminder of loss and heartbreak. In fact the singer is *not* getting along very well without him or her. I'd been made aware of this song, by Hoagy Carmichael, since my mum liked it, and one evening in Vini's room (Vini, like Tony, was doting on me at the time) I'd suggested that we make a recording of it. I sang the words and Vini strummed along. The result was naive, crude and yet rather lovely in a way. When Tony heard it he was keen to record it. I'd sent it to him on cassette the previous November. This is what he had to say about it:

'Your voice sounds so good, very delicate . . . anyway it really sounds beautiful. You must be aware that on three occasions your phrasing/timing is completely off, and you hit a wrong note on five occasions. It doesn't subtract from the charm or beauty of the piece but if you want to have a hit record then you'll have to sort that out, and those things are easy . . . lessons, my love . . . lessons. Take singing lessons. As for the sentiments in the song, I can't bear to think about them. Found the Lew Stone original and made out some of the other lines . . . I don't know about spring, I can hardly bear to think of Christmas. But on.'

This is how it was with Tony. If he was into you then a hit record was possible however diabolical your voice was. And if he wasn't you could have the voice of an angel and he might blank you. I did actually go for a few singing lessons before the recording, with a lady somewhere on or off Albert Square. Until I squared up to the facts about my voice; that I might even be tone deaf.

Did Tony think the song was a romantic message to him? If it was, it was only subconscious. The truth (apart from the fact that I couldn't sing) was that I *had* been getting along without him very well, except perhaps in spring – that spring of 1982. I was so torn, my loyalties so divided. I loved Tony – I always did, but was less sure that I liked him, and definitely didn't trust him to be kind. That was why I was hanging on to the man in London – he was kind. Tony called by the studio and looked very distracted. No doubt he was stressed with a lot going on because of the Hacienda opening night – guest tickets and such. Amazing that he even called in really; it shows how keen he was.

It must have been a difficult time for Tony – Hannett's lawsuit was threatening Factory, and there were money problems at the 'hole in the ground', as Hannett called the Hacienda. There was pressure on Tony, and pressure on me to get back with him. My indecisiveness was agonising, so off I went two days later to see Ivor the clairvoyant. *Pathetic*, I know! He told me that the man in London would bring nothing – that he was moody, and that my happiness was with Tony. I felt resigned then but depressed at the prospect. Why? Because it seemed like a great big trap. A family trap. He wanted me to move into *his* house and have *his* children and be *his* wife and I wasn't even sure if he knew who *I* was. I felt as if I was merely an add-on to his own ego – that he wanted a beautiful woman on his arm more than a personality to communicate with or even someone to love him back.

My mum told me that I should ignore what Ivor said. Interestingly, at the end of his life Tony blamed my mum for our break-up.

It was around this time that Tony made the unusual step of admitting he had been wrong in buying Old Broadway without me and announced that he would sell it. Consequently we set about finding a home together. Unfortunately all the enthusiasm for this came from Tony; I couldn't put my heart into finding a home with a man I was effectively no longer seeing. I clearly remember three of the houses we viewed – all of them lovely, yet somehow I came away feeling very fearful of such a move.

Bruce Mitchell recalled Tony and I visiting him and his wife Jackie at 77 Central Road (around the corner from Alan's flat): 'You were thinking of buying the house next to me that was going up for sale. You came round to our house because these houses were built by one family, one half for the senior members and half for the married sons. You came in your beautiful VW car and as you pulled up outside the house Tony leaned his head out of the window and said, "One trendy couple coming to meet another trendy couple." You looked round the house and when you were coming down the first floor to the ground floor you fell down the stairs. You were showing all your legs. You did well because some people who fell down those stairs went straight through the window!'

I'd forgotten about this incident, but how symbolic that fall was – it could have been Icarus himself. Because I wouldn't go along with this house-and-family scenario, I not only might have 'sealed the death of real happiness', to use Tony's words, but also incurred a struggle thenceforward with my primary needs of bricks, mortar and basic financial security. But it still felt as if I was being bought, only that the price had gone up. And Tony's funny comment to Bruce seemed like posing – we weren't even a proper couple, so how could we be a trendy one?

Much has been written about the Hacienda and the apparently ill-considered business plan – or lack thereof – on which it was built. (See Peter Hook's book *How Not to Run a Club* for a graphic breakdown of this 'folly'.)

I wasn't party to the financial decisions or implications – being a Factory wife and an errant one at that. A streak of chauvinism, along with a streak of Catholicism, ran through the board. As Hooky noted in his book about Rob and his girlfriend, Lesley Gilbert: 'The band didn't have much to do with Lesley. Perhaps it's because Rob did his level best to keep our professional and personal lives separate. He didn't like girlfriends (or, as in Ian's case, even wives) coming to shows. To him, what happened backstage stayed there – and a lot of what went on wasn't particularly compatible with family life. Rob structured things so that we could be different people on the road; it became a bit Jekyll and Hyde.'

Although I have never been able to abide this mentality, unlike Hannett I wasn't concerned about the huge sums of money being eaten up by the club (even if I was managing on very little) – it honestly had my full support. I didn't know then that Tony had put the 'family home' up as collateral against the Hacienda, but in the circumstances would probably not have been bothered. I'd opted for another life. But Tony was pulling and pulling on me. It took him a year, but by 1983 he'd got me away from London.

Howard Jones, aka Ginger, was taken onboard as manager of the Hacienda from as early as 1980, when the idea first came about. He told me an amusing story from that time:

'When we were building the Hacienda we had a directors' meeting in Tony's living room at Old Broadway. Tony always used to video the board meetings. We're sitting there and Tony starts skinning up and Alan jumps up and jumps through the window into the garden. He's standing outside in the garden and all you can see is his head through the slit in the sash window. Tony said, "What you doing Alan?" He said, "I'm not being in a room on video while you're skinning up." Tony said, "Why not?" He said, "If the cops come who are they going to arrest, me or you?" So we spent the entire meeting with us three in the living room and Alan's head in the window between the ledge and the top of the sash.'

Alan told me that he'd been looking at the Bridgewater Warehouses opposite Dukes on the canal at Castlefield before Les Thompson introduced him to the Whitworth Street boat showroom.

Ginger remembered Alan giving several astute reasons for not opening the club in the Whitworth Street building, including the fortune it would cost to convert. Alan tells me that he wishes he'd bought the Bridgewater Warehouse building himself as it was available for £26,000 and didn't need as much work. Ginger says, 'Alan said, "We can buy the building for the price of two years' lease at this other place." To which we all said, "No Alan, you don't understand, we've got a vision."'

Tony had shown me this huge building just after it had closed as a boat showroom. It had a facility at one end of it to allow for the height of a fifty-foot yacht. Sitting in the middle of Manchester this showroom was as unique, in its way, as that which followed it. As ever Tony was exuding huge enthusiasm that matched the huge, cavernous space. As we walked up and down the stairs in one corner of the building he shared his vision with me and the way he told it made sense.

On Saturday, 22 May 1982, Tony took me to the official public opening of the Hacienda. The size of the venue and the exorbitant costs could hardly be justified by the pathetic turnout that night – there were probably only about sixty people and they all looked as if they were from the raincoat brigade (to use a term adopted by Mick Middles when describing a typical Joy Division fan – Ian Curtis being well known for his raincoat). This night Cabaret Voltaire played and they and their fans were a bit similar to Joy Division. Since the Hacienda is fondly remembered as a glamorous, happening disco nightclub (as it became with the onset of Madchester and ecstasy in 1987), my short diary entry about this particular night is perhaps surprising: 'Went to the "Hacienda". The miserable, meagre people there do not deserve all that money being spent on them. Or perhaps they do. It reminded me of a prison. The music was absolutely terrible. All seemed very cold. Tony was ill – looked a wreck and we went home early.'

In purely artistic terms, it must be noted that the vision behind the Hacienda and the expensive Ben Kelly design and cost involved in refurbishing the club proved immensely perceptive, albeit eventually. I truly believe that a large part of this vision came directly from Tony, and that Ben Kelly had the skill to implement it. The very notion of creating a dance arena and inviting the Manchester indie audience in the early eighties seemed little short of bizarre. Tony was quite fond of the bizarre. That was probably why he disagreed with everyone else and put the stage to the side of the club rather than in the more obvious location at the end. When you walked in you couldn't see who was on and the acoustics were terrible, but it was actually more of an interesting place for that, and its layout served the Hacienda's heyday rather well since the DJ booth was directly opposite the stage.

For a time it all seemed ridiculous. If the Manchester indie-rock audience even deigned to venture into the Hacienda they would usually gather unseen in the shadows. Perhaps when a gig was particularly intense they might venture forth, but they wouldn't exactly be dancing and the act of applauding the messenger, the DJ, was clearly absurd.

There were also spectacular teething problems and vast amounts of money wasted. Chris Hewitt, from Tractor Music, said: 'The initial sound and lighting was state-of-the-art but the problem was it needed state-of-the-art maintenance to keep it going. Within the first two days they had twelve sets of studio monitors hung from the ceiling. Very efficient but only fifty watts. Every one of them blew up. Tony rang me and asked me if I'd got a cheap system he could install? I installed it and the cost was nearer £3,000.'

Chris said he was forever being called out to deal with things – from the biggest to the smallest of technical problems. Once it was because the till didn't work and he discovered it was just a fuse in the plug. Once they had hired in a Yamaha piano but hadn't thought about a piano tuner after delivery.

On 3 July 1982 Tony and I took LSD together at Old Broadway as a belated birthday celebration. He showed me some slides that night, as well as a film he'd made and a section of *Brideshead Revisited* that made me cry. Rather inauspiciously we watched Fassbinder's *Despair* on TV. (Fassbinder had died in June 1982, aged just thirty-seven.)

Then we went to the Hacienda. The cavernous open space didn't feel so empty on this night, or if it did, it didn't seem to matter so much because Tony and I were getting on.

Every time I went to the Hacienda I came to love the design and feel of the building more and more. It was a major surprise when, years and years after its closure, the *24 Hour Party People* moviemakers reconstructed the club in a mill in north Manchester's Ardwick. It was absolutely identical! I stepped into it and honestly would not have known the difference.

Downstairs the Gay Traitor cocktail bar felt more cosy and intimate, and balanced well with the big open space upstairs. For the next five years this bar was generally where you would find me.

All the names – Hacienda, Gay Traitor, Kim Philby (bar) were coined by Wilson. Who else would have a clue about their relevance? The gay traitor was Anthony Blunt, a gay art historian who became a spy for the Soviet Union and was described as the fourth man in a Cambridge spy ring along with associates Kim Philby and others. Tony took the name of the Hacienda from a slogan of the Situationist International: 'The Hacienda must be built.'

Tony and I enjoyed this outing, he wasn't under the stress of the club launch, we met up with people we knew and, all in all, were getting along well and having fun.

At the end of the evening we even danced together on that as yet alien area known as the dancefloor. I hesitate to name one of the songs I remember us dancing to. It wasn't anything cool or happening and seems at odds with people's idea of the Hacienda as well as the advertised name of that particular night: 'Funkapolitan'. Still, I think it was near 2:00am so it might have been a wind-down song. I'm pretty sure I never heard it there again. The song was 'Me and Mrs Jones', and I thought it rather appropriate (given that we were married yet seeing each other when other people were involved). With hindsight it could also have been said to be prophetic. More familiar to me was the *Thunderbirds* theme tune, which from 1983 generally let you know it was time to go home.

This night was the calm before the storm. For the next two years I wouldn't know peace of mind anymore. On 6 July Tony rang and said he wanted a 'final' chat. We went to an Armenian restaurant and I told him I'd go back. But then, later in the evening, after a friend called Neville visited, I decided I couldn't go through with it. I felt frightened of being sucked into *his* new lifestyle. Tony therefore said it was the end, and I returned to my mum's. I think he probably showed weakness when he rang the next day and apologised for his behaviour. I said it should be me apologising, but I knew I had more time and that 'final' didn't mean final. Just as with children it is a mistake to waver on a rule, because then the rule becomes meaningless.

I duly went to London, but was aware of a profound stress eating away at me – the pressure of being pulled two different ways.

My basic reasoning was that, as it had been infidelity that destroyed our marriage, if I were to have sex with Tony then I would be unfaithful to K, and that would be the end of that. I wrote in my diary 15 July: 'Tony rang to say the session for the record has to be cancelled. Also cancelled is his affair with Ros (or is it?). I'm so unsure what I should do. Now I feel the pressure full on, but I miss K though it may fade. T is a manipulator and a taker. I hate him and he hates me. *No*, I hate that about him and other things, but I love him.' How's that for a demonstration of how mixed up I was?

Being Tony, he had a literary take on all of this. He rang three days later and said he wanted to talk. I went over and he told me the story of Troilus and Cressida. This Shakespeare play was always one of Tony's favourites and, one day in the last months of his life, he got talking to me about one of its themes – how Cressida played hard-to-get even though she loved Troilus from the outset. He inspired me to go straight out and buy a copy. But in 1982 he was making a different point. I wrote in my diary. 'That was about it. So I'm not his Lindsay.' Troilus dealt with his discovery of Cressida's infidelity by deeming that, though she was tied to him with the bonds of heaven, this Cressida (the one who dallied with Diomedes) was not she.

Tony had referred to this story in one of the love letters he sent while I was in hospital. He first quoted from Yeats, then wrote, 'that thing I found in you . . . and cannot quit . . . and which now I dread has been lost in you . . . Lawrence's diamond beneath the rose . . . though there in two souls, like unique jigsaw cuts,' and continued: 'I'm sorry if I killed it in you . . . still seems to be here in this heart of mine . . . in *Troilus and Cressida* last Saturday night . . . a disappointingly awful production on BBC2 . . . Cressida says to Troilus, "Will you be true?" . . . he replies, "Ay: it is my fault, my vice." And so it seems it is mine . . . nearly a year from that dread Christmas when I decided action was required . . . and no nearer escape . . . all that bosh about Proust and the onset of indifference. Not me so lucky.'

At the end of July 1982 I wrote: 'I have to stop seeing either Tony or K. Feel today it has to be Tony if it's what I want most, or K if it's what "they" want most. Feel bloody miserable either way. I wish I could be a better person. My guilt is enormous.'

The turmoil was certainly evident in my relationship with K. One night I got up to go to the guest room since I couldn't sleep for worrying, but K woke, said he'd go instead and ran off. Half an hour or so later, he suddenly charged into the room and threw a glass of water at me. I got out of bed and laughed. Then I dressed and made to leave, but he walked out to my car stark naked and begged me not to go, so I went back. People were passing by (this was Central London). I swallowed gales of laughter.

On 17 August I took Tony to the station for the first leg of his trip to Hong Kong. He gave me a beautiful painting of cows as a birthday gift. He knew how much I loved those animals and that I favoured vegetarianism after becoming attached to a brown, white-faced cow awaiting slaughter in a corral in Ireland. He also gave me a Lichtenstein card of a crying girl and wrote:

'These cows, a perfect image of the dream we've sadly lost – I love the little calf on the left, as faint and removed as our hopes. When we are older, our lives quite removed from each other, that little dream will still be there, just as the painting's still hung on the walls of our rooms. There will always be a corner of our souls in which we are forever husband and wife. It isn't Catholicism – just the condition of what we were to each other that cannot be erased. Good luck with your-our-record and with dispelling the Boethian mists that cloud your wheel. All is as it should be if only we could see beyond that mist. My love in all its ages. Anthony x'.

This picture has hung on a wall in all the places I've lived since then. Most recently it hangs in my kitchen. But about a month before Tony died, it unexpectedly crashed to the ground. It is sometimes said that a picture falling off a wall can be a superstitious omen of death. Tony would have said that it meant the string had just worn out, or wasn't hung properly. Strangely though, in the middle of the very night Tony Connolly died, another picture came down in my lounge. I knew as soon as I found it the next morning that he had gone. When the cows came down I thought Tony had as well and had to ring him immediately.

Why it came down when it did I don't know, in fact why pictures falling off walls should have anything to do with death is also a nonsensical mystery to me, but the cows falling did seem a sad symbol of the end of all our hopes.

According to Nathan McGough, Tony chose to go to China in 1982 because he decided China was going to be the new world power. He asked Nathan to house-sit so the house wouldn't be empty and, of course, there was also Tabatha to consider, although I went across to feed her fairly regularly and was using Tony's typewriter to work on a play I was writing. In point of fact, though, Nathan lived there for the next eighteen months.

It was a habit of Tony's to take a special holiday every year, even if it meant travelling alone. Endless visits to New York and LA didn't count. In 2005, about a month after I began seeing Tosh Ryan, Tony rang up and invited me to accompany him, at his own expense, on that year's major adventure – Vietnam. It seemed that otherwise he'd be travelling alone. That in itself was not necessarily a first, but inviting me along certainly was.

For the previous year or two Tony and I had embarked on fairly regular dinner outings (about once a fortnight at the weekend). He would pick me up and we'd generally go to the same Pizza Express, where he would always order the same pizza. I would have gone back with Tony then. After about a year of this dinner dating something happened one night and it looked as if he might want the same thing, but subsequently he appeared to pull back from it. I confronted him and his excuse was that he didn't want our friendship to be ruined. Perhaps it's true that it would have been. Just as once he'd been unable to fall in love with anyone but me, now he was unable to fall in love with anyone but Yvette.

Of course the invitation to Vietnam was tempting – never say no to travel is my motto – but I could hardly accept when I'd just started seeing someone else. I didn't want to wreck this new relationship before it had even started.

Six days before Tony's death I asked him, 'What's the best place you've ever been to out of all the places you've ever seen?' I was thinking I'd make a pilgrimage – wherever his favourite place was – to remember him. His reply was not audible, except that I gathered it was a hotel in Vietnam.

'Where?' I repeated. He looked exasperated.

'I can't have a conversation,' he said.

'Okay, just nod,' I said. (God, how insensitive it sounds.) 'Is that where you went that time you asked me to go with you?' I asked.

'Yes.' The word rang out as clear as a bell, with some anger I thought. Was he reminding me what a fool I was not to go? Was he reminding himself what a stupid cunt (his word) I was? Was he angry with me or was he just angry period? Was he even now still capable of revenge? Did I regret not going? Of course. At that moment almost more than I could bear.

Tony wrote to me in 1982 from Canton (now known as Guangzhou). He described our parting at Stockport Station as: 'That strange-tight-neurotic-near-to-tears-full-eyelidded farewell at Stockport was almost worth the fare in itself; what strange reactions we provoke in each other – and was that graveside vow my undoing?'

This is how Tony described Canton:

I crossed the border into Red China at 12:00 – it is now 10:30pm. And I just cannot believe that this land which has fascinated me on and off for fifteen years is more wonderful that I could ever have imagined. Crazy, bustling, bemusing, exhilarating, wildly alone, unique, happy – a joy to be in. The streets of this city of three million are full of bikes – thousands with smiling careering bright-faced Chinese. Buddhist temples with towers that make Kew seem insignificant look down on the triumph of Socialism and Daoism. The honeycombed city full of people and weird shops; strange seven-storey restaurants; street teenagers selling cassettes to the flood of cyclists who swarm over the Pearl River Bridge; deliciously shaped gardens in honour of revolutionary dead; great people's auditoriums; ideograms on hoardings that paint the words 'China belongs to the people'; dark thronged streets 'cause they're saving on public electricity; department stores of crumbling concrete and bizarrely simplistic products; and the cultural parks where hundreds of people listen to amplified folk concerts, ride primitive Ferris wheels, watch a girl's floodlit basketball match/an open-air movie, a pair of TV sets in an open amphitheatre, an acrobatics/ ballet theatre, tea gardens, trees and crowded park benches, lovers on the boating lake and even a storytelling place where perhaps 200 or so old men loll on pews and fan themselves in the evening heat while other old men take it in turn to sit at the raised table and tell into the microphone – stories – old folk tales of heroes and wars and lovers and antiquity.

He also wrote: 'If I had intended to make this the start of my "Lindsay-is-dead-get-on-with-living phase" (Brian's wisdom from Castaneda – "live like a warrior"), then it was the wrong place. More beautiful dresses in one town than I have ever seen before. If the only remnant of my hunger for you is to be this dramatic window-shopping for you, it will be devotion enough. The designs here – both cheap and expensive – are stunning, something to do with their approach to the shoulders and hips as a plane. In the last week I have bought you 142 dresses – they suit you.'

In actual fact Tony returned not with a dress for me, but a Chinese Buddha. (Incidentally, he was referring to Brian Eads, a close friend of his back then.)

By October 1982 my relationship with K was all but on the rocks. On 1 November I wrote: 'Here I am looking at the last of the leaves falling. Like them I'm clinging on to something that cannot be. I'm leaving lock, stock and barrel. Feel calm about it, but a little sad. I am off to seek my independence – nothing and nobody else.'

On 28 December 1982, I wrote: 'For so many months I've written "It's over". It wasn't then – is it now? Tony is off on his annual romance which will occupy at least three months. K really cares more about his work.'

Tony's new girlfriend, now that Ros had gone, was unlikely to be the mother of his children. She was big and jolly and loud and raunchy and colourful. I liked her; she was friendly to me when I met her. I doubted either of them thought it was a long-term thing. She was obviously a station on his road (Leonard Cohen, courtesy of Tony). Short-lived as it was, it gave me a bit more time with K, though I could feel that running out.

On Saturday, 5 February 1983, Tony delivered me a letter and an ultimatum. He said it was to be answered by the following Wednesday or else we were finished. I respected his wishes to bring things to a head but still felt divided and didn't want to hurt or lose K. On the Wednesday in question I suddenly jumped into the Kharmann Ghia and drove down to London. K said, 'Why don't you say hello?' I said, 'Because I've come to say goodbye'.

He cried. I cried. (Not at the same time.) I went with him to deliver a bergere suite and, enjoying his company, wondered if I could go through with it. He advised me to say to Tony, 'We can but try,' reminding me yet again what a decent fellow he was. The next day I packed my things together but felt very depressed about going. Tony rang, seemed annoyed, and said that if I wasn't back by Friday that was it. K and I had a fantastic Japanese meal and I left in tears the next day. Instinctively I wanted to resist the thing I felt was being forced upon me. Even if it might have been the thing I wanted. I returned to Manchester like a weary pupil going back to school.

So on Saturday 12 February I was 'back' with Tony. He took me to an Armenian restaurant and we drank wine. Afterwards I said, 'Where now? I suppose you'd go to the Hacienda?'

'Yes,' he said.

I said, 'Let's go.' I got *extremely* drunk by accident and also because of the pain. Whatever great accolades the Hacienda has since had, this was 1982 and it was dead – and in any case, it paled in comparison to the cultural outings I'd had in London. Plus, like Martin Hannett, I felt peripheral to the board of owners. I was too drunk to drive and passed out. Tony must have undressed me, but that was as far as a physical reunion went.

Although always happy to see Tony and be in his company, I was simply reluctant to move in or even stay at *his* house. He carried on living with Nathan and I carried on living with my parents. But Tabatha the cat was, by this stage, very poorly and so I went around every day with bits of her favourite fillet steak to tempt her. She died on 25 February. I sat with her and stroked her and she purred. Strangely she purred almost to the very end. It was, as they often say, a peaceful death. I've never really got my head around that term though. How can death be peaceful? She only had a moment of pain but it was very, very upsetting and I felt very guilty that I hadn't been there for her in this house. Tony came home shortly afterwards, I was sobbing as I met him in the hall. He smiled broadly and gave me a hug. He just accepted a cat's death as natural, which of course it is, but to me this possessed an element of personal tragedy. It was as if there was no separation between the cat and me. I left Tony with Nathan (who seemed fairly oblivious to the cat's death despite being present), called at my mum's and told her I was driving up to Charlesworth. I was still sobbing as I set off and she called out to me, 'If you're going to be like this over a cat what will you be like when I die?'

'I'll die before you,' I said, a bit melodramatically.

'I hope for your sake you do,' she replied. That reflects the kind of state I was in. Ridiculous. But it seemed more far-reaching than the cat's death. Later I got stoned and mulled over the significance of the letters. Tabatha's initials were T.W. (Tabatha Wild); Tennessee Williams also died the same day (T.W.); T.W. – Tony Wilson. I was going to lose him and there was nothing I could do about it. It was like watching a crash in slow motion. It was fate.

When Tony and I discussed why I still hadn't consummated my return to him I blamed the house as being the basic problem, the reason I wasn't comfortable. I didn't want to bring up the issue of my bond with K since that was a sore point, but I probably should have done. I had enormous guilt about what I'd put him through – the agonies of indecision during the previous year. We'd come to blows in January, literally – my diary description of our row sounded like a catfight. Not good, but evidence of passion all the same. The days when Tony and I rolled around the floor fighting (or loving) had gone. It just felt as if Tony was some kind of Victorian authoritarian figure who was demanding return of his property – me. The same thing that Roger McGough had done over Thelma.

Tony asked me where I would feel comfortable sleeping with him and I said Portmeirion (knowing the hotel was shut for the winter, as it used to be then). The very next day he told me he'd booked it for March. March suddenly seemed dreadfully soon. At least he was happy to wait until then. I was buying time. The simple physical act of sex had taken on gargantuan horror in my mind.

We had a brief respite before then. Tony invited me to Portugal for a Durutti Column gig at the Coliseum in Lisbon. Bruce Mitchell arranged our tickets. He recalled: 'I bumped into Tony somewhere and he said I've got these tickets, got the hotel rooms – you know the first thing Lindsay said? "What are the sleeping arrangements?"'

I was terrifically impressed with the hospitality we received in Lisbon. Miguel Esteves Cardoso and some of his associates greeted us at the airport and Miguel was such a charming host. Miguel is bilingual and already had a love of Manchester and Manchester music, having graduated from Manchester University with a degree in Political Philosophy in 1979. His first of many books, *Escritica Pop*, had been published in 1982. He has an enthusiasm and brilliance of mind that matched Tony's in a weird way (yet is also entirely different). I adored the time Tony and I spent in Lisbon and thus began a love affair I had with the place and the people. I went back each year for the next three years and dreamt of living there.

Bruce Mitchell remembered going sight-seeing that weekend and bumping into Tony and me in Sintra, sitting inside the palace there. 'You're sat on one of the famous buildings of the world,' he said, 'Tony's reading *Remembrance of Things Past* and we're sight-seeing.' The beautiful, mediaeval Royal Palace is straight out of a fairytale and sits atop a high hill, almost perched on a rock, affording a spectacular view. I remember Tony and I looking out at the view over the palace walls that sunny day. A rare moment of peace.

'Wilson said the local guide had written a book about Situationism and Factory,' Bruce continued, 'and Tony introduced me to this guy Miguel, whose wife is there – he says, "This is Miguel and they've got a relationship just like me and Lindsay."' Tony was doubtless referring, somewhat tongue in cheek, to our volatile relationship. Miguel and his wife were also on the brink of a separation, although they had parented beautiful twins.

Miguel formed a label called Fundacao Atlantica, and released an album by Vini called *Amigos em Portugal*. Bruce told me that Vini took a friend called Francesca with him and recorded the album in just two days in Estoril, and that it immediately sold 15,000 copies upon its release.

I was amazed at the reception Vini received at the concert. The hall was packed and he was treated like a real star, whereas in Manchester he was by comparison more or less ignored. Maybe it's that thing about Europeans appreciating art more than the English. *Saudade* is a beautiful Portuguese word for which there is no literal translation in English; the nearest we have might be nostalgia, but it doesn't quite do it. Tony said, 'It's the national mood, a sense of something lost, of intense nostalgia and yearning. Senor Cardoso did his PhD at Manchester on the influence of *saudade* on Portuguese politics in the 10th to 15th centuries. You see, cool guy, a guy to do a deal with. I always think that *saudade* is why the Portuguese, as much as any country in the world, take Vini's intensely romantic guitar to their hearts. Damn sight better than their Fado folk song tradition, which is more whining than romantic. Although Vini wrote a track in this period which was called "Saudade", that's more typical of our carelessness with titles. The piece "Favourite Descending Intervals" from the same collection much more connects to that *saudade* spirit.'

Tony subsequently fell out with Miguel, though how anyone could fall out with Miguel was beyond me. Tony always said that there was just one rule in the music business: never do a deal in Portugal. On a music blog site called Dias Atlânticos, he attempted to justify this logic, but in the end the only reason he came up with was that Miguel and his associates didn't turn up for a gig Vini played in Portugal six months after his album was released. I wasn't at that gig so can't comment, but I can vouchsafe that Miguel was not only at the gig I went to, but treated us like royalty. I have never received such kind hospitality from any company before or since.

Miguel said that he and Tony had a disagreement about royalties: 'Factory paid the artists fifty percent and Portuguese law only allowed us to pay fourteen percent, and export taxes took the rest.

'Tony wrote me a long letter explaining Factory principles and calling me irresponsible. He was right. Of course I never made a penny – or even a free drink – from my label and we went bankrupt long before Factory. But we fell out. We were very good friends and, twenty years later, I realise friendship, business and idealism don't mix. The record is a masterpiece, though. Vini came to Lisbon to record a single and ended up setting down the whole album in one, magical night.

'I had no idea Tony had written about it [on the Dias Atlânticos blog]. Just shows how honest he is. But he's wrong about my not being at Vini's concerts. I convinced the promoters, plugged them and was there with all the other fans, the five or six times he played here. Ah, it brings tears to my eyes, it really does.'

Back in England the Portmeirion date was looming. It was bound to fail and, of course, it did. Whereas our first visit there was heavenly, this visit was hell. All the rooms in the cottages and hotel are lovely, but even so, after we took LSD it took on a slightly sinister aspect. Perhaps that was my mind. It was a mad idea to take LSD, but Tony thought it was a special occasion. I suppose it would have been if I could only just have given myself to him and let everything else go. I couldn't. We sat in the lounge and he watched TV while I worried about everything. As it got much later (and it became obvious we weren't going to make love), the dreadful part was that I suddenly realised there was an upstairs to this particular cottage and the couple inhabiting it were having wild sex.

Tony and I could hear the bed knocking against the wall. I think it was at this point that I decided we were on a bad trip. I remember Tony was eating biscuits and I was just looking at them, wondering whether or not to have one, and he said, 'Go on, do yourself a favour, have one.' He didn't say it nicely. It was said with a sneer and a tone of, 'What is your problem?' Indeed. I regret not making love to Tony that night and every single other night I may have missed. My advice to anyone who loves someone is: love them now, for tomorrow you or they will be gone.

Driving back to Manchester the next day, I knew I'd blown it and that Tony was now writing me off. I couldn't blame him. But in a sense it was exactly that attitude which held me back. I was rewarded for this, punished for that. If love isn't given freely then it isn't worth a fuck. I notice that the original date on Tony's divorce petition was not long after we returned from Portmeirion – 10 April. He'd crossed it out and re-inserted a later date. He must have decided to give me another chance.

It was rather like Paul Morley's tribute to Tony in the *NME*: 'Funnily enough, when I was going through a phase of not quite trusting Wilson, if only because his appetite for experience could seem overwhelming and a little suspect, he would pop up in some way, with a phone call or an appearance on television that reminded you, once or twice in the nick of time, that he was a force for good, and definitely not bad. It was just that sometimes he could be truly, usually tactically, mischievous in how he pursued the goodness.' Quite so. And such tactics made me think that perhaps Tony was bad.

My diary entry for 14 May 1983: 'Wedding anniversary. Six years. Went round to Tony's in a depressed mood. Had gone mad with mum – she said I'd lost my option with K. T was very reluctant to go for the proposed meal with me in a mood. Returned to house and had a clichéd farewell – e.g. he said he was sorry it hadn't worked out, it had been very interesting, he hoped we'd be friends, etc. It was obvious he had something else lined up for the evening. I decided that that, plus my fury at having "lost" K, clinches it.'

One thing about my mum – she was right. Tony was wrong to blame her for the break-up. She was warning me. I only had one option now, and that was fast running out. In my heart of hearts I knew the relationship with K had been damaged beyond repair, and I also knew that Tony had just been playacting with his supposed farewell. In reality I felt he was still there for me with open arms. But K and I still had one last jaunt to take in Paris and, however critical things were between us, everything had been arranged. The journey was a nightmare – lashing rain and storms, K was driving too fast. My mum came with us. Things were dreadfully strained and the first night in Paris was terrible, I didn't fall asleep until after dawn. I behaved dreadfully, made my mum cry and told K to piss off when he asked if I wanted a croissant. I was a monster! Doubtless the stress of the push and pull, my almost violent indecision, was taking its toll. It's hard to forgive oneself; after my mum died I just couldn't bear to be reminded of the horrid person I was to her sometimes. The car broke down on the way back and we arrived in London to find that K's mother had put his dog down, and two days later his beautiful canary – Booey – got out through the window. K said that the bird had to do with my leaving. The writing was on the wall.

Whoever thinks that youth and beauty is aligned with happiness and peace needs to think again. If I could go back I would do it all differently. But perhaps you have to be young and suffer the pains of love to know what you ought to do, and by then it is too late. And the frustrating thing is that those who know – your elders, your parents – however much they want to, they really can't help you. It's something you have to work through by yourself.

It was clear I needed a job and lifting heavy furniture was hardly suitable (though I'd done my best). The marital settlement – £5,000 – had by now run out.

Tony was now wooing me back to the Factory side of things, if not the marriage. He let me put a gig on at the Hacienda. I called it 'The Last Supper' because there were thirteen of us onstage – all drumming, African drumming, with the teacher taking the lead. He was the one who told me that musically I was a virgin.

That summer of 1983 Tony came up with a clever solution, and offered me what he said was a really great and interesting job – one that he'd have liked to do himself. Obviously I was interested, although I felt there was more than a tinge of manipulation hanging around his offer. If I was working for Factory I could hardly return to London.

There now seemed little point in going back there in any case, since things had become so dire with K. I thought that if I removed myself from him then at least he wouldn't be subject to the torture of indecision I was under. I'd messed him around for long enough. And Tony, come to that. But Tony seemed pleased the day he became my boss. If marriage is a power struggle then I suppose he was winning now. Ostensibly – for me, at least – it wasn't that, it was more that I'd chosen to return to the marriage. But I felt he'd somehow forced me, taken advantage of my lack of a proper job, so on my side it was a case of, 'You can take a horse to water, but you can't make it drink.' And I didn't. I still lived at my mum's, and I still resisted, pulling back from intimacy.

The job was running the overseas licensing at Factory. The day I commenced regular work in September 1983, Tony handed me four or five folders jammed with scattered telexes, letters, purchase orders, invoices, contracts, and an empty address box with blank cards. He explained the rudiments of the job and said it was very important that I made a note of contact details on a card for everyone

I spoke to. That was it really. Rob and Alan didn't speak to me about it at all. Rob's girlfriend, Lesley, was by then running the office and was given the title of production manager. For the first week I worked at Old Broadway but then I moved over to 86 Palatine Road (into what would have been the smaller of the two bedrooms). This had been the flat inhabited by Alan; by this point he stayed there only rarely. Lesley was in the main office (the lounge), and Ikon, the video annex, was based in the main bedroom (before expanding into the basement of Tony's Didsbury house).

Tony was right. It was a great job. I really enjoyed it. I ascertained at once that a lot of income had been lost through the lack of an orderly system. I determined to create such a method and to increase the turnover of business. Within six months the license revenue had trebled.

This, of course, was not necessarily down to me so much as the goods I was privileged to be selling. Nineteen eighty-three was a peak year for New Order. They were really, really good then. Listen to *Power, Corruption & Lies* – the raw energy and enthusiasm of youth. They'd learnt Martin's studio techniques and, although the album was self-produced, his influence is unmistakeable. The only thing that slightly unnerved me about that album was Saville's sleeve; a bowl of flowers in a vase painted by Fantin-Latour. It was the sort of image you might choose if buying a card for a geriatric auntie, I rather thought at first glance. But the sleeve grew on me somehow. New Order were a band who'd dragged themselves out of the mire and come up smelling of roses. And the painting was a striking and unforgettable image. There were no words anywhere on this one – just a pantone colour wheel, standing on a silver-grey background on the reverse. The sleeve actually stands out as incredibly special.

Tony and Peter Saville always had an interesting relationship. After Tony's death Saville told me: 'The best thing that ever happened to Tony and I was after Factory when there was nothing practical bringing us together, no reason to meet but we often did, we'd get together when he was in London or whatever. We liked discussing things.'

I can vouch for this. Tony was extremely fond of Saville and it was one of his genuine friendships. Like anyone with influence, it was hard for Tony to know what people really were to him. Saville was different. Tony phoned him in front of me in the last weeks of his life and he seemed relaxed, totally at ease talking to this friend, as if it was the most natural thing in the world to do. And yet these two, as was the case with other very close relationships Tony shared – Erasmus and Tony, myself and Tony, Elliot and Tony, Vini and Tony – fell out pretty badly and didn't speak for years.

'Blue Monday' was recorded in the same sessions at Britannia Row but released separately and earlier as a single – and a hit single at that. Tony inferred that this decision, one taken lightly, cost 300,000 album sales. Computer wizardry mixed with New York dance influences and Barney's voice. It all just worked. Who would have thought it?

Tony often liked to credit Martin for 'Blue Monday', even though he and New Order had gone their separate ways by then. He claimed that Barney and the band used production techniques on this song that they'd learned from Martin. He always said that the breakthrough record was actually not 'Blue Monday' but 'Everything's Gone Green' – that this was the beginning of what he called 'modern music', i.e. using computers.

Every Monday morning the four of us – me, Tony, Rob Gretton and Lesley – had a 'power' meeting. It began and continued with dope smoking (for all but Lesley). I was aware of a fantasy having built itself right here in the scruffy confines of a rented flat. We (well, Rob and Tony) were major-league players now. I used to hum the theme tune of *Dallas* under my breath. Tony and I were the Ewings – Tony had to be J.R., of course! With myself in the role of Sue Ellen – and Rob and Lesley were Bobby and Pamela. I'm not sure who Alan was. He was either not there or, if he was, he'd generally have vanished within ten minutes, on some errand or other.

I don't know if I ever truly got to know Rob. He was very humorous and well liked. People who make you laugh always are. But he could also be a bit of a bully – with his fists and with his opinions. He took the view that he was never wrong, but sometimes in quite an aggressive way. He was a Capricorn and, according to Penny Henry, who set the door up at the Hacienda, Capricorns always think they're right. It's a Capricorn weak spot. And Tony, being a Pisces, tended to reflect the people around him.

In an interview I spoke to Tony about Rob's role. Tony said Rob was the fifth member of the band, and when I asked him what Rob's contribution was he said, 'There is an artistic-ness about Rob which you never see – it's invisible. It evolved with a certain kind of style about the way things were done. The first sleeve they did was crap – that metal scaffolding sleeve for the twelve-inch [*An Ideal for Living*]. But no – you look at New Order now and somehow . . . What defines Rob? He's the head of a record company and he spends four hours in a room one night trying to persuade this band from Blackpool to call their first album "Fuck" and they're going, "No, no." The idea of a record company wanting the band to call the album "Fuck" 'cause no one has ever done it before. They're going, "No, no, no, we want to call it 'Always Now'," or whatever and he's saying, "Call it 'Fuck'." That sums up Rob.'

I asked Larry Cassidy from Section 25 what he thought about that. He commented: 'It wasn't Rob Gretton's record. Anyone can think up a decent title but try writing a decent song. Rob was a good manager but he had a Rolls-Royce band. They sold themselves.' Sadly, Larry died suddenly six months after this conversation.

Tony continued: 'Saville once said to Rob, "I've done all the sleeves, I did it all myself – you and the band have had absolutely nothing to do with it." And Rob went, "Yes we did. We *let* you do it."'

The relationship between Rob and Tony was interestingly volatile, although personally I felt that Rob was pretty clever at getting his way with Tony, even getting one over on him in certain instances (for example, the fifty-fifty split being weighted in his favour so that Factory paid mechanicals out of their half):

TW: Rob wound the fuck out of me. It's like what Lenny Waronker once said: 'That first meeting I had with you and Gretton was the second worst meeting I've ever been to in my life.'
LR: Who was he?
TW: He was the great vice-chairman of Warner Bros in the eighties. And he also produced all the Randy Newman albums.
LR: Why was the meeting so awful?
TW: We met in his big suite in Claridge's and apparently halfway through the meeting Rob and I started fighting with each other.
LR: What about?
TW: I'd say, 'We want this,' and Rob would say, 'No we don't we want that,' and I'd say, 'No, shut the fuck up,' and he'd say, 'Shut the fuck up yourself.' It used to happen quite a lot.
LR: Who won? Who was the boss in between you two?
TW: Neither of us. It was a constant battle.

Keith Jobling humorously commented on just such a battle: 'The whole Factory thing was bizarre, like walking into a sitcom. You'd be going in for a meeting with Factory Records and you'd go through the door, and Rob would be going, said with drawl, "It's fucking not happening Tony," and Tony would be sitting at the desk saying, "Look at it this way, if we don't do it . . ." pulling on a joint, and Rob would say, "We're not doing it, it's too much money, we're not spending that," and Tony would say, "No, you're right, we're not doing it now." But then he'd go, "You know what though, if you think about it this way . . ." We'd just be standing there while this little board meeting was going on. In all the best sitcoms everyone's playing it deadly straight and then you'd go downstairs with Tony on the way to an edit suite, and as we're driving away you'd ask, "What happened there then?" and Tony'd say, "Oh I just resigned." "Why?" "Oh 'cause he's a fucking cunt that's why. And as for fucking Tina [a Factory employee] – she taped my conversation." Then you'd get to the music studio and you'd go in and there'd be Shaun [Ryder] going, "Oh I've dropped it, I've fucking dropped it . . . *Tony*, have you got a torch?" Just one scene after another.'

I look back with some surprise at the timing of events in the second half of the year. Tony had spoken to me about divorce in June 1983. By this point my relationship with K was truly on the rocks as well. Tony requested a conversation and talked for a long time about the pain we would both feel when we fell in love with other people, and how if we divorced at that point then the pain of both things would be too much, so he said he wanted the divorce now. I didn't protest. I just asked, 'When?' He said, 'Next week.' I didn't believe him. But on 17 June I took Tony to the station on his way to yet another trip to New York. He told me that he'd filed for divorce, but that if I wished to return as his wife I should. A week later I went to London at K's invitation to spend a weekend in Weymouth. The sun was shining, I pretended we were reconciling, but once there he told me he had to say goodbye. However upset I was, I could hardly be surprised.

I still had the vague hope that things would somehow work out with the right man out of the two – that all I had to do was sit things out a little longer. Tony's divorce petition didn't feel real; it seemed more like a charade. 'No wonder Tony wouldn't play charades at Christmas,' I thought. 'He doesn't need to; he's too busy with the main act, the charades in his life.' In this act the scene called for marriage and family, and if I wasn't going to oblige then he'd just find someone else. Which was fair enough I suppose.

I still felt that whatever Tony did, however far things went, there was something between us that could never be destroyed. It's a bit like my belief that however bad you are, however much you drink, however many drugs you take, there's a nugget of something precious within all of us that can't be touched by any of it.

The timing was odd. Tony filed for divorce that June yet I commenced work in September. The decree nisi was issued in October and our divorce was made absolute in December. Tony did the whole thing by himself. He described my occupation as 'Antiques Dealer' and gave the reasons for the breakdown as being that I had moved out of our family home and we had lived apart for two years. I thought Catholics didn't believe in divorce and, not for the first time, he reminded me of Henry VIII. He changed the rules of his religion. I reasoned that our marriage vows hadn't been acted out, so why should this divorce be? None of it meant much to me. I should have taken it more seriously.

But the question still lingers in my mind. Why did he offer me the job at that time? Did he want to put the final nail in the coffin with K and then punish me by making babies with someone else? Was it because I'd run out of money and he cared enough to provide basic subsistence through a job at Factory? Did he – as he said – think I'd be good at the job and really want me to work there? He certainly needed someone. Or did he – like me – believe that we would still get back together?

Tony told me years later that he was still in love with me through all of the foregoing but, having messed up so many other women he'd been out with (because of his feelings for me) – principally Ros, who he treated abominably – he'd made a promise at his mother's grave that he wouldn't do that with the next girlfriend to come along. That's how he explained it to me. I can't help but think, though, that what he did next was partly undertaken out of a desire for revenge.

Within two weeks of Tony meeting Hilary, he told her he'd look after her

Above: 'I'd rather watch fucking paint dry.' Tony at Old Broadway, 1983.
Below: Bernard Sumner, New York, 1983.

Above left: Tony and Lesley at the Factory office, 1983.
Above right: Factory office girl, 1983. **Below:** Shades of Brian Clough and Peter Taylor? Tony and Alan on the road in Portugal, 1984.

Opposite above: Alan and Tony lost in thought at a Durutti Column and A Certain Ratio gig in Portugal, 1984. **Opposite centre:** That's my boy: Tony, Hilary and Oliver in 1985. **Opposite below:** Tony with the apples of his eye, Oliver and Izzy, 1991.

Opposite above: Me and some of 52nd Street go for a jaunt – gigging in Wales, 1983. **Opposite below:** Hacienda heat, October 1988.

Above: Alan makes a run from the camera when Factory goes down, 1992. **Below:** 'It's like Chou En-Lai said . . .' Tosh Ryan interviews Tony on the day that Factory closed, 1992.

Opposite: A.H. Wilson and William. **Above:** Tony and the *Unknown Pleasures* artwork, which hung in the doorway of his loft, 2006.
Below: Tony outside his apartment in 2006.

Above: Genius, scholar or twat?

and that he wanted children with her. Nathan, who had lived at Old Broadway throughout our marital separation, recalled that Tony asked him if he could move out 'next week' because he was getting married. But life isn't exactly a shop where you can just order these things. 'Er, I'll have a happy marriage and two kids please.'

I loved my job – Tony had been right about running the overseas license department; it was good fun. It was also great because I was able to get involved creatively with other stuff in addition to running the licensing.

When I was still in favour with Tony (i.e. when there had still been hope of a reconciliation), he let me go ahead with a plan I had to make a single out of the song 'Telstar' (originally an instrumental track by the Tornados). I'd written words to it with the help of my mum that fitted the song really well and, given my diabolical singing on 'I Get Along Without You Very Well', decided that for this venture I would hire the services of a choir boy. I also gathered a few assorted musicians together.

From ACR/Kalima there was the brilliant keyboard player Andy Connell (subsequently better known as one half of Swing Out Sister) and the multi-talented Martin Moscrop, as well as two other similarly creative characters who were more on the outside of what was going on – Wayne Worm and Eric Random. Wayne was a bassist and integral part of Manchester subculture; he was involved with the Film & Video Workshop and was forever messing around with wires and building studios. Eric had earlier been in the Tiller Boys, also with the Bedlamites and Free Agents, and had good taste in music. The recording session went really well and I put a guide vocal down for the choir boy to copy later. On my way out to the bathroom at Strawberry Studios, I heard Andy and Martin messing around on a piano and trumpet respectively, with a slowed-down version of the song.

'That's brilliant,' I exclaimed. 'Let's record it.'

They did this in about ten minutes flat and it features on the B-side (although in view of what happened next it probably deserved to be on the A-side). Unfortunately the very next day I got a letter from the publisher of 'Telstar' to say that adding words to the tune was strictly forbidden. That was a real blow. I knew it wouldn't be a hit in that event. We salvaged things but it didn't correspond to my vision at all. Hooky came in and remixed the whole track; it felt like a drastic haircut and sounded a bit disco when he'd finished. He put my voice through a vocoder so the words couldn't be distinguished. The sleeve was a bit state-of-the-art for its time. Each one had a hologram of a spaceship stuck to it. I'd managed to buy a job lot of these holograms cheap. I called the band Ad Infinitum, inspired by something Tony had typed on the envelope of one of his letters – *Lins Numero Uno Ad Infinitum*.

It was all good creative stuff and certainly beat humping furniture around in the freezing rain. Again, around the time Tony met Hilary I'd been quite inspired by a Section 25 track called 'Looking from a Hilltop' and suggested getting involved in making a video with them. I'd gotten the idea into my head that the crescents in Hulme (since demolished) were romantic and thought we should film it there, which we did. The video features me driving my Karmann Ghia and is inter-cut with other members of the band, one of whom was playing my 'boyfriend'. When we drove off together at the end the passenger door swung open – the sort of problem that develops with older cars (and bodies come to that). This group were equally inspirational to Vini Reilly around that time. He said, 'I thought the Hacienda was amazing. I preferred it when it was empty. One of the best gigs I have ever seen in my life was there – there were about twenty people there and it was Section 25 in their early days and they were just astonishing, brilliant. Way ahead of their time. They lost the plot later on.'

Tony announced his new girlfriend at almost the same time that she became pregnant. Coincidentally this was December 1983, the same month as our divorce. I rang K to tell him the news, naively hoping we could go back to how we were before. I told him that, despite everything, I had been faithful to him all the way through our separation. He told me he hadn't and that he'd met someone. So I'd lost them both. I was gutted. And I could only blame myself. A year or two later he said that he'd lied about that, because he didn't want to return to the relationship after all the upset and the to-ing and fro-ing of the previous years.

By Christmas 1983 I felt I'd ruined everything. I wanted to punish myself and embarked on the first of a series of relationships with men who were either wholly unsuitable or unavailable. The first of these was probably a drug addict and the only guy my mum ever actually voiced her outright disapproval of. Basically I was subconsciously choosing men I could guarantee no stability with. Looking for love in all the wrong places. Perhaps because these were the kind of men I felt I deserved, or because I was frightened of ever being trapped again. Despite having a degree in Psychology, I'm still not sure of the reason I continued to choose destructive relationships from then on. It took me several years to even figure out that that was what I was doing. Self-denial is a wonderful thing. I subsequently had the token affair with a married man (isn't everybody supposed to have one?), but it was too dishonest, not really for me, however wonderful the man was. Ultimately I chose a better scenario – how about men who are ostensibly available but live in another country? Great one that. Actually I'm still doing it! But I consider myself psychologically in much better health. Instead of America, the latest one only lives in Wales.

The speed with which Tony married and began a family with Hilary was alarming. Yet since it was my own stupid fault I'd lost both him and any future family with him, I only blamed myself for what had occurred.

One day soon after Tony and Hilary had moved in together, I had occasion to go round to 36 Old Broadway, since the basement there now housed Ikon's video suite and I had some work to do on the Section 25 film. This basement had its own steps outside but none of its own facilities, so the inner door to the house was left open. I hadn't been introduced to Hilary but felt ready to be friendly to her. My mum always said that if you want to get to know everything about a man, go and have a long chat with his last girlfriend or wife! I knew she couldn't possibly know him like I did. It seemed like a good idea – there was much I could tell her, and warn and prepare her for – but it was naive of me to think she would want to talk to me.

That said, I was somewhat relieved that Hilary was out when I got to the house. I didn't want to cause any upset and I also wanted to keep my job. However, I hadn't been there very long when I heard footsteps walking above us on the kitchen floor and a definitive click to the door that led down to the basement. The Karmann Ghia parked outside was a bit of a giveaway to my presence. Myself and the others had been working for an hour or so when one of them, Malcolm I think, brightly said, 'Fancy a brew?' Again I felt a bit relieved. He hadn't heard what I had; maybe I'd just imagined it. He gathered up the cups and headed up the stairs, only to return with a rather dismayed look on his face. 'The door's locked,' he said. I couldn't blame Hilary but was disappointed to be shut out. I held no ill will towards her and never have.

Bruce Mitchell remembered a day later on when I was working in the second room at 86 Palatine Road and Tony was beavering away in the front room.

'Someone said, "Oh Hilary's coming round," and Tony looked up from his bits of paper and said, "Is Lindsay here?" He didn't know if you were in the office or not! He didn't want to encourage Hilary to come round if you were there.'

My position at Factory felt rather tenuous. How stupid I was to think that this could carry on. I was friendly to Tony when our paths crossed at work and politely asked after Hilary's health and so on. Tony became somewhat aloof; disinterested in me and the work I was doing.

It was a pity because I was good at the job and enjoyed it. It was those years when I was officially working at Factory that I grasped the fact that making money is not a principally male domain, as I'd been brainwashed into believing. I was making a bomb with very little effort. The only problem was that it was all for Factory. I earned just £69.75 a week but it didn't matter to me, I was grateful to have a job.

Tony and Hilary's son was born in September 1984. It changed Tony visibly. I felt redundant, as if I was something of an irritation on a personal level. Tony admitted to me later that he had – at last – been able to cut the cord with me. He'd believed he'd only achieve this by falling in love with someone else. He hadn't managed to do that despite all the lovely women he'd courted, it was as if he was imprinted physically on me. (This also became the case later with Yvette; however hard he tried, he told me, he couldn't fall in love with anyone apart from her.) In 1984 it wasn't another woman but it forged his commitment to Hilary. He'd fallen head over heels in love with his little baby boy, Oliver.

In August 1984 I'd become manager of a Factory soul and funk band called 52nd Street. My appointment ironically coincided with a new release by 52nd Street called 'Can't Afford (To Let You Go)'. How true.

Derek Johnson, the bass player, had asked me if I'd like the job and, since I'd been really impressed by the single 'Cool as Ice', I agreed. However, it transpired that there had been a reshuffle in the group since that record release – the singer Beverley McDonald had left and been replaced by Diane Charlemagne. Tony took the same view of Beverley's role in the group that he earlier had regarding Simon Topping and A Certain Ratio. Namely that she was the star and the group would never get anywhere without her. Indeed, there was a quirkiness about her in a Macy Gray sort of way. But Diane sang like an angel, on a par with the greats such as Dionne Warwick, in my opinion. Mind you, the night I met her I thought we were going nowhere.

I travelled down with the band for a gig in London as a way of getting to know them. The gig was a Factory event at Riverside Studios; one night of a week of Factory London premieres (FAC 121). 52nd Street shared the evening with Quando Quango, Mike Pickering's band. (Mike went on to wider acclaim with M People, and as a Hacienda booker and DJ with an ear for talent such as the Happy Mondays.) I climbed merrily into the front of the van sitting alongside Diane and the driver. She didn't speak a word to me all the way there, remained huddled up, and even appeared to sleep for part of the journey. The boys were laughing and joking behind us in that laddish way. I couldn't imagine Diane performing, but she explained her behaviour to me recently: 'I was happy when I saw it was you – a woman – managing us, but disappointed because, although you were intelligent and beautiful, you were naive and you didn't know the power of your own sexuality. The boys were being disrespectful, they saw you as a piece of meat, but you were a free spirit and didn't see it, you were vulnerable. I had to distance myself from you because I didn't want them to see me in the same light.'

This is an interesting, sad observation. Looking at a photograph of myself with members of the group taken around the time, my naivety and innocence is visibly apparent, despite being nearly ten years older than the others. Also, I had low self-esteem – I knew men found me attractive but had no confidence in anything else I had to give. My mum thought I had more male friends than female for that reason. Thankfully this is no longer the case.

Once onstage Diane emerged from her self-imposed cocoon state and danced and lifted the music to another place – but then didn't speak all the way back. I didn't think she liked me or trusted me at first. But we became true and lifelong friends.

It was obvious where my job at Factory was heading and I was perhaps also naive in thinking I could stay. But when the end came I felt it was outrageously unfair.

Generally speaking Factory didn't bother with promotion. Tony Michaelides (sometimes called Tony the Greek) was very enthusiastic and unofficially helped out. Radio DJ Mark Radcliffe was Michaelides's lodger around 1982-84 and was then presenting a 'Cure for Insomnia' show on Piccadilly Radio. This perfectly placed Michaelides to pick up copies of records from Factory and hand them over to Piccadilly. After Michaelides had promoted Factory's records free of charge for a year, Tony announced one day that it was about time they paid him and he was then given £400 a month.

Mostly the rule in the Factory office was that if you said 'No' in response to people ringing up, you'd be on fairly safe ground. I found this way of dealing with media requests frustrating, unfair to Factory's other acts, and simply not in line with my generally helpful nature. Nathan McGough recalled: 'Factory had this policy, "We don't talk to journalists, we don't do interviews." But okay, so New Order don't do interviews, but all these other fucking bands needed to engage with the media but there was this hostility against it.'

The enigma of Factory lent an air of power and mystique but, as Larry Cassidy pointed out, New Order sold themselves. The other bands needed as much help as they could get, and I was of a mind to provide it if I believed in their talent.

Marcel King was one such.

If I hadn't gone out of my way to help Marcel King's demo go ahead (something Rob had asked me to do), Tony wouldn't have had the ammunition to fire me. It would have been a lot easier if I had just said no – then nothing gets done and no mistakes are made. If you don't wash up you can't break dishes. But I genuinely enjoyed being creatively involved. This was my life now. I was – naturally – between boyfriends.

It was the first week of December when Gretton asked me to arrange a demo recording for Marcel, which A&M Records in Los Angeles were waiting for. In 1974, at the tender age of sixteen, Marcel had had a Number One hit record with 'Sad Sweet Dreamer'. Marcel told me this record came about because someone heard him singing in a shop. He was too young to handle overnight success and seemed bitter about the treatment he'd received from the music business. He was broke, somewhat temperamental, a drug fiend – and yet he sang like an angel. Earlier in the year he'd recorded a great track called 'Reach for Love' and Rob gave me the task of enabling the next single to come together.

I personally arranged the musicians and equipment for a day's rehearsal. I asked Rob whether I should book an eight-track studio or a twenty-four-track, and he told me to see how a rehearsal went but that, since Factory were covering the costs, it would probably be better to book an eight-track.

On Monday 3 December the first rehearsal session took place. This went very well. I could see that they were ready to record immediately and that if we stalled, Marcel might well go off the boil. On the day in question, Factory were overdrawn by approximately £6,000. We'd had a run of bad luck – one of our distributors had gone bankrupt owing us £40,000. Therefore I was concerned about the expense, and told Marcel that we'd record at a simple eight-track studio such as the one we were rehearsing in. He said that he didn't want to bother with that, since the tracks could be master-taped in the same amount of time in a twenty-four-track studio. I told him that Factory's budget wasn't sufficient. He replied that A&M were paying and that he knew this since he'd spoken with them directly, two weeks previously. He asked me to phone them and find out for myself. Marcel didn't have a manager, something Tony felt was essential to an artist's success, and I suppose I took on the role in this case. That night, on my return from the rehearsal, I passed the office at approximately 9:00pm. I knew this to be a good time to phone Los Angeles. I got through to Nancy Jeffries – the same woman that Marcel had spoken to. She said that she'd asked Michael Shamberg (the filmmaker who was by this point also running the Factory US office) to submit a written budget of the studio costs two months previously but that he hadn't done so, and that her company couldn't okay the payment until this had been done. She asked me if I would submit a budget and said that she'd telephone me on Thursday. She, like myself, seemed very keen to move things forward.

When I returned home my mum said Tony had just phoned, worried that I was running up a bill in the recording studio. The following morning I rang and told him that the session had only been a rehearsal and that I was going to submit a budget before booking the actual studio. At this he exploded and said, 'I cannot believe you have done it again – destroyed Michael Shamberg's work.' I said I didn't see why. He said that Shamberg had been negotiating a $3,000 advance for the demo tape. (The written budget I'd worked out came to £2,000.) I explained that A&M needed a budget and he hadn't got around to submitting one, so Tony said, 'Let's finish the tapes and then think about it.'

I wondered why I was being blamed just for trying to sort things out. In fact I was being dismissed, but Tony was angling for my resignation. When I later asked him to give me his actual reasons, by letter, he wrote: 'I was informed by one of the management committee of the Hacienda Club that the head cleaner, who is also a bass player, had not turned up for work because he had gone into studio "for Marcel King" and that "Tony would know all about it". I did not.' But another director – Rob – had asked me to sort the demo out, and it wasn't my fault that he hadn't bothered to communicate this to Tony.

Then Tony explained his reasoning: 'I was aware that Michael Shamberg had been working for three months to get A&M to release a second single by Marcel King. Michael had been responsible for a $6,000 deal for Marcel's first single for A&M earlier in the year. I was aware that he had almost negotiated a $1,000 payment for Marcel to complete demo tracks here in England, of two tracks suggested by A&M themselves. But that money had not yet come through.' No, and it wasn't going to in the absence of a budget. Honestly I didn't regard what I was doing as stepping on anyone's toes. Since I was organising the demo I was best placed to estimate the costs in any case. I was just trying to make the record happen (which, incidentally, it never did). None of the directors had bothered explaining any of the aforementioned or the protocol involved because, if they had, I would have phoned Shamberg first.

Actually, I must admit that Shamberg and I hadn't hit it off too well because a) when I served him a homemade hotpot the first time he came to our house he told me it was boring, b) I thought he brought out arguably the worst record, with the worst sleeve, ever on Factory – Thick Pigeon – and, since he'd been 'honest' about my hotpot, I thought he deserved my honesty about that, and c) our rivalry for Tony's allegiance, probably. Clearly by this point in time it was no contest – he was on much stronger ground than the shifting sand I stood on. Which is exactly why I wouldn't have taken him on.

Tony's letter continued: 'Having failed to locate you that evening, I called Michael Shamberg to ask if he knew anything about the demo recording. NO. He decided to call A&M immediately to tell them Marcel was going in the studio. He called me back twenty minutes later. A&M knew all about it; apparently you had talked personally to Nancy Jeffries, of A&M, and set it up immediately without Shamberg knowing.'

No – Rob had set it up, via me, without informing Shamberg. Maybe I'd overstepped the mark in calling this woman, but I was just trying to move the bloody thing forward. I'd had my work cut out. But I should have known I was dealing with a boys' club, and was obviously on a very weak wicket in any case.

On Wednesday 5 December, Tony told me over the telephone that I was fired and that he would be issuing the customary warning letters. He wasn't clear about when the dismissal would take place, but said that he would like me to stay on and teach my successor the job.

On Thursday, when I arrived at the office, Alan and Lesley were standing together behind the main desk and told me that my return to work was pointless in view of the circumstances. I refused to accept this, and doubtless told them to fuck off. I had business to attend to and stayed for the duration of the day. Tony didn't show up.

The next day he called at the office and I asked him if he'd brought my dismissal notice. He said he thought I'd resigned. I said I had not. He said I had no choice. I told him that I was a 'free spirit', that I did have a choice, and I wasn't going to resign.

Our battle of wills was carrying on even at this juncture. Evasive as ever, he suggested we meet for lunch to discuss the matter, but said that he would prefer me not to carry on working in the meantime. Between tears, as acceptance was slowly dawning, I asked him if he'd been happy with my work. He said he had, that he'd been pleased overall, and agreed that the license revenue had trebled. But he accused me of pursuing a personal vendetta against Michael Shamberg and said that, because of my refusal to do as the company asked, I had no choice but to go. He said I couldn't continue because of my 'disobedience'. That was like a red rag to a bull – if he didn't like disobedience then, now that I'd lost everything he was sure to get an eyeful of it. I was so hurt that I reacted slightly hysterically. In his letter Tony referred to the abuse I had given the day before this, but that paled in comparison to my final swansong. He wrote:

> At this point, I am sorry to say, you became violent and abusive. By violence, I refer to the nature of your language. This persisted throughout the day and then throughout the next day. You continued to abuse the lady who is Factory's production manager throughout the two days. 'You fucking cunt,' is a small example of the insults that persisted throughout this period.
>
> You also attacked me verbally, though as your loving ex-husband it is rather like water off a duck's back. However, your attacks on my partner Alan Erasmus during that two-day period were unforgiveable. Mixing violent language with vicious personal criticism. It got to the point where, if he saw your car outside the office, he was not prepared to go inside. Obviously your behaviour over this period and the complete destruction of your personal relationships with other workers and directors within the company make any suggestion of your return to your post utterly out of the question.

His letter finished:

> We will remain loyal to the original suggested terms of dismissal. Notice, effective as of the end of 1984, three weeks holiday pay to take your salary through to the week ending 19 January and then three months salary as a pay off.
>
> It is not a happy solution; merely the only solution.
>
> Yours, A.H.W.
>
> P.S. Your tax-free payoff – three months – comes to £1,235.00 – please though, return all Factory property and papers. P45 in post. Anthony.

In his letter Tony also referred to my 'appalling behaviour of less than a month ago', which concerned 52nd Street. The only basic instructions I'd been given regarding the license of a particular record to a territory was to first consult the manager of the group in question. Therefore I presumed that in this case I didn't have to consult anyone.

In November, the aptly titled Black Market Records of New York phoned me asking to license the latest record by 52nd Street. It seemed sensible to get a release over there as soon as possible since the record had been out for three months already (on import). The license would enable people to buy it at the standard retail price. I checked firstly with Michael Shamberg – that he'd not had a better offer (i.e. from a more major record company than this one). He spoke of other interest, but he'd mentioned that during earlier calls and it hadn't led to anything concrete. I told him of the offer and he asked me if I'd like him to call them. I said there was no need since they were calling me the following day. The band seemed to favour the idea and liked the label, so three days later I verbally agreed terms with Black Market. Rob Gretton said the license was 'stupid'. I asked him why. He replied, 'If I told you, you wouldn't listen.' I said, 'I'm listening,' but he walked away. In fact Rob generally treated me with contempt once my relationship with Tony was clearly beyond redemption.

I told Tony that I appreciated any efforts Shamberg had made but that they hadn't, so far, been fruitful and I considered speed to be of the essence. I didn't see us as working in competition with one another. I'd thought we were a team. As far as I knew, I was acting for the good of the group and therefore the company.

This is Tony's account of the Black Market saga, as written in his letter:

> While generally satisfied with your work for the company, in particular the liaison established with our foreign licensees, there has been, since your early days with the company in the autumn of 1983, a series of disagreements between yourself and the company's directors over company policy. Throughout the summer of 1984, Michael Shamberg had been working extremely hard to get American licensing deals for

Factory's two black dance acts, 52nd Street and Marcel King. As Factory's man in New York, his main function had become liaison with the major US labels.

In the first week of November, in your other role as manager of 52nd Street, you responded with an enquiry from Black Market Records of New York, by saying 'yes'. As is your right as manager of the band, you decided off your own back to sign with this company. Fully aware that Michael Shamberg had spent the last three months trying to sell the band to either A&M or Elektra, you made no attempt to inform Shamberg. In fact he found out when he went to the Elektra office to again try to tie up the 52nd Street deal, only to be told, with laughter: 'Don't you know . . . they've signed to Black Market?' The personal embarrassment and the damage to Factory's prestige in the States are clear cut.

So many years later – twenty-four to be exact – I read these letters and tried to be objective and sympathetic to Tony's viewpoint. However, although I could be just as bloody-minded as Tony, and although I made mistakes, I still believe it was primarily an emotional decision he made – that if I had returned as his wife I could have done exactly the same things and he might even have praised them.

In later years I often mentioned to Tony – lightly, without blame, even humorously – the obvious unfairness of his sacking of me. He never backed down.

I was devastated; shocked that Tony could be so ruthless. He reminded me of Henry VIII and I felt like Anne Boleyn. A final, quick chop and I was history – our entire lives together, our friendship, my career – over in one fell swoop. Of course, 'Move on, darling,' was one of Tony's expressions – I even considered it as a title for this book. I'd accepted that he'd done that with his new baby and wife. I'd come to terms with it, was grateful that I'd had a job I enjoyed and – even if I had been a bloody fool – at least Tony and I had worked together. Factory felt like a child of ours – the only thing that *had* been born at any rate. And this seemed cruel and totally unjust.

Marcel King and a friend of his, whose name I can't remember, happened to call in the office as I was preparing to leave on the day of the sacking. It seemed so unfair. I wanted others who worked there to speak up for me – Tim Chambers in Ikon I seem to remember as one. I was sure he knew the truth, that he'd heard Rob ask me to arrange the demo. Apart from Tony, they all knew, didn't they? I wasn't trying to sabotage Michael Shamberg even if I didn't think much of his Thick Pigeon. Not a word was said in my defence by anyone. The boss, like the customer, is always right. I was on my own and deeply upset. In reality, though, I was naive to expect justice in this situation or to think anything that members of staff could say would change things. This was more a matter for the board.

Bruce Mitchell remembered that Tony went round to his house for a meeting with Vini after this hatchet job, and he told Tony he'd seen me very upset. Tony just shrugged and said, 'Yeah I know, I've just fired her.' Kind of like, 'Yeah, coffee with two sugars.' In some part of himself he was able to shut the door on compassion.

Bruce said, 'It's hilarious firing your ex-wife.' I agreed. It would be a good scene in a film, and that's what Tony thought mattered in life. Bruce being Bruce had a good quote that came from the PA to Richard Burton and Elizabeth Taylor. There was a bad atmosphere in the house and Burton was stomping about. As it was going wrong in whatever way it was she said, 'And always the farce would curdle the tragedy.'

But I was at a loss to see the funny side then. I still am now. I came down the stairs, crying all the way, and was reluctant to surrender. Marcel came too. I offered them a lift to Wythenshawe. We all got into the Karmann Ghia and then Marcel's friend produced a bottle of champagne from under his jacket. He'd taken it from Alan's fridge – it had been there as long as I remembered going to Alan's flat. At first I was horrified that they could take something Alan had especially kept for some special reason. It was theft in any case. But then it kind of seemed appropriate. Someone said that the best time to drink champagne is at such times – forget celebrations, you don't need it as much then! So we opened it there and then and the three of us drank it sitting in my car outside 86 Palatine Road. My blurry outlook – from the tears, the raindrops rolling down the windscreen and my uncertain future – was blurred further yet softened by the champagne.

The next thing for me was to sign on at the dole office. I still managed 52nd Street (as far as I knew) but had not had any income whatsoever from that. However, one member of the band rang up the very next day to tell me that I was no longer the manager. I told him there were five people in the band and that I would call a meeting to see what their collective vote was.

I could see why I might not be so useful now that I no longer worked for Factory, but – again – it felt like a betrayal. Things turned nasty when, since he didn't have a phone, I called round at the drummer's house in Wythenshawe to tell him about the meeting. The member of the band who had tried to oust me suddenly burst into the house, brandishing some kind of small whip and pointing it at me threateningly. He called me a 'Factory slag' and other choice words. The strength of this guy's venom was quite shocking. We'd been on the road together several times and I thought he'd been loveable, funny and nice to me. Where had all this anger suddenly come from? It surely must have been lying dormant before this. But, as Diane noted, respect was absent from the outset if all these boys viewed me as a piece of meat. With hindsight I wonder if perhaps Rob might have been an influence in some way. This 52nd Street member was quite matey with Rob, and Rob was doubtless of the old school of men who think, for instance, that it's more acceptable for a man to have an affair than a woman. Rob coined the phrase 'Belgian boiler' for Annik Honoré.

If anyone reading this entertains even the faintest notion that Annik was that kind of girl – that her relationship with Ian Curtis was visceral rather than a more platonic love, that she instigated the relationship or seduced him away from his wife – then I implore you to read the excerpts of his letters to her in my previous book *Torn Apart*. Annik has wrongly been vilified and a more dignified and decent woman you'd be hard pushed to find. If Rob thought she was a 'boiler', God only knows what he thought of me. Factory slag? At the very least I should think. There is a beautiful book by Thomas Hardy – *Tess of the d'Urbervilles* – that sums up the double standard men often take concerning women. The truth was that I was deeply insecure and believed, wrongly, that security could only be found in a relationship. I was like a drowning person trying to hold on to a passing wreckage.

I could actually have understood a musician having all his hopes and loyalties tied up with Factory and not seeing a future with me now. But this was the wrong approach. If he'd talked to me along those lines, I would have sympathised with his point of view.

In the event, I was voted in at the meeting by the other members. Hence 52nd Street came with me and left Factory and, despite being on the dole for the next five months, we were fortunate enough to obtain a record deal with Virgin/Ten Records.

Meanwhile, I wasn't going to take this injustice lying down. I put the wheels in motion to take my case to an unfair dismissal tribunal.

The tribunal was held in the centre of Manchester, somewhere near the back of Kendals Department Store. I arrived expecting a fair fight between Wilson and me. I honestly believed it was just between the two of us. Therefore, as I walked up to the door bright and early at 9:00am, I was quite shocked to see Tony walking down the street accompanied by the laughing or smiling faces of Rob Gretton, Lesley Gilbert and Alan Erasmus. What had this to do with them? Perhaps Lesley and Alan were going to say I was abusive in the office and Rob was going to back up Wilson's 'evidence'. I thought this was hitting below the belt. Couldn't Wilson have been a man and fought this particular battle by himself?

Feeling rather disgusted, I took my place in a narrow room with my legal aid solicitor. He was a really nice person and I have often thought of what he said to me at the end of that day, and sometimes sincerely wished I had taken his advice. Unfortunately Tony and his friends were all sitting together in the very next room and I could hear them laughing and joking. It felt like a bad trip and insensitive, rather like they were amused at someone's funeral. They might not have cared but that didn't mean that no one else did.

I felt terribly alone. I wondered what chance I had for a fair hearing on the merit of numbers alone. It was torture as the hours went by – we got to lunch and my case hadn't been called. Then it got to the middle of the afternoon and my solicitor said it was beginning to look as if the case might be adjourned to another day. Still aware of the banter and laughter coming from next door, and the hopelessness of my word standing against four others, I told him that if it was adjourned I didn't want to go on with it. I didn't want to put myself through such an endurance test ever again – it was humiliating and no doubt ultimately pointless. The solicitor agreed in principle. He said that, even if I won, the compensation would be very little since I only earned £69 a week and hadn't even been salaried for very long. But then he said that my divorce was fairly recent and, since there had been no legal representation, I was still within my rights to take a case there. He said I was entitled to claim half the house in Old Broadway and half of the business. He said that as the business had been established using only our marital money I was entitled to claim half of it. I told him I didn't want to do that – we'd already agreed the divorce terms (i.e. the £5,000 I'd already had) and I didn't want to go back on it. Also, I'd consulted the *I-Ching* about suing Tony for a settlement and got, 'The superior man does not go to the law courts.' This unfair dismissal court didn't count – it wasn't about money, it was a question of principle. I wasn't looking for money but vindication. So I dug my heels in, so much wanting to act like the superior man. It's difficult to take the moral high ground when you're broke and with no one to turn to, but my parents were alive then.

The solicitor was horrified and practically begged me to reconsider. The cynical may think he was interested in taking the case on, but I rather think he had my interests at heart. He was right and I should have listened. At one point he even said that I had a moral obligation to go ahead with the case. My own morals seemed to be telling me the opposite. At 5:00pm, the case hadn't been heard and so I took my leave of both him and Factory Records for the last time.

I look back at that young woman who chose to walk away empty-handed with admiration. The woman who writes today is not she. That was 1984. Thatcher's dream of making every person in Great Britain a capitalist hadn't quite taken hold then. Now the worship of mammon grips all of us comrades. We're judged by what we have, not who we are. What use is an honest, non-materialistic outlook in today's greedy, egotistical world? This country is almost bankrupt because of it.

But I also thought then that I had everything to play for, that I would go on and prove my own talent, that I'd claw my way back up – yes, on that fucking wheel of Boethius if you like. Oddly, I was right. The fact that I didn't make any money out of it was simply unfortunate.

I had no idea then that I might struggle to provide for myself. Neither Tony nor I ever did care that much about money and, despite all the rows, never argued about that particular subject. But being absolutely penniless, without any possessions and – worst of all – without a job yet again at the age of forty-two further on in my music business 'career' taught me the most about its value. Money might not make you happy, but not having it can certainly make you unhappy. Tony always had his day job and large sums of money coming in and out of Factory, so perhaps he went the other way. Around the same time that I became more responsible, he became more irresponsible. It was that in part that led to the downfall of Factory.

Just as a matter of curiosity I asked Stephen Lea, Tony's lawyer, when I interviewed him in 2009, what he thought I would have been entitled to if I had followed up on a legal case in 1984. He said, 'I couldn't see you getting less than a six-figure sum out of it. There is an argument to say that whatever Tony's share was on paper, his real interest in the property and business was much greater, therefore your half-share was much greater.' If I had known then how much financial difficulty lay ahead of me, I doubt I would have walked away as I did. The odd thing about that is, if I had taken Tony to court as Martin was also doing at the time, it is highly unlikely that Factory Records could have survived beyond 1984. Between myself and Martin we doubtless would have brought the company down.

34 Most Likely You Go Your Way (And I'll Go Mine)

For the next two to three years I loathed Tony and Factory Records. Yet with every wish I had for their downfall they seemed to prosper more. Of course 'Blue Monday' had charted twice in 1983 and probably would have fared even better if New Order hadn't insisted on playing *Top of the Pops* live, which was a technical disaster. Nonetheless the song was a dance hit that paved the way for the group's newfound success.

One night soon after the sacking my desire to slash Tony's tyres was so strong I almost had to be physically restrained to prevent me from doing it. The next thing I remember was seeing Tony, Alan and Rob all driving around in new cars.

I looked around for likeminded others who hated Factory, but apart from the odd snipe – whispers of 'Fat Tory' records from somewhere far off – I found none. People generally suck up to success and avoid failure like the plague, despite the fact that a sycophantic circus can be ruinous to the personality, whereas failure is often good for the soul.

How my 'friends' fell away once my association with Tony ceased. There were 200 people at our wedding, and I began to wonder if there was anyone left. Admittedly I'd gone to ground somewhat after what had happened, but one day in early 1985 I looked around and was trying to think of any friends who were still actively seeking me out. There were friends I could call upon, but which friends were still calling on me? On the day in question I could only think of two people and neither of them were present at the wedding anyway. They were both misfits – Alan Wise and Wayne Worm. There was also another misfit, Tony Connolly, but he could loosely be described as family.

My rage at Tony fuelled me. I always listened to Dylan in the car in those days and when it got to 'Most Likely You Go Your Way (And I'll Go Mine)' I used to turn it up.

But then my anger began to fade. There were good points in my situation, such as getting rid of sycophants and false friends – better to have none than false ones I think. The worst part of it was regret. At the back of my mind I sensed I would never have a family now. I envied women who had husbands and children. I still do to be honest.

At least I had my freedom, the thing I'd fought for. Although, as my mum used to say, complete freedom is just having nothing left to lose.

It's only in an advertiser's dream or in glossy magazines that life is perfect with a husband and baby. Not long after the birth of her son there was a most awful attack on Hilary at 36 Old Broadway. Hilary had alerted Tony to warning signs since she thought someone had slept in their garage. Despite Hilary's fears, Tony didn't think it necessary to call the police. Then a sixteen-stone, obsessed-with-Tony woman got into the house and slashed Hilary across her face several times. Hilary thought she was going to pass out but managed to distract the girl briefly by giving her a photo of Tony and telling her that she was sure he would want her to have it. At that point Hilary managed to almost crawl out of the house to raise the alarm, but the woman locked the door and was now alone with Oliver asleep upstairs in his cot. Hilary was desperately screaming 'My baby!' as help was obtained. The police came out but it was a neighbouring vicar, speaking to the girl through the letterbox, who managed to get her to open the door. It appeared that she had not even seen baby Oliver, but had been sitting in Tony's office looking through his things.

Unbelievably, almost the day after this Tony went to Japan, where the Durutti Column were scheduled to make a film. This was surely a callous thing to do and it's hard to fathom why he didn't cancel the trip – certainly the group could have managed without him. Was he running away, avoiding the situation? That was sometimes how he dealt with things. He was capable of being a cold fish and held no guilt about anything. Or was it that life and business always went on as usual with Tony? When he was poorly he didn't expect or even want anyone else to change their schedules to fit in with him. And one day he was almost too ill to get out of bed, yet he still went on a final trip to New York.

Obviously it was an enormous challenge for Hilary to come to terms with, and recover from, this dreadful event. Plus the fact that her husband, absent at the best of times, was clearly not giving her the support she needed. I empathised with her and better understood my fear of having children with Tony. He was a man who would never be at home much.

I carried on living at my parents' and it only took five months for 52nd Street to obtain a record deal, at which point we were all able to earn a basic monthly wage.

Managing 52nd Street was terribly hard work, mentally more than anything. Further down the line there were fights and more fights. Sometimes I felt like the mother of squabbling children, but they were full-grown adults. I was sometimes just as bad. My worst feature – as already described – was volatility, shooting from the hip, which never helped to calm the situation down.

The group looked at first as if they might 'make it', especially in America, and with their first single 'Tell Me (How It Feels)'. As soon as success looked likely movements were afoot within the record label to oust me as their manager. They called the group in one by one to turn their heads with words about someone who could really make them go places. But this was when they thought they *were* going places. I was useful for schlepping about, driving up and down the M1, managing their accounts and their tax, negotiating deals, arranging their mortgages, etc, but if they'd have made it I would have been sidelined quicker than you could say 'bastards'. Anyway, they didn't 'make it', so I was allowed to keep my job until they did and carried on with them for five years and three albums. I think it was about three years in when I admitted to myself that I didn't much care for this kind of music anymore and, if I did, it really wasn't worth all the grief. But by that point we were all too bonded in with one another to move on. I cared about them as people but I just wasn't really enjoying it. There were many good times though.

During the five months I'd been on the dole I decided to have a go at launching another label. I had no money, of course, but figured I could do it on a shoe-string if I boxed clever. My plan? Well, pick up where I left off. I got Marcel round to a small eight-track and had him sing a cover of a Beatles song that I felt sure would be a hit. It was 'Yes It Is'. I'd had an idea earlier on, when missing Tony one day, that a girl could record the song, but instead of, 'Please don't wear red tonight,' she would sing, 'Please don't wear a suit tonight, 'cause a suit is the style that my baby wore, yes it is, oh yeah.' It wasn't Marcel's bag at all, but it corresponded with the idea I'd had for 'Telstar' – which I believed would have been a hit if I'd got a choir boy and permission to add lyrics. This was the same principle. But of course it was out of my reach, financially, practically. I've still got the recording by Marcel, for what it's worth. Sadly in 1995 he died of a cerebral brain haemorrhage. He was only thirty-eight.

With hindsight it's a pity I didn't hook up with Martin Hannett, especially if I had known what he was up to and how our paths were yet to intertwine more than once. And, of course, he was a likeminded other who hated Factory. Having heard only Tony's side of the legal case Martin took against Factory, I wasn't as sympathetic towards Martin as I later became. I thought he'd played his cards very badly – but then again, in a different way so had I. In 1985 Howard 'Ginger' Jones and Martin were getting a label called Thin Line started. The pair released the first recordings of the Stone Roses, 'So Young' and 'Tell Me', on this new label. Martin produced the tracks at Strawberry. Oddly, within two years I would be co-managing the Stone Roses without knowing much about Ginger's earlier history as manager of the group.

I had better known Ginger as the manager of the Hacienda from the club's inception to the end of 1983. Having taken on the Roses, he perhaps felt he was better suited to managing them more than an ailing club that was losing money fast. Although a director of FAC 51, after four years of hard work (two years' work before the club even opened), he said he'd had enough. He described the day the crunch came:

'It was Halloween 1983. On my way to the club, I always took Mike [Pickering] in the car with me. He was booking bands. I told Mike I was quitting – because the A&R side of things wasn't going to happen and because I'd been working for four years without a break. Seven days a week. Mike said don't do it. We went into the cocktail bar and Tony's dad was in with his friend [Tony Connolly]. I said I want us all to get together – we've got to have a meeting. Tony [Wilson] said, "I can't, I'm with my dad." I said, "Tony this is really, really important." He said, "Well, there's nothing you've got to say that can't be said in front of my dad." I said, "Well, Alan and Rob have got to be there as well." So we all got together in the alcove on the balcony of the cocktail bar and sat down and Tony Connolly said, "Blimey, I don't believe this." Somebody told me later he was psychic. We all looked at him and he said, "Is this a dagger I see before me?" Then he got up and laughed and walked off. We all looked at each other and Tony asked, "What's this about?" I said, "I resign." It really upset Tony. We'd had an honest relationship believe it or not. He knew I respected him for his intellect and he respected me for my streetwise. He liked people for weird reasons. He said to me, "No, no, you're not quitting. What you're going to do is – you're going to have two weeks holiday, we'll pay for it" – and he looked at Rob and Alan – "take Mal" – my then girlfriend – "with you, everything will be great, and come back – you need a break."'

This isn't quite the way Tony told the story in his book *24 Hour Party People*. He related that Ginger had been asking for a marketing/promotions manager, without which the club could not be a success. Ginger's request was denied and then, Tony said, 'When the axe fell, it was Gretton who wielded it.'

Ginger's version of events isn't too dissimilar at this stage: 'Rob said, "Are you saying you're quitting?" and I said, "Yes." Rob said, "I'm only going to give you one more chance. Are you quitting?" And I said, "Rob, I've told you, I'm quitting." And he said, "Right that's it."'

Did he jump or was he pushed? It sounds like a bit of both to me, although Alan Erasmus maintains that it was the latter scenario. Certainly the friendship between Rob and Ginger was ruined after this. 'I used to go to the Man City match every Saturday with Rob and Mike [Pickering],' Ginger said, 'so it was a friendship, it wasn't just a business relationship. I'd told Rob on several occasions how unhappy I was about keeping the club open seven nights a week. Tony used to come from Granada on Sunday after a meeting and there'd just be the staff and me and Claude playing cards in the DJ box. Tony would say, "Why are we open?" and I'd say, "Ask Rob."'

Hacienda employee Penny Henry remembered: 'We all said it, but Rob wanted the club open every night. He put Greg Wilson on Sundays. Hewan

[Clarke] did Fridays. Greg had all these break dancers; it was like their own private club. There were more staff working than people paying in.'

Incidentally, it was Penny who first noticed, just before opening, that the Hacienda had no cloakroom. She'd had experience of running a club and previously worked for Alan Wise and Roger Eagle, about whom she said, 'Roger has been marginalised. If he hadn't booked all those black acts at the Twisted Wheel – Magic Village, Eric's, etcetera – then people wouldn't have heard that kind of music.'

In 1984, after a robbery at the Hacienda, Penny told me about Rob wielding the axe again: 'Rob gave me the sack because he said it was my fault the robbery happened. The robbery was set up for Ellie [Gray, who was also part of the management team], but she'd gone on a photo shoot so I was there. The men were let in the club by the cleaners. They came down the stairs and I thought it was a joke. I thought it was one of the bouncers playing about with a stocking on. I said, "You've had your fun, now get your masks off." They said, "We're really serious." I just couldn't take it seriously. The police said I was really brave. I was lying on the floor with this gun in my head and stroking the cleaner's head saying, "It's all right, we'll get out of this, don't worry." I even fobbed them off with the float which was about £200.

'I could have taken them to an industrial tribunal but I didn't because I knew the club was in trouble. Tony did agree to give me three months wages. Only Alan Erasmus came and saw me after that.'

Having found the Stone Roses, Ginger wanted to devote his energies to managing them. Yet again he had picked a winner but yet again was too early to enjoy the success.

52nd Street had rehearsed briefly in a hired room in Chorlton around this time, and the Stone Roses happened to be in the next rehearsal room on a few occasions. I thought the Roses sounded pretty terrible back then. It was soon afterwards that I noticed the name Stone Roses scrawled and spray-canned on walls all over town. Someone believed in this lot, but I suspected that whoever it was was either in the band or misguided or both.

Andy Couzens, original member of the Roses, told me he that had stumped up money for their first recordings (released on Thin Line). He also introduced music lawyer Stephen Lea to the band. In later years Stephen was to become Tony's lawyer and was the man Tony called Doctor Gonzo, a reference to *Fear and Loathing in Las Vegas* by Hunter S. Thompson. Doctor Gonzo was the 300-pound Samoan attorney who accompanied the narrator, journalist Raoul Duke, on a drug-fuelled trip to Las Vegas in search of the American dream.

Both Stephen and Andy remembered a pivotal meeting with Gareth Evans (who managed the group post-Howard Jones) and the Roses. 'The meeting began at Eighth Day Café in All Saints,' Andy said. 'Gareth had got very aggressive and was trying to psyche me out – putting his head in my face and things like that. John [Squire] and Ian [Brown] weren't saying a lot about it. Then we went on to the International and Steve [Lea] was there. He'd negotiated a management contract with Howard [Ginger], which we decided we weren't going to sign, and then drafted the letter to sack Howard amongst other things. Gareth was really laying into Steve at the International. Steve had been there on the band's side for a long time and done a lot of work for us for free. Gareth was making it clear he wanted him out of there. Gareth said to me, pointing at Steve, "Who the hell are you that comes with a lawyer attached?" And then he said in the next breath, "And anyway I've done some checking up on you and your practising certificate has expired so what are you exactly?"'

Stephen Lea remembered: 'A band meeting was held at which Gareth Evans tells the group that with him they will have free rehearsal and studio time, a venue to play at etcetera. Then he pronounces, "It's either him or me." Andy Couzens then says, "I'm not having this." So he walks.'

Stephen said that after a minute or two he also walked. He told me he regretted it, because he should have walked out sooner. (Subsequently Gareth employed a conveyance lawyer named Geoff Howard. Whether or not this was a strategic move, Gareth now had hold of the reins.)

Andy Couzens told me that Evans had been gunning for him (Andy) for some time, and apparently even offered him £20,000 to leave the band at one point. (Waving cash around – verbally or literally – was a favourite trick I also observed in Evans. Getting him to part with it was another matter.) As Couzens remembered: 'He'd drop a wad of tenners in front of us from the bar take. It meant fuck all but he kept doing it. But Ian and John kind of liked this flashiness.' Evans took umbrage when, after a gig in Ireland, Couzens flew back to Manchester rather than undertake the long sail back to Liverpool with the others (due to a work commitment). Evans seized his opportunity and used this as ammunition for a full-scale attack. 'He was determined to get shut of me,' Andy said. 'He used to follow me round in his car and call me *nouveau riche*.'

Ginger had been ousted before this showdown. He explained: 'They [the band] all came round to my house and said, "You've got to either quit Thin Line, or quit managing us." I said, "I'm going to stick with Thin Line so it's up to you." So they went straight to the International and asked Gareth to manage them. The only reason they wanted Gareth to manage them was because I refused to pay for rehearsals, but Gareth would let them rehearse free in the International.'

As all of this was bubbling under, in a different club across town, so were the Happy Mondays. This is how Phil Saxe, who was one of the original DJs at the Twisted Wheel, recalled their beginnings: 'I was selling jeans in Manchester – flares. These three girls asked for them – they said they wanted to be different. Within a month I had 600 to 700 customers. I was the only person selling them. And that's how I met the Mondays, they were customers. Then one day I went to see a friend's band at the Hacienda – they used to do a hometown gig on a Thursday night. Mike Pickering would put on three unknown and unsigned bands. I'm watching this band and these three lads come and sit next to me. They said, "Fancy seeing you here." I didn't think that people like the Mondays would ever go in the Hacienda. It was the opposite of what they were about. These three scallies, for want of a better word, were wearing flares and they've got those haircuts and no one in the Hacienda would ever have seen anything like it. So they gave me a tape that night. I listened to it and I liked it, but I liked them more than their music if you know what I mean. They looked great and I thought kids on council estates should have their own bands as well. Music then just wasn't to do with ordinary kids. So I took this tape to Mike to see if he might put them on the hometown gig. Mike said he didn't need to listen to the tape – if you're recommending them we'll put them on anyway. Mike put the Mondays on and at that gig he said he thought I'd want to manage them, which hadn't occurred to me. So I asked them and they said yes. Mike took them to Factory and produced their EP *Delightful*. Bernard [Sumner] produced the second EP. I don't even know if Tony had noticed them at that stage. He got it a bit later; he let me use John Cale for the first album, I think it was only when he got Nathan involved that he took any notice at all.'

Phil told me that he had been sacked because the band wanted Nathan McGough to manage them. Tony told me in interview: 'I always think that the real idealist in the whole thing was Erasmus. Looking back on it – whose master plan was it, when Phil Saxe stopped managing the Mondays – who had the idea of McGough to manage them?' Tony also claims it was Alan's idea in his book. Tony might have asked Nathan to move out of his second marital home but, unlike me, Nathan was still very much in favour with him. I was therefore surprised by Nathan's account of an unfavourable response from Tony when he related to him the news of his appointment as the Happy Mondays' manager.

Nathan remembered: 'He said, "You're not fucking managing this band." He said, "No – because you're always fucking rude to Lesley. Lesley doesn't want you in the Factory office and there's no way you can manage a Factory band if you can't go in the office." Mike Pickering made the peace, calmed it all down. He said, "Tony it's not up to you. It's up to the band, they've asked him, they want him, you need to make this work." So Tony didn't want me even though we were really great friends. He retracted it later though.'

Nathan's disagreements with Lesley and Factory probably arose during his management of Factory band Kalima and his frustration with Factory's policy of zero marketing. He told me: 'Lesley was only going with the company line.'

I pointed out to Phil Saxe Tony's hostile reaction to the news that Nathan was to be their manager, but Phil said, 'I always thought Nathan and Tony concocted that behind their backs. That was the impression I got. Not long after that I got the Head of A&R job and replaced Mike Pickering. I think that was down to Rob. I think to some degree the Mondays wouldn't have happened as well without Nathan though.'

Phil made an interesting point about the Hacienda: 'In those days people who went to the Hacienda would wear suits and short trousers, with socks pulled up. It was a New Order/Joy Division sort of vibe. Everyone thought they were very arty. It was very middle-class, kids didn't go in there from council estates.'

Tony was yet to become Shaun Ryder's biggest supporter and I was yet to co-manage the Stone Roses, but it has always struck me as strange that we became involved – separately yet at the same time – with the emerging next two biggest Manchester bands. We had very little contact with each other then. Our paths occasionally crossed at the Hacienda.

The only legacy I took from my marriage was that I got into the Hacienda for free. The bouncers knew me and always let me straight through. I appreciated that. It was a small gesture that went a long, long way. One of the bouncers in particular I remember as being very kind because I was always too embarrassed to say anything if there was someone new on the door and he just ushered me straight through. This went on for a few years until one day all the bouncers were different. They looked at me strangely and directed me to the paying counter. I thought, 'I'm not having this.' Pointing at Tony's large picture hanging near the door I said, 'Listen, I don't want to name-drop or anything but I used to be married to that bastard so can you just let me in?' Never had a problem after that.

The early years of the Hacienda, when it was at least half-empty, were the best for me. As Vini said, it felt like our club, meeting up with friends. It's odd in view of my demise at Factory, but I really felt at home there.

At the same time that the Hacienda was struggling as a live venue and still yet to find its niche as an acid house and rave club, the International, on Anson Road in Longsight, was the perfect live venue with great acoustics. It opened two or three years after the Hacienda, when the live music scene was particularly vibrant in Manchester, and captured a market that rather bypassed the Hacienda.

'The acoustics were terrible at the Hacienda,' Nathan remembered. 'If they'd put the stage at the end of the club rather than along the side, the acoustics might have been better. But then it would only function as a venue, not a club. Me and Dave Haslam started indie nights at the Boardwalk, which opened in 1985. We would put bands on – loads of people, Sonic Youth and Primal Scream. It was always full and we made money. But then me and Dave would go to the Hacienda on Saturday nights and it was pretty empty. There would be more people in the Boardwalk than the Hacienda.' Oddly enough, the Boardwalk was almost directly opposite the loft on Little Peter Street that Tony lived in to the end. Dave Haslam went on to be a resident DJ at the Hacienda.

The International had formerly been a cabaret club called Genevieve's, and Dougie James (minus his Soul Train) had been tipped off that the club was about to go bump having just had a carpet fitted at a cost of £18,000. Dougie had run Rafters, which had closed down after the Clash performed there and spat at the bar staff amongst other things. The owner, John Bagnall, said he couldn't have that and closed the club. Now Dougie saw another opportunity for a great venue in the International. Hence he and his business partner John Stenson bought into the club along with Gareth Evans and his business partner Matthew Cummings. The four had previously all been partners in the Andalucia Hotel and used money from that to set up the International. Dougie brought Roger Eagle on board to book acts – the two already being something of a double act, since Roger had run Eric's in Liverpool when Dougie had run Rafters. Dougie told me that Gareth and Matthew's job was to take care of the paperwork.

The International was just the right kind of venue at just the right kind of time. Roger Eagle had the *nous* to put on guitar bands that would never have fitted in the Hacienda and yet pulled large audiences – R.E.M. and Echo & the Bunneymen among them. At the same time there were all kinds of bands breaking through in Manchester – the Chameleons, Easterhouse, James, Simply Red, the Jazz Defectors. It was a revival of Manchester after a lull dominated by three bands; the Smiths, New Order and the Fall. Dougie recalls that the club took £22,000 over just three days within a few weeks of opening. 'I said to Gareth we should take the money and put it back into the hotel,' Dougie explained. 'We all knew if we didn't put the money back into the hotel it would sink, which it did. Gareth and Matthew had no intention of putting it back. I'd trusted them to do the paperwork but they hadn't put our names down as directors or shareholders or anything. They intended to cheat us from day one. I had to go to court and it took me five years.'

If I had known this perhaps I might have been forewarned. But I didn't.

Gareth befriended me every time I went to the International – let me in for free and that sort of thing – and seemed genuinely pleasant. It wasn't a chat up; he wasn't interested in me physically, which made a nice change. All the same I was a bit wary. He struck me as a bit of an unsavoury character and yet had a certain charismatic charm and enthusiasm that could be quite compelling. It was never a problem getting 52nd Street to play at the club and it was always a good gig somehow, the whole scene was a bit like Rafters had been ten years earlier, plus the club had a much better layout and proportions.

Gareth told me he was managing this band called the Stone Roses. My low opinion of their music was about to dramatically change. Gareth arranged for the group to play privately for me downstairs at the International and I thought they were unbelievably good. The material sounded head and shoulders above the inferior stuff I'd heard in their former years. As Tony always said about music – it boils down to the songs.

Afterwards I told Gareth what I thought and he asked me if I would like to co-manage them with him and Matthew. He told me that Matthew would be less hands-on than us – that he was an accountant and basically just took care of the paperwork. That, in reality, it would just be me and him. So we began discussing a contract since I had a feeling that Evans was not the sort of man you work with on trust. It transpired that Gareth and Matthew had a contract with the band for a commission of thirty-three percent. I was a bit gobsmacked by that. After all, most managers take no more than twenty percent, and I was only on fifteen percent for managing 52nd Street. Gareth explained the reason. He said that there were four in the group plus himself and Matthew so they had divided everything equally. That was fair, he said. So I said in that case I wanted ten percent, which was less than a third of the share that himself and Matthew were on. Gareth agreed and we drew up a contract – just a simple piece of paper, signed and witnessed.

Another opportunity for financial security beckoned and yet again I blew it.

I don't recall seeing Tony at the International much, although he did turn up if the Mondays or another Factory band were on. Perhaps he felt it would be disloyal to his own club to make an appearance there otherwise. Yet although the Hacienda was a great place to socialise, it wasn't a good place to see a band, and the International was.

Gareth and I set about arranging demos of the Stone Roses so I could take them around the people I knew in London. I suspect Gareth's whole motivation in bringing me onboard was that I had the contacts and he didn't. I remember a recording session at Spirit Studios in Manchester, now renamed as SSR. I think it was there that I met Steve Adge, who was their road manager and general fifth member of the band (rather in the mould of Terry Mason and Joy Division, a Man Friday whose bonhomie and trouble-shooting skills a band just could not be without).

I rapidly recognised a talent for duplicity and showmanship in Gareth. One day I was sitting in his office and he was talking to someone on the telephone. He asked them to hang on as he'd got someone on the other line. He was so convincing I actually looked around for another phone in the room. In point of fact, he didn't even have another line. He waited several minutes and then went back to this person saying he'd just been talking to the head of CBS. Andy Couzens remembered a similar game: 'Gareth kept having pretend conversations on the phone with his banker.'

Another time he came to my house (actually my mum's, which is where I was living). The telephone rang for me two or three times after he arrived, which was badly timed, but my mum played the host and made Gareth coffee. When I came off the phone Gareth said to me, 'That was impressive – did you set that up especially for when I got here?' He thought that because it was the kind of trick he would pull. But I wasn't out to impress Gareth in any case.

I trawled around London on my own with the Stone Roses cassettes since there was little point sending them in the post. I knew several A&R men and could walk into meetings but most of them rejected the tape as being of little interest. I got the standard 'Keep in touch, let me have other material' spiel. I thought to myself, 'If you don't get it now you never will.' It was totally disheartening. There were only two of my contacts who showed sufficient interest to attend a showcase London gig we'd arranged at Dingwalls in Camden Lock in January 1988. One was Geoff Travis of Rough Trade, who I'd known since the early Factory days. The other was Roddy McKenna of Zomba Records, who I knew through negotiating publishing contracts for 52nd Street. Geoff stood next to me when the band went on. Even before the end of the first number he turned to me and said he would sign the band. I felt quite jubilant. I seem to recall that Roddy McKenna arrived late and, when I spoke to him afterwards, seemed slightly less certain about them than Geoff, but was nonetheless interested enough to follow up on it and said he would. Of course by himself he didn't have the power of yes and no as Geoff had. I went backstage afterwards and announced the good news to the band, which went down rather like a damp squib. I couldn't understand why they didn't react with any kind of jubilancy or celebration. Perhaps it was because I was already being set up and stitched up. Gareth intended to work McKenna and his bosses, Howard and Lauder, behind the scenes from day one. According to Mick Middles's account McKenna, his publishing boss Steven Howard and Evans locked themselves in the dressing room with the band at this gig (although I think this must have been at the International rather than Dingwalls). Many years later the band told me they never knew that I had brought McKenna in. But what would they care if I had? What was it that Tony and others with experience, including me, have said about musicians? Selfish children?

Gareth played me and I fell for it. He told me he wanted the group to sign to Rough Trade even though Zomba rapidly came forward with a deal. I remember a gig at the International in May 1988 at which Geoff Travis and Roddy McKenna were present. It was strange because the limited audience – hardcore fans of the Roses from their early days – didn't sit right with the music anymore. They had a goth look about them. I could sense that the band had outgrown their original fanbase.

Gareth told me to keep Geoff happy, but meanwhile was doubtless taking the Zomba crew into the dressing room behind my back. Later, although not hiding a Zomba offer from me, he said he thought independent Rough Trade were more suitable for the group and I agreed. I should have known he was lying and would have gone for the money over everything else. I recall that Zomba offered a £35,000 advance for the publishing and £35,000 for recording.

Gareth cleverly kept the band away from me during negotiations whilst planning the first single with Rough Trade. Geoff Travis, like me, was working on trust to some degree. I didn't see any point in duplicity in this case since I thought Gareth, me and the band were all on the same side. How naive.

Gareth did call me into a meeting with Zomba legals at which Gareth's lawyer, Geoff Howard, was present. I should have seen through the game Gareth was playing but I didn't. He had a skill for playing three steps ahead of the current move (useful in chess). I once told him he was the most deceitful man I had ever met. He smiled and took it as a compliment.

On the day that the group signed to Zomba, Evans drove them down to London and took them to Rough Trade for a marketing meeting. Afterwards they went to Zomba and signed on the dotted line. I didn't even know about the journey, much less what they were up to. I found out the next day when speaking to Reni, the drummer. It was the last straw. I didn't like being played for a fool and I didn't want to work with someone who was a liar and a cheat. I felt really bad for Geoff Travis. He'd been strung along too and had paid for recordings of the group in good faith. He was also the one who first suggested the group work with producer John Leckie. Evans's behaviour was very shabby. Not gentlemanlike in the least. I rang Evans and told him that I never wanted to see him again, our working relationship was at an end, I wanted him out of my life. By the terms of the agreement we'd made he owed me £7,000. I never got it, of course. He called round to my flat in Didsbury the very next day (by this point I'd moved out of my parents') and I asked him what the hell he was doing there when I'd made it clear I wanted him out of my life. 'Oh, that's a shame,' he said. 'I've brought this car round for you.' He pointed to a swish black number, in rather better condition than my Karmann Ghia, which was on its last legs (or wheels). I just thought it was the old game, flash the cash. I told him to get lost. After three months of badgering for my share of the advance he reluctantly gave me £1,000. I called it quits because I didn't want anything to do with him anymore.

I should have taken him to court but I walked away. Again.

I did expect some thanks or recognition, at least, but none came. I thought Tony might pat me on the back when the group became successful – shake my hand or something at least. No. He never mentioned it. It was as if I hadn't had a role in it. That was how everyone else saw it, including the band. That is still how Gareth wants people to see it. He states in John Robb's book *The Stone Roses and the Resurrection of British Pop*: 'I got to know a guy who worked for Zomba and lived in London. He would come down the club. I then signed a deal for the Roses with Zomba.' Why do people always want to take the glory for themselves? Years later the group got rid of Gareth, but it would cost them. This was after he'd made a killing and got them one of the biggest advances in history for their second album after getting them out of their contract with Zomba. Gareth told Mick Middles: 'I knew that contract was no good. That's why I let them sign it.' At the time that Evans was being courted by the US big boys I was working at the Disney-owned Hollywood Records in London, and they too were interested in joining the auction. Hein van der Ree, the MD of Hollywood in the UK, a Hollywood VIP from the States and myself met Gareth at the Blossoms Hotel near Knutsford. I can't quite describe Gareth's behaviour but it was a bit sickening. It was the thought of all that money I think, his ego was well and truly bathing itself in the sacred excrement. The band were led by this greed and it ruined their career, in my opinion. It isn't money that's the root of all evil, it's the love of it.

Legal case followed legal case until the one between the band and Gareth. The group's lawyer called me in as a witness. Gareth's lawyer also telephoned me. I met with the band and their lawyer in London. I said I supported their case against Gareth, but I had to warn them that I'd told Gareth's lawyer I thought they were a bunch of ingrates. Ian Brown was the only one who didn't mind admitting that he didn't know what the word meant. 'It was bad enough only getting £1,000 for getting you a deal,' I said (a few raised eyebrows and laughs there), 'but not one of you ever thanked me for what I did. You didn't even have the grace to make sure I got a copy of the album.' I said this quite nicely, though it was true. When I left the office they all piped up with a rather weak, 'Thank you.' Too little, too late.

After Gareth had secured his huge settlement from his split with the band, I rang him up. By then I was unemployed and broke. I reminded him that, by the terms of our contract, he still owed me £6,000. He said, 'You're stupid,' and hung up on me. For once I had to agree with him. Just like Tony I was bad at making money whilst enabling others to do so. But I don't regret ousting Gareth from my life, even if it may have been in line with his own design.

Over the years I noticed that Tony got more credit for the Roses than I ever did. I suppose because of the Madchester scene and the Hacienda's role in it all and the Happy Mondays. Plus he put the Roses on TV, so he appeared to be giving them a push. They featured on his show *The Other Side of Midnight* in 1989. Tony did once refer to my contribution, but it wasn't complimentary – it was as a funny excuse for the fact that he hadn't picked up on them. 'They were managed by my ex-wife, my ex-business partner Martin Hannett, and two ex-protégés from the Hacienda were also working with them. So everyone who was an ex in my life was involved with the Roses, so I completely ignored them.'

Keith Jobling told me that Tony had a thing about the Roses. Maybe it was a bit like supporting United or City. Keith said: 'He had a real problem with the Stone Roses – as a kind of clan thing, maybe he just understood it as a story – in that if you're on one side then you don't do something for the other side.' The Happy Mondays, of course, were the other team. I think their music has stood the test of time and I wish I could tell Tony that in this particular rivalry of ours my opinion now is that his band were the better of the two.

On 30 June 2007, on one of our Saturday nights when Tony was obviously very poorly, we'd gone to bed but stayed up a bit later than usual watching a programme called *The Seven Ages of Rock*. It was quite good. At one point the Stone Roses came on – it was from a gig at the Empress Ballroom in Blackpool in 1989. Tony said with some excitement, 'That's my footage, that's my Granada footage!' and I said, 'Oh yeah, and it's my fucking band.'

Nineteen eighty-eight was a strange year because it contained two unlikely events, both connected with revival.

It was the year that Tony and I found each other again, forgave each other again, and loved each other again. Something had changed between us when our paths crossed at the Hacienda.

I don't think we had even spoken to each other between 1985 and '87 but, as ever – even in this case – the ice thawed and the hate fell away.

Perhaps it was rather as Peter Saville described his own reconciliation with Tony after a supremely bad fallout in 1990. When I asked how they became friends again, Saville replied, 'We missed each other.'

If anyone had told me when Tony sacked me that we would be friends again for life, I would have been doubtful. But if anyone had said we'd be lovers again I would have thought, 'Impossible, absolutely no way.' That's why I always think you should never say never. You just never know. I think we put too much emphasis on feelings – but feelings can change. Then again, some feelings just never go away.

Nineteen eighty-eight was also the year that there was an explosion in music, another revolution of sorts. There was house music, which led to acid house, and the Hacienda became massive overnight, literally overnight it seemed to me. I'll never forget the night I went to the Hacienda and it was suddenly an entirely different place from what it had been before. For the first four years it had lost money hand over fist. Information about the exorbitant sums that were squandered are detailed in Hooky's book. But this night it was wild! Totally packed, hot, steamy, I think there was a pool – maybe it was Hot Night. Even if it wasn't it was hot! People were interacting; it was as if 1,000 people all knew each other and were the best of friends. They seemed slightly jubilant, as if they were on some wacky drug. Most of them probably were.

I never really got the connection between ecstasy and clubbing myself. The first night I tried ecstasy I was expecting it to be like some kind of mild LSD, and therefore best to take at home (or someone else's home). Later, when I tried it in a club setting, I could see why it made house music (or any kind of music) more interesting, but that was about it. Maybe I'm just not really a clubbing kind of person.

Back in 1986, Factory had organised the Festival of the Tenth Summer (ten years since punk). This consisted of ten events held over a week, and the festival had Tony's fingerprints, vision, energy and enthusiasm all over it. It was rather like a colourful and early In the City event (Manchester's yearly music seminar set up by Tony and Yvette Livesey in 1992 and continuing to the present day), and even had a daily lunchtime seminar at the Hacienda's Gay Traitor bar billed as 'The New, New Music Seminar'. As usual, Tony wrote the notes for the ten events, and injected the fuel of enthusiasm that orchestrated the content to come together. It all culminated in a major concert at G-Mex with the Smiths, New Order, the Fall, OMD and such like. It's a testament to Tony that he and Factory reinstated Manchester's prominence in the country's music scene at that time. Interestingly, the Happy Mondays played at Rafters during that week and Vini remembers telling Tony that he thought the Mondays were the best gig out of the whole lot. On reflection Tony had to agree with him. His belief in and commitment to this band was yet to become paramount.

Phil Saxe thought it was Nathan McGough's involvement with the Mondays that made Tony take notice of them. Nathan recalls his first sighting of the Happy Mondays in 1985: 'I first went to see the Mondays with Rob Gretton when they supported New Order in Macclesfield at the leisure centre. Rob told me they sounded a bit like Echo & the Bunnymen only different. As soon as I saw them I wanted to manage them, but they were already managed by their dad and Phil Saxe. It was an instant attraction for me, I loved it, I felt it was dangerous. On the way down Rob said the band were like pure boys. I said what's that? He said pure boys are like scallies; they wear wedge cuts, and cords and trainers, but they're really into LSD. It wasn't really a working-class drug at that point, nor pot for that matter. They had an element of menace about them, not violent, just something dangerous. One night I was working at the Hacienda and Shaun Ryder came up to me and said, "We've fired Phil Saxe." This was like early '88. I said, "Are you just telling me in passing conversation or are you telling me that the management position is free?" He went, "What the fuck do you think?" I said, "Are you asking me to manage the Mondays?" He said, "Of course I am you knobhead."'

The Stone Roses and the Happy Mondays had come from completely different places. The Roses were more of an indie band wearing tight jeans and paisley shirts, and their early audiences hailed from a gothic rock scene. When the Roses played the Hacienda they seemed somewhat out of place in a Chicago-based funk environment, whereas the Mondays came from a funk background and blended in more easily with the Hacienda club ambience. Both groups began around 1985 and the more time that passed, the more it became apparent that despite having no real similarities they appealed to the exact same audience. I'm not entirely sure why the Roses fit in with a rave scene. They changed their look to flares, T-shirts, rave shirts, and Reni's trademark beanie hat.

It was almost like watching the International and Hacienda clubs slowly converge into one happening scene. The Roses and the Mondays were looked after respectively and separately by me and by Tony. Both bands got their break through our efforts, and we were also like them – two disparate entities slowly merging.

Things had turned around slightly for the Hacienda in 1986. At Erasmus's suggestion – if not badgering insistence that went ignored for some time – Paul Mason came in from running a club called Rock City in Nottingham. He was the first manager with proper experience. I remember meeting him and initially thinking we weren't going to get along too well. He seemed very serious and not especially friendly – hardly surprising given the clean-up act that befell him. It's likely that he took a dim view of my free entrance, especially in light of all the scams going on there. His job was to prevent wasteful expenditure; hence he quickly put an end to nightly openings. And after all I was only an ex, so why should I be getting freebies? I put my foot down at that though, taking the view that this guy and this club wouldn't have been here in the first place without my marital money. If a court of law would have seen it that way, why couldn't anybody else? Because I walked away, that's why. Same with the Stone Roses.

They gave Paul a very fancy car – according to Hooky it cost £30,000. Doubtless he deserved it because he had a very tough job on his hands. And I got to keep my free pass.

Green shoots were actually visible at the Hacienda as early as October 1984, with the launch of Mike Pickering's Nude Night. Mike had done well booking bands for the Hacienda, but having taken his band Quando Quango to New York, he returned with impressive new ideas regarding DJ mixing from Danceteria, the club that had inspired this whole thing in the first place. He was probably playing house music before anyone called it that. Simon Topping (Tony's A Certain Ratio 'star') would sometimes join in the set with US-based, Latin-feel experimental music. Simon and Mike recorded one of the first house records, 'Carino', under the name T-Coy (supposedly standing for 'Take Care of Yourself') with Ritchie Close.

I remember when Nude Night began. The reason was down to Tony Connolly, Tony's dad's live-in partner. Connolly liked a drink and one night I was at the Hacienda and he wandered in, without Sydney, very much out of it. He was harmless enough though. I watched him dancing around one of the pillars near the main dancefloor. It began to take on the look of a pole dance, even though the pillar was square. I think he was taking the piss somewhat, or maybe the yellow-and-black stripes got him going. The next thing he did was to slide his trousers down slightly, very slowly and somewhat erotically in time with the music, with his back turned toward the pillar. Suddenly a bouncer or two appeared and chucked him out. He was barred after that. For life! I was a bit annoyed – after all he was family. But what really got to me was the name Nude becoming the biggest-named Hacienda night, and beginning so soon after this event. The word Nude was splashed everywhere, all over any promotional material. I remember Flesh Night as well. I thought Connolly himself might have inspired it.

In 1986 the Hacienda had its first band-less packed night. It happened to coincide with the publication of A-level results that same evening and many of the club-goers were celebrating sixth-formers. Mason had run a student night in Nottingham and knew it made commercial sense (and as Tony later observed, Stella at a quid a pint was the drug to do the business). That summer Tony was in China again and, according to Mick Middles, when Tony heard about this night from Paul Mason he decided to forestall the club's inevitable closure (in light of losses sustained). It was given a temporary reprieve.

I'm not going to give a diatribe on house music or acid house because, like Tony, I didn't totally get it. I suspect Mike Pickering was a pioneer of house and the first to bring it to the Hacienda. He came from those roots; that funky stuff that preceded the raves, Chicago-based minimalist funk music. He was playing decent stuff.

But as Nathan pointed out: 'Tony created the space for it to happen. No one knew what was coming but, without the Hacienda, that spark would not have lit when it did. Liverpool didn't get acid house until two years after Manchester. I am from Liverpool and I used to come to Manchester a lot. For weekends. But it was cliquey . . . there wasn't a big central space. The Hacienda was an amazing space and it was radical. There wasn't anywhere else like that in the UK. If you wanted to see bands in a club, they would be grotty, shitty places where your feet would stick to the floor and, if you wanted a nightclub experience, it was all chrome and velvet. The Hacienda was completely radical because they took the model from New York. People didn't really know how to use the space because it was so big.'

Although it was Phil Saxe and Mike Pickering who first made Tony aware of the Happy Mondays, and it was to take him some time to become their biggest fan, I wonder if that group, like Joy Division, would have been as successful without Tony in the equation.

Tony had long been interested in developing film and video, as witnessed by the inception of Factory's Ikon arm and the release of a Factory compilation video (*IKON 1*) in 1981. Interestingly, Tosh remembers showing Tony his new Sony Betamax Portapak video system the year before this and Tony's response to it. Apparently Tony said, 'Wow, that's fantastic, you could make your own porn movies!' Domestic video systems were not widely available then. A whole new world of visual creativity was about to open up.

Keith Jobling and Phil Shotton, aka Bailey Brothers, were soon to become Tony's film and video protégées after a chance meeting with Nathan, then manager of Kalima, led to Keith and Graham Proudlove making a Kalima video. As mentioned previously, the basement at 36 Old Broadway had been turned over as an edit suite, and while working down there Keith recalled meeting Tony for the first time. Tony told them that he'd just spent a fortune with Jonathan Demme (New Order's 'The Perfect Kiss' video apparently cost £160,000), yet he liked their work better. The timing was perfect since Tony was just about to put the Mondays on Factory, and he asked Keith and Phil if they'd like to help on the video. 'We turned up,' said Keith, 'we had Richard Heslop with us and Phil. Graham had gone to London by that point. It was outside the Hacienda, Wilson pulls up in his Jag and he gets out and he says, "Is anyone else here?" We said, "No," but then we had a mate, John, who arrived from London – he had this massive American car and he was coming up for the weekend and we'd asked him if he'd like to help. The band turned up and they had this dead young kid with them. We said, "Right, what we going to do, Tony?" Then he turned round and said, "Look I'm really sorry but I've just got to go and do something at Granada, I'll be back in about an hour, can you guys just crack on?" So we said to the band, "Get in the car," and we started filming. That was "24 Hour Party People".

'So we just kind of made it up. This young kid was in the middle of the video – kind of [a] car-theft, joy-riding kind of movie. Years and years later I said to [Mondays drummer] Gary Whelan, "How's your little nephew doing?" He said, "Who do you mean?" I said, "You know, the kid in '24 Hour Party People'." Gary went, "No, he's not my nephew." So I said, "Who was he with?" And Gary said, "He was with you. We were all asking each other why had you brought this kid." So he'd gate-crashed it. The film got a lot of attention – it was on *The Chart Show* and we just carried on working from that point onwards.'

Tony later became so enthused by the Bailey Brothers that he hoped to make a full-scale movie entitled 'The Mad Fuckers'. I always understood that this title came about because, since the film had a somewhat similar plot to '24 Hour Party People' – car theft and joyriding – the title was a derivation of 'mad for cars'. The project was a tad ambitious even for Tony, and production was eventually halted when the requisite millions failed to materialise.

The dual rise of the Roses and the Mondays culminated in 1989 when they were both on *Top of the Pops* on the same night that November. It was a strange moment watching that. I felt there was some kind of musical twinning between Tony and me, like stars orbiting separately but under the same sun. Despite their bitter dispute, Martin Hannett had also come back into orbit, having produced the Mondays' second album, *Bummed*. This had been Alan and Nathan's idea.

'It was after *Bummed* that Happy Mondays went on *Top of the Pops*,' Nathan remembered, 'November 1989. There was a four-track EP called *Madchester*

(Rave On). Keith Jobling came up with the concept of Madchester. Because Manchester was in full fucking flow at that time. The Hacienda and ecstasy . . . being in the Hac on a Saturday night was like watching the Storming of the Bastille. It was literally full-on energy. And he came up with the idea of changing the "n" to a "d" in Manchester. Madchester was born and just seemed to completely capture the spirit of that moment. Then Central Station Design did a great logo for it. So they called the EP *Madchester (Rave On)*. It was a brilliant piece of marketing. That sold shedloads.'

Tony felt that Shaun somehow filled the gap left by Ian Curtis. Shaun's wife, Joanne Ryder, told me: 'My guess why they got on so well was: one being Salfordians who are very deeply passionate about their roots, [and two] Tony recognised in Shaun the lyrical genius that Shaun is and with this, between them both, they managed to put their mark in our music history, which is priceless.'

Tony thought that 'Atmosphere' had the same feeling for him as 'Lazyitis' later had, and got enthused by Shaun's poetry to the point of hailing him as a modern-day Yeats. 'Shaun's poetry was post-modern, concrete, it's about words and word association,' said Elliot Rashman (who began managing the Mondays in 2005 after Tony 'ordered' his help sorting out the mess they'd gotten into). 'Making phrases do jobs and being able to sum something up in some unique way. The way I see it is: it's like, from it leaving his thought processes in his brain to coming out of his mouth, something happens and it comes out twisted. At first you think that's a load of rubbish and then the next day you're thinking it's fucking brilliant – his take on it. And having spent a lot of time with him, say if you ask Shaun about a movie he'll give you an incredible appraisal of it that's actually a proper analysis. He has a skewed view of things that actually cuts a lot of crap out. He summed up global warming in a song called "Somebody Else's Weather". That's what we all have now, somebody else's weather. It's not our weather, it's somebody else's. When he recorded "Somebody Else's Weather" he took all his clothes off in the studio and he's got words all over his body and he was reading the lyrics. Brilliant. His writing might not look like any of those modern poets such as Simon Armitage, but I think it's as valid. I think also he has a take on his people, if you like. He came from estates in Salford where to be intelligent or clever was regarded as a weakness. He's had to hide his light under a bushel. He's very knowing, Shaun. He absolutely loved Tony.'

Tony believed in a thirteen-year cycle theory – he'd worked out that the Beatles happened in '63, punk in '76, and acid house in '89. He was convinced about it until 2002 came and went without leaving a mark, never mind a cultural revolution. Although I seem to remember that he invented some spurious youth culture nonsense somewhere in the world for that year, rather than admit he was wrong.

Vini had this to say in 2009: 'Acid house led us down a blind alley. That was the last revolution, but we are all waiting for the next revolution. We are back to boy bands and girl bands.'

I think Tony respected the fact that I was surviving in the music business without him despite walking away empty-handed. I was glad I had because I got to keep something more precious than money, and that was his friendship.

Perhaps because we'd effectively had the worst bust-up imaginable, the making up part was very, very special. Also, there was the fact that I had irretrievably lost him as a husband and father to my children – now there were no plans to make, no traps to fall into, nothing but just let's share another moment in time. And, of course, inevitably this was going to be short. It had to be. We couldn't have gone on sneaking around, having an affair for long. In that sense it was similar to the time we spent together before his death. I totally appreciated his worth again.

I don't remember how it came about. But I found these diary notes:

Friday, 15 July 1988
Plane to New York was delayed approx three hours. I began to panic when people were boarding and he still hadn't showed up – decided he definitely wasn't coming. Wondered what to do, whether to still go or not, went to the phone, maybe he'd got a message to my mum about why he couldn't come. Just then espied him walking as cool as you like – dashed to a seat and imitated calm, picked up a book, but I was breaking down just like a little girl. He said he'd been watching the cricket in the lounge but seemed to be concerned about standing with me as we boarded the plane, which further broke my cool and the tears began to flow – so I put dark glasses on. He went up the stairs to first class and I took my place in the centre of the downstairs bustle. Once in my seat I cried my eyes out. For once I felt grateful for the conversation of the two Americans

on either side of me – otherwise I probably wouldn't have stopped. Mid-flight Tony came down to check on me but I felt awkward speaking to him then just as he hadn't wanted to speak to me at the airport.

I hated Tony's play-acting when we got there. 'Can I offer you a lift?' he asked in the luggage reclaim, but most of the tension seemed to dissolve once we got into the car, a Mercury Cougar – I loved it – and he drove fast and expertly on the freeway. We were tired though, but happy, when we stopped off and had some supper and coffee. We arrived at Lake George soon after midnight (5:00am to us) and checked into the Lake Crest Motel. It seemed kitsch with flashing lights by a pond.

Saturday, 16 July 1988
Woke at 6:00am and woke him but slept till 7:00. I lay awake till 8:00 while he slept then I kind of woke him. I was so hungry. We had bacon and eggs and French toast and maple syrup. Went to Fort William Henry. Watched a display with a grenadier firing a gun in a cannon. Back to the motel to change room – moved up – beautiful view of the lake. King-sized bed. Drove to another Fort – Ticonderoga. Very tired in the car. He phoned home. Got ferry across to Vermont, stopped for lunch in a diner and back home. The sun came out so he put shorts on and went to the lake, where he hired a windsurfer and I sat and read Jeanette Winterson, *The Passion*. He actually crossed the huge lake and I worried when he disappeared. Finally he returned, we drank a beer and went home again. Took some ecstasy at 6:00pm. Sat on the balcony listening to New Order – he watched Jesse Jackson at the convention and compared him to Martin Luther King. The sun was falling but hot, I wanted to get a speedboat but we slowly meandered down to a bar when a thunderstorm and heavy rain broke. Marooned inside we met a couple who were down from a ski resort twenty miles away. Walked back arm in arm – so nice, the freedom to do that.

Sunday, 17 July 1988
Managed to sleep till 8:00. Went to mass. How odd – were we husband and wife or adulterers? I became very emotional during the service, the reading was 'The Lord Is My Shepherd' – he leadeth me beside tranquil waters where he resteth my soul, etc, and there was another reading about uniting after a period of division. It all seemed apt and beautiful but I had to control my tears as they weren't the order of the day. Finished with a sweet song about peace. The heat was terrible and we were longing to jump into the car and blast on the air conditioning but even so, if I could keep one moment from the weekend it would be when we walked away from church, hands entwined, with the others. I could feel the time we had slipping away. Maybe that's why I remember so well how happy I felt then. We drove to the Sagamore – a nice hotel – and had lunch on the

terrace. I had just finished the last strawberry when the heavens entirely opened. Again we were marooned, the rain was torrential. He left me in a gift shop whilst he phoned home. I had to laugh when he went to get the car – barefoot with trousers rolled up to his knees.

Back in New York he put on his business hat for the New Music Seminar. We parted in a New York subway. I looked at him through a grill that seemed to symbolise the end of our freedom together.

I had left him a note in pencil before I returned home (ahead of him). He enclosed this note with his letter to me from Morgans Hotel, 21 July. He wrote: 'I have been crying. In Mr Curtis's words, there are still "tears in my eyes". How well you write. How simply and how powerfully.' My note read:

Memories fade like the red of an old eastern carpet washes delicate pink after years of daylight. The times we shared – funny, they all seem happy now, as sweet as the days just passed; your soul in retreat with mine by a tranquil lake; and the only pain I can remember now was this one, the sadness for loss of you, mixed with a terrible fear that a day would come when we would no longer wake up together except by chance. There is no sense in either of us.

The last time I ever saw Tony was Wednesday, 8 August 2007. I hadn't seen him since the previous weekend when he said, as I was leaving, that he would call me. I couldn't imagine that being possible given his poor health – he could barely speak for one thing, and was incredibly weak. So I had set off that evening determined to visit him in any case. Remarkably he called me just as I was leaving. A man of his word. I didn't know it – he did – but the word this night was the last goodbye. The previous night, when I'd picked out Tony's bundle of letters from a suitcase, I chose one at random to read and it was the one from Morgans Hotel. The contents made me cry, because it seemed as apt in 2007 as it had in 1988. Tony's letter from 1988 went on:

Our kinship is of this life and all this life. Of course 'all this life' will not be for waking up together; but some of our life, from San Francisco to Lake George; from Charlesworth to some other place – the room is not yet booked. Really can we ask for any more? I am happy. You have made me happy. Though there are still tears in my eyes and talking to you like this is making them well up just a little. You say the past seems – all happy. For me, glorious; and yet your first lines, the words of a carpet dealer, remind me that those days were as near to unbearable as any I can remember. My mum dead in Manchester and I in California – my wife dying in London and I in Manchester, and her changing her name.
Such and for all the past, I cannot recall before the tenderness in your

eyes – through those 42nd Street bars – at today's last kiss. Easy symbolism there, but welcome in its way, and our love has not just grown older – it has also grown. When we have so much – a crime to ask to have it all.

He ends by referring once more to my note to him: 'I know it's crazy, but I know it makes sense, for us perhaps the life of chance, like Winterson's heroine, is natural. Could we ever succeed as creatures of habit? I love someone whom I will only wake up to by chance. Fine. Thank you. Yours, Anthony x'.

Despite the premonition of separation from the subway bars, we did meet as lovers again later that year. I travelled to Los Angeles, where 52nd Street were finishing off recording their third album. Actually the producer, John Barnes, had sensibly sent the band home to put an end to all the squabbles, and was now finishing the songs with the fabulous voice of Diane Charlemagne. That was where I came in. I stayed with Diane for about two or three months as she finished off the songwriting and vocals. The upshot of all this was that the band regrouped and, under the new name Cool Down Zone, the resulting album was entitled *New Direction*. Although the record label understandably called a halt to any more expense, I thought it a great pity because at last the group were getting along well; plus there was a song on there that I truly loved and would for all time. Ironically it had nothing to do with the band at all. The music was written and played by John Barnes, who had worked on piano and keyboards with Michael Jackson. Diane wrote the lyrics and I was privileged to be in the studio as the two of them put the track down in a matter of minutes. I thought it was beautiful. It was called 'When You Call'. It was never released as a single.

A dormant hit, perhaps. I wonder how many wonderful songs are lying around having never been put into the machine – the commercial jukebox that the media keeps locked in a stranglehold spelling death to creativity. Also, I wonder how many talented musicians there are all over the world who are never appreciated, and who remain unable to support themselves through their life's work.

Almost everyone I interviewed commented that most record companies would never have gone near Factory bands then – let alone now. 'Had Factory not existed,' Vini Reilly said, 'I don't think a record company would have touched Joy Division at that time. No one knew that Ian was going to be as good as he was, or that the group were going to be so hugely influential, no one could have foreseen any of that.'

'The thing I worked out quite quickly,' said Keith Jobling, 'when you see him [Tony] introduce that punk stuff on TV. Well, who else would have gone to the bother of doing that? Nobody else in the country gave a toss about that. The record industry didn't particularly give at toss. Nobody was at the time . . . and yet he was saying, "Wow, look at this."'

Tony also had business in LA around the same time as me, and timed his journey to coincide our travelling there. For this trip we didn't travel on the same plane (neither of us was going to fall for that one again) but, since we both arrived on the same day, Tony romantically suggested we meet at the Hacienda Hotel – one mile away from LAX Airport. I took a shuttle and he hired a car and drove us on from there. We had a lovely couple of days before I joined Diane. I stayed with him at the Chateau Marmont and he took me to Long Beach, where we visited the Queen Mary (now a hotel, it wasn't then). Even after I moved into the apartment with Diane he came the next weekend to take me out. He took me to Watts this time (Tony's trips were always educational). He enthusiastically told me about the severe riots that had occurred in this neighbourhood in 1965 and the racial tension and poverty that he believed had engendered them. It was the stuff of revolution to him. We were happy but my clock was audibly ticking.

Because I wanted children, and because of my age then (thirty-six), it seemed I must move on from Tony. It was a crazy suggestion but he said that if I hadn't met anyone with whom I wanted to have a child within a year, then we would have one together. I didn't see how we possibly could. He was devoted to his son, Oliver, then only aged four, and he told me he would never leave. I didn't want him to either. But nor did I want to be a single parent. It was too late for us.

With hindsight I regret ending our affair and, perhaps more bizarrely, regret not having a child with him – even in those circumstances and at that late stage. Because I never did find another man to share marriage and children with. I couldn't accept a compromise. But it's useless to have regrets. With all its imperfections life is still magical, and in another way absolutely perfect.

I had a great time living in LA those next three months, going to the studio every day on Melrose Avenue, being creative, keeping healthy with good food, exercise, yoga and generally becoming at one with the LA lifestyle. It reminded me of the old days at Strawberry with Martin and Tony. I felt completely at home in this studio and happily stayed hour upon hour, day after day.

Tony and I had only one more illicit meeting. (My mum used to say that when she was a child she thought adultery was something that adults did – and how right she was!) This meeting took place in a lovely hotel in London. I remember it because it was the same night as the Lockerbie Disaster, 21 December 1988. Odd somehow to think that Noel Gallagher was auditioning for Inspiral Carpets at the same time.

Christmas is the worst time of all to be in an affair. You can't even receive a message from the person you love (especially in the pre-mobile, pre-text, pre-email era). You need really strong self-esteem to carry on with an affair, because it makes you beat yourself up – it just seems all wrong, however bloody right it also feels. Especially when there is a child or children involved. And especially at Christmas. Impossible.

I think women aged thirty-six to forty-five are very vulnerable where men are concerned if they haven't had children but want them. I felt I had to move on to the next available candidate as soon as possible if I was to have a family of my own.

I told Tony we had to separate, even though it could only ever have been him and even though, subconsciously, I ran a mile from any man who looked capable of commitment.

Tony Connolly always said that the most important thing in life is to have a clear conscience. When your conscience isn't clear it is easier to relate to that statement. I was able to rationalise the guilt away; I was Tony's first wife, this was hardly a casual affair. But it didn't feel fair – to Hilary or to me.

I agree with Connolly – peace of mind is *numero uno*. But I don't necessarily moralise about affairs.

We didn't know it then, but in a very short time Tony was to meet the young Yvette and – well, I wonder, if I had stayed, would he have remained loyal to me then? Of course it sounds ridiculous to use the word loyal when he was being dishonest to his second wife, the mother of his child. This is what he had to say about that to me then:

And you were right; I was wrong to deny when you said, 'You love Hilary, don't you?' Of course, in my way, I do. For my way is to add that word 'enough', and indeed I love Hilary enough to stay with her. Be cynical, and yes, I do not love Lindsay 'enough' to leave my new wife and son. But then do I really not love you. My tears – oh yes – I have been crying a little while writing this. I'm careful the stewardess doesn't notice. They're so tactful in CLUB class anyway. My tears say something quite different. Till death do us part, I think. We both had a fairly good go at parting, but our twinned souls don't really allow it. For better or worse kid – it was a sacrament.

When Tony met and became bowled over by Yvette Livesey in 1990, he followed the same route with her that he'd taken with me. A clandestine affair is safest abroad. He took her to New York while he attended the New Music Seminar again. Their relationship began as it ended, since it was also the last place he ever took her or ever visited in his life.

While discussing the stress that Ian Curtis had been under, Tony told me in interview: 'I'd been with Yvette in New York that summer of 1990 and we'd masqueraded that she was Keith Allen's mistress, that she wasn't with me. Keith Allen – the great comedian – he was part of the team. He became part of it when he came to Manchester to do a drama in '87, hanging out at the Hacienda, everyone's mate; he became part of the Mondays crowd and all that.'

Tony was on a high, literally and metaphorically. He was understandably cock-a-hoop then. Not just about his new love but about the cultural youth revolution that had his own Hacienda and city as its focal point. Drugs were always 'cool' to him, but around the Happy Mondays period his love of drugs bordered on reverence. That summer of 1990 Tony ran a New Music Seminar in New York which, with his penchant for sound-bites, he entitled, 'Wake Up America, You're Dead!'

Tony had an unusual ability to stir things up. He was very brave when you think about it, going into situations like this with all guns blazing. He took a stab at America for starting a house music evolution that was going nowhere in the country where it began. Steve Sutherland documented the entire event in *Melody Maker*. With his predictable aplomb when it came to confrontation, Tony began: 'Good morning, ladies and gentlemen. Welcome to the New Music Seminar. The rest of the shit going on in the rest of this building is the Old Music Seminar. This is the New Music Seminar.'

He continued: 'I'd like to begin with a quote. The quote is: "The kids wanna dance." That does not come from Manchester or Madchester 1989 or the Hacienda or Ibiza in 1987; it comes from the Family Dog in San Francisco in 1964. You used to know how to dance here. God knows how you fucking forgot.

'What people in America don't seem to know is that the music which has come out of Chicago and Detroit in the last ten years has so changed British pop music – not only dance music but also rock music – that now, if you're a British rock group and you cannot play rock music in the style to which you can dance, and with the rhythms that have come out of America but that have been ignored here, then you aren't a rock group that matters. You're dead.'

Tony loved to boast and boast he did, about his club the Hacienda, in which kids were going wild and dancing like crazy; about the DJs such as Pickering who brought the music to England. He somewhat smugly introduced Keith Allen as a doctor of the Post-Freudian Therapy Centre in Geneva and a world expert on drugs. He told an uneasy audience: 'It's so strange in America, you're so embarrassed about fucking drugs aren't you? It didn't do Guns N' Roses any harm.'

He was obviously on dodgy ground promoting drugs. Safer perhaps was his declaration: 'I think if we talk about the fulcrum moments, one was when the Balearic all-night Ibiza dance attached itself to house music in the beginning of '88, and the other great moment was when people like Ronnie and Paul Ryder, the drummer and bass player of Happy Mondays, began to be able to put the dance rhythms out of Chicago and Detroit into rock music. They soon became the first generation of British groups with the Roses and Inspiral Carpets and now there's a dozen or more.'

Derrick May, a Detroit house producer, was eventually wound up enough to rise to Tony's challenge and complain: 'Dance music has been fucked up. You've got all these motherfuckers who don't know shit about where the shit comes from, they don't have no fucking idea what the fuck is happening and they're making money and they're fucking up the scene. Dance music is dead. I hate to say it. I do it for a living. I love it. I do it as an art, okay. But I know that when I have to sit back and see some bullshit Adamski shit . . . that's bullshit. On the charts! Number fucking one! Okay?'

Clearly this was the confrontation Tony was looking for. He had touched a nerve, and May spoke with true venom and passion about the problems of being black and making music from the heart that is then turned around by drug-taking idiots and 'stuffed down motherfuckers' throats'. The row was like an exciting edition of Tony's *Upfront* show. In fact, Tony asked May if he'd like to be on his TV show.

The personal insults began to fly thick and fast, with May finally screaming at Tony to shut the fuck up, but then taking his leave on this note: 'I don't have to stand up for my manhood. You can argue with yourself. You can pull out your little two-inch penis and dog yourself, okay? I'll see you later. Good night. And thank you very much, crowd. It's been nice.'

Who else but Tony could be so infuriatingly smug and funny and stir things up as well as that? Not a bad PR stunt either, since two nights later the queue outside the Sound Factory for a Hacienda presentation, 'From Manchester With Love', stretched for over a mile. Happy Mondays and 808 State played to a complete sell-out.

But for all of that the Hacienda was not without its problems. In 2006 Tony told me: 'The night we opened the Hacienda, after it had been closed for four months due to the gang violence back in 1990, we'd got a whole new door done with a new metal-proof gate and a new metal detector at the centre, and there's a massive queue round the block and I'm thinking "fantastic", but I get to the door and there's Leroy and he says, "Sorry Toe we've got a problem, the metal detector's not working," and yes [it was working], but the floor is metal so it keeps detecting it. Oh my God, only us.'

In September 1990, following up on Alan Erasmus's great idea to venture into the world of classical music, Factory launched its classical arm with three events across the length of the country – in Glasgow, Manchester and London. Composer Steve Martland had already released a record on Factory back in 1989, a 20th-century contemporary piece entitled *Babi Yar/Drill*. These Factory events showcased other classical artists along with Martland and Durutti Column, namely I Fagiolini, Red Byrd, Rolf Hind and Graham Fitkin.

I'd just begun working with Hollywood Records as Head of A&R (although I was in a department of one). Hollywood was a Walt Disney company and their London branch was a new office with exciting possibilities. The managing director, Hein van der Ree, took me on because he remembered me doing the rounds with the Stone Roses demo when he was MD of Phonogram Records and his then A&R department rejected the band. Alas, the group I signed to Hollywood – Natural Life – were not destined for success. The only member who 'made it' was Shovel, who went on to join M People, Mike Pickering's band. It so happened that Tony and I were in Scotland at the same time, since I was checking out a group in Glasgow when the Factory Classical event was being held at the Tramway Theatre Museum.

Just as Tony had wanted Thelma to meet me fifteen years earlier, now Tony wanted me to meet Yvette – a sure sign he was deadly serious about her. With his taste for style and finery, Tony had asked Jane Lemon (my friend and partner of ACR's Jez Kerr) – who had been working at Factory for a couple of years – to organise a dinner party at Rogano's Oyster Bar. There were probably about ten of us at the table.

No doubt Tony had researched this restaurant beforehand. When, years later, he would pick me up in the country, we would set off for some recommended eatery that he'd found in one of his manuals and the food never failed to impress. Sometimes he'd find a gem locally that I had no idea about. Another habit of his – apart from guidebooks on food and hotels, wherever he happened to be – was to buy a map of the area. In the early days I couldn't understand why he would insist on buying a map when we were only just passing through somewhere. It spoke of clutter and wasteful expense. I hadn't seen anything yet! (That was before the Hacienda.) As I've gotten older, I've learnt to appreciate people's foibles rather than be irritated by them. This foible of Tony's reflected both his enthusiasm and thirst for knowledge and adventure.

Bar and club owner Ross McKenzie became a close friend of Tony's and was sitting at his bedside to the end. Before the pair met Tony had made an impression on Ross due to an episode of *The Other Side of Midnight*, in which Tony was driving around in his Jag pointing out buildings. One building Tony was raving about with his usual enthusiasm was, like Rogano's in Glasgow, built in the art-deco style of the 1930s. It was the *Daily Express* building on Great Ancoats Street in Manchester. Rogano's was styled after the Queen Mary liner, built on the Clyde in 1935. This helps explain Tony's zeal when taking me round this very ship in 1988 at Long Beach, Los Angeles.

I like to think that, just as Thelma had, I went to the meal with Tony's wellbeing in mind. I genuinely wanted him to be happy by whatever means. But when I saw him walk in, looking like the cat who'd got the cream, with a stunningly attractive young woman who was at least twenty years his junior, my old sabotage instincts came to the fore. It is true that there's nothing quite like the bloom of youth, but it didn't sit right somehow. I wasn't alone in thinking that (although it felt like it then). Keith Jobling told me: 'It was as if he'd gone out and bought himself a beautiful Harley Davidson.'

Tony was puffed up, oozing vanity. I wanted to instantly deflate him, to remind him of something he didn't want reminding of – that this is not the way to feel good about ourselves. I vented my feelings slightly with the odd note of sarcasm. That wasn't a good idea and, if I had been older and wiser, I would have held my tongue. It was like water off a duck's back to him anyway. I was reminded of one of my mum's sayings, written in her book of thoughts:

'First thought: No mature man would look at (i.e. seriously consider) a seventeen-year-old girl.

'Second thought: There are no mature men.'

Yvette was nineteen, Tony was forty.

Perhaps I sensed that I had irrevocably lost Tony in some way. I'd certainly lost sexual power over the man – something I'd held for so many years without using or appreciating it. Now it was too late, I was supplanted. I don't really believe it was something I'd ever particularly wanted, wishing instead that he would love me for me, not as an object. He didn't see it that way. He was in love or he wasn't. And now that he'd fallen hook, line and sinker for Yvette, he would never again be in love with me. Tony and I often spoke about sexual love and he would always give the case for the power of it, how it's in all the classics – *Othello*, Proust, Greek mythology; basically it's everywhere – and how it meant everything to him. He once wrote to me: 'We should never be friends. There was too much passion and love to degrade it like that.' And in another letter, when it looked unlikely that I would return to the marital home, he wrote: 'I'd like to think we could be deep friends . . . and yet that would mean losing my passion for you . . . and in a sentimental sort of way I'm quite attached to that passion. I think I would sacrifice a highly valued friendship with Lindsay Wilson – just to feel my heart beat faster in thirty years' time if I caught sight of your car in Manchester.'

All these feelings were welling up during this Glasgow meal but I was unable to process any of it. I feared for his vulnerability over his adoration of this young girl. I thought he was a fool, feeling angry that he couldn't see she was out of his league were it not for his status. In the midst of the meal I went to the ladies and Jane joined me. I expressed my doubt, anxiety and irritation about Tony's new situation to her. She didn't see a problem. So then I wondered out loud if I might not just be a bit jealous? 'Jealous with a capital "J", I'd say,' she replied. So I took that on board. Perhaps she was right. I still cared for him and on some level I probably always would be a little bit jealous. We did go on to share an everlasting friendship, but it would take me a while to accept that this was the end for us – the rest of his life, in fact.

Having fallen head over heels in love with Yvette, Tony might have thought at first that he could have it all. But though he could lie through his teeth, and did indeed try to live with the deception of his new love, he wasn't the world's best at acting.

This was proven in 2005 when he played a part in the film about Tristram Shandy, *A Cock and Bull Story*. It was another Michael Winterbottom-directed production featuring Steve Coogan as the title character, made three years after *24 Hour Party People*, and I like to think that film came about as a result of Tony talking about the book. He was so literate, he really did know a lot about it and loved it. It was a fantastic film, but this is what Keith Jobling had to say about Tony's role in it: 'He was dead chuffed being in the Tristram Shandy film and when I saw it I thought he couldn't act, which was kind of quite endearing. It's ironic because he was a very good Tony Wilson but I wanted him to be someone else. I was hoping he'd surprise everybody and not play himself, not play Tony Wilson, but he couldn't.'

And this is what Tony's lawyer, Stephen Lea, had to say about him: 'I think Tony was an open book. I mean, he couldn't keep a secret to save his life. He was beautifully indiscreet at times.'

But the most positive man in the world *was* keeping a secret, and was also beginning to know what desperation felt like. In an interview with me, Tony said that Hooky had seen through the charade of Yvette being with Keith Allen. Tony discussed it when relating to how Ian Curtis must have felt:

TW: Hooky was there [in New York] and then one night at the Tribeca Grill under Nero's restaurant, I was there and Hooky comes up and says, 'You and that chick then?' and I said, 'No, no, she's here with Keith

Allen.' Hooky's line was, 'Don't shit a shitter,' which was quite funny. Don't bullshit a bullshitter. I said, 'Okay fine.' So Hooky knew all about me and Yvette at that point. So then this is like a few months later, and Hooky says, 'How's it going, Toe?' I go, 'Fucking shite, Hooky.' Hooky went, 'Oh well, now you know how Ian felt.' I kind of went, 'What did you say?' He says, 'Now you know how Ian felt.' I said, 'Hooky I can't believe you said that – I spent the last week driving round in a mist thinking that's how Ian felt – how did you know?' To which he said, 'Why do you think I left? It was the second time I'd gone to the top of our house and opened the window ready to jump out. And I thought, "Fuck me, this is what Ian did, I'm not doing this."' He'd had exactly the same experience, which was: I can't stay in the marriage and I can't leave the children. When there is an unsolvable problem the solution is leave.
LR: If you commit suicide, though, you are still leaving your children.
TW: It doesn't feel like that. It feels as if you are solving the problem for everybody. I think you get to the point where it's the only way out of the unsolvable. At the time, before I had my own experience, I always thought it was to do with the fact that Ian thought he was helping everybody. He thought he was messing everyone's life up – his daughter, his wife, his lover – so that's what I thought for eight years until my own experience with the kids and Yvette in '90. Certainly in '80 and for the following ten years I thought it was to do with that. That he was helping everybody and he thought he'd do everyone a favour. But that changed to be the irresolvable problem was resolved. That's my personal explanation.

Tony carried on with the deception and generally treated Hilary badly, although she didn't understand why. On one occasion he phoned Hilary from London and she told him that if he didn't change his attitude he shouldn't bother returning home. He didn't. Two weeks went by and she didn't know where he was. Rooting through his office she found Yvette's passport and noticed that the dates and stamps of countries, including the USA, tallied with his own. So now she knew. She also found out his address in a village in Cheshire – a rented cottage in Comberbach – and went there one afternoon. Hilary said that Yvette answered the door and told her that she was just waiting in the house as Tony was expecting a BT engineer and had to be at work. Hilary responded that she wasn't stupid and asked her to give Tony up – especially if it wasn't that serious – because he had two children at home. She said Yvette told her that Tony didn't want Hilary anymore, he wanted her now.

Obviously it must have been excruciating for Hilary, she'd recently given birth to a baby girl and – having a scarred face – now had to witness Tony leaving his family for a beautiful and much younger woman.

Having been Tony's mistress myself, and knowing that his relationship with Hilary wasn't on solid ground – sadly and probably in part due to the hasty basis of it – I wasn't even remotely surprised that he was having an affair. But I was genuinely shocked when Tony left his family. It went against everything he'd told me or seemed to believe in. Still, increasingly that is how it often is in this modern world, and Tony's commitment to, and love of, his children always remained paramount.

Soon after this Tony was dropping his children off at the house and Hilary told me that she looked out of the window and saw Yvette holding Isabel (then aged one). This became the one and only occasion Hilary remembers when she totally lost her temper. She flew out of the house and punched Tony hard enough to give him a black eye, which he had to wear make-up at work to conceal. Yvette handed the child to Tony as Hilary then began to go for her. She ran towards the car – Yvette jumped in and Hilary could hear the lock and electric windows winding up. However, it was an open top and the roof was down. Hilary reached in and picked Yvette up by her pony-tailed hair and smacked her in the face.

Tony was not a man to waste time on guilt or regret. He always took a philosophically positive view of things. Perhaps that was partly why he subscribed to the concept of praxis. He told me that praxis meant doing something first and then inventing the reasons for doing it afterwards. I found this a rather convenient philosophy, and suspect he was a bit prone to inventing reasons for his actions. For example, he described his situation with Hilary to me: 'I was in a marriage that didn't have love or passion in it – and that was on either side. Hilary wasn't in love with me either. For many years I worried that she was but she wasn't, and we both married out of convenience. We had children who we adored.' This was not necessarily Hilary's viewpoint or rationalisation of the situation, however.

In 1984, for the BBC documentary *New Order: Play at Home*, Tony described praxis as 'doing something and then only afterwards finding out why you did it'. This makes more sense – the idea that things are not intentional, they just happen. We don't understand the reason for it at the time but perhaps later we do.

Once Tony had left his family and his affair with Yvette became legitimate, he forced my friendship with him to go underground. I remember once he came round to visit me in the early nineties and was sitting comfortably drinking coffee when his mobile rang (the mobile was a bit of a brick, in fact I think it might have been his car phone). He took the call and then froze – he looked terrified and had to rush out of the house. Yet he was doing nothing wrong, we weren't having an affair, we really were 'just friends'.

I thought this was a sign of insecurity and weakness. He was being ruled by fear.

But for the first year or two with his new love, between 1990 and '91, my friendship with Tony was acceptable. Was it because I was in the music business? I was invited to the opening of Factory's new offices and went with my then boss, Hein van der Ree, MD of Hollywood Records. The new offices on Charles Street, near the BBC, were opened in September 1990. They were plush, stylish and impressive. I was honestly glad for Tony and for Factory that they'd been able to do this. Not a trace of my old bitterness. Besides, I'd survived and was in the business myself.

I congratulated Tony, 'Well done, I love this place,' etc. Tony had a rare moment of doubt. So rare in fact that it's probably why I remember it.

'You don't think it might be a bit pretentious?' he enquired of me. 'A bit over the top?'

Well, how should I know? 'No, it's fantastic,' I said. I just assumed he'd done it because he could. I mean, he wouldn't overreach himself would he? He never had before. But yes, yes, yes. He would.

Tosh Ryan, who opened his Basement Video Project on the same road in 1989, had earlier offered £40,000 for the same building, but then withdrew his offer having seen the costs involved in restoring it. His landlord was the same guy who was selling the building. Tosh said, 'The basement was scary, it was wet and horrible. The water from the River Medlock was running right up the wall of the basement. The outside wall against that river was just completely saturated. I think the water was getting in. I thought, how would you get that sorted out? You couldn't. Alan decided to do it. It must have cost hundreds of thousands to do. What they had to do was – they got a very expensive pile driver in and pile-drive these steel girders into the river bank so that the water was diverted off the wall while they repaired and tanked it. They had to get permission off the council to redirect the river. I thought they were daft looking at it. They paid £70,000 to buy it; they paid Ben Kelly a fortune to make the entrance look like a Victorian tiled toilet. The roof was shot, a complete mess. I estimate they spent three quarters of a million just doing that place up.'

Without doubt the exorbitant costs of this building played a more than significant part in the downfall of Factory. But Tony didn't care about money, he cared about art. Sometimes he overplayed his hand and ought to have considered the practical side of things more, as in this case. But in a sense he was able to achieve things with his cavalier attitude that a penny pincher never could have. The Hacienda is one example of that. Vini Reilly related another, smaller example of this trait: 'I saw this nice-looking Stratocaster in a music shop called Sounds Great, so I took it down and asked the guy there if I could have a go on it. He plugged it in and after about two minutes I just looked up and said, "This is *my* guitar. This is what I've been looking for all these years. I want this now." I had no money on me at all. This guy was called Gary that managed the shop and he said, "Vini, do you realise what you've got there?" I didn't know what he meant. And then he showed me that it was a custom-made guitar, hand-made from start to finish by one guy in a custom shop and it was £5,000. [The Strat that Vini already had cost a more usual £250-£300. He'd had loads of work done to it but it was nothing compared with this Strat]

So I just rang Tony from the shop and he was in the Factory office, and I just said, "I've found a guitar." He was always very interested in guitars and asked what it was. I described it to him and said, "Look, I've just got to have this Strat." He just said, "Put Gary on." He spoke to him and sorted it out. After he'd finished speaking to Tony, Gary said, "Right, it's yours." And I walked out of there with a Stratocaster that I'm still playing today. I will never ever get rid of it because it's so perfect.'

Martin Hannett died in 1991. Do we only begin to recognise and cherish people when they are dead? Martin who was so broke when he was alive and yet so talented.

Luckily I got to spend some time with Martin again in the year or two before his death, and by chance was involved with his last project. It wasn't a happy sight to see how much his weight had ballooned, and how heavily he was drinking, but underneath he seemed somehow just the same. In 1989, before I got the job with Hollywood Records, I was working as a talent scout for Polydor Records, and Martin brought my attention to a band called the High. He thought they were brilliant and that in itself was enough to get me going, but I was impressed by them anyway and pleased that Andy Couzens from the Stone Roses was a member. John Williams was then Head of A&R at Polydor, and after I told him about the band he recalled: 'I went to Manchester to see them rehearse. I was thinking of signing them to Polydor and we had some discussions. They knew that I was a record producer. At the beginning of 1990 I was no longer working for Polydor but still in contact with the High, and the idea was that I would co-produce a single with them with Martin Hannett. We thought that with my pop leanings and his left-of-centre approach we might create something interesting together. So we agreed to produce "Box Set Go" at Strawberry Studios.'

London Records (part of Polygram) had by this stage come onboard to sign the group. Martin, John and I had a drink together to talk about it and everything was amiably agreed. However, when it got to the recording, things didn't go so well. John continued: 'We'd start at about eleven in the morning and Martin would turn up about three or four a bit the worse for wear. I don't know what he was consuming but he was drinking a lot and doing a lot of stuff. He would get to the stage where he would be absolutely incoherent. It was very hard to understand the sentences that were emerging from him, and I pretty much produced the record myself. When we finished it we talked about making the album, but I said to the band that really it was very hard co-producing a record – either get him to do it or I'll do it. It was pretty obvious that, whilst Martin had been a genius, those skills were no longer so evident. So the band and I produced the album, called *Somewhere Soon*.'

John recalled Tony – in that loyal way of his, always keeping an eye on his extended family (however errant) – popping his head round the door at

Strawberry on one of the days with the High. I asked John what he thought of Martin's talent at that time and he responded: 'I think Martin was a producer who liked to find his dreams in recording methods, whether that meant piling lots of effects on things to make it sound weird or just experimenting with sounds, but I think by that stage to try and catch simple recordings and making hit records – I don't know whether he was about that. I was probably the last person in the studio with him.'

When I heard the news of Martin's death on the telephone I was in the Portobello Hotel in London, oddly a hotel at which the four of us – me, Tony, Martin and Susanne – had stayed, and at which I had met Leonard Cohen. The tears rolling down my face were evidence of my affection for Martin. I made my way down to the lobby to find a bride and groom both dressed in white. It felt as if I was dreaming. I was just leaving to return to Manchester and when I got to Euston, somewhat eerily, Leonard Cohen's song 'Suzanne' was playing in the café area. It was a poignant moment somehow, as if my own personal finale with Martin was closing on a musical note.

In 1992 Tony and Yvette publicly launched the music convention In the City. It was to be their baby and provided them both with a mutual and musical endeavour. I often wondered if perhaps Tony had learned from the error of leaving me out of his creative ventures. And besides, how else was a busy man like him going to find time to share much of his life with a partner? He understood the importance of that now. Though he always gave her the credit for its success, said that the venture was her idea and often told me how good she was at the job. Reporting on how Yvette had spent a year selling the event, the *Daily Mail* wrote: 'Former beauty queen puts the fizz back in pop.' In the City certainly was a feather in the cap for Manchester. Previously there had really only been Midem in Cannes and the New Music Seminar in New York.

The emergence of In the City, however, accentuated the problems within Factory. Although Factory was involved with In the City's initial stages, with business conducted from the Charles Street offices, Alan felt that Yvette didn't have the necessary music-business experience to front the seminar. In the City may have been the straw that broke the camel's back with regard to what Alan describes as a difficult business relationship with Tony by this point.

Elliot Rashman and Andy Dodd, former managers of Simply Red and partners and directors of So What, provided financial support for In the City at its outset, investing £25,000 into it. This was technically a fifty percent shareholding in the conference. It was this, along with a personal loan of £15,000 that Elliot gave Tony some years later, which caused a schism between the pair. Elliot told me: 'When Andy and I split up and closed So What, Andy gave me his share of In the City because, in Andy's words, it was "worthless". Certainly we never earnt from it. We never saw a penny. Tony and Yvette did all the work. I would do the odd panel and I came up with the "hypotheticals" for it, which I took from Shelley Rohde, a wonderful press and TV journalist and [L.S.] Lowry's biographer, who worked with Tony for some years at Granada; she invented it for the BBC. So I ended up with fifty percent supposedly worthless shareholding and told Tony that I would give it to him.'

Since I was officially in the music business in 1992 and also at a safe distance living in London, Tony was pleased to arrange a free pass for me to attend In the City, along with a huge number of other attendees no doubt. There was a real buzz about it that first year. Or so it seemed to me.

As well as suggesting the 'hypotheticals', Elliot brought the concept of a music manager's forum to In the City, so that managers could share ideas and protect their musicians. He got together several notables, such as Ed Bicknell, and the forum is still in existence today. Ed Bicknell was a friend of legendary Led Zeppelin manager Peter Grant, and they were both speakers at the first In the City conference. Peter and I got chatting, and I happened to be travelling back to London on the same train as him and Bicknell. I found Peter's life story quite interesting – as managers go he'd been the opposite of me. I was too soft. He erred more on the side of fierceness. Subsequently I went down to his house in Eastbourne and interviewed him for a BBC Radio Four programme that Bob Dickinson was organising. I interviewed Bob Geldof for the same show. It was questions about what you'd do on the last day of your life. I think I hurt Peter's feelings, because he sent a huge bouquet of flowers to my London address and I rang him to make sure he was clear that I wasn't attracted to him. I'm wiser now. I'd just say thank you very much. All the same I agreed to accompany him to an event at Silverstone at which we drove around the track in his Porsche, registration 'BAD 1'.

Tony very much championed Yvette as his new and equal partner to run the conference and rather left his erstwhile Factory partners out in the cold. Tony expressed his view to me that Alan and the other directors became slightly jealous when Yvette came along, because they were 'heterosexual men in love with each other'. Alan says this isn't true, but rather that he wanted Tony to be happy and it was purely Yvette's lack of music-industry experience that made him doubt her subsequent appointment as CEO. Clearly he was hurt to find that Factory's initial investment into the seminar became as valueless as So What were to find theirs.

Elliot explained his falling out with Tony after In the City had taken up an office near the loft on Little Peter Street: 'Tony and Yvette were having some kind of a tax problem with In the City in that, whatever they were paying themselves to avoid tax, had to be paid in a dividend. And if you are paying in a dividend all the shareholders have to have dividends also. So he asked me for my fifty percent shareholding. Initially I had no problem with simply handing it over, but then I heard that Tony was about to do a moonlight flit from his office space, which was rented from my friend Chris Joyce. He'd been there at least a year and apparently owed a year's rent. Chris was a friend who had helped me out after I had left So What – he'd offered me an office in the same small block on Little Peter Street. Chris was really distressed because losing all that revenue would have been disastrous financially for him. I was really angry with Tony – Chris was his friend also – and said I'd only hand over my share in In the City if he paid his rent arrears to Chris. I was so pissed off that I also told him to pay back the £15,000 he owed me while he was at it. I think Tony then thought I had reneged on our deal, which I suppose I had, but it was me championing Chris. I thought they were being disrespectful to him. If I had my time again I don't know if I would do that, actually, given all that's happened since. They paid Chris because I forced them to. Whatever the tax liability was they were looking at was much bigger. So they moved out and paid me, and for about four years Tony and I didn't speak. Or he didn't speak to me. Early on I sent him a letter saying, "I would much rather have you as a friend than as a creditor because all your creditors get fucked." I discovered later he hadn't been shown the letter, which saddens me. I know that Yvette was very unhappy with what had happened and saw it as a bad deal. I don't think she's ever forgiven me. But I also think that In the City didn't cost them anything to set up. Andy and I put the money up, but they built themselves into the overheads and did okay out of it. And any company setting up has to do that for all the shareholders, not just half of them.'

Fortunately Tony and his friend let their grievances go approximately four years before Tony's death. 'I heard Tony had some sort of brain aneurysm,' says Elliot. 'It really freaked me out so I rang him to ask if he was okay. He said, "Yes, but I thought we aren't talking." I said, "No, we're not, but I just wanted to check you're all right." It was a couple of years before we talked again. A couple of years before he died we were reunited through the Happy Mondays. I'd been approached by their drummer on a number of occasions to manage them but had always run a mile. Then out of the blue I got a phone call from Tony in Australia ordering me to get involved because they were in a real mess and Shaun was about to go to prison. This was the first real contact I'd had with Tony since our fallout. I reluctantly agreed to see what I could do, and ended up managing them for about three years. Trouble is it was an enormously costly experience for me, emotionally as well as financially, so I don't know if this was Tony's gift to me or his revenge . . . But I suppose if I hadn't done it – which I only did out of respect for Tony – we would never have made up. It's really scary to me to think that he might have died without us settling our differences. As it was, we became really close again after his diagnosis and I spent a lot of time with him – especially in that last six months. We would just chill out together, watch DVDs and exchange books to read. That's something I really miss now, not being able to talk to him about life, art, everything.'

However, in September 1992 neither the schisms nor reconciliations that eventually followed had yet occurred, and Tony looked for all purposes like a man with the world at his fingertips. Riding high (in April – shot down in

May, the song 'That's Life' goes). Yep, it's that old Boethian wheel again. In November 1992, only two months after the launch of In the City, Factory Records went into liquidation.

Tosh Ryan was tipped off that the company was going down the night before, and stood outside the offices filming who and what he could from first thing in the morning until everyone had left the building. Tosh was a bit of an archivist then. He'd filmed Martin Hannett's funeral and I remember a) that it seemed a bit sick somehow, but b) I was annoyed that he didn't film me – obviously I wasn't one of the movers and shakers. I told him this later and he said that it wasn't him holding the camera in the church.

Tosh caught Tony on his way into the building that fateful November morning and Tony, with his usual bad acting, pretended there was nothing wrong, that it was just another day in the life of Factory.

Tosh described what happened when Rob Gretton turned up: 'Rob threatened me and said, "Don't you ever point a camera at me again or you'll have me and these guys to deal with," pointing to henchmen bouncers from the Hacienda. I just laughed and told him to fuck off.'

When asked at lunchtime who was winning Tony replied, 'The musicians are winning.' Incidentally this has always been misquoted – even by Tony – as, 'The music is winning.' I've seen the video.

Later Nathan McGough commented that the Happy Mondays had just cleared £300,000 of un-recouped royalties so were celebrating. Too right the musicians were winning.

At the end of that long, hard day Tony came clean about what had occurred. He was still smiling and found time to be philosophical when asked to comment. I have to take my hat off to him; he was great in a crisis. He said, 'It's what Chou En-Lai said when he was asked whether the French Revolution was a good or a bad thing and he said, "It's too soon to tell."'

An interesting conversation then occurred between Tony and Tosh:

TR: What a right-winger he was [Chou En-Lai].

TW: Well, he did his bit for keeping people fed.

TR: I've been there from the start on this one.

TW: Yeah, you're the one who told us . . .

TR: . . . How to do it.

TW: Yeah, you told me how to do it. You're the one who told us not to employ a musician who gives us doctors' notes a week in advance of rehearsals.

TR: There'll be a whole load of Durutti Column records in the building that won't shift.

TW: They shift all the time, that's the surprising thing about it. Plus this track called 'Otis' keeps being used very fruitfully for Vini on advertising projects – things like tampons in Australia.

Eric Longley, who came on board as managing director of Factory in 1991 when things were already in a financial mess, was quoted in John Robb's book as saying, 'The usual suspects are the Happy Mondays but in reality they had no more to do with it than New Order, Northside, Cath Carroll or any of the other artists.' He specifically mentioned: 'Hooky was deep into Revenge, which proved singularly uncommercial. Factory signed the Adventure Babies for more money than they were worth – as it happens the public agreed with me on that one. We also launched Cath Carroll with an expensive promotional campaign, spending nearly £250,000 on an album that sold less than 4,000 copies as I recollect.' Both the Mondays and New Order were supposed to be making an album but apparently partying respectively in Ibiza and Barbados, and appeared not to be getting much work done. Gone were the days when masterpieces were polished off in just two weeks.

Cath Carroll gave me the following comment:

'Oh dear, I feel like the Mrs O'Leary's Cow of Factory Records. This [Eric's statement] is the closest I've come to hearing actual sales figures but Eric's number sounds about right. I have never actually seen a Factory royalty statement or sales statement; we didn't get anything for the two Miaow singles either. £250,000 was the amount Factory set aside for the recording and promotion [before Eric came onboard], so it's not like we surprised them with a bill at the end.

'If the promo "shirt box" package given away at the Ronnie Scott's showcase for the album is any indication of the scale and intensity of spending, I am sure we rang the quarter-of-a-mill bell. Oddly enough, the recording in Brazil didn't constitute too big a part of the budget, but that is usually what people point to when they wish to illustrate foolish excess.

'Tony, bless him, had this sort of vaudeville impresario/masochist thing where he liked to make out his bands were somehow killing him or taking him for some sort of Bill Grundy-ish ride. It was part of the act. He did get his ankles chewed on a regular basis by Chris Smith the accountant and Rob Gretton – can't blame them, I suppose. Anyway, I shall always be grateful for Tony's chivalry and the label's generosity.'

When the news broke to me I was very sorry to see the end of an era. I reminded myself that this was what I'd wished for in those weeks and months after Tony sacked me. But I took no comfort from that. This stone-cold dish of revenge was no longer one I wanted to serve.

'It was a tragedy that Factory never carried on,' said Elliot Rashman, 'and again I think that what Tony did was – everyone else got the benefit of it. New Order walked away without any recourse to helping Tony at that point. They walked away and they let Factory go under. And they let Tony go under. And they let Alan go under. We should have rallied round Tony. And I think that was a tragedy. Roger Ames [London Records] got this, which has been under-utilised ever since. And it's now partly run, it's owned, it's licensed to Warners.'

Tony Michaelides and his company TM Promotions have been the regional radio promoters for Factory from the early eighties to this present day. Before Factory went down Michaelides had been given a number of cheques for £5,000 that had each bounced. He said at that point he was owed £15-18,000 and his business depended on the money coming in. He recalled a lunch in a Chinese restaurant next door to his office on Princess Street. Rob, Tony and Alan were all present. During the lunch Rob suddenly piped up with, 'Don't you think we should pay our mates?' (Though that, of course, was easier said than done.) Michaelides cashed in the money from some insurance policies to save his business and Rob eventually came true to his word, in a sense. When New Order went to London Records they had their own in-house promotions network, but Rob insisted, 'Tony Michaelides is doing my fucking promotion.' He got London to pay Michaelides £500 a month and Rob paid the same sum, so after fifteen months you could say he'd been paid back.

The same couldn't be said of other creditors who were also friends. Dave Greatbanks ran Real Recordings (who specialised in cassette copying), and at the time of the collapse Factory owed him £25,000. Like Michaelides he'd been fobbed off in the run-up to this. At £16,000 down he'd been asked to carry out more work for Factory and, upon requesting some funds before doing so, was summoned to a meeting in the Lass O'Gowrie, the pub opposite the new Factory offices. The minute he walked in they shouted out something along the lines of, 'Greatbanks is here, he can get the round in,' so Dave said it actually cost him to attend this meeting and, of course, no money was forthcoming. Nonetheless Greatbanks, like Michaelides, has no bitterness. Mainly because Tony had put so much work his way – in effect helped him to make the business in the first place, so he could hardly be too angry about it.

And obviously, there were many creditors who weren't friends.

Stephen Lea remembers that it was soon after the liquidation that Tony got in touch with him: 'Lawyers were parasites in the successful Factory days as far as he was concerned. He wouldn't ever phone me, the first time Tony ever phoned me was when he was in the shit with Factory. I hadn't heard from him for ten years. Factory had gone and there were threats of bankruptcy on the horizon and actions against directors, and I believe John Kennedy [music industry lawyer and executive] said to Tony, "You need to get a lawyer, stop it, this is getting stupid." At that stage he phoned me up and he said, "You always said I'd need a lawyer one day and you were right," and I went, "Well, you're only ten years too fucking late but never mind."

'That was the first thing I did for Tony – help him get out of the Factory organisation without it being too painful. It could have got very painful for him. It was round that time there were all these loose ends, the liquidator and his lawyer – Tony and Alan Erasmus in particular were under attack. They were protected so long as they didn't end up becoming insolvent at the end of it all, or having proceedings taken against them. It was very much, let's sort this out as best we can and get on with it.'

The week after Factory closed, Alan Erasmus had no choice but to sign on.

Clearly it was fortunate that Tony had kept his day job and also now had In the City each and every year. I went to the conference for two years running but on the second occasion things went awry. Tony had met up with me a month or two beforehand and, over lunch, shared a worry he had about things with Yvette. I was well and truly in the role of confidante. But then he was for me too. Things had yet again gone disastrously wrong in my own love life and Tony reassuringly told me that I was just mentally ill and it was nothing that Prozac (or five years in psychotherapy) wouldn't cure. I actually took his advice on the Prozac for two days until my head hurt and I felt peculiar. Although I don't believe I'm mentally ill (Tony seemed to think a lot of people around him were mentally ill), in a sense Tony was right, I did have a hormonal/chemical imbalance causing volatility and he understood something about it. It is in part thanks to him that I have been able to work it through and become psychologically healthy. But, as far as giving advice back to him went, it was so obvious he was totally in love with Yvette and my suggestion therefore made sense to him. I more or less said, 'Well, if she still wants you [in bed and in life], why not just go with it without worrying about anything else?' This pretty much followed the line of the enlightened contract between Martin Hannett and Susanne O'Hara that had been witnessed and signed and read: 'Get on / Get on with it / And get it on.'

Tony seemed visibly relieved at the suggestion.

However, during In the City I was walking down a corridor and Yvette and I crossed paths at a doorway, and I remember smiling quite warmly at her and thinking that, whatever rivalry there might be between us, it was an honest smile since I'd inadvertently fought her corner. Tony told me later that she might have seen my smile as a smirk or something. Or maybe she was just annoyed that I was attending the conference. Whatever, the next day I was with Scott Piering (a great guy and Radio One plugger who promoted 'Blue Monday', sadly also deceased) to attend one of In the City's gigs. Tony and Yvette came out as we were standing on the pavement to go in. Tony rushed over waving his finger accusingly at me. 'We've got a bone to pick with you,' he said. I noticed Yvette quickly shot round the corner, out of sight. 'Why did you snub Yvette when you saw her yesterday?' I was horrified since – if anyone hadn't let on to anyone – I'd a strong impression that it was Yvette who blanked me. I couldn't be bothered explaining. I just slapped Tony across his face, as if trying to knock some sense into him. He was totally stunned, he wasn't expecting that, why would he? It felt really great; I wished I'd done it a long time ago. So great, in fact, that I tried to do it again, but he was prepared for it this time and blocked it. 'I won't let you ruin this, me and Yvette have worked really hard for this,' he said threateningly, between gritted teeth. Needless to say, that was the last In the City I ever attended. And Tony and I didn't speak much for the next year or two. Nor did Tony ever speak to me again if he was with Yvette.

Yet again, although somewhat distanced from one another once more, by coincidence Tony and I were similarly enthused by a new computer revolution, and both separately working on our own contributions to it at the same time.

Tony was very fond of quoting Manchester as the birthplace of the computer. Alan Turing researched computer development at Manchester University and by 1951 had invented the first stored programme computer, although Tony always claimed that this was in fact the very first ever actual computer. He said that when another mathematical genius friend of Turing's designed a punch-card programme for the computer, it then played a version of 'God Saves the Queen' followed by 'I'm in the Mood'!

I went to visit a friend and colleague of Tony's and mine, Nick Clarke, currently lecturer in Digital Media Design for Manchester University. We took a short walk to Sackville Park directly opposite the UMIST building, where a statue of Turing sits on a bench, holding an apple (which he poisoned with cyanide and died after taking a bite out of). Some people believe that Apple computers were paying homage to this when they designed their logo of an apple with a bite taken out of it. Others believe this was just to enhance their early catchphrase, 'Take a byte out of an Apple.' Either way, Turing is regarded as one of the founding fathers of the Apple computer.

Odd then that Tony generally disapproved of Apple computers as compared with PCs. In 1993 I bought my first Apple Macintosh – a portable Powerbook (which now resembles something out of a museum). Tony poo-pooed it and said that Apples were for geeks and I should have got a PC. It was like the difference between City and United to him. Nick noted the same quirk in Tony: 'He enjoyed having a dig at Apple as I was a Mac person. He couldn't stand the whole concept. I tried to explain how the Mac was the first proper system to try and attempt to work with a human being, rather than against, but he didn't take that argument. He dug himself in so deep that he didn't want to move out. He'd say, "I'm still not moving, you still can't tell me that OS X is better than Windows XP."'

Funny, though, that Tony had the last word in this battle.

I had bought the Apple computer in an attempt to re-invent a career for myself after losing my job at Hollywood Records. It was a final parting of the ways for me from the music business. I suppose I'd done pretty well surviving for as long as I had. I packed up everything in London, came back to my mum's house (my father had died in 1990) and went to California for four months to try and kick-start a CD-ROM called *The Women's Disc*. I misjudged the CD-ROM format, believing it had a solid place in future technology. Thus, just as I was busily inputting data for a computer programme concerned with astrological compatibility in relationships to contribute toward this project, Tony had a meeting with Nick Clarke because their mutual friend Keith Jobling thought Tony was sure to be interested in the CD-ROM phenomenon. Nick reminded me of that time: 'For many people the CD-ROM was the first popular mass device. At the time the amount of data you could fit on a floppy disc was only about 1.8 megabytes at the most and a CD-ROM could hold 600 times that. It was pre-internet but it was the first time in our lives, beyond say going into a library, that we had the ability to have a lot of information next to us on a personal computer. Philosophically it was fascinating because of the access to data that we'd never dreamt possible.'

Both Nick and Tony were somewhat nervous of meeting one another – Tony because, as Nick said, 'He'd never met a computer geek before' (Nick was then senior lecturer in Computing and Design at Salford University), and Nick because 'I was still fighting with a system that says that computers will never replace pencils. I know the pencil will always exist but the pixel is mightier than the pencil these days.' Nick wasn't sure of the best way to explain to Tony where the future lay, but he brilliantly showed him a children's story called *Grandma and Me*. This was a simple interactive CD-ROM that allowed you to click on the characters on the screen, plus there was music and sound. Nick recalled: 'Tony absolutely adored it. He hadn't realised that you could interact with something. If you think about it everything is pushed towards you, but this actually allowed you to engage with it. The relationship between the user and the computer became different and philosophically he understood that.'

Tony being Tony, this meeting was a catalyst for brainstorming something innovative. Nick continued: 'As Tony was of a mind to – and I saw this as a regular pattern that emerged over the years – he would get like-minded people together and talk, so we'd often have meetings. He held court. Often I would be subjected to having to justify things. These meetings went on for eighteen months; it was like Tony's computer club really. Factory Too was starting up,

I think he was revitalised, the darkness had gone and he could see the light, as it were. The people that stuck together out of this particular project, or idea, about interactive media, were Keith Jobling, Graham Newman, John Machlin and myself.'

As a record label Factory Too probably failed yet, to my mind, the most exciting product on Factory Too came out of Tony's 'computer club'. This was possibly a result of the teamwork involved – as with the original Factory, Tony needed other talented people around him and was not suited to running a company as a director without that.

The intrepid foursome (Machlin dropped out) were driving back from a tour of Tony's beloved Jesus College at Cambridge one day, as Nick recounted: 'The conversation rolled on and on through the night as Tony drove, still rolling joints and changing gear – I don't know how you do that – and Keith said, "Why don't we just get something together and do something instead of talking about it?" Then Tony said, "We've got to give it a name." One thing that everybody shared was football and Tony said, "Well, why don't we call it the Boot Room?" I liked that idea 'cause you boot up a disc, don't you, you boot up a computer? The other definition of the name is that it is where all tactical decisions are made about the football game.'

So the Boot Room was born and the team set up a computer in the office on Little Peter Street. Tony managed to persuade London Records to fund a Durutti Column CD-ROM version of *Sex and Death* which, in its own way, was revolutionary for the time. Essentially it would allow data and music to exist on the same disc, with the same high-quality audio as you'd expect from any CD player. Tony's plan was to discontinue the physical CD of *Sex and Death* and make only the CD-ROM-plus product available.

To turn this album into a narrative wasn't as simple as it may sound. As Nick remembered, 'Nobody had ever done that before and the technology hadn't been invented, in a sense, to do it. We're talking about an average processor speed here of a computer of being many, many, many more times less than what we've got today. I mean very slow, watches are faster these days than computers in those days. And the resolution, the size of the screen was also very restricted.'

Eventually the team built a twelve-sided object and, using Post-it notes, began to stick related information together. Naturally there were cat-and-dog fights about what should be going in and what should be taken out. But Nick perceptively remarked, 'Tony could calibrate to the very centre of what was good and to the very edge of what was good as well. That was a unique gift. He could deal with the whole thing – outside intellectuals, people on the periphery, people right in the centre – some people can't calibrate but he could. We did a full history of Buenaventura Durruti written partly by Tony and narrated by Jimmy Hibbert [ex of the Albertos]. Marcus Greil contributed, he wrote a special piece.' Other specialities on the disc included some of Vini's answer-phone messages that he'd kept – hundreds of hours of messages. When clicking on the screen a generator randomly selected one of the eight recordings that were chosen. You might have got Tony saying, 'Hi Vini, I'm trying to get hold of that Morrissey cunt. Cunt. Do you know where the fuck he is?' or, 'Hi Vini, Tony here. Just got out of a meeting in London. We have a new record company. Keep working darling.'

Nowadays this CD-ROM is something of a cult object. Tony's 'revenge' or last word on the PC and Mac battle was that, although both versions of the Durutti Column disc were made, now only the PC format works. The Mac version doesn't since Nick hadn't anticipated Apple's move to a UNIX operating system.

While Tony was busy with all this, I was in California trying to kick-start *The Women's Disc*. I was optimistic, falsely as it turned out. I spent a lot of time and energy getting to know a software team, developing a presentation pack, etc. I think it was the first time I actually saw Tony since the debacle in which I'd slapped him, but he happened to be in the area (near San Francisco) and since he was interested in my project he said he'd call in. I got to the studio some minutes after Tony and he was already engrossed with the guys, picking their brains and getting the same information in ten minutes that had taken me about two months to set up! When I walked in he was so engrossed that he barely glanced up at me, just murmured, 'Hi kid,' in a dismissive way. I nearly wanted to smack him again. It wasn't because he had the resources I lacked to build a CD-ROM (although that irked slightly); it was his apparent dismissal of me when in fact I'd arranged for him to meet these guys knowing they could be helpful to him.

Around this time (April 1994) Tony planned to make a CD-ROM of the Hacienda but neither this, nor my *Women's Disc*, was ever made. Technology was, and indeed still is, changing fast. That said, Tony presented the first TV show about computers and software, *The Program*, in 1995. Keith Jobling thought of the name. Some of its archive (which had been given away as a free disc with *Personal Computer World*) can be viewed on YouTube. Nick Clarke, who appeared on the programme, pointed out: 'Fifteen years ago, a long time, even then computers were still the stuff of geekdom, but Tony was trying to bring it out of the closet. He was trying to evangelise people about technology through the medium of TV.'

My own computer project having failed to lift off, I came back from California with my tail between my legs. I hadn't wanted to leave but I was completely broke. The only money I'd made there was as a Feng Shui consultant (having attended an intensive course). I owned nothing – no car, house, flat, and only my mum to fall back on. I was forty-two. After a short bout of depression I picked myself up and actually made a living for two years – as a Feng Shui consultant.

Things weren't exactly booming for Tony either. His later incarnations of Factory Records – Factory Too, F4 – weren't successful for all of his enthusiasm. He particularly raved about a group called Raw-T, yet his claims that they were the best band in the world didn't make it so.

Tony and I remained somewhat estranged, yet friendly, for the next few years. I kept in touch with his father and Tony Connolly but in 1996 Sydney had a severe stroke. When he became well enough to leave hospital Connolly had a bit of a fight on his hands to take Sydney back home with him. Sydney's sister and Wilson were understandably concerned that Connolly might not be up to taking on full-time care, since Connolly wasn't exactly well himself and drank to great excess fairly frequently. A meeting was held at which Sydney, who was partly paralysed and unable to speak, pointed at Connolly when asked where he wanted to go and mouthed the word 'Tony'. Certainly Sydney had a better quality of life with him than he would have had in a home. A year later, in April 1997, Sydney died. I went to the funeral with my mum. Tony was there, as was Rob Gretton. After the Catholic mass (which seemed to me to have absolutely nothing to do with Sydney) the cortege had quite a long drive from the church in Eccles to the graveyard in Hollins Green near Warrington. This was the same cemetery where Tony's mum had been buried with Ted, her first true love. The lines Doris had written on Ted's tomb were: *Eheu fugaces labuntur anni. Hinc illae lacrimae.* The words are a poignant reminder of love and loss, something along the lines of: 'Alas our fleeting years have passed. Hence these tears.'

My mum and I were at the back of the cortege following the posh black cars driven by the Factory directors. We were in a battered Ford Fiesta. Connolly told me that Wilson rolled and smoked a joint while driving his car behind his father's coffin. I was a bit shocked since it seemed like sacrilege (and he also had the children in the car with him). But perhaps not. Tony insisted on being himself no matter what the circumstance.I had no idea that day that my mum was ill. She died four months later. I had a very difficult time but Tony was quite supportive. Two years later I had sold her house in Gatley and found something cheaper. My sister helped me out so I could get a two-up two-down that wasn't a grotty flat in Stockport. A week before moving, though, I was having serious last-minute doubts. Tony said, 'Let's go up there so I can see it.' We drove together and when he saw the house from the outside he said it was great and that I mustn't have any worries about it. With his knowledge of routes he told me a quick way into Manchester. It is sufficiently far out that I don't go in very often but that isn't such a bad thing really. He reassured me.

In 2004 Tony Connolly died and joined Sydney out at Hollins Green. Tony, as ever, was there when he was needed. I'd always thought Connolly had money. Two months before he died we were heading to a pub when he suddenly said, 'Stop here,' pointing to a posh-looking Italian restaurant. We walked in and he immediately pronounced, 'A bottle of champagne please.' The waitress said, 'But you haven't even looked at how much it is.' He said he didn't care. Then he said he was going to make me cry. There was a Steinway piano and he got up to go and play it. I thought, 'My God, he's going to really embarrass us.' People were delicately dining. And then he played the most exquisite piece, I honestly did cry. The diners just thought he was supposed to be there. I never even knew he could play. And then again, that January of 2004, after a pub lunch, Connolly and I went to see Peter Saville's exhibition at Urbis. Connolly was too ill to walk and had no interest in the exhibition, but I was taking a skirt back to Hobbs and he managed to stagger there with me. He sat on the couch and ended up buying me loads of clothes. When I protested that he mustn't spend so much he got really annoyed. I didn't see how he could afford it. He'd sold the house he had when Sydney died and given half the proceeds to Tony. It was only about £20,000 each. I knew that must have gone so was concerned he only had his sickness benefits. But if I said anything he always said, 'I've got money, don't you worry about it.' He had been a jewel thief in his day and an active member of the underworld, so I thought he was up to something, but when he died there wasn't enough to pay for a funeral. What a character he was!

Tony (Wilson) and I met at Connolly's flat. We found a will leaving everything to Tony. When we later found out the real state of affairs, Tony gallantly paid for most of the funeral costs. I put forward what I could. I paid for the carving on the tombstone of Sydney and Connolly. Connolly had written 'We'll meet again' under Sydney's name. He wanted the words 'I told you so' to go under his own, a comic aside that even the most skeptical couldn't argue with, since he literally had.

Incidentally, the funeral didn't go off without a hitch. Tony was absent and incommunicado even while I was trying to sort everything out. I decided to switch funeral directors at the last minute to save £1,000. Then I had to sign documents because I couldn't find the deeds to the grave. I wasn't strictly family and it was all going to get very complicated so, for the sake of simplicity, I said I was Connolly's sister. I felt like I was anyway, and besides he didn't have any family and his partner was my father-in-law. The next thing it all blew up and the funeral looked like being off and Tony told me what a bloody idiot I was. He was really shitty to me; he was absolutely furious. He had to run round at the last minute and, using his influence and a cheque, ensured it all went ahead.

The funeral went well in the end. Tony came with Izzy and Oliver, who both looked lovely. Oliver behaved like a gentleman, walking by my side behind the coffin as Izzy walked behind with her dad.

Tony didn't want anything from Tony Connolly's flat except the photos in two chocolate boxes and a piece of the Hacienda floor that he'd given to Connolly as an ashtray. One night in July 2007, when Tony knew he was beaten for sure, he suggested looking through these boxes. Sydney had lovingly cut out every newspaper clip of Tony. They seemed to start around 1976; there was one in February of that year that said he was the North-West's most eligible bachelor and that he received 200 fan letters a week. Three months after that he was my boyfriend and I thought what an idiot I had been – our lives together I threw away and now he's dying and all youth gone from us.

42 There Is No
Future in Nostalgia

In 2000 the filming of *24 Hour Party People* began, prior to its general release in 2002. As said, the first I knew of it was when Tony came round with the script and I discovered my major role in it was having sex with five men, one after another in sequence. With hindsight, seeing how comedic the film was, maybe I should have let it go. The idea was to convey the destructiveness of the 'revenge fucking'. But I was a bit peeved that no one had spoken to me and felt rather betrayed by Tony's response to my objection ('Well, we'll just have to have you having sex with someone you did have sex with then'). In a sense that was worse! But I couldn't really object if it was true. It just annoyed me that I had to be portrayed as a sexual part of the movie. I mean, why the hell did I have to have sex with anybody? Nick Clarke also thought that the film took a misogynistic view of my role in Tony's life.

As a result of that evening with Tony I got to meet Frank Cottrell Boyce, the writer of the screenplay, and he was a really lovely person who listened to my story and adapted the plot somewhat. But the film still had me and Howard Devoto having sex in a toilet at the Russell Club, which I knew had come from Tony – this is how he saw it in his imagination after I'd told him about the conversation I'd had with Howard when he was on his way to the gents. I took umbrage and made threatening noises to Michael Winterbottom and producer Andrew Eaton, which I partly regret because I think Winterbottom is a cool director and I've got the utmost respect for his filmmaking. But I didn't know it then – he could have been anyone.

People's opinions about the movie differ, however. Some people who knew Tony and Factory didn't like *24 Hour Party People*. For instance, Alan Wise said to me about it: 'It started off as being a serious thing and then it became a comedy and Tony – who was the main character – had a lot more gravitas as you know. He wasn't such a comical character, he was much more serious and the people around him treated him much more seriously because he was the one with education and knowledge and they didn't treat him comically, they treated him with awe. That's not how it was portrayed. The movies will want to take not the reality – which is of no interest to anyone – but the myth. Look at the inaccuracy of it – no one is interested in what really happened to you. This happened with Nico. The last person I could imagine sucking someone off in a lift is Nico [as is portrayed in Oliver Stone's film *The Doors*] – no one is really interested in Nico, she is dead, but they are interested in that story and these things that they imagine people do which they don't.'

I found out later from Tony (alias Eric) McGahan that Alan had invited him to see the premiere of *24 Hour Party People*. (McGahan once played with the Fall and worked for years with John Cooper Clarke.) They went along and after watching a few minutes of it McGahan said to Alan that he couldn't believe how stylishly made it was. He was waiting for when the location would move on to Manchester, but it turned out that Alan had steered him in to see a different movie instead. It was *Mulholland Drive*.

Miguel Esteves Cardoso also didn't care for Tony's portrayal in *24 Hour Party People*. He said, 'Coogan wasn't like Tony at all, it wasn't his personality. Tony believed in what he did. He wasn't a chancer. He was a hopeful person. Coogan was vain. Tony is a tremendously serious, honest and artistic person. He makes jokes and was much joked about, but he's a real Renaissance man, absolutely caught up in art and subversion. His – and thus Factory's – main inspiration was always the May 1968 Situationist uprisings, added to a very Manchester sense of fuck-the-expense beauty and style.

'There's no hypocrisy; no Janus-faced bullshit; no real ambiguity at all. He wouldn't play well as comedy, in my opinion, except for being excessively earnest. Though playful and conscious of inherent contradictions – Factory Records was more luxurious than Sinatra's Reprise label, the one it resembled most – it was Tony's mini-tragedy to be working in a culture, Manchester's, which is based on deprecation, suspicion and general piss-taking.

'The funny thing is, of course, for those lucky enough to know the Mancunian spirit, is that this is their deepest expression of affection and respect.

'I wonder whether the rest of the world – the audience for this film – appreciates this.'

'When I first saw the film I was upset,' said Nick Clarke. 'I had no sense of humour about it at all. I was fuming when I came out. I rang up Keith and he told me not to take it seriously. I was personally angry because of the fictional portrayal in a sense. Ian turns up, somehow he's managed to get a bus all the way from Macclesfield to Charlesworth. He knocks on the door, you've got a joint in your hand, "Is Tony in?" "No, do you want to come in for a cup of tea?" "No, I've got to get off." First of all I know for a fact that you and Tony looked after him.'

Paul Morley writes in his book *Piece by Piece*: 'Anthony H. Wilson leaves a message on my answer machine. He's been fretting at the idea that the film will signify the end of his journey. He's keen to explain that, as always, he's actually only just beginning. "There's the things I'm doing now that just make the movie irrelevant to me . . . big development projects in Liverpool, lots of things in Manchester to do with moving the city on . . . I just want to get it over that just because they make a movie about your life, it doesn't mean that it's all over. Life does go on. Okay, God bless, bye love."'

Certainly the movie changed Tony's life, but one wonders what Tony actually thought of the film. Nick Clarke observed: 'There was a kind of dichotomy going on in Tony's mind at the time – you know, is this the best thing or is this the worst thing?'

Overall I thought it was a great movie – funny and very enjoyable. To have someone of the calibre of Steve Coogan play Tony was a huge honour and, however unfunny things might have seemed at the time, it was in line with Tony's optimistic outlook to look back on it all as comedy. I felt that whereas *24 Hour Party People* was, as Tony once observed, 'a collection of lies that somehow manages to tell the truth', the later film *Control* was, in my opinion, a collection of truths that somehow managed to tell a lie.

That said, *Control*, directed by Anton Corbijn, was beautifully shot. Interestingly the idea to make a film about the life of Ian Curtis originally came from a young writer named Michael Stock, who first approached Annik Honoré after obtaining her email address from Michel Duval (who ran Factory Benelux, a European branch of Factory). She had remained silent about her relationship with Ian for over twenty years, but after speaking with Michael was somehow convinced to disclose the contents of her private letters from Ian.

As Annik says, 'It was upon his insistence and the enthusiasm he showed that I spent hours in the attic looking for those letters that I had hid somewhere . . .' When I visited her in Brussels much later to interview her for the book *Torn Apart*, I was amazed when she handed them to me without my even asking, particularly as I thought she had decided to renew her silence (in the absence of a movie at that stage). There was something very sacred about the letters, which proved vital in understanding that Ian's relationship with her was no mere affair on the side.

Michael Stock had also contacted film producer Amy Hobby, who then took up an option on the book *Touching from a Distance* by Debbie Curtis. However, when the option came up for a yearly renewal Amy was in the process of dissolving her partnership and requested that it be transferred to a new company name. She said she 'got a sort of wall of anger, then silence that I never really understood'. Subsequently Amy, along with Neal Weisman, optioned *Torn Apart* for their film, and for a while it was a two-horse race alongside Anton's project. Tony, who was an executive on the *Control* option, told me that his job was to 'fuck off the rogue film'. I speculated that his might be the rogue film and that the £12,000 advance he told me he was getting might have something to do with his loyalties!

He said rather that it was because Amy hadn't sent Debbie her option money – a seemingly spurious reason. In any case, that film wasn't to be and *Control* was. I found it hard to watch – the dramatisation of a personal tragedy with style triumphing over truth. Some of the dialogue and the characters were all wrong to me – Tony's especially. He wasn't a wally; he was a sexy guy. Still, I know the film was well made and, if I hadn't lived it for myself, I might have enjoyed watching it. But the very idea of enjoying this particular tragedy is anathema to me, of course. It's funny looking back that Tony and I were again on rival teams over this. And what the hell did it matter that he 'won'? He lost his life the year the film was released.

As mentioned, the *24 Hour Party People* filmmakers had the most amazing replica of the Hacienda built in a huge warehouse in Ardwick. I felt a bit emotional when I visited it; the detail of the set was so immaculate it really was like being back at the club again. Tony wept when he saw it. At the end of filming a big party was held there. Nick Clarke told me: 'Tony had got the tickets for the fantastic recreation of the Hacienda. I met him at a Krowbar on Oxford Road and he duly turned up very agitated – you don't normally see Tony agitated but he was. The bar was full of students and quite busy and he said, "Let's get out of here." So we got in the Jag and went down to Atlas. This was the first and last time I saw him take a drink. He still seemed very, very agitated. I asked him what was wrong and he mentioned some other personal things that were going on. Then he said, "What do you think is the coolest thing to do tonight?" I said, "Well, I guess this is one of those questions Tony that's gonna be right or wrong. You've already got the answer haven't you?" "What do you think the coolest thing is to do?" he repeated. I thought I'd play his bluff so I said, "Not to go to the party." He went, "Exactly. Let's not go." I looked at him in slight disbelief for a couple of seconds and I went, "Okay," and we never went. You know what? I felt quite relieved and I know he did as well. The relief I felt was because I wasn't letting him down.'

In view of the above I wonder why Hooky said of that night: 'Paul Mason was there, everybody was there. That evening I walked up to Barney and said, "Fucking hell, all that's missing is Rob Gretton."' Actually no, the person who breathed life into the whole thing had chosen to be absent. I wasn't there either, not that New Order or anyone else were likely to notice or care about that. 'Blow blow thou winter wind, thou art not so unkind as man's ingratitude.' I'm not referring to Hooky, but Shakespeare could have written that about musicians – almost every one I've ever known anyway! They never truly appreciate the talent of those who helped them, instead choosing to believe in their own. I feel sure that no amount of fame and money would have made Ian Curtis forget, and, if it had, he would have walked away from it. I don't think Ian cared about fame and money in any case, and therefore it's ironic that he has become an iconic star, but I believe it could only have happened in his absence.

Tony's life changed for the better after the release of *24 Hour Party People*. His profile and job prospects improved. Even *Granada Reports* appeared to bring a peace offering by reinstating him (a short-lived event since Tony accidentally used his habitual F word on live teatime TV).

Anecdotes were born from the movie. Nick Clarke reminded me of one he loved, when Steve Coogan was asked what the nicest thing Tony ever said to him was: 'Steve thought for a minute and said, "It's quite easy this. I was doing that scene where a guy from London Records [played by Keith Allen] comes up and he's all flash, and Michael Winterbottom made us both improvise." Coogan made this statement up, off the cuff, about why it was good to go to London. Done in a single take. So the nicest compliment was Tony said to Steve, "You know that scene when you were with Keith Allen? When people asked me that question I'd never been able to answer it but I do now, I use your answer." This perfectly describes a part of Tony, [and] if you knew him personally you would thoroughly understand why that is so funny and why it was such a lovely compliment. Underneath there was a massive amount of warmness and generosity ticking over in Tony.'

What actually happened in the film was that, while making the 'deal' with Roger Ames, having been offered £5 million for the company, Tony explains that he must be labouring under the misapprehension that Factory have contracts with their bands. ('Artists own all their own work, Factory owns nothing. The bands have the freedom to fuck off.') When Ames/Allen realises he no longer has to deal with Tony/Coogan, Coogan says that his epitaph will be that he never literally or metaphorically sold out. That he protected himself from ever having the dilemma of having to sell out by having nothing to sell out. So that must have been the answer Tony used.

When the film had been about to come out Andrew Eaton suggested that Tony write a book of the film. Tony embraced the idea because, as he said in the foreword, 'a novelisation is the lowest form of art which is right up my street'.

Although the rumour was that he wrote his version of the story to pay his VAT bill, Bruce told me: 'He got half his advance to start him off. It got near Christmas and he wanted to buy his presents and he needed money, so he got on to them and asked for the rest of the advance. They said, "Well have you got the manuscript?" He said, "Oh no," so he had to finish it off really fast. The story goes that he found some really old speed and copped that down his neck and rushed it out. It reads like James Ellroy.'

Speaking to Mick Middles in 1996, in the offices of Factory Too, Tony stated: 'It's all time, isn't it? Writing . . . writing a book. Time to research and concentrate. That's one thing I haven't got and I will never have . . . excuse me [phone rings].'

I was disappointed that Tony's first book was a novelisation and, as a lot of people do with books, flicked through it, regretting that Tony hadn't written something original. Why do we judge a book when we haven't even read it? No wonder the worst insult Beckett could think of in *Waiting for Godot* was 'Critic'! When I actually properly read Tony's book I thought it was bloody fantastic and very entertaining. In fact it contains a lot of Tony's original truths, whilst being written in the comedic vein of the film.

With the written word, as in life, Tony always made an impact. He could have been a great writer, no one will now know. Even his diary jottings in this book indicate as much. He had great wit, and his wit had depth. He was always at once thought-provoking and entertaining.

His writing first surfaced in the 1977 listings magazine, *New Manchester Review*, in which he penned a two-page article about Debbie Harry. The article was well received in Manchester and perhaps slightly subversive. It was an article laced with enthusiasm, fun and – typical of Tony this – sex.

'Some women make you melt,' he wrote at the start of the article, which concluded with the line, '. . . look at me. A pool of water.'

A top local television presenter writing about sex! Positively subversive. It's just a pity that Tony never got to write that book about sex he'd planned as his next missive.

Although Tony never found the time to write at length, those short sharp samples would shine through. In the sleeve notes for Vini Reilly's non-Durutti Column (and non-Factory) album, *The Sporadic Recordings*, Tony wrote about his love affair with the guitar, the only instrument I ever heard him play. 'I don't need a guitar anymore. I have Vini. I'm pleased about that, because I love guitars,' he concluded. (Perhaps this reveals the real reason Tony bought Vini the expensive Stratocaster – in a sense he was buying it for himself, living guitar-vicariously through Vini.)

It's possible that, had Tony lived to a greater age, and had he slowed to a more sedate pace, his writing might have seeped more and more into his work.

Before he died, Tony was writing columns in the newspapers and he was re-inventing himself as a broadcaster on the radio.

In 2006, he wrote a weekly column in the short-lived quality newspaper, *North West Enquirer*. To the surprise of many, it was a general sports column and he simply revelled in it. Whether writing about golf, football or rugby, it was fired by unbridled enthusiasm and depth of knowledge. Tony would have made an excellent sports writer. He once stated how much he admired the football reports of his old Granada colleague, Bob Greaves.

Tony loved sport. Even when he was so poorly he could barely walk, I took him down to the BBC to appear on a radio programme about football or something. Keith Jobling recalled: 'I had a ritual where I would go round to Tony's house on Superbowl nights and watch the Superbowl till it finished, which was like 4:00am. We would do other stuff in a similar kind of weird way, where there would be a boxing match on and we would meet somewhere and just go and watch it. Tony was absolutely besotted with sport. He just loved the stories of sport. He loved it all.'

Incidentally, on the subject of sport, it is well known that Tony revelled in being a 'red' and was a fanatical supporter the season when United won the 'treble' (League, Cup and European Cup).

In the mid-1970s, whilst it is true to say that Liverpool and Leeds have always been 'rivals' of United's, Manchester City were the traditional and local rivals – especially after City had effectively relegated United towards the end of the 1973-74 season by beating United 1-0 at Old Trafford. My brother, Roger – a massive City fan – had somehow managed to convince Tony to use a City 'Young Supporters' club pen on *Granada Reports*, which he had agreed to do, I suspect, on the basis of impressing the young sibling of his new love. However, whilst probably only him and Roger knew he was using the City pen on air, he still made a point of snapping the pen in two pieces at the end of the programme as if to illustrate his hatred of City!

In 2007, Tony's writing surfaced yet again. This time it was in the form of a lengthy guest chapter in *Mersey: The River that Changed the World*. This coffee table affair, published by Bluecoat Press, celebrated the achievements associated with the river that defines the North-West region.

Tony wrote: 'If I care to think about it, and for this book I care deeply, it should be no surprise that every phase of my life has been touched, sprinkled religiously perhaps, by the waters of the River Mersey . . . as a Lancashire lad, it is this river which rises in the black-brown moors to the east and kisses the Irish sea in the west that flows through my homeland.'

Tony could have gone a long way with the pen (as long as it wasn't from Man City). I miss the words he will now never write and the thought-provoking words he will now never say.

For Christmas (2004 I think it was), Yvette gave Tony the Weimaraner dog Tony christened William (his heroes' name – Shakespeare and Yeats to name but two). William was just like the dog that appears on New Order's original 'Blue Monday' video. The dog appears in various artistic poses on chairs and things (which later collapse) – actually William and that dog were works of art just by themselves. Thereafter Tony's visits were always accompanied by a loud woofing and pounding coming from the back of the car, followed by the inevitable walk come rain, hail or shine. The first evening I ever met William I seriously doubted the wisdom of Tony caring for a dog in an apartment (however large) with no garden, and with his extremely busy life travelling hither and thither and hence constant visits to the kennels. He later confided that he had been harbouring doubts himself before that particular night, although Tony subsequently always said how brilliant it was of Yvette to buy him this dog. It was a cold winter's night and we walked in the drizzling sleet with the dog yanking our arms off. I took the lead because Tony seemed to be nursing yet another cold and needed to use his handkerchief. But it rapidly transpired to be the dog, not me, who was in control; I had to run to keep up with him. We hastened to my local pub, where there was a welcoming fire, and thankfully the dog was tolerated and didn't go berserk. Somehow in this moment all seemed well again and the dog was allowed, even welcomed, and thereafter William always seemed to be a joy and to make Tony laugh.

Actually that's not entirely true. William was very wild and Tony didn't have him under any kind of control. In May 2006, following Tony's radio show *Sunday Roast*, at which I had been a guest, we went off with William to a nearby Café Rouge in Salford Quays. Tony tied the dog to a railing and as we perused the menu he subsequently took a phone call. The next thing I knew someone was shouting our way. 'Is this your dog?'

'Yes,' I meekly replied, as Tony was too busy to answer.

'It has just bitten my wife on the arm,' the man shouted, at which Tony abruptly ended his phone call and began shouting back almost as fiercely. I was quite taken aback. I knew that William was wild, but jumping up and biting a passerby was totally unexpected and rather in a different league. The couple were visiting Americans. 'My wife's arm is bleeding!' the man continued. I didn't blame him for being angry. I thought this was going to cost Tony a fortune. But Tony seemed to be shouting as if it was the woman's fault – that she must have put her arm out, because William wouldn't just jump up willy nilly. The man vehemently disagreed and I had to sympathise because William had been going crazy tied to the railing, jumping up and down like a mad thing. Tony offered to drive the couple to the nearest hospital, an offer that was declined, and much to my amazement they left us – in peace were it not for the fact that we had William with us. We had to move him somewhere safer out of the way of passersby.

Keith Jobling told me: 'That fucking stupid dog was bonkers. I'm standing there and the dog is chewing my coat – I said to Tony, "This coat cost £150," and Tony said, "It's only a coat."' He loved William, you see.

Paul Morley, with his usual perceptiveness, aptly described the dynamic between a man and his dog in his book *Joy Division: Piece by Piece*, when Tony and William visit the set of *Control*: 'His dog runs amok, causing chaos, shitting all over the wires, bumping into scenery. Wilson keeps grinning at everyone as if the trouble the dog is causing is absolutely nothing to do with him.'

The support Tony showed when he put me on his *Sunday Roast* radio show to promote the publication of *Torn Apart* in 2006 was terrific. By coincidence it was thirty years to the day we'd met and twenty-nine since the day we married. It was out of character for Tony to *speak* to me in public, let alone mention our anniversary, which he did on air. Only eighteen months previously he'd actually blanked me in Urbis when he walked past me with Yvette – as if he wasn't speaking to me. I felt as if I'd been punched in the stomach. We'd shared a friendly dinner only a week or so before that. I assumed he was banking on the fact that Yvette wouldn't be listening to his radio show. Or perhaps she was away. Now the interview can be heard on YouTube.

Tony and I had begun meeting regularly around the time I'd commenced interviews with him in 2005 for *Torn Apart*. It was funny looking back at a very early interview I did with him. In fact it was a typical example of how our rows might develop. I had a dodgy tape recorder and didn't get off to the best start. He was very judgemental about that. He started telling me a story from the *24 Hour Party People* film, which I hardly needed to hear (and wasn't based on truth in any case), so I rudely interrupted and said, 'Can *I* ask the questions?' He replied, 'No, you can't.' I must admit I got irritated. I think the story about Ian calling him a cunt was his next bit of old news. Leading with my chin, I told him that Pete Shelley and Buzzcocks watched the film in their tour bus and thought the portrayal of Ian as stroppy and aggressive was out of character and so did I. Tony said, 'Then you are completely and utterly fucking wrong,' but admitted he'd only witnessed Ian's aggression this once. It finished up with him saying that if I just wanted to give opinions I shouldn't be doing interviews and that I was 'absolutely shite at this'. To compound things, at that point my dodgy tape player stopped working. Tony's comment was, 'Get yourself a fucking tape machine.'

To be fair, this was only the second interview I'd ever carried out (Pete Shelley being the first). And it is a bit odd to be interviewing your husband, ex or not, and have him talk to you as if you were someone who wasn't there and/or hadn't seen the film. I resented it. I mean, I was actually there. And my memory, bad though it is, is just as intact as his was.

Fortunately subsequent interviews were rather more productive. The talks I had with Tony around the book about Ian were inspired and inspiring. Actually Tony was a dream to interview, apart from his insistence on repeating several of the same stories, as if to emphasise the fact of their truth (therefore making me all the more suspicious).

But if we became reacquainted in the last five years of his life, it was in the last five months that we truly shared something special. In every sense of the word we became companions again. He might not have valued our friendship that much before this but I know it meant a lot to him at the last. I'd also learned from previous experience the privilege and sacredness of being present with someone who is dying, and this time I found it easier to accept that there was nothing I could do except just be present.

Just before Christmas 2006 Tony found out he was seriously ill – having thought he'd got a type of flu that wouldn't go away for about two months.

Early one Sunday evening in late November 2006, I was getting changed as Tony had arranged to pick me up to go out for dinner (invariably Pizza Express, where he always had the exact same pizza). The phone rang. 'I've still got this flu virus thing, it's still not gone away. I'm feeling a bit unwell with it,' said Tony.

I gaily replied, 'Let's leave it then, get yourself well,' but privately thought it a weak excuse. I didn't offer to go up to the loft. He'd always been a bit funny about me going up there, as if it might betray Yvette in some way. (They were living separately by this point, though still working together.) About an hour later the phone rang again. 'How about if we met somewhere halfway? Then I can walk William as well.'

'Are you sure you're up to it Tony?' I asked.

'Yes, I'm fine.'

Had he read my mind? Did he know I was thinking he was making a crap excuse because he couldn't be bothered?

We met at TGI Friday's, an odd choice of his. I'd never been there in my life but it was a suitable halfway point between us. On my arrival he was already sitting at the bar, drinking a soft drink. I ordered red wine. We talked, I thought maybe he wasn't quite himself but the virus thing didn't ring true somehow. He seemed guilty that he'd tried to cancel me so late and ordered some food and more wine (for him as well), although I'd had my tea by then and was only being greedy joining in on that. Afterwards we wandered in Sainsbury's car park with the dog, trying to locate the path through to the park. When we got down there the place was eerily knee-deep in mist and the air choked with dampness and, no doubt, fumes from passing overhead vehicles lighting their way through the dark winter night to the nearby airport.

I later felt guilty about this night. This walk might have been a surreal step into Tony's lungs – the mist a symbol for the yellow fluid encased there.

One night in late December I was in a changing room at John Lewis (a stone's throw from this walking place) trying on some top or other. The phone rang and it was Tony, he sounded much brighter but his news was bad.

'It turns out I really was ill all along, it's a bit more serious than flu. One of my kidneys is diseased but I'm having an operation to remove it straight after Christmas.' He explained that he'd had some fluid on his lungs but that had all been sorted out so he didn't feel so bad, just tired, and he'd be fine once he had the operation. We arranged to spend New Year's Eve together as both of us happened to be at a loose end that night.

On Christmas Day Tony called round to Bruce with his usual book gift. He apologised for telling him he was ill on a day such as this. He compared this announcement to a scene in Proust's *Swann in Love*, when Swann knows he's dying and goes round to tell his best friend, where they are all dressed up and going out for dinner. Swann makes his announcement on the doorstep, upon which his friend scolds him: 'How ill mannered of you Swann, have you no sense of propriety or occasion? Don't you see we are just about to go out to dinner? Your news has ruined my evening.'(Incidentally, at the beginning of the book Swann falls in love with a girl below his station. He's completely obsessed with her and marries her. He tells the same best friend about it, who then remarks, 'Well, I'm sorry to hear that Swann, of course we can't possibly receive you.')

On New Year's Eve I called at the loft since Tony was clearly too tired and unwell to drive. I had no idea that he had cancer, having actually bought his statement that he had a diseased kidney and that all would be well once it was removed. He was beautifully dressed in a gorgeous suit and we set off together for a meal he'd booked nearby. We'd barely got down the road when he asked me to stop at a cash point because, although he'd got credit cards on him, he was concerned they might be full up and the meal was going to be expensive ('But I'm paying for it,' he said quickly).

I thought, 'Heavens, I never imagined Tony would be that broke that a credit card wouldn't work.' I couldn't be bothered stopping and felt that the outing itself was taxing enough for Tony. I insisted that in that event we would put the dinner on my credit card, since I knew it could stand it. Mind you, I was saying that without a clue what meals like this cost on New Year's Eve. We were heading for a restaurant in Castlefield by the canal, called Choice, one we'd been to not that long ago with Tony's daughter Izzy and her friend after a night out watching the Fall. (Izzy's friend was a huge fan – Alan Wise got us all in free.) The food had been gorgeous and not all that expensive, I thought.

However, when the bill came, I was shocked to see that it was nearly £200 and therefore somewhat horrified when Tony's credit card didn't work. Feeling rather weak I handed my card over as promised, but in point of fact my card wasn't accepted either – there was a problem with an overload of card transactions taken at the same time. So Tony did end up paying for it at a later date.

It is a bit strange when I think about Tony and money. One minute his credit card would be full up and the next he'd be paying for something outrageously expensive. Throughout his life it always seemed that large sums would enter and exit his account and he wouldn't give a damn so long as it kept on flowing.

Steve Lea, Tony's lawyer, told me, 'Three months before he died he paid for the Happy Mondays to go to Coachella [an annual music festival in California] on his personal credit card because there was a problem and he'd given his word that they'd be there.' When Tony was bravely facing the rigours of intensive chemotherapy, I remember he'd cheer himself up by talking about that forthcoming trip and how he was going to show Los Angeles to Oliver. That was his reward to himself I think. He introduced the Happy Mondays onstage at the event.

Something similar happened after this when the Happy Mondays were due to play for In the City New York. Elliot Rashman told me, 'Tony wanted Happy Mondays to play and we were prepared to do it for no money, but we needed the expenses. They had been booked to play two dates and that would be 4,000 tickets. I went mad because they put both dates on sale at the same time – something you never do. You sell out one show at a time. After two weeks they had sold just 180 tickets and just one week before, they had still sold only 180. Tony was really ill – it was only about three months before he died – but he was in New York with Yvette. I had told him that the money needed to be advanced first because Happy Mondays had no cash flow at all. Tony said, "Don't worry, we've got the money." And I could hear Yvette screaming in the background, "You haven't got any money! What are you talking about?"'

The voice of reason, perhaps, but Tony just didn't care – the gig was the thing. Elliot said that he eventually made the tough decision to pull the gigs because he didn't want the Mondays playing two disastrously empty shows in New York, and to save Tony and In the City from looking really bad.

Tony always said that the most profound moment of his life was when he interviewed Cardinal Arns. This was back in the seventies – he told me about it then but I doubtless took rather a dim view of anything to do with religion. We had a priest who regularly called on us and I sensed that his motive was more in the interests of financial gain than our spiritual succour. My grandmother was an Irish Catholic raised in a very poor part of Dublin. Her priest regularly collected money from the keenly poor families in the area, but when the priest's huge estate was made public following his death my grandmother absolutely abandoned her faith in the church. But Cardinal Arns is a bit different. He espoused liberation theology, which aims to support the poor and oppressed and to overthrow the sin of exploitation. Himself one of thirteen children of German immigrant parents, he became Cardinal Archbishop of Sao Paulo, Brazil. The first thing he did was to give up the wealth his station afforded (such as the palace he was expected to live in) and spread it amongst those less fortunate. He also expressed support to Fidel Castro. What a guy! The church, and indeed the world, needs more of these people. Both Tony and the Cardinal were highly educated men of great intelligence and I only wish I could hear the interview now. Why haven't Granada done that – unearthed some of this fascinating material and work of Tony's and given him the kind of send-off he deserved?

Tony told Andy Fyfe about the profound moment for *Q* magazine. He also told me about it several times, but Tony had a way with words. He said, 'Towards the end, and I'm a good altar boy and playing theology with him and all that, and I said, "But Cardinal, are you saying that to be rich of itself is a sin?" And he leaned back and said with a grin, "Yes my boy," as if to say, "It's only taken me forty-five minutes but you've finally got it."'

In many ways In the City had perfectly placed Tony and Yvette to go on with their project to improve and re-brand Pennine Lancashire. They had lots of alliances, such as with Pat Kearney on the council. In the City was a big move in that direction because it attracted people to the city. It attracted money and investment. Tony was very interested in how that process worked. Bob Dickinson stated: 'I went to some kind of big exhibition connected with Pennine Lancashire and Elevate in London, in Whitehall. Tony was there with Yvette and Jack Straw, MP for Blackburn, who was then the Home Secretary, and I interviewed them as one interview and Jack Straw separately. It was very interesting, watching Tony knocking around with cabinet ministers, and he was loving it and it felt like it mattered. That part of the country needed investment then and this was before the recession. It was an exhibition of Asian art to open at Blackburn Art Gallery and it was linked to that regeneration project.'

Alan Wise took a somewhat dimmer view of Tony's activities. He said, 'The silliest I ever saw him was when Yvette turned him into a corporate man.'

Tony was a regenerator, however. As Bob Dickinson also observed: 'That corridor that takes you down Whitworth Street to Castlefield, the Hacienda is just right halfway along that, and the idea of regeneration seems to have spread like a virus, down those railway arches, which is now all clubs, down to Castlefield, which is now all bars. When the Hacienda closed it was a really bad thing. That was the end of the Madchester phase but it was the beginning of another phase that wasn't pop culture, it was maybe pop culture transmuted into architecture and urban planning.'

Tony was an activist who had an enormous impact on the growth of the city he loved, but his illness was to curtail many of his activities as soon as 2007 got underway.

Tony first went into Christie for chemotherapy on his birthday, 20 February 2007. He was to endure days and days of this, and basically never moved off the bed during this time. I visited him the night before and ironed his pyjamas and dressing gown. It was as if he was going on his holidays. As ever he was indomitably optimistic.

The first time I visited him that week I burst into tears at the sight of how ill the chemo had obviously made him. Izzy, his daughter, was in the room and, though I'd only met her a few times, she came straight over and gave me a hug. That meant a lot to me. I didn't think Tony could see me as his back was turned but he said, 'It's supposed to be making me better, you silly bugger.' Bless his heart for going through that and remaining so positive. I felt so tender in that moment. I sat at the end of the bed and, as his naked feet were exposed, began to massage them gently.

When the game was up Tony wept openly; at the time of our last outing, after we listened to 'Love Will Tear Us Apart' at the Opera House. That sunny evening when I arrived at the loft I was greeted with loud, optimistic music which rather belied my sombre outlook. Oliver, who had been a tower of strength for Tony throughout his illness, was the DJ. The track shifted to Happy Mondays' 'Bob's Yer Uncle'. Tony was choosing the songs for his funeral.

Another time I remember his tears was a lunchtime I called at the loft. I found him sitting on the sofa in his dressing gown, with a kebab on his knee that Alan had brought round. His favourite. Sadly he could manage very little even of that, but he was eating again, and he was up.

Now that Tony was ill all his projects had to be put off, although he cared about them as much as ever. He told me that when he saw the artwork that Saville had done for the Pennine Lancashire project that summer, he was moved to tears. It is an exquisite graphic contour that evokes the rolling hills of the area and stands as a flag, literally and metaphorically, for regeneration.

14 May 2007
Told Tony about Tosh ending our relationship only a week after my cat was run over and Tony exclaimed, 'Who gives a fuck – who cares?' Whilst I understand no one else can feel the loss like I do I suddenly exclaimed back, 'You know what I need, a boyfriend who does care – that's exactly the point.' We were having dinner at the Highwayman, a very sad affair because he told me they have seen new growth cancer cells since the chemo. He's sure though that the Sutent, which he starts today, will work. I'm not as positive. But after dinner we take the dog round the park. It's lashing down with rain and cold too. The dog doesn't feel it but we do. Yet somehow there was poetry in these moments – walking huddled together under his umbrella.

Reading that diary extract now I see how selfish it was of me to speak about my upset over a cat and a boyfriend (even though it was a bit raw having only happened the week before). Also, maybe I misunderstood Tony – he might not have meant 'Who cares?' about the cat, but rather about Tosh (in other words who gives a fuck that Tosh had called it off? – I'd thought he was being callous about the cat being killed). Tony had been through such a lot, only to be told that it hadn't worked, so a relationship problem must have seemed petty and minor to him. The chemo was awful. I honestly felt he suffered more having that than actually dying. Elliot told me that Shaun Ryder, who visited Tony at Christie during his chemo treatment, said it was one of the most chastening experiences of his life.

That night all Tony's hopes were pinned on Sutent. He had absolute faith in the professor and in the drug. But another worrying problem reared its head (not that he seemed especially concerned, after all it was only money). The National Health would pay for Tony's first month of treatment, but from then on it was going to cost £3-4,000 a month. Not only that, but if he took up the option of paying for it, then all other treatments – X-rays, blood transfusions, anything – had to be paid for privately as well.

It seemed shocking that you couldn't be given a life-extending drug on the National Health, and the drugs were just so unaffordable for most people. The lad from Salford – or the Salford in the lad – rose to the challenge and found a campaign and a cause to carry him through his last two to three months on earth. And, as ever, he made things happen in that department.

Meanwhile, on the practical, money side of things, Tony's friends were getting busy. Nathan McGough explained: 'BBC Four were making a documentary about Factory Records so I was asked to go to Wood Lane, to be interviewed. The chap who was directing it said he'd seen Tony a week or two before and that it wasn't looking good. That was a real shock to me; it was the first time I had any sense of Tony being in real danger. This director mentioned that Tony had to go on expensive medication. I called up Oliver and he confirmed that Tony had had the first month and this was the only chance he had of beating it. There was a real sense of hopelessness that he didn't have the funds to go with it. Tony was a really admired and respected person in the industry. I just said to Oliver there's a lot of money in this business and there must be people out there willing to help. I asked Oliver if he would let me speak to people privately and help raise some money to sort this out. Yvette was getting on a plane to New York but I texted her and she said anything you can do would be amazing. So I contacted a few individuals, on the basis of non-disclosure, who I thought might be able to help. People got back to me instantly. The first person I contacted said, "Yes, I'll put £20,000 into the fund. Where do I send it?" Within a day or two I was able to contact the family and say I've got enough money to pay for the next five months of treatment. Before you knew it £100,000 had been raised. There were cheques still coming in when he died.'

Elliot Rashman also set about raising money. He said, 'Tony was very reluctant to have people raise money for him. He was very proud and I threw lots of suggestions at him and he would bat them all away. You know . . . a concert blah blah. In the end I said, "We are gonna do this. We are not asking you to get involved. Even if you don't use the money, we are going to do it and it's there for you." And for me it wasn't about the Sutent. It was about thinking he is not going to be well enough to work. He had high overheads and the idea would be to take care of all the overheads. It was just being practical. All I knew was that Tony was terribly ill and was completely broke.'

Like Nathan, Elliot was able to use his influence: 'Nathan and I didn't coordinate it but he had his list and I had mine. People were unbelievably generous. Stuart Prebble was great but the greatest was Richard Madeley. Stuart Prebble was the guy who put together *World in Action*. He was one of the originators of it. He was the head of it. I had got to know Stuart Prebble through a guy called Steve Locke, who was a Granada producer-director. So I had known Stuart Prebble and I phoned him and said Tony's short of money and he said, "No problem." Then I got Richard Madeley's email. I just emailed him and got an instant reply – he was horrified that Tony was so ill and unable to access potentially lifesaving medication. He said, "Anyway I can help at all. Of course I will put money up but how can I help in other ways?" I said, "I don't know any Granada people, I know some music people," and he said, "Leave the Granada people to me." So he raised all this money from the Granada people and he went round the Granada lot and the TV lot and raised it – a huge amount and really quickly. He was incredibly complimentary about Tony and Judy was very, very, very emotionally upset about it. He pulled out all the stops and we had this great email dialogue. He was very witty and got on with it and just did it. I had never watched *Richard and Judy* in my life until then and I became a Richard Madeley fan. But in the end I felt we failed. Naively I thought once Tony had Sutent it would be a lot better.'

I know it still meant a great deal to Tony that his friends did this for him. He was both touched and honoured. I also know how amused Tony was by Richard's text messages at this time. One of them that made Tony's day had something to do with the Pope. Richard told me: 'I texted him [that] I'd been rustling around a bit and talking him up, but was probably going a bit over the top because Stuart Prebble had said to me something like: "Look, Rich, I know Tony's a top guy but we're not trying to get him elected Pope."'

For all of these efforts, the real hero was, of course, Tony himself. He was an activist to his final hour, campaigning for the drug Sutent to be made available to all on the NHS. It was a selfless act; he knew it was too late for himself but he empathised with those for whom it might really be a lifesaver. As his friend Ross McKenzie said, 'He was very, very brave and dignified – I admired the way he dragged himself out there to beat the drum for this good cause, going round the news stations when he was so ill. That was jaw-droppingly wonderful. He had steely determination. He had a really sharp tongue occasionally. I've heard him tear a strip off people on the phone and things like that. If he felt someone was letting him down or letting the cause down then he'd let rip.'

Many other people admired Tony's campaign. Penny Henry, an ex-Hacienda employee, remarked, 'I thought he was amazing in the last part of his life –

what he did for people with kidney cancer I thought was unbelievably brave and wonderful. Somebody else would have just crawled into a hole. He was just so brave. I really respected him for that.'

It wasn't just how Tony was in public that I admired. It was also how he was in private. He was truly brave and had, I think, that unknown quality – the thing we never know if we ourselves have until we are tested (whether or not we are brave or a coward).

Tony's health really took a downturn after a trip to New York that he took with Yvette in mid-June.

The idea of the journey was to promote In the City there and Tony's rave band – Enter Shikari. He said he hadn't seen anything as exciting as them since the Sex Pistols. He'd played me some tracks of theirs in the car (as he had done with his earlier rave band Raw-T), and when I said I didn't much care for it (either of them) he took that as evidence in their favour. In other words that oedipal rock thing – if the older generation disapprove, it proves how good the music must be. I never related to that idea, my parents liked the Beatles as much as I did. My mum was into Mick Jagger in the sixties more than I was, I think even she fancied him!

Tony loved New York so much that I wondered if he wanted to see it one last time in any case (though in point of fact he was pretty much confined to the hotel bedroom). The morning of the journey he told me he rang Yvette to say he didn't think he could make it. However, he subsequently rang Alan Erasmus to ask him if he would help get him down the stairs. This seemed the most daunting task of all to Tony; God knows how he could entertain the thought of a transatlantic flight. Alan had helped Tony up the stairs after his debilitating chemotherapy and now they both used all their strength to get him down. So it was that Tony made it to the car and the airport, but he told me he was sick on the plane. It was while Tony was in New York that he stopped eating properly. Just like with our pets – we only really fear the worst when they don't eat.

We had planned to go to Italy together when he got back. It was to be a week of resting in some warm sunshine. And our farewell, perhaps. He showed me the fax booking of a hotel outside Rome. Of course there was no way he was well enough to go and he apologised profusely. I told him it was the least of our worries. He thought he might be well enough to go to Portmeirion but he wasn't.

His dissolution struck me as rapid then. One day, I noticed he'd put his will out on a table – right beneath the place where I hung his bed linen to dry. (I had taken to changing the bed every week – how quickly I fell into my old role of looking after minor chores; fairly major, though, when you are unwell.) Tony knew that was where I hung the washing, so why had he placed the will there, where I couldn't help but see it?

Although it would have been in my nature to comment, I decided against saying anything as he was so ill. I went in his bedroom and said I was going out for a walk. It was the only way I thought I'd manage to keep my mouth shut. He suggested I call in at the Central Library to see an exhibition that had moved him to tears (in fact he nearly broke down when he told me about it). It was called *Queen and Country* by Steve McQueen and commemorated British soldiers killed in the Iraq War, with their photographs duplicated on postage stamp sheets and viewed on pull-out wooden panels. (It took me a while to find these hidden amongst the tables and echoes of people working in the library.)

Perhaps because I am opposed to war in Iraq, Afghanistan, or anywhere at all in fact, I wasn't moved to tears, however tragic it was to see those young faces now entombed in a wooden panel. But I realised that life and death isn't a political issue and Tony understood then the true sorrow, meaning and value of a life lost. I felt ashamed of my petty thoughts about a stupid will – what the hell did anything matter? – Tony was about to lose his whole life, just like all these young men.

Dear Tony dragged himself from his sick bed so we could go out for my birthday on 2 July. We went for dinner at Zinc. I'd found out that day, after a phone call from Tosh – our first contact for three months – that he'd been seeing his ex-girlfriend after breaking up with me. I felt betrayed and upset (hell hath no fury and all that). It was also very hard as before leaving, Tony, Oliver and I watched a DVD, filmed fifteen years earlier, of a very young Oliver, baby Isabel and dad Tony. My regret was so intense seeing this happy domestic scene at Old Broadway. Old Broadway the family house he'd bought with me in mind. And the family I never had. Longing for something that can never be. Longing for Tony to be well again. This sorrow was compounded by my having been seemingly overthrown for another woman by my last lover. I was hurting. At dinner I moaned, 'Tosh never loved me.' Tony got annoyed that I was talking about it, and I can hardly blame him. 'Do you know how boring this is?' he said. 'I've got cancer. You've got dysfunctional relationships with men. We've both just got to get on with it.'

I think he was pretty angry but he didn't really show it (except for the fact that he let me pay for dinner). Erasmus told me much later that I blew it with Tony, as he was about to ask me to move in with him. Tony told him on Tuesday 3 July that he didn't want me to as I had talked about Tosh all evening.

Of course I regret being so insensitive – it was just a pity that I'd gone straight from the phone call to Tony's loft.

Tony's health seemed to pick up a little bit in early July – perhaps it was a period of remission. He and Yvette attended Barney's wedding. Shortly after this I was round at the loft again and Tony told me what had happened as he was leaving the wedding. He said that it was a standing joke between Barney and him, that Barney has always blamed Tony for things going wrong – for the Hacienda (money losses), for his divorce (Tony had invited *Smash Hits* to LA without telling the band, resulting in some photographic suggestion of Barney's infidelity), for the fact that Barney had recently put diesel instead of petrol in his wife's car (because he was distracted thinking about Tony) and so on. Tony joked with Barney that he hoped he wouldn't be blaming him for this – i.e. his wedding day, I suppose. Barney replied that actually he was, and pointing to the grounds around his house, he said that if it wasn't for Tony he wouldn't have any of it; he'd gone from a two-up two-down to all this. As Tony related this to me the tears rolled down his face. I couldn't help but sarcastically remark that since I'd met Tony I'd gone from a detached house to a two-up two-down. At least it made him stop crying. But the next thing was he got me crying (although he called it snivelling), because he told me he and Stephen Lea were trying to sort some money out for me.

Steve told me about this later: 'I was interested to know when he knew he was beaten. I had an afternoon in May or June with Tony where I picked him up, drove him to Blackburn, met Yvette, had some lunch at Tony's favourite place up there. Then we went to the accountant's so that he could get his bollocking and everything else. I'd had a couple of meetings with him at the loft, when he talked about what he wanted the will to say. On the way back from Blackburn he said, "And now about Lindsay." I went, "Yeah." He goes, "I feel quite guilty about her. I ought to get her £10,000." And I went, "Right." So he said, "How you gonna do it?" I went, "Hang on a minute, what do you mean how am *I* going to do it?" He said, "I thought when I'm gone you can sort it out when you're doing the will." "Oh yeah Tony, that's really easy for a lawyer to fiddle a bloody estate so I can whip £10,000 out for your first wife." I said, "Tony you can't ask that of me it's not fair." He said, "What can we do about it?" We hummed and hawed. Within the estate I couldn't see how we could have done it.'

Tony may have known the game was up, but he was still kidding people. For example, he told Nathan the same story as me about the clot being the problem. Nathan remembered: 'I had a conversation with Tony the month before he died when he was having his first scan after the treatment. He sounded terrible, he said he was really weak, he'd got a terrible blood clot on his lung and could hardly walk. He was on drugs to thin his blood but he said, "The good news is the drugs that you raised the money to pay for are working. The tumour has shrunk. I can't tell you how grateful I am to you. I feel shit now but in two weeks time I'll be better. I love you Nabs." I never spoke to him again.'

All through his life Tony was fond of the phrase, 'Two weeks.' If he said he'd call you in two weeks, it generally meant you couldn't rely on that call.

But there is always an element of denial when someone you love is dying. You need to believe in a miracle and so you do.

19 July 2007

Told Tony about the opening night of the Hacienda exhibition at Urbis yesterday. I said that the amount of people there showed how important it was and that they'd like the Hacienda back. He said, 'No, what they wanted was memories.' 'What good are memories?' I asked (so much wanting Tony to live and not just leave me with those). He replied with real conviction somehow: 'Memories are a very beautiful thing.'

Vini Reilly recalled his last meeting with Tony in the hospital. Our conversation was as follows:

VR: We just spoke and chatted very gently about things. I told him, I didn't know much about . . . none of us knew what was going to happen but, given the person that he was, that he didn't have anything to be afraid of . . .

LR: You said that to him? That he didn't have anything to be scared of? Why? Did you think he was?

VR: Yes, I think so. Well, we all are, aren't we?

LR: The Catholic judgement thing.

VR: Yes, definitely. If you are born a Catholic, you are stuck with that, aren't you?

LR: Are you a Catholic?

VR: Yes. The last thing he ever did. He was really tired . . . very poorly, and I had to go and let him get some rest. I said, 'It's just like a trip. You know, when you take some acid. What you have got to do is just go with it. Just let it take you along with it. Just let it take you where it's going to take you and see where you end up. That's how you should be doing this.' When I said I was going he raised himself up just a little bit and gave me a victory sign.

LR: That's peace, as well, isn't it? You saw it as victory?

VR: Yes. Just that he wasn't beaten. He was dying, but he wasn't beaten.

Tony's last exchange with Nick Clarke was rather similar. Nick related: 'Shortly before his death there was an email exchange, he was too weak. I said something about the worst things coming to the best people and how utterly sad I was about it. He wrote back in Italian! Essentially the translation would be, "I will be victorious to the end." It was almost like, it's going to take a lot to get rid of me.'

I last saw Tony on the Wednesday evening before his death on the Friday. It was just the two of us that night. I told him then that, just as Scarlett O'Hara had said, I knew I would get him back 'tomorrow' – because I felt absolutely sure that our connection would continue in some form or other. Where there is love it is certain. My mum told me that when she was dying – I doubted it then but now I'm as sure of it as I know she was. I told Tony about astral travelling – both mine and my mum's experience of leaving the body. Was this not proof of something existing outside of, independent of, the body? He shook his head somewhat despairingly. Wanting to change the subject, he told me to tell him about a silly phone call I'd had with Tosh that had gone badly. He looked nonplussed when he heard the story. He wanted to hold my hand and I was amazed how small his hand seemed. I said, 'Where is your faith, Tony?' I said we are spirit and we go back to spirit, from where we came; that it happens every night when we go to sleep. And he did go to sleep then. I looked at his face and it didn't look like him somehow. The familiar gap in his teeth was the only thing remaining of his youth. I was holding his hand with both of my hands, one under, one over, and they got uncomfortable so I gently took them away but he slept on. He seemed in a deep sleep. It was getting late so I decided to leave. I didn't say goodbye but tiptoed out. He didn't wake.

A very kind nurse stopped me on my way through the doors. She asked me how I was. I was a bit taken aback – it was only Tony I was concerned about. She asked me if I wanted bereavement counselling. I said no. But how considerate and how wonderful all those Christie nurses were throughout Tony's stay and treatment.

Besides, I didn't need bereavement counselling. I was absolutely certain I would see Tony again. The very next day in fact.

Wrong.

He knew it was our goodbye, the nurse even knew. Why the fuck didn't I know? Denial is like shock, it helps to get us through. However desperately I wanted to be with Tony on his last day on earth, I had to respect his wish that I wasn't there when Yvette was. Of course I wanted to make it as easy as possible for him.

On the day of Tony's death Bruce remembered assisting Tony to pass water, obviously it was embarrassing for his daughter. Ross McKenzie was there. Tony whispered, 'Small victories Bruce.' Tony was referring to a conversation the pair had shared thirty years earlier, about the 'small victories' of Shukhov in Alexander Solzhenitsyn's *One Day in the Life of Ivan Denisovich*. The book is an unflinching account of the torments endured in a labour camp. On the day of the small victories he'd found a broken piece of hacksaw and successfully put it under his mattress.

Bruce sent me the following paragraph from the novel: 'Shukhov went to sleep fully content. He'd had many strokes of luck that day: they hadn't put him in the cells; they hadn't sent the team to the settlement; he'd pinched a bowl of kasha at dinner; the team-leader had fixed the rates well; he'd built a wall and enjoyed doing it; he'd smuggled that bit of hacksaw-blade through; he'd earned something from Tsezar in the evening; he'd bought that tobacco. And he hadn't fallen ill. He'd got over it.

'A day without a dark cloud. Almost a happy day.'

I think to make a literary reference such as this on the same day as your death is nothing short of outstanding. Also it was a personal tribute to Bruce – to their shared discussions and the enjoyment Tony got from them.

A few of Tony's other friends were also gathered along with Bruce at Christie when they heard the end was very near.

'There was Leroy Richardson, Alan Erasmus, Keith Jobling and me,' said Elliot Rashman. 'He was far too ill for visitors but somehow managed to tell Ollie to let us in. It was terrible seeing him fighting for every breath – he'd been given the last rights by then. He clasped my hand and pulled me close and tried to tell me something but he couldn't get the words out. I told him I loved him, kissed him and said goodbye. It was incredibly emotional. He died shortly afterwards. It still haunts me that I couldn't understand what he was saying, though my wife says he was probably just telling me to "fuck off".'

Since Tony was finding speech uncommonly difficult, he made a touching tribute to Keith by kissing his hand. Ross McKenzie kindly phoned me on the Friday afternoon and told me how Tony was coping, and Alan Erasmus called me as soon as Tony died.

As Elliot said, 'Manchester just isn't the same without him – it's more grey and corporate. It's weird walking around the city and not seeing him anymore because he used to walk everywhere and you'd often just bump into him. He still lives inside my head though. I often hear his voice telling me to, "Move on, darling, let it go."'

Funny that. I had a very vivid dream ten months after Tony's death. I dream about him all the time actually, but this particular dream had an entirely different quality. When I awoke from it tears were falling down my face.

This is the dream as I wrote it in my diary:

I was relieved to see Tony looking much healthier – almost chubby but not in a bad way. He seemed to be doing one of those late-night shows – *The Other Side of Midnight* or something – and enjoying feeling passionate about one thing or another (to do with music). I had said something stupid and – watching a video reel playing this back – I cringed somewhat. But Tony seemed not to notice and bounced over to me with his usual buoyancy, optimism and affection. Delighted as I was to see him looking so well, I began to get upset that his life had been cut so suddenly short (in the future that was already past). Tony brushed it aside philosophically and said something to the effect that everyone left the set exactly when they were meant to and that it was all perfect. 'Oh no,' I protested and felt tears falling at the thought of the awful truth. 'It was much too soon.' Tony's arms were around me and he was comforting me as he said, 'See it as a good memory and move on.'

I had feared Tony's funeral would be a media circus but it wasn't – the press, TV and general public were very respectful and quiet. The town hall flag was at half-mast. The city was in mourning. The bells sounded. Send not to know . . . I was prepared to take a back seat inside the church, the beautiful Hidden Gem, but became alarmed when I saw that Bruce Mitchell was standing at the door and, in almost bouncer mode, made sure I went upstairs. It suggested that my role in this funeral, and therefore Tony's life, was – like the role of women in synagogue life who are dispatched to the women's gallery upstairs – inferior.

Tosh consolingly remarked that I could look down on people. I looked at those in the front and second rows and wondered why they were near his coffin when I was not. Several strangers were at or near the front; Geoff Travis and his partner on row two, Tony's Buddhist friend, Neville, and others. Had I imagined that I'd stayed in Tony's bed most Saturday nights these last several months? The priest kept referring to Yvette, Oliver and Izzy as though they were a family. Even he was in on the conspiracy. Yvette sat separated from the children on the left front row of the church and the mother of Tony's children, Hilary, was also mysteriously somehow banished to the back. Thelma McGough was sitting on the far right front row with the children. People would have thought she was their mother. Yvette sat beside Tony's lawyer, Steve, on the far left. Richard and Judy and sundry others sat front centre. I felt as if I was in a theatre, looking down on a play, not at the funeral of a man I'd loved for thirty-one years. Something inside me almost wanted to laugh slightly hysterically – like the widow in *Women in Love* who behaved bizarrely at the graveside. This is what Tony went for every time – the fantasy, the image – even the lovely old priest, Father Lynch, played to this tune, although apparently in 1991 he had told Hilary that she could make no appeal to him regarding Tony's departure from their marriage, despite her being the mother of his young children, since, in the eyes of God, she and Tony weren't really married.

Tony's children were a shining example of love, not just for their father but also for one another. Throughout the service they sat huddled together, comforting each other. Whatever mistakes had been made, Tony seems to have been a good father to them both and loved them dearly.

Tony's beloved childhood friend Sean spoke, and received a rapturous applause, no doubt because he spoke from his heart. And coming from a lifetime's friendship, he flew in to be with Tony for his last hours on earth. How beautiful that guy was, weeping sincerely. So Tony was not without genuineness around him, he had Sean and he had his children.

Richard Madeley also spoke with genuine feeling. He almost broke down when he said it was just unbelievable that Tony had gone. Actually that might have been because he hadn't quite gone yet. He was still playing stage manager.

Nathan said of the service: 'In all the years I knew Tony I never heard him confess his faith for Catholicism or talk about religious faith in a meaningful way. So the funeral . . . was like a high Catholic mass. I didn't think it was a celebration of his life in a meaningful way. There was a lot of talk from the priest about how we are all carrying sin and, not to be rude, but I just felt that this was absolute bullshit. We should be celebrating this man's life and we were just celebrating the church and praising God. I mean it was a great send-off. But I felt it was all wrapped up in this pomp of Catholicism and that pissed me off. I mean, it was what he had requested. But I had shared a house with him for a couple of years . . . at Old Broadway, after he separated from you. I don't ever remember Tony on a Sunday morning getting up and going to mass. Fair enough . . . I know when people are dying they look to religion . . . they look to faith as some kind of salvation. But there was a great turnout for his funeral and I just felt that people should be talking about him. There were some good tributes made at the end. It did, from what the priest was saying, seem that he got to know Tony and Tony would come to the church. It really surprised me, because I thought I knew Tony very well and was close to him. But I didn't know that he was deeply religious.'

All the same, Nathan couldn't help but laugh when he saw the plaque on Tony's nearby coffin. It read: FAC 501.

I thought Tony's love of Catholicism was like his love of his mother and Manchester – inbred, immoveable, an ever-fixed mark.

Outside there were around nine black limousines to follow the hearse as it made its way up Princess Parkway. My first thought was, 'What the hell is that costing?' Not that Tony didn't deserve such an entourage, but bear in mind – flashback to only eight months earlier – New Year's Eve 2006, when Tony suspected there were not sufficient funds available on his credit card for the dinner. My second thought was, 'Why was I, his first (and only in Roman Catholic eyes) wife, who was there bringing food and staying in his bed to the end – why then was I not given a place in one of these?' Not that I minded, as I preferred trundling along in Jane Lemon's people carrier with people I considered to be real friends. But Tony did have many genuine friends. Thelma was sitting in one of the limousines and jumped out to greet me as I walked past. She had genuine tears.

I was disappointed that, as Jane's car was parked at the back of the town hall, we failed to catch up with the cortege at all stages since we were so well behind.

The burial was dignified and peaceful. It was the closest I got to Tony's coffin and a farewell. But the after-service wake was something of an ordeal for me. Firstly, one had to use one's pass to get in. Understandable for someone with such a profile, but I was still upset about his funeral being invitation only since my sister had been refused a pass when she telephoned In the City to ask for one. For God's sake, she was his sister-in-law and had also been Head of Year to Tony's son, Oliver, at Cheadle Hulme School. Besides, shouldn't *anyone* be allowed to mourn the passing of someone? In death we are all the same. Dead.

I doubt that my sister would have attended Tony's wake since we went then from a beautiful church to a club – One Central Street, run by Tony's good friend Ross McKenzie. Music and chattering people round the bar. A good empty space seemed to be near the chicken and rice soup that Dimitri had kindly brought in from his restaurant (at my request) as it was Tony's favourite. I detest small talk at the best of times, but the trouble with wakes is that the deceased person doesn't always even get talked about all that much.

It felt like a nightclub – well, it was a nightclub, but the atmosphere wasn't really conducive to someone genuinely grieving.

I felt deeply uncomfortable and wanted to leave. Tosh (who I hadn't seen for over four months) had rung after Tony died and suggested accompanying me to the funeral. I nearly said no – after all, Tosh was with someone else and I thought his presence might make me feel worse. But something made me say yes and he was in fact a huge comfort.

At the graveside Vini Reilly had suddenly turned to Tosh and me and, in his own funny, quirky way, suddenly announced that he and I belonged together because we both like to argue. Actually we don't, but the thing is, Tosh grew up in the Wythenshawe school of hard knocks and he's got a really tough streak, and he's able to stand up to me. It was because of the rows that we'd broken up, but much to my surprise Tosh turned to me and said that he was available. So at the wake I was looking for him, I needed a friend to turn to and he felt like my best bet. And so it was we got back together – ironically with Vini Reilly playing cupid and at Tony's graveside, despite all the sparring he and Tony had, me and Tony had, me and Tosh had. And the good news is that two or three years on – guess what? – the rows have virtually stopped. At our age you just can't be doing with rows. Tony would be amazed. And pleased, I think. At last my insecurity has abated – but it took maturity and a man of iron to break it, a bit like taming a wild horse. Dougie James said that Tony wasn't strong enough to stand up to me. Despite all of Tony's huge strength, I think that, when in love, women were his particular weakness, his Achilles heel. But it was thanks to Tony that I was finally able to face up to the fact of my destructive 'illness' and deal with it once and for all. I only wish I could have done it when we were first together. I believe we then might have shared a happy life together.

For two nights after the funeral I couldn't sleep because of the anger I felt. Actually I was hopping mad. I'm not sure who with – but mainly with Tony for preferring fantasy to reality, even for his funeral. Surely the harsh reality cannot be denied here at the grave? Well he's managed it, stage-managed it, I thought. Yvette told David Nolan that 'he would have *loved* his funeral. The coffin was black and had cool silver handles on . . . Tony would have wanted a cool funeral. He got a cool funeral.' Yes, I agree with her. The funeral was everything he wanted it to be, and if a man can't have what he wants at his own funeral when can he? But it's that old style versus substance, presentation versus content discussion I began earlier in the book. I just needed to say goodbye and cry and I couldn't.

Besides, the man I loved wasn't always cool. He was vulnerable, sometimes angry, he made mistakes, he got hurt, and he wore rubbish boots for a photograph.

His funeral was very cool but that was a public persona, it wasn't really him. And yet it was like him sometimes to put up a front and hide behind it. That was a part of him that made me angry. The way he denied our friendship for instance. So strange to be livid with someone who has just died. I was fucking furious. It reminded me that a relationship with someone doesn't automatically stop when they are dead. It carries on, and on.

I had not shed a single tear. Me who can cry over a pathetic movie or the funeral of someone I barely know. And then, in my fury, I picked up the phone and called Father Lynch. I told him who I was and that what I had to say was in the nature of a confession. I have never given confession before. One of the things I mentioned was how absolutely furious I was with Tony. And how could I be when he was dead? And then my tears flowed. What a blessed relief! Tears for all of it. It certainly was an unburdening. Father Lynch was very kind. He suggested that I visit him; he said that he was sure it was because of Tony's prayers that I was talking to him. Though I found this a bit unlikely I liked the comment he made when I told him how angry I was with Tony – he seemed to think it perfectly natural and acceptable. He relieved me of the block I had about it and helped me to accept it. I suppose that is the great thing about confession, Tony always said that the Catholic religion is full of wonderful ritual. Anger is often part and parcel of loving someone, and is always a part of grief. It doesn't necessarily negate love as I thought it might have. Other people who loved Tony were grieving, and here was I shouting at him as he lay in the cold ground. You twat. Yes, the man I loved was a real twat sometimes. But mostly he was just the man I loved.

And then my anger left me.

At Tony's funeral I felt cheated somehow of a formal goodbye. I never said goodbye at our last meeting, not even goodnight – something that grieved me on the day he died.

In a way, though, I did have my own private goodbye ceremony. This diary note speaks of it:

13 August 2007
Visited Tony in the Chapel of Rest. His face looked more like him than

my last sighting of him alive, oddly. The struggle now given up, he looked restored to himself. Yet so still. Tony wasn't one to be still. Not even a word from his lips. Lips that should speak, if not kiss. I wept, of course. And then I stopped – he didn't like snivelling, and it felt as if I could talk to him. So I said a few words. Something mundane. I don't remember exactly what. Could have been that his hair looked nice; I noticed it had been washed and the curl had gone back into it. He must have left it a long time without washing it when he was ill. I did help him have a bath at his loft but I think a hair wash was just too exhausting for him. Then, feeling silly, talking to a corpse, I got up to go. I'd just left the room and was about to say goodbye to the kind man who showed me in when I suddenly said, to myself if not to him, 'I can't leave, not just yet.' But I wanted, needed, to sit down next to Tony. The kind man brought a chair in for me and said to take as long as I liked. I asked him if I might take a lock of Tony's hair. He said it would have to be with the agreement of his next of kin. 'His son or daughter?' I asked. He mentioned Yvette's name and I really didn't think I wanted to bother her with it. I was sure that Oliver and/or Izzy would be sympathetic but both their mobiles were switched off. The kind gentleman offered to phone Yvette. I said no at first but then reluctantly agreed. He disappeared and I looked at Tony. He seemed to be glancing heavenward, tutting slightly. 'I'm causing trouble again, aren't I?' I asked him. 'Yes,' he silently muttered. The gentleman returned and said that Yvette's phone was also switched off so there was nothing he could do. 'Oh, never mind,' I said, and consoled myself by putting my hands through Tony's hair. It was a gesture I'd made a thousand times before, but the sadness of this last occasion was too much. The tears fell down my face again as I said at the same time: 'It was only a lock of hair, I don't even think anyone would have noticed.' 'I'll get the scissors,' the kind gentleman suddenly remarked. After handing them to me, I thought he'd stand by as I cut the lock but he disappeared again, as if it was something intimate just between me and Tony. But then I noticed him nervously looking through a partition window – perhaps he was worried I might, after all, be some kind of obsessed fan who had really come in to give Tony a punk haircut especially for his funeral?

Such a sad love story. It could have all been so wonderful. Perhaps it really was in its way. Useless to blame either of us for the mistakes, and yet I do. (Myself mostly.) In truth, we all have feet of clay. I look back at the betrayals – whose was the worst? – we were both just as bad as each other. And so . . .

And throughout all Eternity
I forgive you, you forgive me.
As our dear Redeemer said:
'This the Wine, and this the Bread.'

William Blake
'Broken Love'

Before us lies eternity; our souls
Are love, and a continual farewell.

W.B. Yeats
'Ephemera'

Acknowledgements

You would not be holding this book in your hands if it were not for these four people – Bob Dickinson, Mick Middles, Anthony Ryan Carter and Sandra Wake (in alphabetical order). They know why. So if you want to, you can blame them. It was not my intention to hurt anyone, however, and I hope the book does not offend.

I'm not making any dedications except, obviously, I'd like to especially thank the above four (the *sine qua non* of the book) and even more so Tony (the *sine qua non* of the story). Is there any point in thanking the dead? Perhaps not but I do anyway, from the bottom of my heart, for he was a truly exceptional human being. There are several of these who seem ordinary and are unseen by the world – my mum was one, much missed, but thankfully some of her special brand of wisdom appears in these pages.

I'd like to thank Chris Charlesworth, who added an encouraging sprinkle of his old editing magic at the beginning of this journey, and Tom Branton, who, with a wisdom that belied his age and a steady hand, steered me through to the finishing line. He understood the difficulty I had in letting go – I would never have finished this book if it had been left to me. Quite simply I didn't want to (ever). Perhaps because, in the manner of magical thinking (as described by Joan Didion), continuing to write the book was a very good way of keeping Tony around. Tom consoled me when he quoted Paul Valery: 'A poem is never finished, only abandoned.' Or, as Tony would have said, 'Move on, darling.'

Also Coco Wake-Porter who did a superb job with the cover sleeve and the photographic layout.

In addition I'd like to sincerely thank (also in alphabetical order):

Barry Adamson, Steve Atherton, Lawrence Beadle, John Brierley, Richard Boon, Cath Carroll, Larry Cassidy, Diane Charlemagne, Nick Clarke, Vivienne Clore, Andy Couzens, Kevin Cummins Doreen Curtis, Lynn Daley, Howard Devoto, Yvonne Ellis, Alan Erasmus, Miguel Esteves Cardoso, Dave Greatbanks, Dimitri Griliopoulos, Penny Henry, Chris Hewitt, Annik Honoré, Peter Hook, Steve Hopkins, Michele Howarth, Dougie James, Keith Jobling, Howard (Ginger) Jones, Phil Jones, Jeremy Kerr, Fran Kersher, Andrew King, Stephen Lea, Chris Lee, Jane Lemon, Richard Madeley, Pedro Magalhaes, Terry Mason, Thelma McGough, Nathan McGough, Ross McKenzie, Martin Moscrop, Tony Michaelides, Bruce Mitchell, Paul Morley, Ged Murray, Liz Naylor, James Nice, John Nichols, Susanne O'Hara, Elliot Rashman, Roger Reade, Vini Reilly, Neville Richardson, Katja Ruge, Joanne Ryder, Peter Saville, Phil Saxe, John Scott, Vicki Shelley, Chris Smith, Vivienne Starr, Bernard Sumner, Mike Sweeney, Gene Simon Taylor, Peter Terrill, Les Thompson, Dave Tomlinson, Simon Topping, John Williams, Hilary Wilson, Alan Wise, David Wood.

Bibliography

Books: Cummins, Kevin. *Manchester: Looking for the Light through the Pouring Rain*. London: Faber, 2009; Curtis, Deborah. *Touching from a Distance*. London: Faber, 1995; Hook, Peter. *How Not to Run a Nightclub*. London: Orion, 2009; Lee, C.P. *Shake Rattle and Rain*. London: Harding Simpole, 2000; Lee, C.P. *When We Were Thin*. Hotun Press, 2007; Middles, Mick. *From Joy Division to New Order: The Factory Story*. London: Virgin, 1996; Middles, Mick. *Shaun Ryder: Happy Mondays, Black Grape and Other Traumas*. London: Independent Music Press, 1997; Middles, Mick. *Breaking into Heaven: The Rise and Fall of the Stone Roses*. London: Omnibus, 1999; Middles, Mick and Reade, Lindsay. *Torn Apart: The Life of Ian Curtis*. London: Omnibus, 2006; Morley, Paul. *Nothing*. London: Faber, 2000; Morley, Paul. *Joy Division: Piece by Piece*. London: Plexus, 2008; Murray, Ged. *Dead and Alive: 24 Years of Pissed Up Party Pictures*. Manchester: Logoprint, 2008; Napier-Bell, Simon. *Black Vinyl: White Powder*. London: Ebury Press, 2001; Nice, James. *Shadowplayers: The Rise and Fall of Factory Records*. London: Aurum, 2010; Nolan, David. *You're Entitled to an Opinion*. London: John Blake, 2009; Reynolds, Simon. *Totally Wired: Post-Punk Interviews and Overviews*. London: Faber, 2009; Robb, John. *The North Will Rise Again. Manchester Music 1976-1996*. London: Aurum, 2009; Seierstad, Asne. *The Bookseller of Kabul*. London: Virago, 2002; Sharp, Colin. *Who Killed Martin Hannett?* London: Aurum, 2007; Warburton, John with Ryder, Shaun. *Hallelujah! The Extraordinary Story of Shaun Ryder and Happy Mondays*. London: Virgin, 2003; Wilson, Tony. *24 Hour Party People*. London: Channel 4 Books, 2002; Wray, Ian and McPherson, Colin. *Mersey: The River That Changed the World*. Liverpool: Bluecoat Press, 2007. **Periodicals:** *NME*, *Sounds*, *Melody Maker*, *Uncut*, *Mojo*, *Manchester Evening News*, *City Life*, *Guardian*, *New Manchester Review*, *Q*, *The Face*. **Websites:** YouTube, Cerysmatic Factory, Metafilter, Wikipedia, Joy Division Central, FUC51, Martin Hannett, In the City, Factory Records, Music Week, The Quietus, Situationist International, New Order Online, Rock's Backpages, Times Online.